Gombrowicz's Grimaces

Edited by
Ewa Płonowska Ziarek

Gombrowicz's Grimaces

Modernism, Gender, Nationality

STATE UNIVERSITY OF NEW YORK PRESS

Production by Ruth Fisher
Marketing by Fran Keneston

Published by
State University of New York Press, Albany

Printed in the United States of America

For information, address the State University of New York Press, State University Plaza, Albany, NY 12246

Library of Congress Cataloging-in-Publication Data
Gombrowicz's grimaces : modernism, gender, nationality / edited by Ewa Płonowska Ziarek.
p. cm.
Includes bibliographical references and index.
ISBN 0–7914-3643–8 (alk. paper).—ISBN 0–7914-3644–6 (pbk. : alk. paper)
1. Gombrowicz, Witold—Criticism and interpretation. I. Ziarek, Ewa Płonowska, 1961– .
PG7158.G6692G64 1998
891.8′5373—dc21 97–15682
CIP

10 9 8 7 6 5 4 3 2 1

Contents

Acknowledgments

With great pleasure I would like to acknowledge many friends and colleagues who supported and read this book. I would like to thank Stanisław Barańczak, Halina Filipowicz, Marjorie Perloff, Jean-Michel Rabaté, Susan Harris, and Herman Rapaport for their encouragement and support for this project in its early stages. I would like to express special thanks to my colleagues Barbara Green and Graham Hammill for their perceptive readings and illuminating comments. I am particularly indebted to all the contributors for their enthusiasm, understanding, and exciting work—they have shown me aspects of Gombrowicz's text I have not seen before. And finally, I would like to thank Małgorzata Bąk and Sean O'Brien for their invaluable help in preparing the manuscript for production.

I am very grateful to Kathy Psomiades and Hilary Radner for their friendship and warm support. My very special thanks go to Krzysztof Ziarek for his insightful comments, wit, and unwavering belief in this project, and to my son, Łukasz, for his patience and a sense of humor.

Sections of this work appeared before in print. Beth Holmgren's essay was originally published in *Polish Review,* vol. 33, no. 4 (1988). The revised version of this essay is included in this book by permission of the editor of *Polish Review.* Hanjo Berresem's article, "The Laws of Deviation: Physical and Psychic Aberrations in the Novels of Witold Gombrowicz," draws on the longer argument presented in his book *Lines of Desire: Reading Gombrowicz's Fiction with Lacan* (Evanston: Northwestern UP, 1997). Valérie Deshoulières' essay, "Witold Gombrowicz: Toward a Romantic Theory of Incompleteness," was originally published in French in *Littérature* no. 97 (1995). I thank the editors for the permission to reprint and translate the essay into English.

Grateful acknowledgment is made to Tomasz Olbinski for his permission to use his artwork for the cover design and to the publishers who have generously given permission to use quotations from the following works by Witold Gombrowicz:

Cosmos and Pornografia, trans. Alastair Hamilton, copyright 1985 by Grove/Atlantic Inc., by permission of the publisher.

A Kind of Testament, trans. Alastair Hamilton, copyright 1973 by Temple University Press, by permission of the publisher.

History, trans. Allen Kuharski in collaboration with Dariusz Bukowski, published in *Periphery: Journal of Polish Affairs,* vol. 1, no. 1, copyright Allen Kuharski, by permission of the editors of *Periphery.*

Diary, vols. I, II, and III, trans. Lillian Vallee, copyright 1988, 1989, 1993 Northwestern University Press, copyright for the world market Quartet Books Ltd., by permission of Northwestern University and Quartet Books Ltd.

Trans-Atlantyk, trans. Carolyn French and Nina Karsov, copyright 1994 by Yale University Press, by permission of Yale University Press and Rita Gombrowicz c/o Agenzia Letteraria Internazionale.

Ferdydurke, trans. Eric Mosbacher, (New York: Grove Press, 1961) copyright Harcourt Brace & Company, by permission of Harcourt Brace and Rita Gombrowicz c/o Agenzia Letteraria Internazionale.

List of Abbreviations

The references to the following English translations of Gombrowicz's writings included in the body of the text are denoted by these abbreviations:

C	*Cosmos* in *Cosmos and Pornografia.* Trans. Eric Mosbacher. New York: Grove P, 1985.
F	*Ferdydurke.* Trans. Eric Mosbacher. New York: Grove P, 1961.
D I	*Diary* Volume 1. Trans. Lillian Vallee. Evanston: Northwestern UP, 1988.
D II	*Diary* Volume 2. Trans. Lillian Vallee. Evanston: Northwestern UP, 1989.
D III	*Diary* Volume 3. Trans. Lillian Vallee. Evanston: Northwestern UP, 1993.
KT	*A Kind of Testament.* Trans. Alastair Hamilton. Philadelphia: Temple UP, 1973.
M	*The Marriage.* Trans. Louis Iribarne. New York: Grove P, 1969.
P	*Pornografia* in *Cosmos and Pornografia.* Trans. Alastair Hamilton. New York: Grove P, 1985.
T	*Trans-Atlantyk.* Trans. Carolyn French and Nina Karsov. New Haven: Yale UP, 1994.

References to other of Gombrowicz's works are marked separately in the text.

Ewa Płonowska Ziarek

Introduction

Reading in the Void: Lessons in Interpretation

How does one read Gombrowicz? In particular, what does it mean to read Gombrowicz in the nineties in the United States? Let us open this question with two remarkable scenes of interpretation from Gombrowicz's novels, *Cosmos* and *Ferdydurke:*

> There was an oppressive profusion of possible links and associations . . . How many sentences can be created with the twenty four letters of the alphabet? How many meanings can be deduced from these hundreds of weeds, clumps of earth, and other small particulars? (*C,* 36, trans. mine).[1]

> Well, then, why does Slowacki arouse our admiration, love and ecstasy? . . . Why? Because, gentlemen, Slowacki was a great poet. Walkiewicz, tell me why! Tell me, Walkiewicz. Why the enchantment, the love, the tears, the exaltation, the magic? Why are our hearts rent? Tell me, Walkiewicz! . . .
>
> "Because he was a great poet, sir," said Walkiewicz. (*F,* 44)

The first of these citations might be read as a somewhat familiar dramatization of the postmodern indeterminacy of meaning, as an uncontrollable proliferation of interpretations, or, as Michel Foucault would say, as the literary performance of the "ponderous, awesome materiality" of language.[2] The second fragment, probably one of the most famous and hilarious scenes in Gombrowicz's texts, displays an ingenious literature lesson during which the ruptures of literary language are translated into the emotional raptures of readerly admiration reserved for the great writers. As the force of the pedagogical instruction inculcates in the students the love of the great writers, "the awesome materiality" of literary language is quickly mastered by the chorus that dutifully repeats that "we love Slowacki because he was a great writer." Eventually, the profusion of meaning is safely contained by the institutionalization of both literature and interpretation. The tension between these two moments—between the excess performed by literary language and the institutional framework of interpretation—is symptomatic for many of Gombrowicz's texts, which not only call attention to the plurality and the tenuous character of meaning but also dramatize the infinite variety of social and institutional games for making sense we have at our disposal. In the words of *Ferdydurke,* "there is nothing like school for inculcating a love of art" (*F,* 47).

Although he knew that the forces of pedagogical instruction are inescapable, Gombrowicz attempted to fight the institutional framing of his own texts through a single but nonnegotiable requirement for his readers: the prohibition of boredom—a prohibition that can make many a literary critic tremble. If Gombrowicz has been spared boredom, which is so often an unfortunate counterpart of that quiet, systematic, academic or pedagogical labor, his reputation has been shaped by two quite different institutional effects of sensationalism and obscurity. In fact, sensationalism and obscurity surrounded him most of his life. Gombrowicz, who started to write at the age of sixteen, acquired for the first time some measure of international reputation at the age of fifty-four, when his first novel, *Ferdydurke,* published in Poland in 1937, was translated into French in 1958. Certainly, the unusual circumstances of his life, where the linguistic, cultural, and political barriers tended to conspire against him and separate his work from his audience, have contributed a great deal to the shape of Gombrowicz's reputation. Most of his texts were written in Argentina, in a country where he found himself by chance and where he could not at first even understand the language; published in Paris, where they were available only to the narrow circle of the émigré community; and banned in his native Poland, where he was considered a dissident writer.[3] As he writes in *Diary,* "Today I awakened in the delight of not knowing what a literary award is, that I do not know official honors, the caresses of the public or critics, that I am not one of 'ours' . . . But I made my debut three times (once before the war, in Poland; once in Argentina; once in Polish in emigration) and none of these debuts spared me one ounce of humiliation" (*D* II, 180).

My own encounters with Gombrowicz have been marked by both of these twin pressures of obscurity and sensationalism. I read him for the first time in the fall of 1980, as a first-year student of English literature at the Warsaw University. These were the times of the Solidarity activism, of the excitement about the imminent political and cultural thaw, of the exhilaration that comes from the conviction that one is a part of the explosive history in the making. The possibility of reading Gombrowicz for the first time—thanks to the rare privilege, granted to all university students and professors, of accessing the forbidden books grouped in the University's Library under the infamous rubric of *cimelia*—seemed like one more symbolic gesture of dissident activity aimed at the regime.

The whole ritual of censorship surrounding the forbidden text—the waiting period, the forms to fill, the examinations, the identity verifications, the limited time (the books on *cimelia* could be read only for two hours at a time in a designated reading room)—all of this assured me in advance of the incredibly subversive qualities of this text. If the great pedagogue Pimko could materialize from the pages of *Ferdydurke* and ask: "Why do we love Gombrowicz?" I would have answered him with a rapture of excitement of my own: "Because he was a dissident writer!" and received the familiar patronizing pat on the back. When I finally started reading Gombrowicz, I could hardly contain my disappointment: what could possibly be dangerous in this surreal story about the thirty-year-old writer dragged back to school by an old pedagogue, Pimko? In fact, what could be more innocuous than this, intellectually fascinating to be sure, text about immaturity, form, artificiality? What could this "fantastic poem describing . . . the tortures of man on a Procrustean bed, the bed of Form" (*KT,* 59) have to do with other forbidden activities like occupational strikes, street demonstrations, and the like?

Unlike the enthusiasm or sincerity of the real struggles, *Ferdydurke* seemed to be bent on destroying any ideal of political authenticity by submitting it to the duel of grimaces:

> Could there be a higher degree of lunacy? Here was Mientus challenging Siphon to a duel of grimaces . . . Grimaces! What an appalling, what an agonizing weapon! . . . Some of us trembled at the thought of Mientus's bringing out into the broad daylight the dreadful weapon which no one had yet dared to use, except after taking precautions to ensure solitude and secrecy. (*F,* 57)

It was not easy to shake this scene from my mind, to bracket it off from the events taking place in the streets, even though Gombrowicz repeatedly claimed that "the role of the 'committed,' progressive intellectual teaching humanity which path to take seemed . . . both too pretentious and too frivolous" (*KT,* 55). Reading Gombrowicz at that moment did not produce an easy allegory of totalitarianism (I heard about this interpretation even before knowing the text) but was like a demystifying warning against uncritical glorification of dissidence itself—a sobering caution against monumentalization of both repression and freedom, a corrosive parody of politics based on authenticity, liberation, or collective enthusiasm. In its place, Gombrowicz seemed to be redefining political struggle as a matter of strategies, of artificial poses, ingenious games of signification, indeed, as the endless duels of grimaces.[4]

My other remarkable reading of Gombrowicz occurred many years later, at a very different geographical, intellectual, and institutional location. A few years ago, Marjorie Perloff invited me to give a paper at the MLA panel she organized, a panel devoted to Eastern-European intellectuals, with David Antin as the respondent. I rather dreaded the prospect of giving a paper at an MLA Slavic panel. The peculiar institutional position of Slavic studies in the American academy, the marginalization and the isolation of the "second" Slavic literatures, was just too discouraging. I was confronted with a different void, created this time not by the active political censorship but by the quiet institutionalization of knowledge.[5] As usual, I was astounded how theoretically adept we are to deal with what, after Deleuze and Guattari, we call "minor literature" and how practically incapable to extend this mode of interpretation to new objects of study.[6]

Despite my reservations, I admired too much the gesture of a critic like Marjorie Perloff, willing to use the power of her reputation in order to open up alternative spaces for intellectual inquiry, to turn this invitation down. For that occasion I tried to read Gombrowicz along with another prominent Eastern European intellectual, Julia Kristeva, by focusing on their similar preoccupations with nationality as a signifying form. There is nothing like an MLA convention to make one realize how far apart these two figures are situated in the institutional landscape despite the proximity of their geographical origins, historical positions, and intellectual interests. As the marked difference between the receptions of my work on Kristeva and Gombrowicz shows, the audiences interested in Kristeva and the audiences interested in Gombrowicz do not occupy the same intellectual location or institutional status. This disjunction, which structurally resembles institutionalized schizophrenia, not only circumscribes the possibilities of knowledge but also reflects the effects of the politics of ignorance. In contrast to the dramatic ritual of censorship, the hierarchies of knowledge operate silently and invisibly, but produce equally powerful effects.

These three reading lessons—Gombrowicz's own dramatization of the institutional Form containing the interpretative possibilities of the text and my own experiences of the different effects of such forms—are symptomatic of the difficulties and opportunities for the reception of Gombrowicz in the United States today. On the one hand, the current state of the debates about the philosophical and political crisis of modernity, the ongoing reflection on the intellectual and institutional effects of literary theory, the interdisciplinary dialogue between philosophy and literature, the critique of the Eurocentrism and imperialism of Western culture, the interest in the subaltern identities and literatures, and, finally, the discourse on the signification and politics of sexuality create an intellectual climate that should be receptive to so many of Gombrowicz's artistic preoccupations and interests. Even more so, reading Gombrowicz in the context of American intellectual life could enable new and exiting revisions of Gombrowicz's work—to mention just one most obvious example, it would allow for reclaiming the centrality of homosexuality in his critique of aesthetics and culture, without reducing its importance, as is still the case in Gombrowicz criticism, to the sensational biographical secret.[7] Yet, on the other hand, these new interpretative possibilities are contained and severely limited by the institutional Form and the politics of isolation surrounding the so-called second Slavic literatures. Gombrowicz's case forces us again to reexamine not only the range of our objects of study and the still overwhelming confinement of the debates about modernity to the Western intellectual traditions, but ultimately the very presuppositions of the theoretical debates that make such a confinement possible.

Cultural Hybridity and the Postures of Biography

There are many critical portraits of Gombrowicz now available in English which would seem to make the extended gesture of the biographical introduction somewhat superfluous.[8] One of them is provided by Maurice Nadeau, Gombrowicz's French publisher, who in his preface to *A Kind of Testament* presents Gombrowicz as "one of the most original writers of our day," "an exceptional individual, a character quite out of the common, whose work, exemplary in so many ways, will continue to be profoundly *perturbing*" (*KT,* 13). Wojciech Karpiński, in his superb introductory essay to Gombrowicz's *Diary,* gives us a Nietzschean portrait of Gombrowicz: "the affectingly cool critic of European tradition, the diagnostician of the disease afflicting contemporary thought, the great artist and the great moralist. If I were to designate a worthy successor to 'the joyful science' of Nietzschean criticism and poetry in twentieth-century literature, I would answer: Gombrowicz in his *Diary*" (*D* I, xiv). For Gilles Deleuze, Gombrowicz belongs, together with Joyce and Borges, to the most interesting avant-garde writers transforming the legacy of the Baroque into experimental modern writing.[9] And in his introduction to the recent English translation of *Trans-Atlantyk,* Stanisław Barańczak presents Gombrowicz as both a rigorous philosopher and an unsurpassed stylist: "Probably no other fiction writer in modern world literature can match the almost intimidating consistency and precision of Gombrowicz's system of ideas."[10]

In addition to these critical portraits, there are, of course, numerous autobiographical gestures performed by Gombrowicz himself. It is hard to imagine a writer so willing to indulge in autobiographical confessions—*Diaries, Wspomnienia Polskie* (Polish recollections), *A Kind of Testament,* not to mention the many autobiographical intrusions into his literary works—and yet remaining so elusive. The ironic opening of his *Diary* is a characteristic example of Gombrowicz's teasing performances of self-disclosure:

> Monday
> Me.
> Tuesday
> Me.
> Wednesday
> Me.
> Thursday
> Me.
> Friday (*D* I, 3)

If, despite these numerous critical introductions and dazzling autobiographical performances, we nonetheless return obsessively to the question formulated some years ago by Czesław Miłosz—"Who is Gombrowicz?"—it is because the pervasive "me" of Gombrowicz remains an enigma, a titillating cipher, a carefully orchestrated puzzle to which there is no one solution.[11]

This persistent movement of self-disclosure and concealment is not just an aesthetic game Gombrowicz plays with his readers but, rather, a rigorous reenactment of the hybrid sense of his cultural and social positions. In his autobiographical reflections, written shortly before his death and published as *A Kind of Testament,* Gombrowicz gives us not only the basic events of his life and the main concerns of his work but also a crucial figure of "in-Betweenness" for interpreting his life. Born in 1904 at a small country estate at Małoszyce, Poland, Gombrowicz belonged to a family suspended between land and industry, between country and city, between the upper- and lower-middle classes:

> In that Proustian epoch at the beginning of the century, we were a displaced family whose social status was far from clear, living between Lithuania and the former Congress Kingdom of Poland, between land and industry, between what is known as 'good society' and another, more middle-class society. These were the first 'betweens,' which subsequently multiplied until they almost constituted my country of residence. (*KT,* 28)

Since the time of his childhood, the spaces of in-between tended to multiply in Gombrowicz's carrier, conveying a sense of cultural hybridity as the most characteristic feature of his life and work.

One of these in-betweens was the tension between law and literature. To please his father, Gombrowicz studied law, but after his father's death most of his energies were to be devoted to literature. Despite its mixed reviews, his first collection of short stories, *Memoirs of a Time of Immaturity,* published in 1933, already earned him, as Gombrowicz himself admits, "a certain prestige in *avant-garde* circles." Gombrowicz started frequenting literary cafés in Warsaw, in particular café *Ziemiańska,* where he had his own table and was usually surrounded by young aspiring writers. The collection of short stories was soon followed by a play, *Ivona, Princess of Burgundia,* and by his first major novel, *Ferdydurke,* published in 1937. Attacked by the nationalist press, *Ferdydurke* was nonetheless regarded as a major artistic accomplishment, giving Gombrowicz the reputation of one of the major, and certainly most interesting, writers in prewar Poland. Through the literary friendships with Tadeusz Breza, Adolf Rudnicki, Zofia Nałkowska, Witkacy, and especially, Bruno Schulz, Gombrowicz soon became an established figure in the Polish literary world. As he himself wrote, "Witkacy, Schulz, and myself [are] three people attempting to direct literature to the new tracks"[12] (trans. mine).

Gombrowicz did not have the opportunity, however, to enjoy this literary reputation for long. In August 1939, he was invited (or rather invited himself) to participate in the inaugural voyage of the ocean liner Chrobry to Argentina. He was supposed to be a cultural representative of sorts of the new Polish state, which regained its independence in 1918 after almost 150 years of partition under the imperialist rule of Prussia, Russia, and Austria.[13] Ironically, his short literary mission to Argentina turned into twenty-four years of exile, and the transatlantic journey was soon to become the all-embracing metaphor for the cultural in-betweenness constituting Gombrowicz's "country of residence." The twenty-four years in Argentina constituted an extraordinary period in Gombrowicz's life: a period of extreme destitution and intense liberation, of historical tragedy and personal rejuvenation, of loneliness and new friendships (in particular, with Cuban and Argentinean writers and intellectuals, like Virgilio Piñera, Alejandro Rússovich, and Ernesto Sabato), of remarkable textual and sexual experimentation.[14] As Gombrowicz writes of those sexual practices, "He had hardly anything to do with the Polish émigrés and his friends were mainly young Argentinians. Homosexual experiences with lower class boys he picked up in Buenos Aires" (*KT,* 21). And then he adds, "I was nothing so I could do anything" (*KT,* 116). This sense of unlimited possibilities despite severe poverty inspired the major works written during this period: *The Banquet* (written in 1944), *The Marriage* (written between 1944 and 1947, first published in Spanish translation in Buenos Aires in 1947 and then in Polish in Paris in 1952), *Trans-Atlantyk* (1952), *Diary* (started in 1953 and continued until his death), *Pornografia* (1960), and *Operetta* (started in 1955, published in Paris in 1966).

For all these reasons—economic, political, literary, and sexual—Gombrowicz's Argentinean adventure lends itself easily, as Wojciech Karpiński suggests, to controversial mythologization and even to glorification, a process started no doubt by Gombrowicz himself. As he confesses again and again, "the bitter, tragic, poetic taste of the first seven years had left its mark on me"; "never have I been so much of a poet as then, in those hot streets packed with people, completely lost" (*KT,* 85–86). He frequently stages his arrival in Argentina as a radical break, a destructive yet liberating delivery from the past—the trauma and excitement of a second birth: "I was suddenly in Argentina, completely alone, cut off, lost, ruined, anonymous. I was a little excited, a little frightened. Yet at the same time, something in me told me to greet with passionate emotion the blow that was destroying me and upsetting the order I had known up to now" (*D* I, 130).

In these mythologizing moments, Gombrowicz identifies with Argentina completely, and he associates it with the type of writing he always aspired to achieve:

> What is Argentina? Batter that has not yet become cake, or something that is simply unshaped, or, perhaps, a protest against the mechanization of the spirit, the reluctant, devil-may-care gesture of a man who is removing himself from a too automatic accumulation—an intelligence that is too intelligent, a beauty that is too beautiful, a morality that is too moral? In this climate, in this constellation, a genuine and creative protest against Europe could arise if—if the softness found a way to make itself hard or if the indistinctness could become a program, a definition. (*D* I, 72)

In this ambiguous and controversial figure of Argentina as both "something that is simply unshaped" and the "a genuine and creative protest against Europe," we will find all the crucial aspects of Gombrowicz's aesthetics: Argentina, like other cultures that Gombrowicz considered "minor," became an ally in the struggle with the domination of European culture, with the automatism of forms, with the mechanization of modern life, and with the rigidity of the signifying economies that reached their final state of completion. Argentina offered Gombrowicz not exactly an escape but the possibility of a second beginning, and thus of a certain distance from form in its manifold cultural manifestations: nationality, aesthetics, morality, religion, social status, personal identity. It enabled a passionate "protest against Europe" without congealing this protest into a program, artistic or otherwise.

Invited in 1963 to Berlin by the Ford Foundation, Gombrowicz returned to Europe (but not to his native Poland) to find fame, illness, and death. During these six years, he wrote his last novel, *Cosmos* (1966); the third volume of his *Diary;* the autobiographical reflections of his life and work, *A Kind of Testament;* and the whimsical lectures in the history of philosophy from Kant to structuralism, called "A Guide to Philosophy in Six Hours and a Quarter." He witnessed the numerous translations of his work, the successful performances of his plays at the major theaters in Europe, and received the prestigious International Publishers' Prize for *Cosmos.* He died in 1969 in Vence from a heart attack. As a friend, who met Gombrowicz for the first and last time during his funeral, tells me, it was only fitting that in his last journey Gombrowicz was followed not by literary figures but by a crowd of young hippies.[15]

The Embarrassments of Form and Other Aesthetic Matters

The question of Form is of such an enormous importance in Gombrowicz's writing and it is posed in such an original manner that no responsible introduction to his work can possibly overlook it.[16] If one is tempted, however, to do just that it is because the somewhat disreputable (or even, as Marianne DeKoven says, "blunt" and "banal"[17]) ring of the word *form* in the context of Anglo-American modernism and its criticism, dominated first by the hegemony of New Criticism and then by the long overdue revolt against it, can create misunderstanding of Gombrowicz's work from the outset. To avoid the likely reduction of form to literary style, or to the claims of autonomy for the work of art, we have to recall Gombrowicz's own complaints that the "view of Form has often been interpreted somewhat too narrowly" in modern literature:[18]

> I must admit that the forms of the novel do not interest me particularly. It seems to me typical of over-refined cultures, like the Parisian culture, to tend to reduce the gigantic problem of Form to the elaboration of ever new models of the *nouveau roman,* to literature, and, worse still, to literature about literature. (*KT,* 72)

If Gombrowicz resolutely refuses to confine the problematic of Form to the realm of aesthetics alone, or to reduce it to the talk of "literature about literature," it is because he poses it at the fundamental level of language and the social forms of signification.[19] When seen in this light, Gombrowicz's concept of Form has to be considered simultaneously, as Jerzy Jarzębski argues in his seminal essay, as a linguistic, sociological, philosophical, and psychological as well as an aesthetic category.[20]

Another central obsession in Gombrowicz's work is the question of the subject, or, to be more precise, the effect of the signifying forms on the formation of subjectivity. In *A Kind of Testament* he formulates this question in following manner: "If I am always an artefact, always defined by others and by culture as well as by my own formal necessities, where should I look for my 'self'? Who am I really and to what extent *am* I?" (*KT,* 77). If Gombrowicz is troubled by the reduction of Being under the pressure of language, it is because the effect of Form appeared to him to be nothing short of amputation—a cut destroying the illusory fullness of Being in order to enable the possibility of subjective enunciation:[21]

> ". . . I must perform a still more radical operation! I must amputate myself from myself!"
>
> I suppose that Nietzsche might have formulated my dilemma in these terms. I proceeded to amputate. The following

> thought was the scalpel: accept, understand that you are not yourself, that no-one is ever himself with anyone, in any situation, that to be a man is to be artificial. (*KT,* 58)

Despite his relentless emphasis on the exteriority and artifice of linguistic expression, Gombrowicz refuses to see Form merely as an obstacle inhibiting a more authentic identity or true "inner" self. That is why Form becomes in Gombrowicz's work synonymous with the vulgarized word for face. The misleading desire for authenticity or unmasking could lead, therefore, only to a tragic de-facement, to a loss of one's constitution: "Not that man should get rid of his own mug—for beyond it he has no face—here one can only demand that he be conscious of his artificiality and confess it" (*D* II, 4).

Although in Gombrowicz's texts the speaking subjects have "no face" beyond the form of their expression, it does not mean that they identify with these signifying forms without a struggle. The struggle with Form is expressed in Gombrowicz's work as the conflict of two contradictory desires, the desire for order and expression on the one hand, and on the other an equally strong, although experienced as illegitimate, desire for the unfinished and the chaotic, for the state symbolized as the always already lost immaturity:

> Man, as we know, aims at the absolute. At fulfillment. At truth, at God, at total maturity . . . To seize everything, to realize himself entirely—this is his imperative.
>
> Now, in *Pornografia* it seems to me that another of man's aims appears, a more secret one, undoubtedly, one which is in some way illegal: his need for the unfinished . . . for imperfection . . . for inferiority . . . for youth.[22]

This conflict of desires is disseminated in Gombrowicz's fiction through numerous antinomic configurations: Cosmos and Chaos, perfection and inferiority, value and waste, high and low, mastery and slavery, innovation and obsolescence, maturity and youth, cultivation and "under-development," West and East.[23] In a way, Gombrowicz resolves these antinomies in a Kantian manner, that is, by showing that both absolute formulations are false and inaccessible to experience. As Stanisław Barańczak argues, "complete identification of the individual with the extreme of Form would mean dissolution in the conventional, that is, spiritual death; complete identification with the extreme of Chaos would mean absolute isolation, that is spiritual death again."[24] This precarious position of the self suspended between two deaths—the death of inarticulation and the death of enunciation—is, in the end, Gombrowicz's formulation of the being of the linguistically constituted subject—an answer to the question: "to what extent *am* I?"

The traumas of articulation, which always already entail a deformation of the speaking self, are not confined in Gombrowicz's work merely to the private psychological space.[25] Gombrowicz's obsession with the condition of the speaking subject goes hand in hand with his explorations of the "interhuman" character of language, or, what he sometimes refers to as "interhuman church." In this intersubjective domain, the problematic of signification is intertwined with the question of nationality, ideology (Gombrowicz describes, for instance, the rise of fascism and communism in prewar years as the demonic "period of formal mobilization" [*KT,* 58]), and culture in the most general sense. As an artist and social critic, Gombrowicz has been fascinated by "the colossal pressure of pre-established Form elaborated by culture" (*KT,* 74). In *Trans-Atlantyk* and *Diary,* this fascination resulted in the extraordinary analysis of nationality as a signifying form—an analysis that anticipates in many ways Benedict Anderson's influential work. Gombrowicz's interest in intersubjective character of signification bifurcates, however, into different lines of inquiry: it leads to the exploration of the general social conditions of signification, on the one hand, and, on the other, to local interactions with others, so frequently staged in his works through the figure of the duel.[26] If the first aspect explains Gombrowicz's interest in structuralism, the second illuminates his fascination with Sartre's and Buber's philosophy, each in a different way describing I/Thou relations. The relationship between "social forms of being" and the dynamic "deformations" produced in the singular encounters with others can be best explained through the contrast between the notion of language conceived as the general rules of signification and the notion of language as specific linguistic performances.

In order to account for Gombrowicz's virtuoso performances with his scalpel/pen that carves out the question of Being as the question of signification ("to be a man is to be artificial"), numerous critics have stressed the affinities between his work and poststructuralist theories, especially those of Derrida and Lacan. In his 1967 interview given for the French journal *La Quinzaine Littèraire,* Gombrowicz himself points to such proximities:

> "The 'structure' of structuralists is not the same as what I understand by 'form,' I assure you. I read here and there, a little of Greimas, Bourdieu, Jacobson, Macherey, Ehrmann, Barbut, Althusser, Bopp, Levi-Strauss . . . Foucault, Genett, Godelier . . . , Marx . . . Lacan and Poulet, and also Goldmann, Starobinski, Barthes . . . As you see, I am very current.[27] (Trans. mine)

This slightly ironized intellectual genealogy, which resembles so closely the reading list of my graduate students taking their exam in critical theory, encourages numerous comparisons with poststructuralist thought. No wonder that for contemporary critics Gombrowicz becomes a kind of poststructuralist *avant la lettre,* just as the earlier generation of readers saw him as the precursor of the debate between existentialism and structuralism.[28] Since Gombrowicz regarded himself as a prophetic critic of structuralism before structuralism actually took place ("I Was the First Structuralist"), we can only imagine the glee with which he would have proclaimed himself a poststructuralist *"avant tout le monde."*

Queer Gombrowicz and the Study of Modernity

But let us return, before we get ahead of ourselves, to Gombrowicz's place in the context of literary modernism since this context was one of the defining moments in his literary career. As we have seen already, Gombrowicz's emphasis on the aesthetic and sociocultural significance of Form and on the hybrid character of cultural identities undermines many familiar and comfortable binary oppositions operating in both the traditional and revisionary assessments of modernism, as, for instance, the opposition between aesthetics and politics, individualism and collectivity, the assertion and the negation of the autonomy of the work of art.[29] If we also recall Gombrowicz's simultaneous use of both the experimental and popular modes of writing (for instance, the genre of the detective story and the gothic novel in *Cosmos,* the popular Baroque memoirs in *Trans-Atlantyk,* or musical comedy in *Operetta*[30]) as well as his engagement both in the philosophical reflection on the constitution of subjectivity and in the cultural criticism of nationalism, then we will have to reconsider another fundamental division in the study of modernism, namely, the divide between high and popular culture.[31]

This double movement of bringing Gombrowicz's work to the debate about modernism while at the same time contesting some of the parameters of this debate is the first task this collection hopes to accomplish. One of the main questions *Gombrowicz's Grimaces* poses is about the significance of reading Gombrowicz at the moment when the term *modernism* itself undergoes a crisis in the wake of the cultural contestation of its normative presumptions and intellectual legacy.[32] How can Gombrowicz's work participate in the current discussions about the significance of literary modernism in the context of nationalism, aesthetics, sexuality, and the broadly conceived tradition of modernity?

The second task of the collection is to initiate the in-depth study of Gombrowicz's texts in the United States. These two goals are closely interrelated. Given the institutional marginalization of Slavic studies in the American academy, to place Gombrowicz in the context of the recent debates on modernism without close attention to the specificity of his work can be misread as yet another gesture of academic legitimation or belated advertising—an attempt to prove that the value of the experimental Slavic literature is comparable to the achievements of the Western avant-garde and thus merits equal critical attention. This game of legitimation usually assumes the form of "Reading Gombrowicz with . . ."; for instance, with Kant, with Sartre, Nietzsche, Lacan, Deleuze, Derrida, in my case, with Kristeva, or any other famous Western figure of considerable status and intellectual currency. As Gombrowicz sardonically observes, "inflating oneself with Sartre one says, with a patronizing tone, Gombrowicz."[33] There is, however, another way of situating Gombrowicz in the study of the modern period. To bring Gombrowicz to the debate about modernism and modernity can also entail an interrogation of the significance of the normative status of modernism from a position that is marked by an uneven distribution of cultural, national, aesthetic, and sexual values.

This move is encouraged by Gombrowicz himself, who so frequently rethinks the value of European modernism from the hybrid locations of the "secondary" European and non-European cultures:

> The passages in my diary when I mention "Polishness" have only been read very superficially by western readers. I was almost told: "You'd better cut all that . . ." It is high time that the heirs of superior cultures stopped turning up their noses. Instead of "Poland," put the Argentine, Canada, Romania and so on, and you'll see that my allusions (and my sufferings) can be applied to most of the globe. They concern all secondary European cultures. Look at them still closer: you'll see that they constitute a poison which may affect *you* too. (*KT,* 53)

"Polishness" is, no doubt, one of the most complicated and controversial figures in Gombrowicz's texts. When he addresses his Polish readers, Gombrowicz becomes one of the most uncompromising critics of the legacy of Polish nationality, which, throughout most of its modern history, has functioned as the "nationalism-without-a-state." In particular, Gombrowicz refuses to distinguish between the tradition of the struggles for national independence from the imperialist rule of Russia, Prussia, and Austria and the xenophobic nationalism also produced under the conditions of colonial occupation.[34] In reversing the ethos of the struggles for decolonization, Gombrowicz, with the usual mixture of lucidity, arrogance, and provocation, claims to "liberate Poles from Poland." When Gombrowicz addresses his Western audience, however, he embraces "Polishness" as a trope for the numerous forgotten peripheries of European culture. Refigured as the privileged location of writing itself, these peripheries become a dangerous "poison," a secret weapon in the contestation of modern cosmopolitanism. I would like to focus here in greater detail on only two effects of this contestation, on Gombrowicz's revision of the avant-garde legacy and on his exploration of queer sexuality.

For Gombrowicz the passionate protest against the constitutive features of European modernism leads to a rethinking of the temporal structures of the avant-garde itself and eventually to a formulation of a different mode of experimental writing. As many critics observe, the avant-garde criticism of modernity depends on its claim to be a step ahead of its historical moment, in advance of its contemporaries.[35] By writing from the periphery, frequently perceived as "lagging behind" the development of the Western history, Gombrowicz brackets the revolutionary and proleptic claims of the avant-garde and juxtaposes them with the experience of cultural obsolescence or belatedness. This strategy is most strikingly deployed in *Trans-Atlantyk,* where the degraded and obsolete Baroque style is used to describe the modern experience of exile. By foregrounding uneven developments in the peripheries and the cosmopolitan centers, Gombrowicz's dialectic of innovation and obsolescence calls attention in his texts to what Rita Felski calls "nonsynchronicity," or "dissonance between the discourse of those intellectuals mourning or celebrating the death of their own guiding meta-narratives and the very different perspective of other disenfranchised groups who are beginning to gain access to the public constructions of their own genealogies."[36] This dialectic not only disrupts the temporal structures of the avant-garde but also calls attention to the intimate relation between "speed" and the cultural and aesthetic values of modernity.[37]

Another important contribution Gombrowicz's work makes to the debates about modernism is by exploring the relation between "cultural in-betweenness" and sexuality. In many of his works, but in particular in *Diaries* and *Trans-Atlantyk,* the aesthetic experimentation is intertwined with the contestation of the privilege of masculinity and with the explorations of the cultural significance of queer sexuality. In the context of Western modernism, these parallels between modern aesthetics and the performance of homosexual identities have received significant attention, thanks to the groundbreaking work of Richard Dellamora, Eve Kosofsky Sedgwick, Ed Cohen, and Jonathan Dollimore.[38] As most of these queer theorists argue, experimental aesthetic practices allowed modern writers like Wilde and Proust to find alternative cultural spaces in which same-sex desire could be reclaimed and revalorized. When seen in this perspective, Gombrowicz's work presents an extraordinary continuity between his articulation of Form and his performance of sexuality. Let us compare, for instance, Gombrowicz's stress on the linguistic deformations of the speaking self with his description of the crisis of the heterosexual masculine identity:

> So what could be the cause of that inner disorder, which turned a reasonably happy boy like me into a bizarre monster, lured by deformity, by all existing aberrations? I was . . . an abnormal

> being who could never admit to anybody what he really was, condemned to hide for ever, to conspire. Erotic impulses dragged me downwards, toward the gutter . . . I was 'between'. And I was an actor. (*KT,* 37–38)

In Gombrowicz's descriptions of both sexual and aesthetic practices we find a similar emphasis on theatricality, performativity, deformation, and especially on the artificiality of all linguistically constituted identities. Just as Gombrowicz destroys the notion of an "essential" national identity, so, too, he resists what Michel Foucault so brilliantly diagnosed as the reification of sexual practices into "essences."[39] These parallels between textual and sexual experimentation allow Gombrowicz to subvert the homophobic representation of homoeroticism as an unspeakable "aberration" and to turn it not only into the condition of art but also into the fundamental condition of being a speaking subject.

In thinking about sexuality, Gombrowicz returns again to the figure of in-betweenness, which, as we have seen, characterized so many aspects of his life and work. This transitive and hybrid sense of sexual positions reminds me of Eve Kosofsky Sedgwick's meditation on the word *queer:*

> Queer is a continuing moment, movement, motive—recurrent, eddying, *troublant.* The word "queer" itself means *across*—it comes from the Indo-European root *twerkw,* which also yields the German *quer* (transverse), Latin *torquere* (to twist), English *athwart.* Titles and subtitles that at various times I've attached to the essays in *Tendencies* tend toward "across" formulations: *across genders, across sexualities, across genres, across "perversions."* . . . Keenly it is relational, and strange.[40]

For Gombrowicz, too, the notion of sexual in-betweenness tends to stand for so many crossings (or perhaps, in his case, for all those "trans" formations)—the crossings of languages, cultures, continents, genders, social positions, historical moments—that, in the end, it merges with the all-embracing metaphor of his work, namely, the trans-Atlantic journey. When homoeroticism becomes linked with textuality and form, then this "in-betweenness" is linked to the refusal of both the antinomic formulations of modern aesthetics and the binary oppositions of sexual difference.

In Gombrowicz's work, the "in-betweenness," or queerness, eroticizes all other aspects of relational or hybrid identities without losing, however, its specific reference to sexuality. As the already cited passage from *A Kind of Testament* suggests, this figurative dance of generalization and particularity allows Gombrowicz to expose the ever changing values of hybridity and homoeroticism in different cultural locations. With a painful sobriety, Gombrowicz remarks that the "in-between" position is more likely to be associated with creative energy when it is seen as a figure for textual experimentation alone; yet, when it refers explicitly to homosexual practices, it is all too often linked in homophobic culture with monstrosity, degeneration, and fear. Nonetheless, the transitivity of sexual identities in Gombrowicz's work also opens a possibility of intervention as it implies that the valorization of same-sex desire can be changed in different cultural sites. Thus, if the early crisis of masculinity is figured in a *Kind of Testament* as a "monstrosity," the Argentinean experience of homoeroticism turns this "degradation" into "the blossoming of youth" and the passion for life.

By examining the sociopolitical consequences of Gombrowicz's aesthetics, in particular the role of artistic innovations in the contestation of gender norms, cultural identities, and nationalism, *Gombrowicz's Grimaces* demonstrates the significance of Gombrowicz for the comparative study of modernism—the significance thus far only intimated in the frequently repeated claim of American reviews: no consideration of twentieth-century literature is conceivable without including his work. This importance is evident in the very range of the disciplines represented by the contributors to this volume—comparative literature, Slavic studies, Latin American studies, theater studies, German literature, and French literature. By making available some of the more creative scholarship on Gombrowicz to the critics and students of the modern period, this collection hopes to make a twofold intervention in the debates about modernism. First, it participates in the current project of rethinking the ambiguous legacies and mixed genealogies of modernism in the larger cultural and political contexts. Second, this book also argues that this revisionary project is largely incomplete because of the confinement of literary modernity to the American and Western European canons, evident even in the work of such important critics as Rita Felski or Andreas Huyssen. By bringing Gombrowicz's work into the very center of the debates on modernism, the contributors to this volume concur with Rita Felski that "the history of the modern is thus not yet over; in a very real sense, it has yet to be written."[41]

Gombrowicz's Grimaces; or, The Outline of This Project

Reflecting the crucial issues in the study of modernism, the collection is composed of three parts, each one focused at the same time on the central preoccupations in Gombrowicz's career. Starting with the considerations of Gombrowicz's aesthetics (part 1), the volume proceeds to address the ways in which the experience of cultural displacement—Gombrowicz's exile in Argentina and France—informs his literary career (part 2) and ends with a discussion of the relationship between experimental writing and the critique of nationality and the heterosexual model of masculinity (part 3). The post/script analyzes the history of the reception and translation of Gombrowicz's texts in the United States and provides a critical discussion of the secondary works available in English. Taken as a whole, the collection presents Gombrowicz not only as a major avant-garde writer but also as a theoretician and a cultural critic of modernity.

The first part, entitled "Gombrowicz's Aesthetics: Writing, Self, Performance," develops the implications of Gombrowicz's concept of Form. The essays in this section situate Gombrowicz's aesthetic reflections and his literary practice in the context of the poststructuralist theories of writing and performance, European literary traditions, and Gombrowicz's own philosophical interests, ranging from Kant to structuralism.[42] Although diverse in their approaches, all three of the essays return to the central preoccupation in Gombrowicz's texts—to the struggle between the anarchic hybridity of the self and the "formal imperative," which threatens to submit writing to the "tyranny" of the dogmatic forms of dominant culture.

The second part, "Modernity and the Trajectories of Exile," reexamines the relation between exile and modernism by taking into account Gombrowicz's problematic and often conflicted relation to Polish, Argentinean, and French cultures. Building on Gombrowicz's interest in hybrid and subaltern identities, the three essays in this section argue that the concept of exile has to be reconceived beyond the twin topoi of modernism—the nostalgia for origins and its opposite, the naive celebration of displacement—if it is to function as an enabling condition of literary production and cultural criticism.

The third part, "Gombrowicz's Provocations: National Forms, Queer Sexualities," explores the cultural implications of Gombrowicz's philosophy of Form. Rejecting the formalist readings of modernism, the essays in this section focus on the complex relation between aesthetics and politics, between Gombrowicz's critique of nationalism and his explorations of queer eroticism. By making the question of homosexuality central for understanding both Gombrowicz's aesthetics and his contestation of national culture, these essays address the often ignored topic not only in Gombrowicz's scholarship but also in the study of modernism.[43]

The collection starts with Tomislav Longinović's essay, which explores the complexity of Gombrowicz's aesthetics by engaging poststructuralist theories of writing and autobiography. Focused on Gombrowicz's literary autobiography, *A Kind of Testament,* the essay discusses Gombrowicz's preoccupations with the performative aspects of being in the context of Nietzsche's *Ecce Homo,* Derrida's autobiography, and Kristeva's notion of the abject. The essay argues that "Gombrowicz's performance of the 'self' takes place on the stage of writing, which is for him a place of struggle between the dark, abject desires . . . and the formal imperative which demands that abjection be transposed into literature."

In contrast to Longinović's theoretical reflection, Valérie Deshoulières's essay, "Witold Gombrowicz: Toward a Romantic Theory of Incompleteness," explores the specificity of Gombrowicz's aesthetics in the context of the European literary tradition of "paradoxical romanticism," extending from Keats and Hölderlin to Baudelaire and Musil. Fascinated with the fragmentariness, porosity, and incompleteness of the work of art, this type of romanticism is equally seduced by the "immaturity," anarchy, and the essential plasticity of the self. Focusing on Gombrowicz's self-portrait as a modern chameleon—as a strange "agglomeration of different worlds, neither one nor the other"—Deshoulières suggests that this poetics betrays an affinity both with Keats's description of poetic character as "every thing and nothing" and with Musil's formulation of modern subject as a "man without qualities." Yet, if Gombrowicz affirms the anarchic plasticity of the self as the possibility of the poetic experience, this affirmation emerges only in the aftermath of a long struggle with the historical determinations of subjectivity, such as nationality, religion, and literary tradition.

Dorota Głowacka's essay, "The Heresiarchs of Form: Gombrowicz and Schulz," explores Gombrowicz's and Schulz's critiques of *mimesis* within Polish literary traditions. Despite critics' insistence on their "literary kinship," both writers, Głowacka argues, denounce such affinity in order to proclaim the inimitability of their texts. By engaging Philippe Lacoue-Labarthe's work, the essay investigates their pronounced repudiation of the mimetic moment with respect to each other and to literary models as such. By insisting on the condition of absolute solitude, both Gombrowicz and Schulz challenge the paradigm of representation, grounded in the politics of form. In so doing, they obey an ethic-aesthetic imperative, which they define, in contrast to the mimetic ideal of adequation, as the movement of transcendence.

Focused on the detailed psychoanalytic reading of Gombrowicz's major novels—*Ferdydurke, Trans-Atlantyk, Pornografia,* and *Cosmos*—Hanjo Berressem's essay, "The Laws of Deviation: Physical and Psychic Aberrations in the Novels of Witold Gombrowicz," develops the philosophical underpinnings of Gombrowicz's aesthetics. Following Gombrowicz's interests in the Kantian antinomies, the essay presents Gombrowicz's poetics as a fictional deconstruction of the classical architectonics of reason. If Kant resolves the antinomies of pure reason by privileging the interests of the practical reason, Gombrowicz's characters remain suspended in the catastrophic space of the in-between, attracted equally to the moral dictates of the law as well as to the irrationality of pathological desires. The only exit from this catastrophic in-between is the collapse of the divided subject into a state of pure enjoyment, or what Lacan calls jouissance. Traversing the mysterious "roads by which Kant-the-child and Kant-the adolescent changed into Kant-the-philosopher" (*Diary* I, 184–85), Gombrowicz offers us a confrontation with the Kantian philosophy worthy, indeed, of Lacan: as Berressem suggests, Gombrowicz in fact "becomes Kant dreaming of being Sade."

Opening the section on the relation between modernist poetics and the trajectories of exile, Marzena Grzegorczyk's study focuses on the Argentinean legacy of Gombrowicz's writings. This topic is of enormous importance for understanding Gombrowiczean views of literature and culture and, yet, frequently ignored because of the lack of the necessary knowledge of the double, Argentinean and Polish, literary contexts. Approaching Gombrowicz's writings as a source of cultural theory of hybridity, "Formed Lives, Formless Traditions: The Argentinean Legacy of Witold Gombrowicz" discusses the ways in which Gombrowicz's call to decompose the oppressive discourse of the state and nation has been interpreted by the intellectuals and artists of Buenos Aires. In particular, the essay focuses on Ricardo Piglia's 1982 novel, *Artificial Respiration,* in which one of the main characters is openly modeled after Gombrowicz. The essay ends with a theoretical reflection on the paradigms of cultural self-construction in hybrid cultures and points to the limitations of Gombrowicz's views of subaltern identities.

In his essay, "Gombrowicz, Dialectically Speaking: Of Lyricisms, Dissidents, and Politics," Piotr Parlej discusses the notion of exile in the context of Polish dissident literature by focusing on Gombrowicz's rewriting of dialectics. As Parlej argues, the dialectical mode of writing allows Gombrowicz to overcome modernism's tendency to simplify aesthetic experience and to separate art from politics. At the same time, this postdialectical position enables Gombrowicz to contest the excessive valorization of lyricism in the name of authenticity that came to characterize Polish dissident writers in communist Poland. By avoiding both the modernist and socialist-realist temptations, Gombrowicz occupies a unique position in the postmodern landscape of Europe and his native Poland.

In her "Defamation in Exile: Witold Gombrowicz and E. M. Cioran," Katarzyna Jerzak explores the relation between modernism and exile through the comparative study of Gombrowicz and E. M. Cioran, a Romanian artist writing in France. Faced with the difficulty of representing the "second" Europe, a minor literature, and a lesser language, both writers could embrace the condition of exile as the possibility of writing only through the complex strategies of defamation directed at nationality, religion, literature, and even their own writings. On the basis of Cioran's and Gombrowicz's writings, Jerzak argues that defamation becomes a modern form of ascesis as well as a defense against the cultural ideologies.

In her reading of *Trans-Atlantyk,* "The Scar of the Foreigner and the Fold of the Baroque: National Affiliations and Homosexuality in Gombrowicz's *Trans-Atlantyk,*" Ewa Płonowska Ziarek initiates a long overdue discussion of homosexuality in the context of Gombrowicz's critique of national identity. In order to escape the complex legacy of Polish nationalism, Gombrowicz redoubles the figure of the exile in *Trans-Atlantyk* by more "dangerous" tropes—by "obsolescence of the Baroque, on the one hand, and the 'exotic novelty' of gay eroticism, on the other." Either too outmoded or too proleptic, these two interrelated liminal figures—the aesthetic and the erotic significations of marginality—are perpetually excluded from the historical narrative of the nation and yet re-emerge as the fissures within the national identity and open an alternative space for hybrid collectivity.

Drawing on postcolonial theory and gender studies, Agnieszka Sołtysik's essay, "Witold Gombrowicz's Struggle with Heterosexual Form: From a National to a Performative Self," examines the three volumes of Gombrowicz's *Diary*. By reconsidering Gombrowicz's idea of Form in the context of Erving Goffman's and Judith Butler's theories, she argues that the concept of performative identity (as opposed to the essentialist national self) informs not only Gombrowicz's critique of nationality but also all significant aspects of his poetics. In particular, this shift from the national to the performative subjectivity is crucial for understanding a highly neglected topic of Gombrowicz's homosexuality, which, nonetheless, shapes his key concepts of Youth, Immaturity, morality, and style.

Allen Kuharski's essay, "Witold, Witold, and Witold: Performing Gombrowicz," discusses Gombrowicz as a queer voice in Polish literature and contemporary theater. Starting with Gombrowicz's proclamation in the *Diary* that he does "not believe in a non-erotic philosophy" or desexualized idea, Kuharski discusses the intrinsic relationship between style and the performance of queer sexuality in three of Gombrowicz's texts: *Diary, Pornografia,* and *History*. Kuharski examines Gombrowicz's contestation of the conventional gender identities and his desire to liberate himself from the masculinity that men, obsessed by the fear of femininity, fabricate among themselves, in the context of Judith Butler's performativity of sex. As he argues, most of Gombrowicz's texts dramatize the disjunction between desire and the conventionalized performance of sexual norms—a disjunction that results either in the parody of heterosexual courtship or in the breakdown of its prescribed scenarios. This rejection of conventional masculinity—especially of "the militarized heterosexual male body"—is interrelated with Gombrowicz's leftist and pacifist politics and with his rejection of nationalist mythology.

In the concluding article, "Witold Gombrowicz in the United States," Beth Holmgren provides the analysis of the reception of

Gombrowicz's texts in America and, in so doing, also gives an extensive bibliography of the critical texts and reviews available in English. Confronted with the few and highly inadequate "second-generation" translations (mostly from French and German rather than from the original Polish), Gombrowicz's first critics by necessity focused on introducing and defending the importance of Gombrowicz's writings to American audience. Unfortunately, this trend of "introducing" persisted and eventually entirely dominated Gombrowicz's American scholarship, leaving little room for an in-depth study of his works, study that has been flourishing, for instance, in France. Because of the lingering insidious perception that Gombrowicz is "a Polish writer rather than a great writer" on the American literary market, Holmgren suggests that Gombrowicz critics might put the label of "great writer" to new strategic and parodic uses to start the critical conversation on Gombrowicz's work going. The growing availability of the first-rate translations of Gombrowicz's important texts, culminating in the recent publications of *Diaries* and *Trans-Atlantyk,* makes such a serious and long overdue critical encounter possible.

This is, indeed, the main task *Gombrowicz's Grimaces* hopes to accomplish.

Notes

1. My translation is based on the Polish edition, *Kosmos, Dzieła,* vol. V, ed. Jan Błoński (Kraków: Wydawnictwo Literackie, 1988), 29.

2. Michel Foucault, *The Archeology of Knowledge and The Discourse on Language,* trans. A. M. Sheridan (New York: Pantheon, 1972), 216.

3. For a discussion of contemporary of Polish émigré literature, its vexed relationship to the literature produced at home, and the difficulties in reception, circulation, and interpretation of this body of work, see "Forum: Polish Émigré Literature," ed. Halina Filipowicz, *Slavic and East European Journal* 33 (1989): 157–216. Halina Filipowicz's "Fission and Fusion: Polish Émigré Literature," 157–72, is particularly informative in this respect.

4. How Gombrowicz would react to the Solidarity movement is, of course, only a matter of speculation. For an interesting example of such a speculation, see Ewa Graczyk, *O Gombrowiczu, Kunderze, Grassie i innych ważnych sprawach.* Eseje (Gdańsk: Wydawnictwo Marabut, 1993), 90–93.

5. For a discussion of the reception of Gombrowicz in the United States, see the section "Who needs Gombrowicz" in *2b: Polish American Academic Quarterly* 2 (1994): 74–80. For a discussion of the criticism in English, see Regina Grol-Prokopczyk, "New Gombrowicziana" *The Polish Review* 26 (1981): 83–86 and Beth Holmgren "Witold Gombrowicz in the United States" *The Polish Review* 33 (1988): 409–18. The extended version of this article is reprinted in this volume.

6. Gilles Deleuze and Félix Guattari, *Kafka: Toward a Minor Literature,* trans. Dana Polan (Minnesota: U of Minnesota P, 1986), 16–28.

7. For an autobiographical refection on his "deeply erotic" friendship with Gombrowicz, see Alejandro Rússovich, "Rússovich o Gombrowiczu," *Teatr* 9 (1995): 10–12. For a critical discussion of the major trends in Gombrowicz criticism, see Janusz Sławiński, "The Gombrowicz Case," *Literary Studies in Poland,* vol. X, *Gombrowicz,* ed. Hanna Dziechcińska (Wrocław: Zakład Narodowy im. Ossolińskich, 1983), 107–13; Zdzisław Łapiński, "Gombrowicz and His Critics" *Literary Studies in Poland,* 115–26. See also the special issue of *Twórczość* 11–12 (1986).

8. There is also a proliferation of the so-called "portrait studies" in Gombrowicz criticism. See for instance Tadeusz Kępiński, *Witold Gombrowicz: Studium portretowe* (Krakòw: Wydawnictwo Literackie, 1988), or Kazimierz Głaz, *Gombrowicz w Vence i inne wspomnienia* (Krakòw: Wydawnictwo Literackie, 1989).

9. Gilles Deleuze, *The Fold: Leibniz and the Baroque,* trans. Tom Conley (Minneapolis: U of Minnesota P, 1993), 81–82.

10. Stanisław Barańczak, "Introduction" to *Trans-Atlantyk,* trans. Carolyn French and Nina Karsov (New Haven: Yale UP, 1994), xi.

11. Czesław Miłosz, "Kim jest Gombrowicz?" *Gombrowicz i krytycy: Wybór i opracowanie,* ed. Zdzisław Łapiński (Kraków: Wydawnictwo Literackie, 1984), 185–200. As Karpiński eloquently suggests, for Gombrowicz authenticity, including his own, "was one continuous duel of grimaces. He tore one mask after another" (*D* I, viii).

12. "Witkiewicz, Schulz i ja, trzej ludzie usiłujacy wprowadzić literaturę na tory nowe." Witold Gombrowicz, *Wspomnienia polskie, Wędrówki po Argentynie* (Warszawa: Res Publica, 1990), 92.

13. The three partitions of Poland took place in 1772, 1793, and 1795, respectively.

14. For an excellent collection of the responses of the Argentinean intellectuals to Gombrowicz, see Rajmund Kalicki, ed., *Tango Gombrowicz*

(Kraków: Wydawnictwo Literackie, 1984). For Gombrowicz's own recollections of his life in Argentina, see, in addition to the *Diary,* his *Wspomnienia polskie. Wędrówki po Argentynie,* 141–205.

15. A story reported by Marzena Walicka.

16. For the most comprehensive discussion of the various possibilities of interpreting Form, see Jerzy Jarzębski, "Pojęcie 'formy' u Gombrowicza," *Gombrowicz i krytycy: Wybór i opracowanie,* 313–46, and "Między chaosem a formą: Witold Gombrowicz" *Prozaicy dwudziestolecia międzywojennego,* ed. B. Faron (Warszawa: Wiedza Powszechna, 1972), 181–218. See also Zdzisław Łapiński, "Ślub w kościele ludzkim" (O kategoriach interakcyjnych u Gombrowicza), *Twórczość* 9 (1966): 93–100; Jan Błoński, "O Gombrowiczu" *Pamiętnik Literacki* 8 (1970): 47; and Artur Sandauer, "Witold Gombrowicz—człowiek i pisarz," *Gombrowicz i krytycy,* 103–27.

17. Marianne DeKoven, *Rich and Strange: Gender, History, Modernism* (Princeton: Princeton UP, 1991), 12.

18. For a succinct discussion of Gombrowicz's attitude toward literary traditions, both Polish and European, see Michał Głowiński, *Ferdydurke Witolda Gombrowicza* (Warszawa: Wydawnictwa Szkolne i Pedagogiczne, 1991), 29–30, 78–85. For Gombrowicz's criticism of art, see Małgorzata Szpakowska, "Gombrowicz-teoretyk sztuki," *Gombrowicz i krytycy,* 347–64.

19. To indicate the scope of Gombrowicz's reflections on form, I discuss his "formal imperative" in the context of Wittgenstein's elaboration of language games in the context of social forms of life. See my *Rhetoric of Failure: Deconstruction of Skepticism, Reinvention of Modernism* (Albany: State U of NY P, 1996), 201–17.

20. Jarzębski, "Pojęcie 'formy' u Gombrowicza," 313–46.

21. This linguistic effect of amputation described by Gombrowicz has been frequently compared to Jacques Lacan's linguistic reinterpretation of castration. See, for instance, Ewa M. Thompson, *Witold Gombrowicz* (Boston: Twayne, 1979), 150; and Hanjo Berressem, "Witold Gombrowicz: *Cosmos,* the Case of the Hanged Sparrow," *Polish Review* 36 (1991): 145–59.

22. Witold Gombrowicz, "Preface" to *Pornografia,* trans. Alastair Hamilton, *Cosmos and Pornografia* (New York: Grove P, 1985) 5.

23. For an extensive discussion of antinomy in Gombrowicz's aesthetics, see Kazimierz Bartoszyński, "On How Gombrowicz's Antinomies May Cause Problems in Literary Interpretations" *Literary Studies in Poland,* 95–106.

24. Barańczak, "Introduction," xii.

25. For an analysis of the "crisis" of language in the larger context of modernism, see, for example, Richard Sheppard, "The Crisis of Language" *Modernism 1890–1930,* ed. Malcolm Bradbury and James McFarlane (London: Penguin, 1976), 323–36; Irving Howe, *Decline of The New* (New York: Horizon, 1970), 15–27 and Astradur Eysteinsson, *The Concept of Modernism* (Ithaca: Cornell UP, 1990), 35–49. For a view of modernism as a "culture of crisis" see Matei Calinescu, *Five Faces of Modernity: Modernism, Avant-Garde, Decadence, Kitsch, Postmodernism* (Durham: Duke UP, 1987), 123–25.

26. I discuss this bifurcation at great length in my *Rhetoric of Failure,* 212–17.

27. Witold Gombrowicz, "Byłem pierwszym structuralistą," trans. from French Maciej Broński, *Gombrowicz filozof,* ed. Francesco M. Cataluccio and Jerzy Illg (Kraków: Znak, 1991), 145–46.

28. For a discussion of this debate, see Witold Gombrowicz, "Przewodnik po filozofii w sześć godzin i kwadrans," translated from French into Polish by Bogdan Baran, 71–128; and Renato Barilli, "Sartre i Camus w *Dzienniku,*" trans. Wiktoria Krzemień, 227–39, both in *Gombrowicz filozof.*

29. For a useful synthesis of the recent debates about modernism, see Eysteinsson, *The Concept of Modernism,* and Peter Nicholls, *Modernisms: A Literary Guide* (Berkeley: U of California P, 1995). See also, Jochen Schulte-Sasse, "Foreword: Theory of Modernism versus Theory of the Avant-Garde," *Theory of the Avant-Garde,* by Peter Bürger, trans. Michael Shaw (Minneapolis: U of Minnesota P, 1984), xix–xxix. For some of the most interesting revisions of modernism, see Bridget Elliott and Jo-Ann Wallace, *Women Artists and Writers: Modernist (Im)positionings* (London: Routledge, 1994), 1–48; Mary Russo, *The Female Grotesque: Risk, Excess and Modernity* (New York: Routledge, 1994); Rita Felski *The Gender of Modernity* (Cambridge: Harvard UP, 1995), 1–35, 207–13; and Andreas Huyssen, *After the Great Divide: Modernism, Mass Culture, Postmodernism* (Bloomington: Indiana UP, 1986), 3–64;

30. For a discussion of Gombrowicz's uses of popular literary forms, see Maria Janion, " 'Ciemna' młodość Gombrowicza," *Gombrowicz i krytycy,* 510–29.

31. Huyssen, *After the Great Divide,* 3–16.

32. For an excellent discussion of the crisis of modernism and its genealogies, see Felski, *The Gender of Modernity,* 1–34.

33. Quoted in Konstanty A. Jeleński, "Bohaterskie niebohaterstwo Gombrowicza," *Gombrowicz filozof,* 156 (trans. mine).

34. For an informative account of the history of Polish nationalism see Andrzej Walicki, *Poland between East and West: The Controversies over Self-Definition and Modernization in Partitioned Poland,* Harvard Papers in Ukrainian Studies (Cambridge: Harvard Ukrainian Research Inst., 1994) and *The Enlightenment and the Birth of Modern Nationhood: Polish Political Thought from Noble Republicanism to Tadeusz Kosciuszko,* trans. Emma Harris (Notre Dame: U of Notre Dame P, 1989). Gombrowicz's critique of Polish national identity is an object of perennial controversy in Gombrowicz's criticism. For the recent articulations of this issue, see, for instance, Włodzimierz Bolecki, "Prawdy niemiłe," 29–34, and Aleksander Fiut, "Ucieczka z Europy," 100–106, both in *Kresy* 12 (1992); Leonard Neuger, "Polskość jako cel" *Teksty Drugie* 1/2 (1991): 10–23 and Jacek Zychowicz, "Ideologia polska" *Miesięcznik Literacki* 1 (1989): 43–51.

35. For an excellent discussion of the temporality of the avant-garde, see Thomas Docherty, "Postmodernism: An Introduction," *Postmodernism: A Reader* (New York: Columbia UP, 1993), 14–21.

36. Felski, *The Gender of Modernity,* 208.

37. As Docherty argues, "the question of the avant-garde is therefore, fundamentally, a question of the intimate relations between speed and politics." *Postmodernism,* 18.

38. For the discussion of the relation of modern experimental aesthetic practices and the discourse of male homosexuality, see, for instance, Jonathan Dollimore, *Sexual Dissidence: Augustine to Wilde, Freud to Foucault,* (Oxford: Clarendon UP, 1991); Richard Dellamora, *Masculine Desire: The Sexual Politics of Victorian Aestheticism* (Chapel Hill: U of North Carolina P, 1990), Eve Kosofsky Sedgwick, *Epistemology of the Closet* (Berkeley: University of California P, 1990); Ed Cohen, *Talk on the Wilde Side: Towards a Genealogy of the Discourse on Male Homosexuality* (New York: Routledge, 1993); and the excellent section "Between the Pages" in *The Lesbian and Gay Studies Reader,* ed. Henry Abelove, Michèle Aina Barale, David M. Halperin (New York: Routledge, 1993).

39. Michel Foucault, *The History of Sexuality,* vol. I, *An Introduction,* trans. Robert Hurley (New York: Random, 1990).

40. Eve Kosofsky Sedgwick, *Tendencies* (Durham: Duke UP, 1993), xii.

41. Felski, *The Gender of Modernity,* 212.

42. For an informing analysis of the philosophical underpinnings of Gombrowicz's aesthetics, see Francesco M. Cataluccio, "Gombrowicz filozof," trans. Katarzyna Bielas, 5–21, and Andrzej St. Kowalczyk, "Gombrowicz—

Husserl. O fenomenologicznych motywach w *Dzienniku,*" 206–26, both in the collection *Gombrowicz filozof.*

43. In her discussion of the relation between language and erotic desire, Aleksandra Okopień-Sławińska does not consider homosexuality as an important issue. "Wielkie bergowanie czyli hipoteza jedności *Kosmosu,*" 698–702. In an otherwise interesting discussion of the intersection between Gombrowicz's "erotic myth" and his concept of Form, Janusz Pawłowski likewise ignores the significance of homosexuality although he wonders about Gombrowicz's strange obsession with secrecy and conspiracy "Erotyka Gombrowicza," 550. Maria Janion briefly mentions homosexuality in the context of Gombrowicz's use of the gothic form in her " 'Ciemna' młodość Gombrowicza" (521–29). All three articles are from *Gombrowicz i krytycy.*

PART ONE

Gombrowicz's Aesthetics: Writing, Self, Performance

Tomislav Z. Longinović

1

I, Witold Gombrowicz:

Formal Abjection and the Power of Writing in A Kind of a Testament

> I don't know who I really am, but I suffer when I am deformed. So, at least I know what I am not. My "self" is nothing more but my will to be myself.
>
> Witold Gombrowicz, *A Kind of a Testament*

The recognition of the authorial "I" as the floating signifier which attaches itself to the "will" of the writer constitutes one of the central insights of Gombrowicz's autobiographical writings. The radical divestment from the essentialist conceptions of the "self" enunciated in Gombrowicz's statement points away from the high modernist search for meaning and truth, which are supposedly contained by the human subject. Instead, the perpetually exiled writer returns to the posturing that foregrounds the performative aspect of being: "My 'self' is nothing more but my will to be myself" (*KT,* 77).[1] Following Nietzsche's footprints in *Ecce Homo,* Gombrowicz displays a similar compulsion to leave a definite interpretation of his life and work in a short autobiographical text entitled *A Kind of a Testament.* Sensing that the end of life is near, both Nietzsche and Gombrowicz fear that after their death they could be misunderstood and taken for what they are not. Nietzsche opens *Ecce Homo* with this concern: "Seeing that before long I must confront humanity with the most difficult demand ever made of it, it seems indispensable to me to say *who I am.* Really, one should know it, for I have not left myself 'without testimony.' "[2] In order to prevent misreading of his works, Nietzsche leaves his philosophical testament, hoping that it will clearly define the scope and extent of his "I" within the context of Western thought.

Gombrowicz's textual performance is similar, although far more parodic than Nietzsche's autobiographical concern. The title of the English translation captures Gombrowicz's hesitation to take up the writing of a literary testament with a straight face, since he is too well aware of the limitations placed on him by the demands of such a grand genre. Instead, the confrontation with one's mortality forces him to stay true to his parodic relationship to reality and leave "a kind of" a testimony about his life and work. "A kind of" or "as if" are the perfect linguistic signifiers for the position Gombrowicz occupies both as a creator of absurdist prose and as a human being in search of his own "I." In this "kind of" autobiographical effort, where the writer confronts both his physical mortality and his desire to continue his life-in-writing, one can sense the anxiety related to the future in which the name will remain as the only guarantee of the value of the written. "What returns to the name never returns to the living," says Derrida as he works through the textual layers of Nietzsche's *Ecce Homo.*[3] In other words, the recognition and misrecognition that may take place in the future will never come back to the writer-as-a-body, but will always return to the writer-as-a-name. Name will sustain and project itself beyond "the living," continuing to support the identity long after the body ceases to exist. When Gombrowicz speaks of the "self" he does not know, it is a name speaking of an "I" whose fluid boundaries will gain a clearer outline only at the moment of author's death.

"I don't know who I really am" (*KT,* 77). The complex relationship between writing and identity which ends with less certainty is manifest in Gombrowicz's desire to bridge the gap between the two in his life and work. A desire of the writer "to be" through the written word has obssessed him beyond metaphysical assumptions of the identity of the lived and the written. My reading of *A Kind of a Testament* rests on identification of the paradoxical nature of writing which reflects the failures of modernity: people created by mass culture, like the Youthfulls in *Ferdydurke,* are as unreal as any literary character. Their desire to be like the others evokes a sense of formal abjection in the first-person narrators who dominate Gombrowicz's poetics of prose. His struggle to escape from the grip of the "inter-human," a formal imperative which crushes their demonic individualism, brings the reader closer to the degraded, infantile and humorous: "I suffer when I am deformed" (*KT,* 77). His rejections of traditionalism, nationalism, and patriotism are all attempts to free himself from the grip of others, whose massified thought and action have led Europe into numerous bloodsheds and moral failures. His desire for absolute freedom from Form has deeper roots in the recognition of abjection that causes his suffering. This horror of being, which lies at the inception of literary articulations, is a point theoretically elaborated by Julia Kristeva in her analysis of Western subjectivity.

Gombrowicz's testament is shaped by the struggle to formulate the "I" according to the authorial desire which is placed in perpetual conflict with the demands of the established forms. "Where have my assaults on Form got me? To Form. I broke it so much and so often that I became the writer whose subject is Form. That is my form and my definition. And today I, a living individual, am the servant of that official Gombrowicz whom I built with my own hands" (*KT,* 154). Yes, the assault on the established forms can lead only to the creation of other forms. The "living individual" has become the function of the name and can continue to exist only as an appendage to "Gombrowicz," the name that has assimilated the "self" by using its life and energy to inscribe itself in the history of Western literature. The "self" finds itself in quotation marks which define the fictional and arbitrary quality of its appearance; "I" is nothing more than a manifestation of the "will to be" without the name which would carry its "life" beyond the present, evanescent moment. The metaphysical desire for being and the struggle for recognition by the other are transferred to Gombrowicz's poetics in a maxim found in the postscript to *Ferdydurke: "My work must become myself."*[4] This statement certainly includes the inverse meaning as well: I will become my work. The borderline between my life and my writing will be made invisible and each act I perform in the "private" sphere will be already inscribed as a part of my esthetics. The inverse meaning manifests itself in Gombrowicz's appearances in his novels: by naming the protagonist and narrator of *Cosmos* Witold, he insists on identifying the narrative "I" with himself. The avant-gardist dream of merging "life" and "art" finds its incarnation in the practice of writing, which erases the boundaries between the creator and the created. At the same time as the opposition between writing and living is blurred and called into question, the status of what is real and what is imagined becomes very problematic.

Writing appears as a power with a transformative potential, since it carries a promise of bringing the desired recognition to Gombrowicz who has felt "abnormal, twisted, degenerate, abominable and solitary" ever since his childhood (*KT,* 37). He sees writing as a performance that can turn this feeling of constant inadequacy into poetics: if one cannot reach the literary heights achieved by Goethe or Shakespeare, why not explore the sphere of one's own personal pathology? "That slimy pulp of Formlessness in me spilled onto the book—but not to spread like a stinking puddle, no, not at all! In order, rather, to shine with all the colours of the rainbow, to glean with humor, to ennoble with poetry and to attain divine innocence in absurdity" (*KT,* 41). The reality of one's degradation is what constitutes the origins of "I" that emerges from "Formlessness" through the power of writing. Gombrowicz's performance of the "self" takes place on the stage of writing, which is for him a place of struggle between the dark, abject desires that drag him into the depths of dissolution and the formal imperative which demands that abjection be transposed into literature. The writer's "I" claims a double origin, one in the "slimy pulp" which characterizes his most secret desires for the disorder of the instinctual realm, the other in the "divine innocence" which aspires to poetic heights. Writing has the power to assemble these opposing domains into an absurd reality, providing the "I" with a temporary respite from its torments. By helping the "I's" emergence from the "slimy pulp of Formlessness," writing structures reality, which for Gombrowicz has a very different meaning.

"I consider myself a dedicated realist," he claims. "One of the main objects of my writing is to cut a path through Unreality to Reality" (*KT,* 31). Gombrowicz's Reality is obviously not a reality produced by mimesis or a democratic consensus on what is real but a reality peculiar to one's own subjectivity, a reality derived from a "will to be." The task of writing is to attain "Reality" by finding a way out of "Unreality" which surrounds the "I." The discovery of Reality, which is actually never achieved by Gombrowicz's writing, is connected to the gradual takeover by the "I" of all the aspects of the narrative. The narcissistic dimension of writing, which identifies the "self" with the "world," subsumes all the aspects of prose to the all-encompassing scope of the narrator's "I." That is why Gombrowicz's characters appear as cartoonish representations of certain aspects of misguided humanity in the twentieth century. "True reality is the one that is peculiar to *you.*"[5] Reality is for Gombrowicz that which often hides itself from humanity, or that which the humans would rather forget or repress. The "immaturity" and "subhuman greenness" which continue to obsess both him and his works are built into the foundation of his poetics. Instead of striving to stress differences in the experience of reality, dominant culture demands uniformity and conformism as it suppresses the weird, the impolite, and the eccentric discourses within itself. The pressure that Gombrowicz feels from "Unreality" comes from within: "Within me I felt something obscure which nothing could bring to the light of day" (*KT,* 33). This remote, dark, and unknown realm hidden "within" is what constitutes the unreality that plagues Gombrowicz and his narrators. The striving of that subterranean realm within to come to the light of day is what nurtures the desire for writing. This obscure realm within needs to find a voice, a discourse, or an inscription that will allow it to become Reality. Writing allows Unreality to attain a symbolic form, as it struggles to become "literature." This concept of the real is very close to that of Lacan, who treats this register of experience as something that constantly remains foreclosed from the subject, yet determines his actions in most fundamental ways.[6]

A quest for deciphering the meaning of "reality" underlies most of the narratives constructed by Gombrowicz. For example, the narrator and characters of *Cosmos* are subjected to a torrent of absurd events and clues that proliferate around them, initiated by Witold's and Fuchs's accidental sighting of a hanged sparrow. "There is a sort of excess about reality, and after a certain point, it can become intolerable," says Witold, the narrator-protagonist of *Cosmos* (*C,* 66). The unbearable reality derived from the obscure depths of "interiority" is combined with the "exteriority" of writing as the absurd reality is constructed for the reader. The desire for order that may at some point appear and relieve the oppressive burden of this unreal reality by discovering its purpose haunts Witold as he interrogates himself: "What was I looking for? A basic theme, a *Leitmotiv,* an axis, something of which I could take firm hold and use as a basis for reconstructing my personality here? But distraction, not only my own personal, inner distraction, but also that coming from without, from the chaos, profusion and excess of things, preventing me from concentrating" (*C,* 87). The process of constructing the narrative is identified with the process of self-creation, as the "I" searches for the ever shifting ground of reality. Gombrowicz admits that "*Cosmos* is a novel which creates itself, as it is written" (*KT,* 137). This metafictional dimension of creating the narrative without a firm plan is revealed several times in the narrative itself, as Witold complains of the chaotic structure of reality. "It was chaos, like putting my hand into a ragbag and seeing what came out and whether it was suitable . . . for building my house with, and my house assumed pretty fantastic forms" (*C,* 118). The identity and reality depend on the chance operation that guides the construction of the narrative. Reality is chasm and a chaos which haunts the "I" whenever it tries to step on any type of *terra firma* of identification. Repeating Nietzsche's autobiographical performance, Gombrowicz locates the double origin and existence of this obscure, yet real, chasm in childhood and youth, which were dominated by the parents. While Nietzsche confronts the reader with a riddle of his "dual descent" by claiming that he is "already dead as his father" and "still living and becoming old" as his mother,[7] Gombrowicz spells out the origin of his artistic inclinations clearly: "I am an artist because of my mother" (*KT,* 29).

Because the mother is the embodiment of formlessness and unreality, she teaches the writer some basic mechanisms about form and reality by negative example. Mother is instability itself, since she cannot guarantee reality as a logical order. "It was she who pushed me into pure nonsensicality, into the absurd, which was later to become one of the most important elements of my art" (*KT,* 30). Gombrowicz's rejection of the mother bears all the marks of abjection, a force of "immaturity" that haunts both the identity he is trying to manufacture and writing which makes its elusive permanence possible. The lack of Form cannot be allowed "to spread like a stinking puddle" since that would abolish the artistic "I" and submerge it into the attractive, yet feared, realm of unbridled instinct and low culture. The abject reality must not be allowed to penetrate the art directly, but only as an esthetically transformed configuration. Interestingly enough, Gombrowicz identifies this domain with the mother, which Kristeva has theorized as a source of abjection for a majority of "true" writers.[8] The "stinking puddle" of formlessness which "I" inherits from the mother is something that continues to disturb any attempt at unified identity. Abjection is the force that provides space for ambiguity, defies externally imposed boundaries, and sees order as a threat to the reality which emerges from the obscure depths. That reality is saturated with disgust, violence, and nonsense, and mother is blamed for the failure of reason to restore order to the destructive reign of desire. Gombrowicz's mother is constructed as a chimera of unreality, while the father is seen as a purveyor of a heritage of "lucidity, his level-headedness and his sense of discipline" (*KT,* 29).

Gombrowicz constructs the father as order itself, an instance that prevents the maternal disorder from continuing to perform its destructive work without a check. The role assigned to the father in the game of double origins is that of a form-giver, a guarantor of a family name that will continue to carry the "I" beyond the transitory realm of death. "My father? Handsome, tall, distinguished, very proper, punctual, methodical, not very broad-minded or artistic, a practicing Catholic but no bigot" (*KT,* 28). Paradoxically, the father appears as the image of upper-class mediocrity that Gombrowicz sets out to ironize throughout his literary opus. Yet, as a "real" father, he provides a place from which guilt and shame caused by one's "abnormality and degeneracy" can be fully experienced and transformed into a literary value. The very condition of apprehending one's difference from others lies within this identification with the father's name and position, since only then can one discover what is hidden beneath the perfect external form of discipline and order. This paradoxical identification with the father as an expression of the "proper and methodical" allows Gombrowicz to examine the other, less appealing side of his personality. The maternal world of formlessness, the "stinking puddle" which constantly threatens one's sanity and normality, the unreality that forces Johnnie to flee at the end of *Ferdydurke* with his face in his hands—all these are symptoms of the unfathomable obscurity that cannot and should not be known.

Yet, the power of writing allows one to perform the catharctic act of externalizing abjection by way of metaphor, parody, and allegory, which turn the everyday into the absurd. Speech (at first) and writing (later) introduce the symbolic as a force which gradually hollows out the abject by providing it with communicable articulation, while the ambiguity continues to follow Gombrowicz throughout his life: "That was the source of my relationship with all that is repugnant, disgusting, horrible—for, though it disgusted me, yet I felt drawn to it, not to say attached to it" (*KT,* 39). This ambivalence is solved by the constant return to the origins of one's ego through writing: the source of inspiration is the defiled muse of abjection. *"The abject would thus be the 'object' of primal repression,"* Kristeva affirms in *Powers of Horror*[9] (Kristeva's emphasis). Gombrowicz intuitively accounts for the work of primal repression (*Urverdrängung*) which is at once repeated and revealed: the maternal within the "I" continues to corrupt the proper, ordered "reality" by its formlessness as it perpetually exchanges one metaphor for another. The paternal is the external shell in this process of masking and unmasking within the medium of writing, while it provides a configuration which Gombrowicz sees as essential in the creative process. His lifelong preoccupation with the ability of writing to simultaneously construct and deconstruct any given identity is predicated on the effects of this primal repression. The maternal and paternal legacy therefore appear in yet another hierarchical configuration within the "I" whose power is derived from the writing that imposes its "Form" on others, subjecting them to various types of "deformations." Those who are active and creative impose their form on those who are its passive recipients and consumers. The form assumes two separate functions: first, it is a tool of self-creation which allows an author to project the identity he desires by literary means; second, the "I" created in this way has the power to fashion other identities, through the construction of literary characters and their relationships. The reality created by the "I" articulates its own conflicts, which are transposed into a form of a parodic existential drama. The "I" and its reality can never be fully known and accessible, since that would signify the surrender to the conventional, the boring and the predictable. This desire for perpetual transcendence of its own limits places the "I" on the side of life itself, since the surrender to forms and limits imposed from the outside can only bring about its death. "I" is therefore conceptualized as an "oscillation around an inaccessible center," while at the same time it constantly "endeavors to be the assertion of an identity" (*KT,* 77). Oscillation is a repetition with a difference, a constant forward and backward motion of signification which can never fully reach the plenitude of meaning or being. Although identity is striven after, it is always perceived as a construction dependent on identifications which take place outside the domain and control of the authorial "I." This undermines the possibility of a complete or serious identification and leads the "I" away from identity. The impossibility of identity to ground itself as a stable and recognizable center parallels and predates some of the most important insights of Derrida: "Or else we might say that 'différance' was the center that allowed the play of differences among themselves, while withdrawing itself from that play."[10] In other words, the "inaccessible center" cannot be fully reduced to a definition or a formula, since the center itself is fluid and constantly shifting. The writing which oscillates around it is therefore aware of its performative nature, while at the same time always attempting to reach for the inaccessible. The center is dispersed and dissipated through the act of writing, as the "I" continues to take on different external masks and shells. Writing lays bare the effects that form has on the creation of the "I" and its multiple and often contradictory identifications. This is essential for understanding Gombrowicz's poetics, which is predicated on "cutting through" the immense layers of unreality which everyday life and interpersonal relationships throw his way. Writing is the only practice which can embody these contradictions without trying to impose a preconceived, rational order on them. It examines "unreality" by turning it into the "reality" of the written, which for Gombrowicz has the status of enunciated desire of the subject "to be." Being is equated with writing, while the relationships to others are seen as the negative but inevitable confrontations with them and their institutions. While writing provides some hope for authenticity, the world of others and their artificial relationships cause the subject to fall into the "interhuman" sphere of unreality. The "interhuman" space opens up a multitude of possibilities for misperception, misrecognition, and miscommunication. The unreality plunges the "I" into boredom and desperation, since its life is perceived as the effect of conventions people are subjected to as they engage in a dialogue.

Gombrowicz's narrators are irritated by the triviality and predictability of characters and situations which surround them as they endlessly seek an exit from the world of oppressive social decorum and falsified human relationships. The act of narration which creates form and reality is something that oppresses the narrator, although he is driven to continue the process: "How exhausting was this superabundance and excess from which new persons, events and things constantly emerged. If only the flood would stop for a moment" (*C,* 109). The escape is usually found outside the bounds of reason, in the exhilarating absurdity of nonsensical clues whose interpretation turns into a narrative fuel for the entire novel. The "I" of the narrator is usually obsessed with the problem of knowledge of its surroundings, which supposedly hide the secret truth behind the proliferation of insignificant and often absurd clues. In *Cosmos,* the main narrative axis is established between the "hanged" entities that the narrator first discovers and then acts upon: a sparrow, a piece of wood, and, finally, a cat. One of the main concerns of the narrator is his inability to tell the story "as it really happened," since the infinite number of events have constantly to be forgotten in favor of an ordered "reality." The exasperated narrator Witold asks himself: "Will no one ever be able to reproduce the incoherence of the living moment at its moment of birth? Born as we are out of chaos, why can we never establish contact with it? No sooner do we look at it than order, pattern, shape is born under our eyes" (*C,* 31). The desire for disorder, caused by the failure of the universe inherited from the mother, persists in the face of this compulsive ordering of reality. It is indeed the telling of the story, the construction of the narrative pattern that creates order out chaos while precluding Witold from establishing a direct contact with the "incoherence of the living moment." Writing has the power to lend form and provide order even in the hardest of cases, when one is confronted with such absurd events as the hanging of the sparrow in the middle of the forest. The ability of writing to create sense out of nonsense by laying bare the effects of form is something that intrigues and even frightens Gombrowicz: "For me nothing is more fantastic than to *be* here, now, and to be *as I am,* defined, concrete and not someone else. And I fear Form as if it were a wild animal!" (*KT,* 134). This fear drives the "I" to escape the reality of unreality caused by the form and to constantly expand its boundaries. "I" perceives itself as fantastic in any "defined and concrete" form. The existence shaped by Form is the source of the "fantastic," as the "I" attempts to escape its effects and fears for its own independence from it. But, the realization that escape from one Form leads to the creation of another causes the author to fear it "as if it were a wild animal." Writing is a paradoxical process which promises liberation from Form, while imposing its own at the same time. Subjecting oneself to the tyranny of Form leads to the gradual ossification of the "I" and its slow departure into death and oblivion. Gombrowicz's prose gives the expression to this anxiety of the "living individual" confronted by Form: "Do other people share my anxiety? To what extent? If a man doesn't see Form as I see it, in its autonomy, its perpetual malleability, its creative fury, its caprices and its perversions, its accumulations and its dissolutions, its intricacies and continual confusions, what can *Cosmos* mean to him?" (*KT,* 134). The drama of Form is at the bottom of the creative process which reproduces the drama of self-creation. The fact that every identity depends on that of the other, however hard it strives to be autonomous, illustrates how deeply Form penetrates relationships between humans.

Gombrowicz was obsessed with the problem of form and identity throughout his life and writing career. In a 1964 entry to his diary, he rethinks his exile in Argentina upon landing in Berlin: "If this tourism did not leave me barren, it was because, luckily, as a writer used to manipulating form, I could undertake the shaping of my person from this new position, in this situation . . . but wasn't Argentina one of my predestinations, since as a child in Poland I did everything I could to march out of step in the parade?" (*D* III, 109). The advantage of the writer in exile is the ability to subject his life to the laws of form as if it were a literary text, especially since he has stopped envisioning himself in essentialist terms since he was a child. "Marching out of step" and becoming an other is fully realized only in Argentina, where the operation of self-creation has to begin all over again. Exile is perceived as a beneficial condition in this process of distancing from one's own roots, which are perceived as obstacles to the process of artistic and personal self-creation. This process includes the gradual rejection of all identities that were unconsciously imposed at some time on the author's life.

Gombrowicz's disdain for any form of shared inter-human project, and especially for that of national belonging, matures fully only after he settles in Argentina. It is especially his Polishness that begins to irritate him: "I had to break with Poland and turn against it" (*KT,* 56). The native country, similarly to the maternal realm, has to be rejected in order for the "I" to experience the sense of boundless freedom and rejuvenation. The national belonging has the potential of leveling differences and dulling a sense of subjective encounter with the world. "A Pole is a Pole by nature. Whereby the more a Pole is himself, the more will he be a Pole. If Poland does not allow him to think and feel freely, it means that Poland does not allow him to be himself fully, that is to be a Pole fully . . ." (*D* II, 14). This paradox of becoming a Pole by rejecting Polish nationalism underlies most of Gombrowicz's thinking about collective identities. Polishness is oppressive if it is imposed in its vulgar, populist form. It operates by using stereotypes and leveling the possibilities for individual variance. "Thus my desire to 'overcome Poland' was synonymous with the desire to strengthen our individual Polishness. I simply wanted the Pole to stop being the product 'of' an exclusively collective life and 'for' a collective life" (*D* II, 15). Like any other ideology, nationalism has the power to mold and stabilize identities according to the interests of the collective. Needless to say, this process imposes the most oppressive forms of identity onto the individuals who have a strong need to be different. While the silent majority may accept this vision of Polishness, Gombrowicz sees the strength of the Pole in the exact opposite. "I strove for a Pole who could take pride in saying: I belong to an inferior nation. With pride" (*D* II, 15). Instead of glorifying his country as the superior product of civilization, this type of Pole would reject the collective illusion and ground himself in the reality of inferiority. The only way to really love Poland would be to admit its real position of a secondary European country and accept it as such. Any other way could lead one into the delusion of collective Form, which extends its malignant influence both among the Poles in Poland and those living in exile.

This collectivization of being is unacceptable for individualists like Gombrowicz, who seeks a way out of any massified vision of reality: "To break away! To keep one's distance! The writer, the artist, or anyone who attaches importance to his spiritual development, must feel no more than a resident in Poland or Argentine, and it is his duty to regard Poland or Argentine as an obstacle, almost as an enemy" (*KT,* 57). The rejection of one's nation is a duty, since it breaks the chain of identifications which begin with the family and continue to restrict the writer throughout his life. To break away and keep one's distance from any identification with a collectivity is a process which is only reinforced for Gombrowicz in Argentina. He is able to turn exile into an experiment performed on himself, by himself: the writing of the diary allows him to achieve the greatest possible distance from his roots and create an ever changing persona for himself. The power of writing to constitute the "I" through the "manipulation of form" leads him out of the "parade" into exile, which is also the moment of tremendous artistic liberation. The author describes the atmosphere of departure from 1939 Poland as the escape from "the feverish din of European radio speakers," which emit "the stifling fury of nationalists" (*D* III, 108–9). What he encounters in Argentina is the silence of the land which knows nothing of him or his work. "A silence like that in the forest, a silence such that one hears even the drone of a tiny fly after the commotion of the previous years, makes a strange music—and in this ripe and overwhelming silence, two exceptional, singular, specific words began to make themselves audible: Witold Gombrowicz. Witold Gombrowicz" (*D* III, 108). The silence of Argentina is welcome because the name of "Witold Gombrowicz" can now become audible; the trans-Atlantic exile is therefore constructed as a space where one is finally free from the constricting environment of European nationalisms and its totalizing demands by becoming an "I" which knows no bounds or national allegiances. The name of "Witold Gombrowicz" is not yet perceived as a form of oppression for the "living individual" since it emerges anew in a completely alien linguistic and cultural environment. The age-old traditions which prevent the artist from having a sense of freedom by placing constant demands that his art serve the nation are dismissed as a noise of history which drowns subjective, personal voices. Argentina offers silence, distance, and freedom from history that makes the emergence of "Witold Gombrowicz" possible.

But, at the same time, the emergence of the name-in-exile is difficult because that name means nothing in the Porteño literary salons: "Alone, lost, cut off, alien, unknown, a drowned man" (*D* III, 108). Gombrowicz in Argentina stops being identified with his name; this creates a simultaneous sense of liberation and desperation. At the same time as hunger, cold, and homelessness begin to threaten it, the "I" feels rejuvenated by the fall into poverty and uncertainty: "I, Mr. Gombrowicz, plunged into degradation with passion!" (*KT,* 86). Degradation is a guarantee that life will prevail over the demands of Form for definition, order, sense, and identity. Finally, the dark realm of abjection that had plagued him while he was living his upper class life is fully externalized: Gombrowicz is destitute and free from the oppressive bonds of "good society" he left behind in Poland. He begins to share a destiny of those whom he could only observe across the invisible, yet inpenetrable, boundary that divided the nobility from the peasants. Remembering his youth on the family estate, he realizes that the comfortable life of the Gombrowicz family depends on the servants. "They were the ones who really worked, while we simply ate the roasted geese" (*KT,* 32). What oppresses him the most is the unbearable boredom of the family drawing-room, as he secretly begins to adore "the pantry, the kitchen, the stables, the stable lads, the farm girls" while social and economic degradation becomes his "ideal forever" (*KT,* 33). The provincial culture of the landowning class demands denial of the physical and instinctual aspects of life, while that of the peasants reveals "life" in all of its aspects. "The servants! the servants! They knew what life was about" (*KT,* 32). This romaticization of the existential vitality and freedom of the peasant and the servant serves as a narrative device for the imaginary liberation the author constructs through the process of his "becoming through abjection."

In Buenos Aires, Gombrowicz encounters the life and freedom of the have-nots, an encounter that is followed by the transformation of his personality. He embraces youth as the only "value in itself" which is able to guarantee the rebirth of the "I" in this new, trans-Atlantic realm. "Here, youth, already degraded as youth, was subjected to a second degradation, as rural youth, proletarian youth. And I, Ferdydurke, repeated the third section of my book, the story of Mientus who tries to fraternize with a stable boy" (*D* I, 132). The new life that "I" embarks on in exile feeds off this new "fraternization" with youths from Retiro, which challenges the established boundaries of both class and gender. At the same time, the "I" from the fictional world of *Ferdydurke* becomes identical with the "I" of the living experience in Argentina. The postulated world of writing finds its form in the lived experience of exile, bridging once again the gap between "art" and "life." Denying that his associations with the doubly degraded boys from the Retiro are motivated by erotic attraction, Gombrowicz affirms his desire for youth itself that leads him to seek out these relationships. The "I" discovers its own youth in these boys and excludes women from the sphere of identifications on esthetic grounds: "For a man, youth, beauty and grace in a woman will never be as final in their expression because a woman is still something else and she creates a possibility of that which to a certain biological extent rescues us: a child" (*D* I, 132). In other words, male youth is "final in its expression" because there is no hope of continuity through the biological extension; women can extend their youth by bearing children. Male inability to create life lends a tragic dimension to their youth and beauty, causing a nostalgic identification and temporal regression for Gombrowicz. "I" sees the possibility of rejuvenation in homoerotic encounters with the boys who possess that paradoxical quality of youthful degradation which gradually evaporates with age. The discovery of oneself in the other is tragic because there is a perception that youth is perishable and irreversible: “My own because it was also mine, it [youth] came to life in someone like me, not in a woman, but in a man, this was the same youth that had cast me off, now blossoming in someone else” (*D* I, 132). This narcissistic longing for the boys from Retiro turns them into mirrors used by Gombrowicz for imaginary returns to the world of his own youth. The other is never understood as other, always as an extension of oneself. The desire for “beauty and grace” within the same gender is the desire for the past, when “I” possessed the same youthful paradox of the degraded, yet authentic, life. Youth appears as the idealization which the “I” needs in order to sustain its struggle for authenticity and the preservation of its narcissism. Others are incorporated into the “I” as a direct function of this narcissism, never loved as others in their specificity and difference. The boys from Retiro never have names in Gombrowicz’s autobiographical writing, but they always appear in writing simply as “boys” whose main quality is contained within their physique. Love of the other is never possible, since the energy of the “I” is always centered around the act of rejuvenation and self-creation through writing. The recognition of one’s past within the other serves the purpose of placing the origins of the “I” within one’s own youth and degradation. That is why women and boys can be treated only as resting places along the road of perpetual self-discovery through writing, never as the aim of the journey itself.

“Love was refused me, once and for all, from the start, but was that because I couldn’t give it a form, an expression of its own, or because I didn’t have it in me? I don’t know. Was it lacking or did I strangle it? Or maybe my mother strangled it” (*KT,* 33). Mother emerges again, this time as the strangler of love, which cannot find its way out and fashion a proper, acceptable form in reality. The oppressive Form of amorous relationships, which involves mutual idealization and admiration, creates one of the most bizarre spectacles in the theater of interpersonal relationships. Gombrowicz’s lovers are always grotesque caricatures acting under the spell of conventional expressions of love. The three honeymoon couples from *Cosmos* exhibit all the forms of love in “good society” during the final excursion in the novel, as they exhibit “superficial and frivolous gaiety” (*C,* 97). Cousin Isabel from *Ferdydurke* is also the incarnation of an object that does not deserve to be loved since she lives perpetually "in the expectation of meeting someone to whom she could belong" (*F,* 266). Love appears in Gombrowicz's novels as the most compromised of human relationships because it is so dependent on idealization. And idealization is exactly what Gombrowicz poetics constantly tries to undermine. Those whose identities are too stable and well defined cause him endless irritation, since they close off their human potential for degradation and play roles assigned them by the "interhuman form." Since humans are not willing to confront their immature side, they find a way out by overidentifying with their gender roles and seeking fulfillment through mutual idealization of the loved object. After divorcing himself from the sense of national belonging, Gombrowicz attempts to break with yet another identification that he feels is an obstacle to "life." Gender roles produce an excess of reality, turning masculinity and femininity into petrified models whose demands ruin those who identify with them too closely. It is especially masculinity that bothers Gombrowicz, since it constitutes the main pressure inflicted on his own "I." "I knew the masculinity that they, men, fabricated among themselves, goading each other into it, mutually forcing each other to it in a panic-stricken fear at the woman in themselves" (*D* I, 145). The appearance of the woman in the midst of masculine identity causes men to repress her at the expense of enhanced manliness which is fabricated through various homoerotic games. That sort of male bonding is repulsive to Gombrowicz, who would rather overcome all traits of massively imposed identity. Instead of identifying with the assigned gender role, Gombrowicz attempts to overcome identity once again and achieve a transgendered position of someone who is male only by the accident of birth. "In order to prevent this, I had to find a different position for myself—beyond man and woman—which would nevertheless have nothing to do with a 'third sex'—an asexual and purely human position from which I could begin airing these stuffy and sexually flawed areas" (*D* I, 145). The power of Form that influences both sex and gender is so strong that "I" feels compelled to go beyond the constricted binarism of identities and manufacture a position "beyond man and woman." This desire to create an "I" beyond identities is seen as the driving form of life and youth. To be unable to evade identification with Form means surrender to old age and death.

The life behind the name "Witold Gombrowicz" can continue as long as its protagonist continues to affirm immaturity, surprising both himself and those around him. Once there is no more energy for combating Form, a kind of metaphysical entropy, combined with the awareness of biological aging, begins to assail Gombrowicz. "This awareness: that I have already become myself. I already am. Witold Gombrowicz, these two words, which I carried on myself, are now accomplished. I am. I am too much" (*D* I, 172). Like Nietzsche, whose *Ecce Homo* is subtitled *How One Becomes What One Is,* Gombrowicz has a sense that he has finally become himself and that any further experiments with Form will always be contained within the realm of those "two words" that somehow fix his identity, as death inevitably closes in. Gombrowicz's name subsists on the body of writing like a parasite, feeding off its power to give birth to Form, while constantly attempting to escape its "creative fury." The "I" can have a Form only because writing constantly transfers its power back to it, constructing an endless chain of identities which are continually assumed and then rejected. Gombrowicz's "will to be" is actually a "will to write," to inscribe oneself as a Form in all its plurality and multiplicity. Therefore, Form "becomes the tool with which man is shaped," a form of writing which converts various aspects of the "self" into literary objects. The triangular loop among the artistic "I," the power of writing, and the Formal Imperative assures that "Witold Gombrowicz" is remembered as a name for a particular approach to literary creation within the traditions of the European avant-garde.

Notes

1. Gombrowicz's *A Kind of Testament* was originally published in French as *Entretiens de Dominique de Roux avec Gombrowicz* by Editions Pierre Belfond in 1968. The book supposedly evolved from a series of conversations with Dominque de Roux about Gombrowicz's life and work. However, the preface to the Polish edition of *Testament* (Warszawa: Res Publica, 1990) claims that Gombrowicz refused to be interviewed by de Roux, but constructed the entire text of the testament in the form of the self-interview.

2. Friedrich Nietzsche, *Ecce Homo, The Portable Nietzsche,* ed. and trans. Walter Kaufmann (London: Penguin, 1968), 217.

3. Jacques Derrida, *The Ear of the Other,* ed. Christie V. McDonald, trans. Peggy Kamuf and Avital Ronell (New York: Schocken, 1985), 7.

4. Witold Gombrowicz, "Postscript," *Ferdydurke,* trans. Eric Mosbacher (New York: Penguin, 1986), 273.

5. Gombrowicz, "Postscript," 273.

6. For the concept of the real *(réel)* in Jacques Lacan's work see *Écrits* (New York: Norton, 1977), especially the chapter "On the Possible Treatment of Psychosis."

7. Nietzsche, *Ecce Homo,* 222.

8. See especially the case of Louis-Ferdinand Céline in Julia Kristeva, *Powers of Horror: An Essay on Abjection,* trans. Leon S. Roudiez (New York: Columbia UP, 1982).

9. Kristeva, *Powers of Horror,* 12.

10. Geoffrey Bennington and Jacques Derrida, *Jacques Derrida,* trans. Geoffrey Bennington (Chicago: Chicago UP, 1993), 78.

Valérie Deshoulières

2

Witold Gombrowicz:

Toward a Romantic Theory of Incompleteness

"It would be interesting," suggested Gombrowicz to Dominique de Roux in 1968, "for someone to take the trouble to classify all my adventures with Form. He may find rules of which I am unaware" (*KT,* 72). Anticipating this wish or striving to satisfy it, critics generally anchor the analyses of Gombrowicz's novels and diaries in the study of "the conflict between man and Form." From Bruno Schulz (who was among the first to have understood what was at stake ethically and esthetically in *Ferdydurke*[1]) to Lakis Proguidis (who linked in an original manner the problem of Form in Gombrowicz to the joy of countless possibilities enumerated and developed in Rabelais's *Le tiers livre*[2]) passing through Jacques Volle (whose definitive work, *Gombrowicz, bourreau martyr,*[3] shows how Gombrowicz's poetics feeds on the dynamics of paradox and, in opposition to Hegel and Plato, sacrifices Form on the altar of beauty), Gombrowicz's commentators feel that in order to render his work intelligible, they need to take a close look at the roots of his concept of Immaturity.[4] As for making an attempt to classify—itemize, hierarchize, organize—*all* of the adventures of the man who consistently refused to identify himself with anything that might define him, one might as well try to establish the identity of a chameleon.

Here I would like at least to focus on the idea, dear to the poet of Form, that before he dares to take up his pen, a writer must abdicate his qualities. In this respect, the image of the chameleon, which recurs in the diaries as well as in the novels and which forms a natural link with the theme of Immaturity, could provide us with an additional key to the work as a whole if only we recognize that it has the power to inflict a deadly wound to idols: God, Essence, Morality, Fatherland, Function, and, generally, to all closed form. It is to Jacques Volle that we owe the intuition that, "Properly speaking, one would have to describe at length the majority of the romantics as unwittingly immature; among the most interesting ones, Keats, Nerval, Baudelaire, Hölderlin, Rilke chanted and incanted their nostalgia, their incurable crack."[5] Gombrowicz's aesthetics and ethics seem indeed to be indebted to a certain "theory of chameleons and sparrows" formulated by Keats and revindicated a century later by a whole series of Leporidae similarly sick with sympathy, such as Robert Musil or Julio Cortazar, who see in this animal, at once one and multiple, the supreme metaphor for the poet.

Plan for Perpetual Mutation

The question that Gombrowicz asks all along in his oeuvre concerns, through his dialogue with Form, the conditions of possibility and the nature of poetic experience. For it is the sense of the possible and not the cult of pure poetry—"the excess of poetry, poetic words, metaphors, sublimations, finally, the excess of condensation and purification of all antipoetic elements, which results in poems similar to chemical products" ("Against Poets"; *D* I, 216)—that makes him repeat incessantly that writing aims to direct the specialist of the particular toward the universal and to take up arms against the spirit of seriousness. We need not be reminded that the author of *Ferdydurke* questions not the intellect but rather its poses and masks. He himself insists on avoiding any misunderstandings and warns his critics against the errors "which they could commit in their accounts by mistaking this book for any old toy unaware of essential problems, or for a satire aimed at one or another level of society, or, worse yet, for a nihilist attack on culture."[6]

Let us, too, avoid any misunderstandings: the reign of Immaturity, certainly inaugurated by questioning the Form, does not, however, constitute as Jacques Volle would have it, "an unassignable *no-man's-land* of psychological life."[7] To see this, it is enough to reread the description of the confusion which rages in the salon of Gonzalo the "puto"[8] in *Trans-Atlantyk:* "A hall large with divers things filled but one upon the other, one with the other, there a Triptych under a Vase, yonder a Carpet upon a Candelabra, an Armchair upon a Chair, a Goblin, a Madonna . . . and Brothel, Brothel, Brothel, and with no shame one with the other couples as it goes, Brothel" (*T,* 91). This anarchy makes the hero suddenly regret that "cheese be not cheese" and for a while distances him from the "Sonland."[9] The nostalgia for Order, for Category, for Form, temporarily confirms the victory of the Father.

The balance to be struck between the ethical and the esthetic for Gombrowicz plays itself out at the heart of the relationship between the univocal and the equivocal. If he remains convinced that plurivocal worlds are thinkable—"Every man has his own vision of distinct reality and . . . the universe is refracted in the mind of each of us in a different manner. To express precisely this idea is the essential task of literature: in other words to represent thousands of worlds conceived by thousands of minds, to express this 'other thing' which transforms either windmills into giants or giants into windmills"[10]—he nevertheless acknowledges that the principle of identity is the main condition of logic and he is not unaware of the fact that, beyond pure a priori, life would be impossible if the relationships of which it is woven were not intelligible and transmitted in a univocal manner. Thus it is less his impudence than the instinct of self-preservation that dictates to him the opening words of his diary: "Monday: Me. Tuesday: Me. Wednesday: Me. Thursday: Me" (*KT,* 112).

In the sciences as well as in practical life, the univocal thinking required by the principle of identity is assimilable to an objectivizing thinking solidary with an imperative: that of repeatability. It is this possibility of reproducing according to a rule or law those phenomena which life requires us to master that alone grounds science and alone permits action. The affirmation of the self is, in this perspective, only an aspect of the belief in the necessity of Form. "Man, in his deepest essence, possesses something which I would call 'the Formal Imperative'. Something which is, it seems to me, indispensable to any organic creation. For instance, take our innate need to complete incomplete Form: every Form that has been started requires a complement. When I say A, something compels me to say B, and so on.

This need to develop, to complete, because of a certain logic inherent in Form, plays an important part in my works" (*KT,* 69).

While univocality, repeatability, or, to remain closer to the Gombrowiczian sensibility, the imperative of Form, may assure our survival, our life—our "motivated" life, Musil would specify—could never content itself with this. On the contrary, life demands that an unlimited space be open to freedom: "It is by repetition that myths are created" (*F,* 72). The very conviction that norms of rational thinking do not proceed from an a priori root, but rather rest upon a process of adaptation to reality, virtually presupposes that thought remains vital and liberates itself from all that might reduce it. To exit logic without getting lost, to escape the easy familiarity of systems without becoming dizzy, that is what is at stake in Gombrowicz's adventures with Form. In spite of their diabolical variety, these adventures converge on the subject of the conception of a world whose becoming is envisaged in terms of possibilities.

The point is not to flee Form but rather to isolate its "deep current . . . so that it should appear as such, like a black river following its own course, opaque and troubled, concealing ever new and unfathomable potentialities" (*KT,* 71). The point is not to flee Form but rather to flee the formalism that is always ready to immobilize and denature it.

The Mug and the Face

The opposition between form and formalism, an opposition that is fundamental to Gombrowicz's work, expresses itself most forcefully through the metaphors of mug and face. While quoting from the speech given in commemoration of Copernicus and the Renaissance by Józef Cyrankiewicz, the vice–prime minister of Poland from 1952 to 1954, Gombrowicz stops abruptly and turns to his readers:

> Enough! it would be pointless to quote any further . . . lend an ear to our twosome and you will see the astronomical distance which separates our two universes—his and mine. Why do I get to say what I think while he is forced to lie? Why am I endowed with a simple human face while he in turn is visibly born under the sign of the mug and the kisser since he fabricates one for himself and for me . . . Quite simply because he is a servant of

> the Party, of History, of the government, of the program—while I am a simple man, a private person, a free man.[11]

A person, one might add, desirous of abandoning himself to the frightful discipline of the free mind, in other words of drawing from existence not forms but that from which they may be fabricated—a close relative in this of Valéry's Monsieur Teste. The "mug" is to the "face" as slavery is to freedom. It is the spirit of seriousness at its stiffest. The mug clearly stigmatizes all those who are missing the tragic truth of life by applying themselves to underlining its traits, all those who are preparing themselves to produce one day "a tragic rhetoric" in ignorance of the "non-tragic aspects inseparable from authentic tragedy"[12]—above all, the pedagogues and other classical pedants defending tooth and nail the values which usually serve as reference to, and contribute to the elaboration of, moral principles. Their principal characteristic, Gombrowicz reminds us, is to reduce all that they touch by opposing themselves to movement and to the contradictions he cannot help but mock. From the academic necropolis, which he dreams of demolishing, to the bourgeois pretensions which he works to unmask, Józio's father dedicates his art to denouncing, behind the "mug," the scholastic compartmentalization of the spirit.

At the beginning of the formalist error is, clearly, the "rump," that "sensation of dwindling in size inside someone" (*F,* 23). The Gombrowiczian hell has something indolent about it: to lose your humanity you need only let yourself go a little. You begin by letting someone make a "rump" for you, and soon you can't move anymore. To be "rumped" is to have failed to spurn the "mug" by means other than silence. In order to remain free one needs more of a combative attitude. The scenario of the fall repeats itself: the "rump" and the "mug" are the rhythm of the tragic history of a man in search of his face: "Having reached this pinnacle, what course is left open to me but that of retracing my steps by way of the various parts of the body to my rumpish starting-point?" (*F,* 71).

The rejection of the "mug," metaphor of dogmatic, petrified Form, inaugurates an apology for Immaturity, of which the strange chapter 5 of *Ferdydurke*—"Philifor Honeycombed with Childishness"—is the manifesto. Gombrowicz sought particularly to defend before the critics this "element of structure," this "twist," this "special passage," this "coda," this "trill," this "fold," this "passageway" without which he would never have been able to "proceed to the left calf." Dismissing both the great Doctor Philifor, native of south Annam, Professor of Synthetisiology at the University of Leyden, and his rival, the anti-Philifor, Professor of Higher Analysis at the University of Columbia, these pages function as an indictment of pedagogy and double as a hymn to childhood; after long study and many quarrels the analyst and the synthetician make peace with each other to sing popular songs together, break windows, and spit on the hats of passersby. Finally rid of their stiffness, the two specialists refuse to choose between gnocchi, "a mixture of eggs, flour and water," and gnocchi, "the higher essence, the supreme spirit of gnocchi, the thing-in-itself" (*F,* 89). For, as Philifor concludes, "everything is honeycombed with childishness" (*F,* 101). And the Professor, losing "the mug of his profession," feels the poet awakening in him: "But their greatest pleasure of all was buying a red balloon and chasing it across country, waiting for the thrilling moment when it burst noisily as if struck by an invisible bullet" (*F,* 101).

Mythology of Character

The ardor with which Philifor and his ex-rival fill their anticipated retreat, and this red balloon which they brandish as the emblem of the rediscovered Saint Immaturity, show clearly the relationship between *joie de vivre* and the renunciation of "character" in Musil's sense of the word, as an ideological belief opposed to free spirit. If Gombrowicz shows himself to be in sharp conflict with all the postwar tendencies which cast anathemas on the "self" (the Church judges it immoral, Science deems it to be in contradiction with objectivism, Marxism declares it to be outmoded and antisocial), his work nevertheless insistently confronts the problem of the articulation of the structure of the self with the historical reality which conditions that self. While recognizing that the functions of permanence and invariability are essential to the self, as philosophy and Freud's successors agree in the end,[13] he allies himself equally with the idea (more Heraclitean than Freudian) according to which the self is essential fluidity. Against the grain of the traditional thematics of introspection, which aspires to grasp a self separate from the exteriority that alters it, Gombrowicz has sought to show the ineluctable relationship between the self and the determinants of alterity. It is this detailed analysis of the relationship between the self and History which leads him to demythologize such notions as character, person, quality.

He believes that the establishment of an authentic science of subjectivity, able to comprehend—to bring together—the variations of the self and the permanence of the cogito presupposes that one no longer opposes exteriority and interiority, subject and object, consciousness and the world. The problem of subjectivism is reduced to "the egoistic contemplation of one's own navel" only in "feeble minds":

> As for those ignoramuses who consider philosophy to be a lot of twaddle because they don't understand a thing, I say to them that it is over an analogous contradiction that modern physicists have racked their brains, stymied by the wave and corpuscular theory of light, by the dualist conception of the electron, by Einstein's continuum, and by Planck's theory. Everywhere, at all times, the most profound thought is dashed against the reef of the duality of interpretation.[14]

Not to be able to imagine a consciousness independent of its object, a consciousness that is not correlative, strikes a brutal blow to the principle of identity. Thus our thought is frustrated by the impossibility of apprehending the human being, who is what he is not, and is not what he is. With the death of pure consciousness the myth of "character" evaporates. How can we be astonished that each of Gombrowicz's phrases serves several gods?

At the beginning of *The Man without Qualities,* Musil writes:

> "It is always false to want to explain the phenomena of a country by the character of its inhabitants. For the inhabitant of a country always has at least nine characters: a professional character, a class character, a sexual character, a national character, a political character, a geographical character, a conscious character, an unconscious character, and perhaps even a private character; he unites them in his person, but finds himself dissociated from them, and in the end is nothing more than a small valley carved by this multitude of streams, a valley into which these streams flow only to emerge and fill other small valleys with other rivulets. That is why each inhabitant of a land possesses still another, tenth character, which is none

> other than the passive imagination of spaces not yet filled; this character gives to man all the liberties but one: that of taking seriously that which forms his other characters.[15]

We might wager that Gombrowicz extracts from this tenth character the force to scoff with the same intensity at the Pedagogues and the Poets, the Aristocrats and the Bourgeois, the Adults and the Teenagers, the Marxists and the Fascists, the Argentinians and the Poles, as so many symptoms to be alleviated. His sense of the possible, hypertrophied, is ill at ease with these arrested forms.

Portrait of the Poet as a Chameleon

Thus, in opposition to all historical phrenology, Gombrowicz thinks that Man surpasses the sum of the qualities which might constitute him. Further, this friend of paradoxes doesn't at all like "Butter too Buttery, Noodles too Noodly, Millet too Millety, and Barley too Barley!" (*T,* 32). His rupture with the fascination for Essence orients in a decisive manner his adventures with Form; it presupposes that there are between these adventures only differences of maturation: on the one hand, forms desired or in the process of being realized, on the other, finished forms which he thinks to be the dead skin of experience. The apology for Immaturity is in reality a cult dedicated to mobility: "The essence of man resides in his development, and this development is accomplished by a suicide continually begun anew."[16] In other words, we must apply ourselves to "killing in ourselves that which is, in order to arrive at that which will be." The bombs thrown by Gombrowicz at the political, social, or literary establishment have as their sole objective the restoring to man of sovereignty over his own creations.

It is necessary to point out here the Cartesian resonances which often mark Gombrowicz's deconstruction of the subject: his flights, his renunciations, and his prevarications seem to us in fact less dictated by a chronic scepticism than by the desire to lose the world in order better to find it again in a universal realization of oneself. Isn't this how Descartes conceives his break with the world in his *Meditations?* Transposed into the language of Gombrowicz, the Cartesian "Epoché" gives more or less this: to rediscover the human demands that one abdicate even its qualities. As for rediscovering oneself, it is better under these conditions not to deceive oneself: "I don't know who I really am . . . My 'self' is nothing but my will to be myself" (*KT,* 77).

Here, the problem of Form in Gombrowicz takes on the appearance of a conundrum that one could phrase as follows: Who changes while remaining faithful to himself, cultivates his essence without renouncing his mobility, and plays tricks on Form in order better to preserve it? Answer: The one who, depending on the place, the individuals, and the circumstances, is by turns "good, stupid, primitive, refined, taciturn, talkative, self-effacing, arrogant, superficial or profound . . . [or] agile, heavy, important, unimportant, bashful, shameless, bold or shy, cynical or idealistic" (*KT,* 51). Does the poet mean by this enumeration anything other than the metamorphoses of a chameleon?

The Creator without Qualities

The rage with which Gombrowicz defends himself against the deformations imposed on him from the outside is proportional to his discomfort when Dominique de Roux asks him to comment on his life in relation to his work: "we were a displaced family whose social status was far from clear, living between Lithuania and the former Congress kingdom of Poland, between land and industry, between what is known as 'good society' and another, more middle-class society. These were the first 'betweens' which subsequently multiplied until they almost constituted my country of residence, my true home" (*KT,* 28). So much for his birth. His youth? It was hardly more clear: "I always found myself 'between' things. I never fitted into anything" (*KT,* 36). Gombrowicz admits to having grown in three different directions which had nothing to do with each other: he was at once "a boy of 'good family,' " an intellectual atheist, and an "abnormal, twisted, degenerate, abominable, and solitary" being that "slunk along, hugging the walls" (*KT,* 36–37). Three realities of equal importance, to the extent that he is entirely in each of them and at the same time is not in any of them. Gombrowicz asks himself: "So what could be the cause of this inner disorder, which turned a reasonably happy boy like me into a bizarre monster, lured by deformity, by all existing aberrations?" (*KT,* 37)

Life goes on, and the author of *Ferdydurke* goes forward always wearing a mask. "I was alone. I lived in private. Secretly. Out on a limb. Hidden" (*KT,* 38). A comedian or a social misfit of absolute sincerity? When we learn that he considers Hamlet his brother, we prefer to be on our guard: any attempt to be "serious, sincere and authentic" would have been a lie, says Gombrowicz of his early fiction, "simply because I was incapable of sincerity and lying is unhealthy for an artist" (*KT,* 42). This paradox has as its main virtue the ability to stimulate the circulation of air in a house where all the inhabitants are paralyzed by what they have done: career, glory, obligations, responsibilities. And beneath the paradox, what are we to understand? Undoubtedly the following: the assembling of contradictions may be the best method of creation.

Gombrowicz claims that he wrote *Ferdydurke* to defend his personality or, rather, his personalities. Indeed, he evokes his situation on the European continent at that time in these terms: "I was an agglomeration of different worlds, neither one nor the other. Indefinite. If I were followed step by step and spied on, my every contact with people could easily show just how much of a chameleon I was" (*KT,* 51). The image of the multiform animal occurs naturally to the author when his interviewer asks him to characterize himself at a given time. This self-portrait as a chameleon allows Gombrowicz to formulate the supreme paradox, the veritable nervous center of his aesthetics—that the character of man resides in his capacity for metamorphosis. By showing how much its qualities, uncertain and doubtful, are at the mercy of circumstances, the chameleon reminds us that it is possible to explore all the nooks and crannies of the world without breaking with the dignity of necessity. For it is in his essence to change.

These osmotic faculties, this exploration of the Possible in the manner of "plasticine figurines which can be modelled indefinitely and turned into the most hideous monsters" (*KT,* 39) are certainly not Gombrowicz's prerogative: "I was not the only chameleon. Everybody was a chameleon. It was the new human condition, and one would have to face up to it" (*KT,* 59). And yet he distinguishes himself from this spinelessness, his absence of qualities nourishing his creativity. Far from thinking that the poetic condition must be subject to the construction of personality, he believes it to be indissociable from lack of character: "I became 'the poet of form.' I amputated myself from myself" (*KT,* 59). We may refine the thought of the author by linking these two propositions as follows: "I have become the poet of Form *because* I have amputated myself from myself."

Even though man has been obsessed by knowledge, it has often been with hostility, as if he feared vanishing in his contemplation of the world. For Gombrowicz, on the contrary, to be a poet means essentially to refuse to become a beetle to the point of eliminating the contradiction: "I attack all Form which ceases to be the comfortable attire of man and becomes a heavy and rigid carapace."[17] Is this not to suggest that only the man without qualities, eager to espouse all forms, to try all bodies, can hope to take now and then the face of the poet? Knowledge, then, consists in losing oneself without reprieve in the physical and the moral, and chameleonism, in falling head over heels in love with the order of nature.

This image of a sponge evoked by Gombrowicz, his insistence on signaling a lack of identity, makes us think of the utopia of attemptism cultivated by Musil's Ulrich. The latter is equally convinced that personal experience is interesting only on the condition that it is purified and enriched by poetic intuition. Even though present in Ulrich, this intuition doesn't act in his life as a stimulant of the Word: the Musilian chameleon wrote his last poetry at the age of twenty. As for the "book to come" that floats for a certain while above his head, making him a relative of the Proustian hero, the journal which he undertakes with the intention of defining the idea of feeling nips it in the bud.

Small Treatise on Romantic Sympathy

While the Professor barricades himself before the osmotic irruption of reality in order better to "adhere to the evidence of his organs,"[18] according to Jankélévitch's formulation, the Poet gives up defending himself and assures the world of his sympathy. It is this division of humanity into chameleons and beetles that Gombrowicz suggests by scoffing at our eagerness to reduce the object to categorizable and petrifiable terms. His refusal to believe in the necessity of an ideology without contradictions leads him thus to reassert the value of a principle that owes much to English romantic poetry and that could be called "the principle of porosity." Gombrowicz's statements on the subject of *Eigenschaftlosigkeit* indeed echo these words addressed one October morning in 1818 by the poet John Keats to his friend Richard Woodhouse: "As to the poetical Character itself . . . , it is not itself—it has no self—it is every thing and nothing—It has no character—it enjoys light and shade; it lives in gusto, be it foul or fair, high or low, rich or poor, mean or elevated—It has as much delight in conceiving an Iago as an Imogen. What shocks the virtuous philosopher, delights the camelion Poet." In this vein the Poet quickly presents himself as the least poetic of creatures: "For no poet is exclusively a poet and in each poet lives a non-poet, who does not sing and does not like singing" ("Against Poets"; *D* I, 218).

It would be wrong then to see in the chameleon only a possible avatar of the unhappy consciousness. I believe that Gombrowicz's metamorphoses go beyond the disenchanted framework of modern relativism: the symptom is blurred to the benefit of a "Defense and Illustration"[19] of receptivity. The analogy of his poetic art with the "theory of chameleons and sparrows" formulated by Keats has the merit of rehabilitating the adaptive faculties of a small animal too often associated with the strategies of urbane rhetoric and Machiavellian politics. The Gombrowiczian chameleon leaves far behind him the air of "honest deception" and illustrates in an exemplary manner this need for Incompleteness experienced by everyone. To conclude, in Gombrowicz there is a redefinition of a series of fundamental themes—Imperfection, Inferiority, Youth, and of course Immaturity—a series whose elements appear in the final account to be less sceptic than romantic, as long as we do not reduce the latter complex adjective to the sickly effusions of the soul at nightfall. However much Gombrowicz likes the dawn and dusk, he mistrusts their dissolving effect. A romanticism, thus, that would send tailcoats, lakes, and pearl-handled revolvers to the accessory shop and would be perceptible only in a certain tenderness toward the fragment: "To me, art almost always speaks more forcefully when it appears in an imperfect, accidental, and fragmentary way, somehow just signalling its presence, allowing one to feel it through the ineptitude of the interpretation. I prefer the Chopin that reaches me in the street from an open window to the Chopin served in great style from the concert stage." (*D* I, 32) Paradoxical romanticism affirms itself again in the will, already expressed by Berlioz, to "do impassioned things coldly": "The more one affirms oneself as a theoretician, the more it is necessary to be solidly settled, rooted, in the poetics of life."[20] And vice versa.

Between Youth and God, there is then only Desire. Desire to be oneself, desire for Art, desire for Form. The rest is literature and is situated at the antipodes of the truth that is movement. Gombrowicz, eternal candidate for Maturity, did not flee Form, but chose, in defiance of accepted categories, the figure of unlimited seduction.

—Translated from the French by Katarzyna Jerzak

Notes

1. A personal friend of Gombrowicz's, Bruno Schulz expressed his enthusiasm for Gombrowicz's writings beginning with the summer of 1938 in the review *Skamander,* issues 96–98.

2. Lakis Proguidis, *Un écrivain malgré la critique: Essai sur l'oeuvre de Witold Gombrowicz* (Paris: Gallimard, 1989), 74.

3. Jacques Volle, *Gombrowicz, bourreau martyr* (Paris: Bourgois, 1972), 79.

4. See in particular the article by Ariel Denis, "Destruction of Form, Formation of Reality," in the issue of *Cahiers de l'Herne* devoted to Gombrowicz in 1971.

5. Volle, *Gombrowicz, bourreau martyr,* 81.

6. Witold Gombrowicz, *Varia I,* (Paris: Bourgois, 1986), 65.

7. Gombrowicz, *Varia I,* 77.

8. *Puto* refers in Argentina to a homosexual.

9. "Sonland," the opposite of Fatherland, is a neologism coined by Gombrowicz.

10. Gombrowicz, *Varia I,* 81–82.

11. Gombrowicz, *Varia II,* 233 (Paris: Bourgois, 1989).

12. Jean-Claude Dedieu, *Gombrowicz: lieux de l'écrit* (Paris: Marval, 1993), 54.

13. In particular, one sees this conception of the self as essential fluidity in Musil.

14. Gombrowicz, *Varia I,* 139.

15. Robert Musil, *L'homme sans qualités,* vol. I (Paris: Seuil), 39.

16. Witold Gombrowicz, *Contre les poètes,* 64 (Paris: Complexe, 1988).

17. Gombrowicz, *Contre les poètes,* 73.

18. Vladimir Jankélévitch, *L'ironie* (Paris: Flammarion, 1964), 19.

19. *La Défense et illustration de la langue française* (1549) by Joachim Du Bellay; a prose manifesto of the doctrines of the Pléiade. It advocated the use of the French language in poetry. (translator's note)

20. Cited by Jean-Claude Dedieu in *Gombrowicz: lieux de l'écrit,* 55–56.

Dorota Głowacka

3

The Heresiarchs of Form:

Gombrowicz and Schulz

The inadequation of all speech must be said . . . I cannot speak of an absence of meaning except by giving it a meaning it does not have.

Georges Bataille, *Conférences sur le non-savoir*

In 1936, the editor of the journal *Studio* invited two literati friends, Bruno Schulz and Witold Gombrowicz, to cross pens in an open exchange of letters. They accepted the challenge to spar, and Gombrowicz dealt the first coup:

> For a long time I've racked my brains over what kind of thought I could fire off to you, dear Bruno, but absolutely nothing occurred to me until yesterday I bumped into the opinion of a certain doctor's wife whom I once met by accident on line 18. "Bruno Schulz," she said, "is either a sick pervert or poseur, but most probably a poseur. He's only pretending."[1]

> [Długi czas myślałem, jaką by tu myślą wystrzelić w ciebie, drogi Bruno, lecz na żadną nie mogłem wpaść, aż dopiero wczoraj wpadłem na myśl żony pewnego doktora, spotkanej przypadkowo w osiemnastce. *Bruno Schulz*—powiedziała—*to albo chory zboczeniec, albo pozer; lecz najpewniej pozer. On tylko udaje tak.*[2]

Gombrowicz, a self-proclaimed rebel against literary hatcheries of the time, strikes against Schulz, a rebel manqué. What is Schulz but a dwarf stooped at the dainty feet of the Muse, if we are to trust his self-portraits in the infamous *Booke of Idolatry.*[3] Gombrowicz dares Schulz's muse to don the garb of a certain doctor's wife and live among the mortals in Wilcza Street. As an acolyte of Form, Gombrowicz pleads with "Bruno," whom he has ensconced at Mount Parnassus, from his own vantage point of disdainful inferiority: "Your form is manifested *in excelsis!* Get back down here on earth! Dance with an ordinary woman! . . . what good would your form be if it were only put into use at two thousand meters above the level of life?" (*LD,* 119).

Can Schulz's sublime pen withstand the thrust of this assault? It is "dear Bruno's" turn to spar. Yet, he will not play idealist Siphon to Gombrowicz's inferior "Mientus"; he will not grimace. In his riposte, he promptly strikes out his opponent's version of "Schulz" from the scenario of the duel. The duel has always been an honorable pastime among the Polish gentry, the lineage which Gombrowicz both claims as his own and spurns as anathema. However, in Schulz's reply, the duel metamorphoses into a *corrida* when the alleged poseur charges with stamina:

> You'd like to lure me into an arena, dear Witold, beset on all sides by the curiosity of the mob, you'd like to see me as the enraged bull in pursuit of the doctor's wife's fluttering banner; her flimsy amaranthine peignoir is supposed to serve as your cape, behind which the thrusts of your sword await me . . . But what would have happened if I had turned out to be an unconventional bull . . . [and] made a rush at you instead? Not to bump you off your feet, O noble toreador, but to take you on my back if this is not megalomania—and carry you out of the arena, beyond the confines of its rules and statutes. (*LD,* 120)

> [Chciałbyś mnie zwabić, drogi Witoldzie, na arenę obstawioną ze wszech stron ciekawością tłumu, chciałbyś mnie widzieć, rozjuszonego byka, w pogoni za wiejącą płachtą pani doktorowej, jej powiewny peniuar koloru amarantu ma Ci służyć za kapę, poza którą czekają mnie sztychy Twej szpady . . . A cóż, gdybym okazał się bykiem wbrew konwencjom . . . i ruszył

na Ciebie z podniesionym walecznie ogonem? Nie żeby Cię zwalić z nóg, szlachetny Toreadorze, ale żeby Cię wziąć na grzbiet—jeśli to nie jest megalomanią—i wynieść Cię poza obręb areny, jej prawideł i kodeksów.] (*Pz,* 685).

What is at stake in this bragadoccio textual sparring, other than a publicity stunt? After all, at the time of the exchange both writers have already attained certain recognition and a modest suite of fans, although Gombrowicz vociferously scorns the literary trends à la mode, and Schulz remains as if happily oblivious to them. As it appears from the above passages, the object of contention was none other than Form itself. While Gombrowicz fulminates against Schulz's "superior" form that apparently soars too high to ever graze the mundane, Schulz mocks what will become known as Gombrowicz's imperative of Form: the endless, ineluctable coming into being of forms in the interhuman realm:

> Let me tell you, then, that what appears to you as some sort of malign force transcending the individual is only a weakness of your own nature. It is the mob within us that applauds, dear Witold; the mob deeply rooted inside, casting spells, gives off its collective grunt, smothers our better knowledge and causes our hands to lift convulsively in blind acclamation. (*LD,* 121).

> [Otóż, co Ci się wydaje jakąś przestępną, ponadindywidualną potęgą, jest tylko słabością Twej natury. To tłum w nas przytakuje, drogi Witoldzie, pokutujący w nas i zakorzeniony tłum wydaje swój pomruk, zagłusza naszą lepszą wiedzę i podnosi nasze dłonie konwulsyjnie do ślepej aklamacji.] (*Pz,* 687)

Granted, in his review of *Ferdydurke,* which appears in *Skamander* in the fall of 1938, Schulz will be the first to point out that Gombrowicz's claim to genius lies in his diagnosis of the problem of Form. Amid the scandal that accompanied the innovative novel's entry into the literary salons and cafeterias, Schulz hastens to salute Gombrowicz's genius. In the letter to Romana Halpern dated October 13, 1937, Schulz describes the "thunderous, dazzling impact" of Gombrowicz's novel, "a book on an altogether grand scale, pioneering and revelatory" (*LD,* 157).

In 1936, however, if Schulz heeds the call to descend from Parnassus, which he hardly claims as his abode anyway, it is to deliver Gombrowicz from the parasitic form in which he has locked himself, in this case as incarnated in the bounties of his proxy—"a certain doctor's wife." From Gombrowicz's point of view, this preposterous yet fleshy form has been crafted in order to lacerate what he sees as stultifying literary schools of Polish antebellum literature, feebly imitative of Western avant-gardes. Gombrowicz is not unaware that buffoonery consigns the artist to the realm of tabloid spectatorship, where he must engage in the acts of repeated exhibitionism (of which the open exchange of correspondence in *Studio* is but a telling episode). By no means does Gombrowicz cringe from the prying eye of the public; moreover, his early attention-grabbers only anticipate his later project of "baring himself" in the *Diary,* published in *Kultura*[4] from 1956 until 1968. In these later acts of diaristic denuding he will also try to strip himself of the forms that have been imposed on him by his Polish, often thumbs-down, readership. Schulz, who does not succumb to the allures of the spotlight, invites Gombrowicz to spurn the crowd's bloodthirsty applause and walk away, "absorbed in intimate conversation" (*LD,* 121). Such a peripatetic communion of intellects, in turn, best describes the project of Schulz the epistolographer, the author of thousands of letters to people who, as he divined, had "a similar inner structure."[5]

Schulz's spiritual configuration, albeit replicated in several of his faithful correspondents, does not resonate in Gombrowicz; in all probability, despite his token gesture, in the open letter, of invitating "dear Witold" to an act of intellectual communion, Schulz does not really expect it to work out. After all, he seems particularly vexed when the critics attempt to conflate Gombrowicz's writing with his own. For example, he rebukes Emil Breiter, a critic from *Wiadomości literackie* (Literary news) who has classified Gombrowicz as a member of Schulz's nascent literary school.[6] In justifying his protest, and it is worth noting that self-effacing Schulz rarely employs defiance as a means of expression, he emphasizes the absolute incommensurability of their inner worlds. At the same time, Schulz exposes the mechanisms that may have precipitated an illusion of such affinity: the unclassifiability of both writers' prose and a superficial stylistic resemblance stemming from their implacable challenge to convention, even if each executed it in an idiosyncratic fashion.[7]

Apart from urging their readers not to subsume their writing styles under the same category, both Schulz and Gombrowicz repeatedly attempt to challenge some critics' fawning endeavors to attribute the most distinguished literary lineages to their writings. For example, Schulz resents being labeled "the Polish Kafka": he explains that his writing could not have possibly thrived in the suffocating atmosphere of Kafka's fictional worlds.[8] Gombrowicz, for his part, meticulously differentiates between his work and Sartre's and, especially on the pages of *The Diary,* cautions against confounding his theory of form with Sartrian existentialism.[9] If anything, he suggests that his own work anticipates and even parodies, *avant la lettre,* the existential novel. Each writer claims the unprecedented status for his own writing and situates himself with respect to tradition in the relation of absolute non-imitation. Prompted by the desire to maintain "the essential autonomy and separateness" (*Pz,* 683), each denies any family resemblance in his own work, although he does not hesitate to attribute it to others. In the already mentioned letter to Romana Halpern, Schulz stands Gombrowicz on the same pedestal with "Freud or Proust," where Gombrowicz would loathe to see himself elevated; and in the review of *Ferdydurke,* he pursues the analogy with Freud even further. Despite refering to Gombrowicz's novel as "a fundamental discovery," opening up a new realm of intellectual phenomena (*LD,* 158), the review ends with a jab at *Ferdydurke*'s claim to absolute, unadulterated lack of literary model:

> Here it is worth remembering, without disadvantage to the undoubted originality of the novel *Ferdydurke,* that this book has a predecessor perhaps unknown to its author—the premature and therefore heirless *Pałuba* by Karol Irzykowski. (*LD,* 164)

> [Warto przypomnieć bez ujmy dla niewątpliwej oryginalności *Ferdydurke,* że ta książka miała poprzednika może nawet autorowi nieznanego, przedwczesną i dlatego nieskuteczną *Pałubę* Irzykowskiego.] (*Pz,* 491)

The present noncommittal encounter between Gombrowicz and Schulz foregrounds preoccupation with Form as the underlying structuring principle of their prose. What is the correlation between this matrix and each writer's insistence on the uniqueness of his own creative effort? In each writer's account, his work is irreducible to any literary school; it renounces the patrimony of the European belles lettres tradition at large and denies the precession of any literary model whatsoever. What is the rationale behind Gombrowicz's and Schulz's pronounced repudiation of the mimetic moment vis à vis "tradition" and, manifestly, with respect to each other?

Philippe Lacoue-Labarthe argues in his essay "Typography" that the insistence on singularity and inimitability is, in all likelihood, a symptom of the writer's "mimetic sickness," that is, of a desire to simultaneously erase and reiterate an imitative gesture at the origin of the text.[10] The primary focus of Lacoue-Labarthe's project is the repression of mimesis in the Western philosophical tradition. The denigration and subsequent eradication of the literary or "fictioning" moment is indicative of philosophy's desire to remain uncontaminated by its other—the text upon which it necessarily relies as a vehicle to bring forth its ideas. At the birth of this tradition is Plato's auspicatious gesture of relegating the artist/mimetician to the outskirts of the Republic, a maneuver that allows the philosopher to assert the hegemony of noumena over appearances in the definition of truth. As Lacoue-Labarthe reminds us, this gesture, which pervades the entire tissue of the Western thought, is inseparable from the concept of the figure construed as finite, discrete form into which the truth enters in order to appear phenomenally. This conception has preponderant repercussions for aesthetics. Since form, based on the order of similitude, allows for the truth to be apprehended, it imposes upon and configures the Western mind and, in consequence, also orders and disciplines its representational paradigm.

Lacoue-Labarthe's critique notes that Martin Heidegger calls into question Plato's reductive understanding of the truth of Being as adequation because, among other consequences, it relegates art to a subservient status: in Plato's cave, art hovers in the shadows at a third remove from the original and bears no direct relation to truth. In *The Origin of the Work of Art,* Heidegger shows that Platonic mimetic understanding of figuration is always presupposed by the incessant "production" or setting up of the figure (*Gestalt*) in the site of the unconcealment of Being. Heidegger's elaboration of the nature of truth in terms of disclosive appropriation releases the figure from purely mimetic constraints. On the other hand, as Lacoue-Labarthe insists, Heidegger's reading of Plato closes off a possibility of a different reading of Platonic mimesis and thus solidifies its understanding as mere deceit, counterfeit, and inadequation. This leaves a different kind of mimetism, a certain inauguratory fictioning moment, present in philosophy at its very inception, unaccounted for. A trace of this pre-originary mimetic instant can be found in Plato himself, especially in the *Republic,* if only through Plato's repeated maneuvers to suppress it and in his evocation of myth, that is, fabulation, as the foundational test of truth in the hierarchy of essences and appearances. In this context, Lacoue-Labarthe insists on the epistemic need to rethink representation in order to unveil a stage prior to the *mise-en-scène* that relies on simple imitation. On that stage, where mimesis is not yet caught in the visibility of the copy but operates as the very process of differentiation, the thinking/creating subject/mimetician has always already imitated itself. Reflected in the mirrors of its own textual production, the "subject" is disseminated in its own copies, inscribing itself in the text as I ("I"). Lacoue-Labarthe concludes that the moment of pre-originary mimetic redoubling not only underlies the Platonic eidetic determination of truth, as elaborated by Heidegger's critique, but also destabilizes the German philosopher's own notion of *aletheia,* which has to rely on the erasure of the scene of writing. The mimetic fragmentation of the "subject," its de-constitution in the figure, threatens any hegemonic claim to the truth: thus, it is understandable that the mimetic threat provokes a desire to eliminate it.

Both Gombrowicz and Schulz are fascinated with the operation of mimicry in which the power of imagination is released in order to transform reality; at the same time, they investigate artistic and ethical consequences of unbridled creativity. On the one hand, imagination allows the artist to challenge existing representational paradigms, grounded in the politics of form; on the other hand, the artist has to ponder the dangers of becoming trapped in the form of his own creation. Gombrowicz's and Schulz's writings display acute sensitivity to the ineluctable enframing of the creative endeavor in the figure and the degeneration of artistry into lifeless forms. Each of them, however, discusses it in a context specific to his work and focuses on entirely different aspects of the process. Gombrowicz wields his pen mightier than the sword against the Polish national form and, with its every stroke, announces himself as "I, who am terribly Polish and terribly rebellious of Poland" (*D* I, 178). Schulz, on the other hand, does not fashion himself opposite to the Polish tradition. Schulz's general artistic concern is the debilitating reification of form, which corresponds to the increasing commodification of art and the abdication of high aesthetics to cheap simulacra spawned by mass culture. The progression of simulacra and the correlative devaluation of art, reminiscent of Walter Benjamin's notion of the shrinking of aura in the era of mechanical reproduction, have severed the artist's vital connection with his mythic roots.

Gombrowicz targets the form that has forged the Polish nation's identity and, as he insists, has long embarrassed itself. Having become a tyrannical yet grotesque agent of history, the Polish tradition can only narcissistically exercise its own empty gestures, in a monstrous spectacle of self-parody. Therefore, Gombrowicz deploys the entire arsenal of his acerbic wit in combating a debilitating mimetism at the core of the nation's history. Against the Polish messianic conception of history, Gombrowicz pitches a vision of history as a succession of forms which constantly mock one another and, in a pandemonium of universal mimicry, mutually expose their own artificiality. He repeatedly proclaims that his task as a writer is to achieve victory over Polishness and to lead the nation out of its slavery to national form (*D* I, 16).

This peculiar thrust of the writer's combat with form is clearly pronounced in the works such as *Ferdydurke, Trans-Atlantyk,* and *Ślub.* For example, in *Trans-Atlantyk,* Gombrowicz, with the help of his henchman "Gombrowicz" the narrator, busies himself with a meticulous reconstruction of the national form in the Polish community in Argentina. The émigré version of Polishness diligently copies the customs of the old country as if the imitation were trying to outdo the original, while the uncanny effect of this spectacle is enhanced by the anachronism of the narrator's Sarmatian idiom. Gombrowicz spins this form through a series of traditional rituals, all of which are marked by the lack of the ritualistic object (the duel without bullets, "kulig" without snow, and the hunt without the game), until it empties itself out and hangs limp, devoid of content. At the same time, the national form immobilizes itself in the Order of the Chevaliers of the Spur, which has been created to redeem terrifying emptiness through "Anguish and Suffering, Agony and Awe" (*T,* 103). Even in the aberrant twists of Gombrowicz's plots in his later works such as *Cosmos* or *Pornografia,* where the national drama recedes to the background, it still continues to seep through the entire tissue of the elaborately constructed reality. It is worth noting that Artur Sandauer, a prominent Polish literary critic whose mordant reviews equal only those of Gombrowicz himself (Sandauer's war cry: "I am nobody's echo!"), insists that these later works are powerless and insipid because they no longer plug into the life of the nation to a sufficient degree. However lacking in critical sensitivity these comments may appear to be, they diagnose correctly the shift in Gombrowicz's writing towards stylistic virtuosity, in which, as Sandauer observes, Gombrowicz only dexterously imitates the former Gombrowicz.[11]

Another strategy designed to pry the writer's individual form from the shackles of its national counterpart is deployed in *Diary*. There, Gombrowicz assumes a condescending tone, oscillating between a homiletic address to "my brothers" and outright insult ("You are the poor relations of the world, who try to impress themselves and others" [*D* I, 6]). The addressee in *The Diary* invariably appears to be "you, people." The distancing effect of the pronoun "you," which wedges itself between the writer and his compatriots, disallows proximity but also wards off the tyranny of communal "we." Gombrowicz does not wish to see himself reflected in another Pole. Sandauer reminisces that in 1956, during one of the more hopeful moments in Poland's postwar history, he tried to coax Gombrowicz into returning from exile and accepting the role of "the pride of the Polish nation." The writer replied briskly, "I am insulted. Pride. Obstinacy. Coolness. Suspicion. Perversity. Refusal to be sucked into the nation. My writing must remain what it is, particularly in its non-commitment to politics and refusal to be harnessed into its service. I pursue one policy alone: my own. I am a separate state."[12]

Bruno Schulz's writing, on the other hand, is inflected by the Judaic tradition of a people born from the Book and continuously narrating itself. According to Jacques Derrida, this metaphor legitimizes itself in the myth of Jews as wanderers in foreign lands, "autochthons only of speech and writing, of Law."[13] For a Jew, there is nothing beyond the Book, which is the origin, the source, and the destination of his journey: even the exteriority of the book is already inscribed in it as the myth of its own origin. Joseph, the narrator of Schulz's stories, worships the Book as the absolute and timeless tabernacle of truth. The Book's spellbinding aura, which emanates from the mythological penumbra of Joseph's childhood, inspires him with a sense of mission to find the coveted Authentic. The quest leads through a never-ending composition of a poetic *midrash,* an apocrypha of the Book, through which the artist seeks to elucidate the meaning of the original verse. In an essay for Stanisław Ignacy Witkiewicz, Schulz explains that the artists never write anything other than the same primordial text: "their creative effort goes into an unending exegesis, a commentary on that one couplet of poetry assigned to them" (*LD,* 111) [twórczość ich jest nieustanną egzegezą, komentarzem do tego jednego wersetu, który im był zadany[14]].

"Reality is the shadow of the word" (*LD,* 117): in the beginning there is text, the word, the blueprint; since the origin of everything was penned in the Book before the beginning of time, "reality" can only imitate the original and continuously write itself in the form of imperfect copies: The narrator gleans the scraps of the Authentic's esoteric knowledge from degenerate mundane manifestations of the Book—maps, calendars, stamp albums. Somehow, only these most degraded imitations of the Book retain the ability to flash the memory of the Great Authentic. Thus, the Book can be partially recovered in the form of its own appendix, on the illicit, dubious margins of the respectable text, the torn pages of an almanac that Joseph chanced upon in the kitchen, "full of refuse and trash" ("The Book"[15]). If the universal Sense, recorded in the Book as a pre-originary inscription, has been scattered in a myriad of everyday texts, in order to gain access to the chamber of Sense, the artist must devote himself to compiling "These earthly approximations . . . like the fragments of a broken mirror" ("The Book"; *CF,* 130). In the undulations of reality-become-text, the Book unfolds while being read, its boundaries disintegrating in the ebbs and flows of interminable exegesis. Joseph's own text weaves itself into the pages of the Book and sprouts a multitude of surplus worlds. Interestingly enough, Schulz explains that the primeval, nonphenomenal text is already a myth—a process of fictioning and storytelling, namely, the movement on the surface of the mirror. Thus, the artist's attempts to make the text cohere and gravitate toward Sense presuppose a moment of mimetic fragmentation, as if the ineffable "original" always imitated its own degraded copy. In his essay on Edmond Jabès, Derrida asks an aposthatic question: "[What if] there is the other of every manuscript and the book is radically illegible?"[16] The supplement of the Book, its transgressive margin which initiates the mimetic split, remarks the text with such radical illegibility. For the exegete, it signifies the impossibility to complete the cycle of reading, because another crevice or labyrinthine chapter always opens up. Yet, this moment of debordering continues to reinscribe the text in a movement of incessant recommencement of interpretation.

Gombrowicz, embattled in the Polish national form, is bound to overlook the Jewish imperative of the Book, which deems a creative effort of bringing into form to be tantamount with an act of exegesis, an endless textual pilgrimage toward the horizon of the Authentic. Gombrowicz writes in *The Diary:*

> One could say that even the average Jew is sentenced to greatness, only because he is a Jew. And not just to greatness. He is sentenced to a suicidal and desperate battle with his own form because he does not like himself . . . I will even go further and say that a Jew who insists too much on being treated as a "human being," that is, as if he were no different from others, seems to me to be a Jew not sufficiently aware of his Jewishness. (*D* I, 81).

In Gombrowicz's imperfect understanding, the Jew's perennial lack of national form, unlike his own condition of exile from Fatherland, condemns him to a pathetic combat with his own form.

Gombrowicz, a self-appointed philosopher of form, repeats that man is both determined by a plurality of forms and an inveterate creator of forms in the interhuman realm: "Each person deforms other persons, while being at the same time deformed by them" (*M,* 15) [I każdy zniekształca innych, będąc zarazem przez nich zniekształcony[17]]. *Ferdydurke,* conceived as a parody of the philosophical tale, proceeds through a succession of encounters between irreconcilable forms such as maturity/immaturity or synthesis/ analysis and writes itself as combustive frictions between them. Epitomized in the duel of faces between lofty idealist Siphon, the lover of Polish romantics, and Mientus, who extols the hoarse and unhewn form of the stable boy, the receding mimetic orders in *Ferdydurke* yield an appearance of a cosmic funhouse. Surrounded by distorting mirrors, the narrator is trapped in the play of reflections, as if absorbed in the specular surfaces. Having been selected to serve as the umpire in the duel, the narrator comments, "My face, the mirror of their faces, was distorted too . . . Sadly my toe accompanied their fingers, and I grimaced and grimaced, well knowing that I was losing myself in my grimaces" (*F*, 67) [Twarz moja, jakby zwierciadło ich twarzy, również pokraczniała . . . Palec mój u nogi tragicznie wtórował ich palcom, a ja grymasiłem i wiedziałem, że zatracam się w tym grymasie[18]. The entire duel of grimaces, in its turn, resonates *ad absurdum* later in the novel, in the combat between Dr. Philifor, the inspired synthesist, and the vulgar analyst Anti-Philifor. Gombrowicz muses, tongue-in-cheek, on the mimetic relation between the mock-heroic battle between the sacrosanct principles of synthesis and analysis and the writing's own paradox of simultaneous composition and disassemblage.[19] Since the formal imperative operates through the principle of mirroring, the text is bound to always duplicate its own form. Hence, in *Ferdydurke,* the two chapters on "Philifor Honeycombed with Childishness" inevitably produce their own spitting image later in the book:

> Another preface . . . I must provide a preface, a preface is required of me, without a preface I cannot possibly go on. It is my duty to provide a preface, for the law of symmetry here demands the insertion of *Philimor Honeycombed with Childishness* as balance and counterweight to *Philifor Honeycombed with Childishness and* similarly the introduction to *Philifor Honeycombed with Childishness* must be balanced by an introduction to *Philimor Honeycombed with Childishness.* Whether I like it or not, I cannot, no, I simply cannot, evade the iron laws of symmetry and analogy. (*F*, 187)

> [I znowu przedmowa . . . i zniewolony jestem do przedmowy, nie mogę bez przedmowy i muszę przedmowę, gdyż prawo symetrii wymaga, aby *Filidorowi dzieckiem podszytemu* odpowiadał *dzieckiem podszyty Filibert,* przedmowie zaś do *Filidora* przedmowa do *Filiberta dzieckiem podszytego.* Choćbym chciał, nie mogę, nie mogę i nie mogę uchylić się żelaznym prawom symetrii oraz analogii.[20]]

The chapter on Philimor climaxes in a rigamarole apocalypse, in which gentlemen of highest social standing ride their wives' backs as a result of an imitative contagion that ripples through the crowd gathered at a tennis tournament in Paris. This outburst of nonsense allows the reader to diagnose the writing's mimetic disorder; yet, in the reality structured according to the ubiquitous formal imperative, there is no remedy to cure the system or to prevent the spreading of the mimetic epidemic.

In Schulz's stories, a mimetic ambiguity stems, first of all, from the doubling of creative agents. While Joseph is the artist of fantastic shapes that discharge mystical energy, his father foils him as the creator of illicit half-forms that threaten to dissolve the very texture of reality. A peculiar psychomachia between the two unfolds against the background of equivocal interplay between the "depths" which shelter the esoteric secrets of the Book and the sham surfaces that constantly threaten to turn the depths inside out. This becomes apparent in the story "The Street of Crocodiles," during Joseph's expedition to the commercial district of illicit pleasures and easy money. There, the city, devoid of essences, blatantly pretends to be itself and exists only as self-parody: a simulacrum town, it bears no relation to reality of which it fraudulently pretends to be a copy. Joseph comments, "That whole manipulation seemed suddenly unreal, a sham comedy, a screen ironically placed to hide the true meaning of things" (*CF,* 66) [Cała ta manipulacja wydaje się być czymś nieistotnym, pozorem, komedią, ironicznie zarzuconą zasłoną na prawdziwy sens sprawy] (*Pz,* 125). The uncanny quality of imitativeness reverberates in another venture, described in the story "Cinnamon Shops," which in itself imitates and distorts the previous tale. The narrator steps into the starry night, which turns out to be an imitation of the artificial sky painted on the curtain of the theater he has just visited. Joseph fails to halt the spectacle of shifting surfaces and to restore the world to its three-dimensionality. In his attempts to descend into the depths of Sense, he is constantly distracted into the cul-de-sacs of the poor-quality copy that forces out good and solid reality.

While Gombrowicz the lampoonist tampers with the figurable by inflating Form to the limits of endurance, lyrical Schulz seems to caress it and press gently at its nodal points. The narrator's drowsy town is rampaged by exuberant, fantastic vegetation, "malformed wrinkled leaves of astonishing lightness . . . that spread until the space under the windows filled with a tissue thin tangle of green pleonasms" ("The Dead Season"; *CF,* 232) [Lekkie formacje listne, wielokrotne, ząbkowane i pomarszczone . . . rosła pod oknem pustą bibulastą paplaniną zielonych pleonazmów] ("Martwy Sezon"; *Pz,* 300]. These wild, illicit forms grow in the regions overlooked by human vigilance. The tangled thickets exploding in the recesses of the sleepy town and the wanton tracks of demented time into which the narrator strays appear as if exuded by the very limit which demarcates the textual center—the alleged mythical core characterized by oneness, indivisibility, and perfect coincidence with itself. They constantly metamorphose across the frame, deriding the finished form. The stories, which abound in images of organic excess and proliferation, seem to overgrow their textual boundaries, incapable of maintaining a respectable, steady contour. The reader is thus invited to promenade along the constantly dissolving edges, on the border between the formed and the formless, between clearly demarcated figures or areas and blurry, chaotic blobs.

This spurious overabundance of nature and the dissolution of conventional shapes correspond to the creationist endeavors of the narrator's father. A respectable owner of a textile store, Father also manipulates in "the regions of great heresy," in order to engender illegitimate half-forms of uncontrollable, metamorphosing matter. To the being sprung from legitimate creation, the heresiarch opposes his masterpiece of protean forms, custom tailored to last for only an instant, after which they are left behind—ossified and useless. Unlike the fruits of the legitimate creator's labor, these "secondary creatures" are purely gratuitous, spawned outside the restricted economy of purposeful beings. The heresiarch defies all art that purports to give things a finished shape because the aesthetic exigency of discrete forms is nothing but "arbitrary tyranny imposed on a helpless block" ("Treatise"; *CF,* 34) [tyrańską samowolę, z jaką rzuca się na bezbronną kłodę] ("Traktat"; *Pz,* 86).

Schulz comments, in the previously mentioned review of *Ferdydurke,* that while man, in his ambition, "reached for the ideal, in reality he was eternally unfinished, botched, patched up and fragmented" (*LD,* 160) [Gdy w aspiracjach swych dociągał miary ideału, sam jest w rzeczywistości wiecznie niegotowy, spartaczony, łatany i niedociągnięty] (*Pz,* 485). Although Schulz bemoans that man's spiritual depths have been replaced by surfaces of mismatched patches, his stories radiate delight in the eternally unfinished and "botched." Only what is carelessly fragmented can uphold the need to mold and stitch together, thus preventing the complacency that comes with the finished form. Schulz now falls in step with Father, who revolts against finishedness and perfection in order to proclaim that "we wish to be creators in our own, lower sphere; we want to have the privilege of creation, we want creative delights" (*CF,* 32) [Chcemy być twórcami we własnej, niższej sferze, pragniemy dla siebie twórczości, pragniemy rozkoszy twórczej] (*Pz,* 82). This manifesto conveys the creationist's supreme wish to spawn beings that, by virtue of their singularity, will always fall outside classifications.

Gombrowicz and Schulz, within the confines of their rather dissimilar agendas, rise to the challenge posed by Form. For both writers, reality is a matter of an inverse relation to Form. It constitutes itself as a movement of negativity in which Form is eroded and appears as secondary with respect to its own inconstitution. Form is created only insofar as its border continuously dissolves and foregrounds its own unlimitation. Hence, the "real" is what escapes the policing powers of form, although at the same time it bulges into a formless or de-formed monstrosity. Gombrowicz inflates Form from within until it quivers and allows for a transient moment of "flight from Form," while Schulz presses upon it from outside, inundating it with left-overs it has itself discarded or excreted. Thus, for both writers the detour from Form becomes the measure of both artistic and ontological authenticity. In this scenario, imagination reigns as the power of eroding the limit and slipping through recalcitrant forms; the prerogative to capture reality in the form of an image is abdicated. Gombrowicz, for whom the vicissitudes of form are inseparable from the nation's historical destiny, foregrounds a redemptive moment of "escape from Form" that momentarily halts the sleepy procession of moribund representations and interrupts the dance macabre tableau that parades itself as a heroic panorama of Polish history. Thus, from behind the contorted, sarcastic *gęba,* Gombrowicz shyly allows for a moment of affirmation which ensures that the history of the nation will continue. For Schulz, the transcendent moment, toward which the artist journeys through the incessant shedding of forms, guarantees the continuation of the exegetic endeavor. Thus, both writers' struggle to overcome Form and escape its mimetic determination yields a peculiar notion of the transcendent realm which lies between forms. It manifests itself in the writer's desire to expunge himself from the restricted economy of form.

Ferdydurke ends with the narrator running away from the face: "and run, run, and run through the whole of humanity. For there is no shelter from face except in face . . . I fled, with my face in my hands" (*F,* 272) [Gdyż nie ma ucieczki przed gębą jak tylko w inną gębę. Ścigajcie mnie, jeśli chcecie. Uciekam z gębą w rękach[21]. The wish to catapult oneself into the pure infinite is impossible; moreover, says Gombrowicz, it is quite amusing how this desire itself fosters the growth of new constellations of Form. At the slippery border of this paradox, laughter bursts out. When, in the marathon "from face to face," the face is pressing suffocatingly close, it is bound to flip into nonsense and crack open. In the last lines of *Ferdydurke,* which are missing from the English translation, writer-the-clown is fingering his nose at the reader: "Koniec i bomba, a kto to czytał ten trąba."[22] Gombrowicz explains in the *Diary:* "Isn't it true that one cannot undermine form by opposing it with another form, but only by laxity in one's attitude towards it? No, it is not a coincidence that precisely at the moment when we most need a hero, up pops the clown" (*D* I, 36). The writer, wearing a jester's hat, assumes responsibility with respect to all those who remain in the yoke of Form: "Bewitched as I was by Form, I was prepared to become its buffoon for ever" (*KT,* 45).

Gombrowicz acknowledges the extent to which he himself has been begotten by the Polish form, and it is only through parody that he can attempt to break free. In Gombrowicz's spectacle where "Art mimicked and mocked art" (*KT,* 42), everything comes out as parody: the writer intends to write a serious work, attuned to the solemnity of the historic moment, "But then [he] wrote something completely opposed to what [he] should have written. Instead of something serious,—laughter, idiocies, somersaults, fun!" (*KT,* 104). What accounts for this clownish twist of the writer's fortune, however, is his prior parodic gesture with respect to himself. In *Trans-Atlantyk,* the last scene of the novel, the national form, grotesquely tumescent, comes apart at the seams, and laughter gushes out:

> Laughter then, Laughter! The Minister his belly clutched, with laughter bammed! And Boom, Bam, Pyckal the Baron by the belly clutched . . . oh Guffaw, Guffaw so much that perchance they Boom. And so from Laughter into Laughter, they with Laughter Boom, with laughter bam, boom, boom bam boom! (*T,* 122).

> [Śmiech tedy, Śmiech! Za brzuch się złapał Minister, śmiechem bachnął! I Buch, Bach, Pyckal za brzuch Barona złapał . . . oj,

> Ryczą, ryczą, aż chyba Buchają. I dopieroż od Śmiechu do Śmiechu, Śmiechem Buch, Śmiechem bach, buch, buch Buchają![23]

This laughter tends to perpetuate itself, growing into infinity. However, just like form, it spreads by mimetic contagion: "Then again, now this, now that, first one, whereupon another, and presently three, four, presently five Bam, Boom with laughter Boom" (*T,* 122). The conspiracy to kill the father and proclaim the rule of the Son, Filistria (*Synczyzna*), is grounded in mimicry: the son will commit patricide per chance, by imitation. Thus, the two mimetic moments cut through each other. As Barbara Zielińska has noted in her essay "Śmiech Gombrowicza," (Gombrowicz's laughter), laughter has an epistemological dimension for Gombrowicz because it mocks and incapacitates Form, revealing its inherent vacuity, falsehood, and surrogate character.[24] However, in the scene of ubiquitous merrymaking, which folds even the reader in its contortions, it is not clear whether Gombrowicz the narrator is laughing with the rest of the cast, as much as "Gombrowicz" the author is laughing at them. Does Gombrowicz, or perhaps "Gombrowicz," fold his mask and run again? Thus, we should perhaps investigate a kind of double laughter—neither redemptive nor absurdist but the laughter that laughs at itself. It is in this twofold sense that Gombrowicz's comment in the introduction to *Trans-Atlantyk* should be examined: "Yes, but I did not want to give myself to anything with my whole, not to any impending shape—I wanted to be something more, something richer than form. This is where laughter comes from in *Trans-Atlantyk*" [Tak . . . ale ja już niczemu nie chciałem się oddawać całą istotą moją, żadnemu kształtowi nadchodzącemu—ja chciałem być czymś wyższym i bogatszym of kształtu. Stąd bierze się śmiech w *Trans-Atlantyku.*[25]] Laughter erupts when Form is duplicated and made to look at itself. To laugh at the form one has to get to know it intimately, so closely as to become it. Jacques Derrida writes, in his famous essay on Georges Bataille, that discourse can be made to dislocate itself only "through close scrutiny and full knowledge of what one is laughing at";[26] only then can it fissure the system by "small comic recapitulation," as does Bataille's general economy of excess and transgression with respect to Hegelianism.

Although Schulz's stories do not resound with belly-clutching laughter, the artist/heresiarch's manipulations always maintain Form on the verge of "splitting its sides." There, every creation which parades in a serious costume carries within itself its comic double. Schulz elaborates the function of this laughter in the exposé on *The Cinnamon Shops:*[27]

> Reality takes on certain shapes merely for the sake of appearance, as a joke or a form of play . . . There is an ever-present atmosphere of the stage, of sets viewed from behind, where the actors make fun of the pathos of their parts after stripping off their costumes. The bare fact of separate individual existence holds an irony, a hoax, a clown's stuck out tongue. (*LD,* 113)

> [Rzeczywistość przybiera pewne kształty tylko dla pozoru, dla żartu, dla zabawy . . . Obecna jest tam nieustannie atmosfera kulis, tylnej strony sceny, gdzie aktorzy po zrzuceniu kostiumów naśmiewają się ze swoich ról. W samym fakcie istnienia poszczególnego zawarta jest ironia, nabieranie, język po błazeńsku wystawiony.[28]]

Individual beings, in the pathos of their well-defined forms, are always only a step away from falling into their comic doubles and sliding into parodies of themselves. This *commedia dell'arte* appearance of reality climaxes in the story "The Comet," in the vision of doomsday when the Earth is about to collide with a comet. By no means was it "a tragic finale as forecast long ago by the prophets, nor the last act of the Divine Comedy. No. It was to be a trick-cyclist's, a prestidigitator's end of the world, splendidly hocus-pocus and bogus experiments" (*CF,* 170) [Nie, nie był to eschatologiczny, od dawna przez proroków przewidziany tragiczny finał i akt ostatni komedii boskiej. Nie, był to raczej bicyklowo-cyrkowy, hopla-prestidigitatorski, wspaniale hokus-pokusowy i pouczająco-eksperymentalny koniec świata[29]]. The eschatological perspective dwindles into a clown's mask, and *theatrum mundi* is revealed to be a vaudeville stage.

Form comes into itself through the complicity of word and meaning, so that it may appear as if it were endowed with sense. Yet, silent laughter in the interstices of Form interrupts this alliance, unchains the word, and pries Form from its solid foundation. Form is laughable because it takes itself seriously, but the laughter which lacerates it is both more and less than the laughter that shakes the belly; the moment it appears phenomenally, it cannot help but to laugh *with*. The laughter of absolute comprehension exhausts the system and produces the moment of *non-savoir*, which interrupts the system at every moment of self-knowledge. It also marks the blind spot of Form where it always folds upon itself. In the moment of this preoriginary mimetic doubling, Form does not recognize its own reflected image—and in this is like Narcissus, the villain and the tragic hero of the play *Mimesis*. This "other" mimetic scene, to recall Lacoue-Labarthe's designation, precedes the constitution of Form through the series of self-identifying procedures. In that case, can the artist truly laugh at himself? Witold Gombrowicz, laughing at "Witold Gombrowicz" the trickster, does not always notice that he also takes himself seriously, and this, says Schulz, is funny. In the last instance, the artist must produce forms unceasingly, trace them in words, and mold them into images, circumscribing the moment of silent laughter where Form slides and tumbles, the rift where between one form and another, always "something is Amiss, and belike Amiss, oh Amiss" (*T*, 5) [Ale coś niedobrze i coś niedobrze chyba, oj, niedobrze[30]], as Witold chants after his arrival in Argentina.

Both Gombrowicz's and Schulz's writings obey an aesthetic imperative whereby the artistic process occurs as a movement that interrupts the mimetic chain and prevents the constitution of a representational paradigm. After all, is not a so-called literary paradigm but another manifestation of the ubiquitousness of form? Does it not always reduce the text to an object of critical scrutiny predicated on the limited and extortive geometry of the reader's vision? The event of writing, the movement of unlimitation which ruins representation, must elude form, and as such, remain non-totalizable. For Gombrowicz as well as for Schulz, writing happens as a gesture of transcendence in which the relation between writing and its eradicated referent does not result from a succession of preestablished concepts and their rendition in language, but always occurs anew as it is being effected. This brings us back to the initial quandary, why each writer has to disentangle himself from mimesis and remain unblemished by resemblance to a previous model. It now appears that if he can uphold his claim to absolute singularity, then, even if Form is inescapable, at some occluded level of the text, he can still maintain a panoptic position from which to master Form. Thus, the writer strives to assume a philosophical stance with respect to Form, that is, to occupy the locality unaffected by mimetic hubris.

Gombrowicz and Schulz cannot converse with each other, yet it is with respect to the other's challenge of form that each is able to gain momentary reassurance of the solid ground, where the mimetic *mise-en-abîme* of the cavalcade of forms is momentarily halted. Hence each writer insists on the absolute condition of his exile: Gombrowicz, *persona non grata* among his compatriots in Argentina; and Schulz, self-exiled to the republic of dreams, a wanderer in foreign lands which open up in the heart of his hometown. This isolation and unaffected singularity allow the artist to usurp the position of absolute exteriority with respect to Form and to counterbalance its insidious power that casts bodies into random configurations. When Schulz describes his "peculiar lot" in his letters, he explains that only profound loneliness is "the catalyst that makes the reality ferment, precipitates its surface layer of figures and colors" (*LD,* 114) [Samotność jest tym odczynnikiem doprowadzającym rzeczywistość do fermentacji, do strącenia osadu figur i kolorów[31]]. The condition of solitude allows the artist to bring forth the figures and, by the same token, to maintain control. Similarly, in a gesture of parodic baptism, Gombrowicz proclaims, "I am an outsider" (*KT,* 93), and he continuously emphasizes this necessary condition of seclusion: "I am alone, that is why I exist more" (*D,* I, 209). Little wonder that these pronouncememnts would give rise to the readings of Gombrowicz's *au rebours* affair with Poland in terms of the myth of a misunderstood genius.[32] In pursuit of uniqueness, Gombrowicz seeks to extricate from the mesh of Form an authentic piece of himself, which would not be a reflection of anything else—Poland or even his own tenacious face. In *A Kind of Testament,* he cries out, "Give me a knife, then! I must perform a still more radical operation! I must amputate myself from myself!" (*KT,* 58).

Yet, the artist always looks in the mirror: only in Schulz's afterlife sanatorium, from the story "Sanatorium under the Sign of the Hourglass," the mirrors are opaque and do not offer the solace of reflection. The artist holds up to himself the mirror of the text. The text holds him up as a mirror and projects itself upon him. Gombrowicz reads the excerpts from the *Diary* in a volume of *Kultura:* the other, refracted "Gombrowicz" does not wink back, yet he makes authoritative comments on the texts authored by Gombrowicz. For the thousandth time Schulz sends out "Bruno Schulz" to chat with his epistolary soulmates. To whom do they really respond? In the stories we read today, which "Schulz" peeks at us from behind

Joseph the artist and Jacob, the demiurgos of illicit creation? Each author moves through his texts accompanied by his uncanny *Doppelgänger.* Always already redoubled, the artist returns to himself disseminated in the shreds of the mirror. That is why both "Gombrowicz" and "Schulz" are caught up in a double function of the narrator/creator and commentator/interpreter. The artist bends protectively over the work of art he is creating, but the text never lets itself be assimilated in the commentary, despite the author's renewed efforts to provide an accurate explanation of his own texts.

The artist's desire for transcendence has been revealed as the moment of exteriority that incessantly traverses Form and bounces it on itself. It transpires in Gombrowicz's distorted grimace and in Schulz's misshapen half-creation, where Form slides into the gap that has always already taken place as I ("I"). The interruption slits open through the artist's own pre-originary redoubling that he cannot know but that precedes and precipitates all the ruses of representation. The artist expresses it as the wish to be authentic, to be the one who holds the mirror. Lacoue-Labarthe translates this paradoxical moment as the simultaneous persistance and desistance of the fictional/fictioning "subject" that, in its refusal to "go" altogether, as Heidegger would like to have it, allows for the impossible possibility of the text.

The escape beyond Form, the impossible desire to occupy the space where Form has not yet impressed itself, is never truly egressive, since the artist discovers that he is already treading in his own footsteps. The above investigation into Gombrowicz's and Schulz's manipulations of Form in their respective neighborhoods and their maneuvers towards each other allow us a glimpse into this essential instability of the mirror. It remains for the reader to ask in what way he or she can listen to the silent laughter coming from the text. How can I ("I") hear? In reply, a derisory guffaw from Gombrowicz. Schulz's suppressed chuckle.

Notes

1. Bruno Schulz, *Letters and Drawings of Bruno Schulz with Selected Prose,* ed. Jerzy Ficowski, trans. Walter Arendt (New York: Fromm, 1990), 117. Further references to this text will be marked parenthetically as *LD.*

2. Bruno Schulz, *Proza* (Kraków: Wydawnictwo Literackie, 1964), 693. All further references to this text will appear parenthetically as *Pz.*

3. *The Booke of Idolatry* (Xięga Bałwochwalcza) is perhaps Schulz's best known accomplishment as a graphic artist. The original *cliché-verre* etchings were printed by Schulz and compiled in portfolios. Most drawings feature the Idolator (usually a caricatural self-portrait) at the feet of the Woman Idol.

4. *Kultura* was a literary organ of Polish émigré literature, devoted to publishing texts that were banned in People's Poland, so-called literature of the other circulation [literatura drugiego obiegu].

5. The expression comes from a letter dated December 18, 1934, written to Rudolf Ottenbreit, a prominent pedagogue and professor of Polish language and literature, in which Schulz extends an invitation to epistolary friendship. In Bruno Schulz, *Z listów odnalezionych,* ed. Jerzy Ficowski (Warszawa: Wydawnictwo Chimera, 1993).

6. In *Wiadomości Literackie* 762 (1938), Breiter writes: "Schulz has already managed to create a literary school which, apart from several clumsy epigons, has yielded genuine talents, which begin, such as Gombrowicz, to search for new and independent means of expression" [Schulz zdążył już stworzyć szkołę literacką, która oprócz kilku nieudolnych epigonów wydała poważne talenty, zaczynające, jak np. Gombrowicz, szukać nowych i niezależnych dróg wyrazu] (*Pz,* 692). The names of Schulz and Gombrowicz usually appear together in the textbooks of Polish literary history, and the view of their literary kinship has been championed by critics such as Artur Sandauer, "Schulz i Gombrowicz czyli literatura głębi: próba krytycznej psychoanalizy," *Osnowa* (1978), 74–88; H. Vogler, "Dwa światy romantyczne," first published in *Skamander* 99/101 (1938); Andrzej Falkiewicz, *Polski Kosmos:* 10 esejów przy Gombrowiczu (Wrocław: Agencja Wydawniczo-Reklamowa, 1966); and others.

7. In a letter to the editor of *Wiadomości Literackie* 26 (1938); quoted in Schulz, *Proza,* 692.

8. In one of the letters, Schulz comments, "I wouldn't be able to create in the atmosphere of such intense terror" [Nie mógłbym tworzyć w klimacie tak ostrej grozy]. Quoted in Jerzy Ficowski, *Regiony wielkiej herezji,* 84 (Kraków: Wydawnictwo Literackie, 1967).

9. A seeming exception to this rule appears in the preface to *Ślub,* where Gombrowicz mentiones that his play aspires to the greatness of Shakespeare's or Goethe's works. However, this half-ironic proposition refers to the desired magnitude of the work rather than any literary resemblance.

10. Philippe Lacoue-Labarthe, *Typography: Mimesis, Philosophy, Politics* (Cambridge: Harvard UP, 1989), 43–138.

11. See Artur Sandauer's "Gombrowicz and Politics," trans. Edward Rothert, *Polish Perspectives* 29 (1986): 33–39. Sandauer attributes this shift to Gombrowicz's growing impatience and disillusionment with the fortune of his novels in the periods of alternate thaws and assaults on the freedom of expression in People's Poland. To a high degree, the waxing and waning of Gombrowicz's texts in the Polish bookstores at that time seemed to be a litmus test of the current political climate.

12. Sandauer, "Gombrowicz and Politics," 33.

13. Jacques Derrida, "Edmond Jabès and the Question of the Book," *Writing and Difference,* trans. Alan Bass (Chicago: U of Chicago P, 1978), 66.

14. Bruno Schulz, *Republika marzeń,* ed. Jerzy Ficowski (Warszawa: Wydawnictwo Chimera, 1993), 43.

15. Bruno Schulz, *The Complete Fiction of Bruno Schulz,* trans. Celina Wieniewska (New York: Walker, 1989), 66. Further references to this text will appear parenthetically as *CF.*

16. Derrida, "Edmond Jabès," 77.

17. The Polish text is from Gombrowicz, *Ślub. Dzieła zebrane,* vol. I (Paryż: Instytut Literacki, 1971), 63.

18. The Polish quotation is from Gombrowicz, *Ferdydurke. Dzieła,* ed. Jan Błoński, vol. II (Kraków: Wydawnictwo Literackie, 1987), 64.

19. For detailed discussion, see Jakób Liszka's "The Face: I and Other in Gombrowicz's *Ferdydurke,*" *Philosophy and Literature* 5 (1981): 62–72. Liszka focuses on the mimetic exchange between the text and its reader, foisted by Gombrowicz's mimetic strategies.

20. Gombrowicz, *Ferdydurke. Dzieła,* 178.

21. Gombrowicz, *Ferdydurke. Dzieła,* 254.

22. In the French translation of *Ferdydurke,* the phrase is rendered as "et voilà tra la la, zut à celui qui lira."

23. Witold Gombrowicz, *Trans-Atlantyk. Dzieła,* ed. Jan Błoński, vol. III (Kraków: Wydawnictwo Literackie, 1988), 120.

24. See Barbara Zielińska, "Śmiech Gombrowicza," *Ruch Literacki* 4/5 (1987): 295–308.

25. Gombrowicz, "Przedmowa do *Trans-Atlantyku*" [1957], *Trans-Atlantyk. Dzieła,* 7 (trans. mine).

26. Jacques Derrida, "From Restricted to General Economy: A Hegelianism without Reserve," *Writing and Difference* (Chicago: U of Chicago P, 1978), 253.

27. In American translation, the volume appeared as *The Street of Crocodiles.*

28. Schulz, *Republika marzeń,* 44.

29. Schulz, *Republika marzeń,* 27.

30. Gombrowicz, *Trans-Atlantyk, Dzieła*, 11.

31. Schulz, *Republika marzeń,* 45.

32. See, for example, Wojciech Karpiński's introduction to the *Diary,* in which Gombrowicz is introduced to the reader as a rejected artist paying the price of unbearable, devastating solitude for his "obstinate, consistent search" (*D* I, viii).

Hanjo Berressem

4

The Laws of Deviation:

Physical and Psychic Aberrations in the Novels of Witold Gombrowicz

> . . . exiguum clinamen principiorum nec regione loci certa nec tempore certo.
>
> Lucretius, *De Rerum Natura*

In his *Diary,* Witold Gombrowicz remarks of his works that all of them take up slight aberrations which they carry to their logical conclusions, regardless of the consequences:

> It is possible and perhaps even certain that my literature is even more extreme and crazy than I am. I don't believe that this indicates lack of control, instead it is a taking of certain charms which are magnified in the books to their ultimate formal conclusions. In me they remain that which they were, that is, only a slight *deviation of the imagination,* a kind of light "inclination." (*D* I, 119, emphasis added)

In what follows, I will take my cue from the fact that in this quote, *deviation* and *inclination* can be understood as both psychic and

---

This essay draws on the Lacanian interpretation of Gombrowicz I presented in my book *Lines of Desire: Reading Gombrowicz's Fiction with Lacan* (Evanston: Northwestern UP, 1997).

physical movements. The same goes for the terms *attraction* and *repulsion,* two other terms that are seminal in Gombrowicz's work. I believe that these convergences are symptomatic for Gombrowicz's poetics and that one can develop from them a general operational principle at work in his writing. This principle invariably brings order and chaos on a collision course, and, by doing so, it "honeycombs" extremes, or, to use a Kantian term that, as many critics have noted, is crucial to Gombrowicz's poetics, antinomies.[1]

The convergences of psychic and physical movements are also important in the context of the eternal fight between order and chaos. In fact, they allow for a mapping of literary and scientific parameters, because precisely these four terms are key notions in two related sciences: René Thom's catastrophe theory, which deals with the modes of change from one seemingly stable system into another one; and chaos theory, which deals with the laws that govern the physical behavior of dynamic, self-regulatory systems, systems that show a "sensitive dependence on initial conditions." In fact images and concepts from these sciences can illustrate and explain the catastrophic and chaotic dynamics that characterize Gombrowicz's works.[2]

A deviation, for instance, can be understood as a physical, a psychic or even as a narrative deflection, aberration, or abduction from a straight path. In physics as well as in philosophy, the technical term for such a small deviation or inclination is *clinamen,* a term introduced by Lucretius in *De Rerum Natura.* In *La naissance de la physique dans le texte de Lucrèce. Fleuves et turbulences,* in which Michel Serres reads Lucretius's book as a first tract on chaos theory, he describes the *clinamen* as "the smallest conceivable condition for the first formation of a turbulence [*turbulence*]" that befalls the atoms in their fall through an "ideal laminar [that is, ordered and smooth] cataract"[3] in which they "do not touch each other" (*N,* 12). This "infinitesimal turbulence" (*N,* 104) is a "differential" (11); a first "detour" that causes an "asymmetry" (43). It is "the minimal angle for the formation of a vortex [*tourbillon*], which appears aleatorily in a laminar flow (14).

This first aberration of an atom from a straight, vertical path through space marks the beginning of atomic interaction and thus the birth of the world.[4] On a macroscopic scale, this microscopically small moment of the beginning of atomic turbulence can be visualized by the suspension of an object into a laminar flow of a fluid or a gas. The deviation(s) caused by this object will (under specific conditions, which have to do mainly with the current's speed and thus, in the case of water, with the inclination of the slope), cause chaotic whirls, vortices, and eddies behind the object.[5] Similar dynamics govern the confluence of two (or more) currents. In a diagram, or flow-chart, these movements can be described as a line that bifurcates and as two (or more) lines that merge, respectively.[6]

Lodged between the Brownian "melée" (*N,* 41) of a turbulent "disorder" and the laminar order lies a milieu that consists of metastable vortexes, maelstroms, and spirals that follow the laws of a "deterministic chaos." This milieu results from the *clinamen,* which, at some point in the cataract, creates "a small angle, and, following from that, a spiral" (*N,* 14). In the "chaotic order" or "ordered chaos" of the open systems in this milieu, "one single movement determines *quo motu* simultaneously the formation and the resolution" (*N,* 117). As Serres states, "the vortex, instable and stable, flowing and equilibrious, is simultaneously order and disorder" (*N,* 40). As such, the *clinamen* and the vortex "belong to both destruction as well as to construction. The dissemination is sowing. The corruption is generation. And *vice versa*" (*N,* 123).[7] In Lucretius's text, in fact, as in Gombrowicz's works, the movement is that of a spiral: "the overall form of Lucretius's poem is a vortex. It closes in on itself without closing in on itself [*il se boucle sans se boucle*]. It dies and is reborn, but somewhere else, in another time" (*N,* 172).[8]

In *A Thousand Plateaus,* Deleuze and Guattari use Lucretius's theory to describe the catastrophic and chaotic ways in which what they call "smooth space"—a heterogeneous "field without conduits or channels . . . wedded to a very particular type of multiplicity: nonmetric, acentered, rhizomatic multiplicities,"[9]

> escapes the limits of its striation. At one pole, it escapes them by *declination,* in other words, by the smallest deviation, by the infinitely small deviation between a gravitational vertical. . . . At the other pole, it escapes them by the *spiral or vortex.* . . . From the smallest deviation to the vortex there is a valid and necessary relation of consequence: what stretches between them is precisely a smooth space whose element is declination and which is peopled by a spiral. Smooth space is constituted

> by the minimum angle, which deviates from the vertical, and by the vortex, which overspills striation. (*TP,* 489)

The "link between the *clinamen* as a generative differential element, and the formation of vortices and turbulences insofar as they occupy an engendered smooth space" (*TP,* 489) is responsible for the emergence of "a physics of packs, turbulences, 'catastrophes' " [*TP* 490].[10]

Ferdydurke

Symptomatically, the birth of the first of Gombrowicz's literary worlds already evokes Lucretius's image of the birth of the world caused by a first *clinamen*—in the same manner in which their deaths evoke the image of a turbulent melée or, in the case of his last novel, *Cosmos,* a vortex—because *Ferdydurke* opens up with a moment of deviation. Gombrowicz takes this image of deviation from Dante's *Divine Comedy,* the most important literary inter-text in the novel. In a passage that takes up Dante's lines

> In the middle of the journey of our life
> I came to my senses in a dark forest,
> *for I had lost the straight path*[11]
> (*Inf.* 1:1–3; emphasis added)

Johnnie states that "[h]alf-way along the path of my life, I found myself in a dark forest" (*F,* 14). This forest, which is already a psychic rather than a physical one, is dark because it is devoid of the metaphysical force of the sun, which, in the *Divine Comedy,* assures that the wanderer does not deviate (although in *Ferdydurke* it is a sun that will at the end of the novel have turned into a gigantic behind). As Dante states explicitly,

> I looked up, and saw its shoulders
> clothed already with the rays of *the planet*
> *which leads men straight on every path.*
> [*Inf.* 1:16–18; emphasis added)

In *Ferdydurke,* another such deviation or deflection is of central importance. It is related to Gombrowicz's fictional deconstruction of the Kantian antinomies, which are the arguably most important touchstone of Gombrowicz's poetics. As Gombrowicz himself has stated explicitly, "after the period in which art, philosophy, and politics looked for the integral, uniform, concrete, and literal man, the need for an elusive man who is a play of contradictions, *a fountain of gushing antinomies* and a system of infinite compensation, is growing" (*D* I, 30; emphasis added). Kant is so important for Gombrowicz because it is precisely as a deviation from the Kantian system that his own poetics unfolds. For Gombrowicz, in fact, the Kantian moment designates the moment just before a deviation, because "[b]eginning with the *Critique of Pure Reason* . . . [reason] began to delineate terrain inaccessible to thinking and to discover that life ridicules reason" (*D* I, 185).

Symptomatically, Gombrowicz invades Kant's system by deconstructing the internal architectonics of the *Critique of Pure Reason,* which, in the chapter "The Architectonic of Pure Reason," Kant himself defines as "the art of constructing a system."[12] The *Critique of Pure Reason* is a fitting target for Gombrowicz, because, like the *Divine Comedy,* it is based on the ideal of a classical architecture.

The chapter "Antinomies," in which Kant puts up four fundamental theses (dogmatism) and their corresponding antitheses (empiricism), is a seminal one in the *Critique of Pure Reason,* because in it Kant in turn creates a touchstone for his *own* philosophical system. The irredeemably oppositional character of these theses and antitheses is taken up by the fact that Kant presents them in two parallel textual columns. The two possibilities are that:

1

Thesis

The world has, as to time and space, a beginning (limit).

Antithesis

The world is, as to time and space, infinite.

2

Thesis

Everything in the world is constituted out of the simple.

Antithesis

There is nothing simple, but everything is composite.

3

Thesis

There are in the world causes through freedom.

Antithesis

There is no freedom, but all is nature.

4

Thesis

In the series of world-causes there is some necessary being.

Antithesis

There is nothing necessary in the world, but in this series all is contingent.[13]

If this state of things is visualized in terms of a cusp-catastrophe, as it is defined in catastrophe theory, the two possibilities present two equally strong attractive forces, with the subject—somewhat like a ball—balancing on what is called the basin boundary, separatrix, or cusp (which is why this kind of catastrophe is called a cusp-catastrophe) between the two craters (fig. 4.1). Kant realizes that according to his own system, which posits that the human mind, rather than a transcendental agency, is the highest arbiter of judgement, there can be no reason to favor one possibility over the other. Accordingly, *Kant's decision to favor the dogmatic theses is derived not from a transcendental dogma or truth but from the very architectonic character of the mind:*

> Human reason is by nature architectonic. That is to say, it regards all cognitions as parts of a possible system, and hence accepts only such principles as at least do not incapacitate a cognition to which we may have attained from being placed along with others in a general system. But the propositions of the antithesis are of a character which renders the completion of an edifice of cognitions impossible . . . As, therefore, the antithesis will not concede the existence of a first beginning which might be available as a foundation, a complete edifice of cognition, in the presence of such hypotheses, is utterly impossible. Thus the architectonic interest of reason, which requires a unity—not empirical, but *a priori* and rational, forms a natural recommendation for the assertions of the thesis in our antinomy. (*CP,* 287–88)

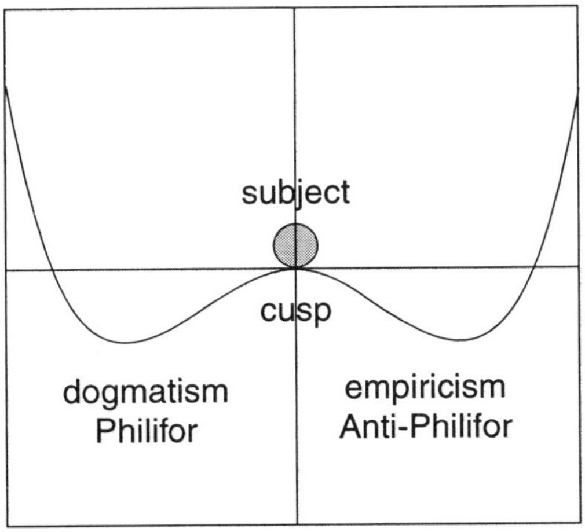

Figure 4.1 Diagram of René Thom's cusp catastrophe applied to the Kantian dynamics. The attractive forces are equally strong.

What, however, if one were to follow, as Gombrowicz does, a deconstructive architecture, whose aim is precisely to not create an ideal, complete edifice? What if one were to stake the logic of irrationality against any inherently rational and reasonable system, because, as he states in the *Diary,* we "can no longer digest the *reasoned God* of Aristotle, Aquinas, Descartes, or Kant" (*D* I, 173, emphasis added). What if, like Nietzsche, one were to proceed from the position that God is a "pure fiction" (*D* I, 173)?

Read against this Kantian background, the chapter "Philifor Honeycombed with Childishness" deconstructs the Kantian antinomies in an almost classical manner.[14] In fact, it can be read as a direct allegory of the overturning and displacement of the Kantian dialectics, whose architectonics it follows almost to the letter—however, only to use what it borrows, the balance of the composition and the beauty of its formal clarity and stringency, for a deconstructive project.

The setup of the scene, as that of the preceding one about the two teachers, one of whom comments that "[p]rices are going up" whereas the other thinks that "they were going down" (*F,* 41), and their respective lessons, is once more strikingly symmetrical. On the one side stands Philifor (the figure of synthesis and the dogma), tall, fat, and bearded. On the other stands Anti-Philifor (the figure of analysis and empiricism), small, skinny, and clean-shaven; here Mrs. Philifor (who, as a wife, is an image of culturally sanctioned love), there Fiora Gente (who, as a mistress, is an image of illicit love); here abstraction and the ideal, there corporeality and the sensual; here order, there chaos; here construction, there destruction. In the hierarchical system in which these opposites are suspended, Philifor stands for the thesis and Anti-Philifor for the antithesis that will forever contradict the thesis but that will always be overcome by it. As in the fight between Siphon and Mientus, the synthesis and the ideal are inherently more originary than the analysis. Accordingly, it is only as a physical reaction to Philifor's syntheses that Anti-Philifor emerges. As the narrator states, "[b]y virtue of Newton's principle of action and equal and opposite reaction, an intellectual phenomenon of such magnitude [Philifor] could not fail to provoke a counter-phenomenon in the bosom of nature" (*F,* 88).

The story recounts the collision of the two men, who before invariably missed each other because "each was prevented by pride from admitting that he was the pursued as well as the pursuer." When they do finally collide, their collision is "a disaster on the scale of the greatest railway accidents" (*F,* 89). As with Siphon and Mientus, in this collision, Philifor's syntheses (because they are *ideal*istic and psychic) are not only more originary but also inherently stronger than Anti-Philifor's analyses (which are concrete and physical). This is why Philifor can state before their final duel that "whatever happens, my spirit will survive and be victorious, for death is essentially synthetic. If he dies, his end will be a tribute paid to synthesis; if he kills me, he will do so synthetically. Hence in any event victory will be mine!" (*F,* 98).

Before it comes to this duel, however, the opponents engage in a "verbal duel," (*F,* 89) which follows and illustrates the workings of the Kantian antinomies to the letter. It starts with Anti-Philifor defining Gnocchi analytically as "a mixture of eggs, flour and water"; a statement that Philifor counters synthetically with "Gnocchi means the higher essence, the supreme spirit of gnocchi, *the thing-in-itself*" (*F,* 89; emphasis added). Although they are victorious, however, Philifor's syntheses are each time subverted and disrupted by Anti-Philifor's analyses. If Philifor has been victorious in the question about the gnocchi, Anti-Philifor attacks Philifor's wife, whom he disassembles analytically; that is, *piece by piece.* Although Anti-Philifor makes Philifor's answer to his wife's "disintegration" impossible—a *slap* in Anti-Philifor's face that would "restore my wife's honour and synthesize the scattered elements on a higher level" (91)—by tattooing two roses and doves onto his cheeks because "slapping roses and doves would be as idle as casually slapping a piece of painted paper" (92), Philifor is successful by turning the slap "analogically" (93) into one administered to Philifor by Anti-Philifor. As he tells his companions, "I cannot slap his face, but he can slap mine! It will come to the same thing. A face will have been slapped and synthesis achieved!" (93). In order to get Anti-Philifor to slap him, Philifor reverts to Anti-Philifor's strategy to deviously attack the opponent's companion; he synthesizes Fiora Gente. First, he attempts to "awaken her annihilated ego" (94) by reciting love stories, but each time, she demands money from him to listen to these stories, which have, on top of it, no effect on her whatsoever. Yet Philifor then uses this very money to synthesize her. When she is confronted with such a sublime amount of money that it can no longer be divided into parts—"[t]he sum had ceased to be a sum, had turned into something impossible to grasp in its entirety, something so tremendous, so inconceivable, that the mind boggled at it, as it does when it considers the dimensions of space"—and thus when it has become more than its parts and can no longer be analyzed, "[s]he rose to her feet, showing every symptom of synthesis—tears, sighs, smiles, thoughtfulness—and said: 'Gentlemen, myself. My higher self!' " (97).

The rigid symmetry of the ensuing duel, which is instigated by the fact that Anti-Philifor indeed slaps Philifor in answer to Fiora's synthesis, and in which "the initiative was Philifor's" (*F,* 99), is a direct figure of the Kantian antinomies. At this crucial point, however, Gombrowicz, as in Mientus's and Siphon's duel, overturns the classical hierarchy of the oppositions—synthesis *over* analysis—*through* a general displacement of the whole system. This gesture defines simultaneously the story of Philifor and Anti-Philifor *and* the structure of the novel, of which this story is a part. Already the relation of the chapter to the rest of the *corpus* of the book points toward this fact because Gombrowicz opens "Introduction to Philifor Honeycombed with Childishness" by explicitly calling it a "digression" (*F,* 70), which is once more, this time in narrative terms, a deflection from a straight path; a deviation from the smooth, laminar flow of the narrative. The digressive character of the chapter is thus both a *formal* device to break up the unity of the narration *and*—because it mirrors the digression that defines the duel described in it—a reflection on and of the theoretical foundation of the story's *content.*

Ironically, it is once more the very symmetry that brings about the dissymmetry. As the narrator says of the duel, "the situation was symmetrical; hence its strength, *but hence also its weakness*" (*F,* 98; emphasis added). The axis of this symmetry is figured by the bullet's path, which is "an imaginary *straight line* drawn between the two duellists." (emphasis added) But what, the narrator wonders, if "Anti-Philifor departed from it? Suppose he treacherously wandered from the *straight path,* basely evaded the iron laws of symmetry and analogy?" (emphasis added) And this is precisely what happens. Anti-Philifor "uttered a savage yell, *deflected the barrel of his pistol from the axis of the situation and fired*" (*F,* 99; emphasis added).

This deviation, or digression, of the bullet figures a displacement of the structural undecidability of the antinomies. In fact, Kant himself had stated that, because the antinomies cannot be solved transcendentally, without some kind of "practical" deflection, they would lead to an eternal oscillation or hesitation, with the subject forever balancing precariously on the brink of the two craters:

> But if any one could free himself entirely from all considerations of interest, and weigh without partiality the assertions of reason, attending only to their content, irrespective of the consequences which follow from them; such a person, on the supposition that he knew no other way out of the confusion than to settle the truth of one or the other of the conflicting doctrines, would live in *a state of continual hesitation.* (*CP,* 288; emphasis added)

At this crucial point, however, Kant introduces the notion of ideals, which form the hinge between the realms of practical reason and pure reason, because "human reason contains not only ideas, but ideals, which possess, not, like those of Plato, creative, but certainly *practical* power—as regulative principles" (*CP,* 335).

On two levels, this is an important moment, because both the Kantian moment in general and, more specifically, within Kant's work, the moment of the folding of practical reason onto pure reason, are moments of a catastrophic bifurcation. On a large scale, as

Gombrowicz has stated in "Guide de la philosophie en six heures un quart," after Kant, one line of philosophical thought develops straight into German idealism as it is represented by Fichte, Schelling, and Hegel. Another one, however, which also curiously originates in Kant, develops into the vitalistic philosophies of Schopenhauer, Nietzsche, Kierkegaard, and existentialism.[15]

Within Kant's work, the mode of the folding of practical reason onto pure reason recapitulates this bifurcation. It is the moment at which Kant succeeds in on the one hand negating a Platonic idealism by setting the limited faculty of the understanding of the subject over and above the realm of pure reason (a move for which Hegel made him pay dearly), and on the other hand in re-capturing, if only for purely architectonic reasons, the realms of reason and the ideal as practical, regulative forces for the subject.

At the moment at which practical reason folds onto pure reason, the notion of the ideal deflects the oscillating antinomies—which themselves remain oscillating in their eternal undecidability—into a specific direction; into the "morally attractive" realm, or crater, of a practical reason that "leans toward" the dogma and toward synthesis. Gombrowicz's analogous deflection, however—a deflection that is, symptomatically, brought about by Anti-Philifor—leads into the opposite realm, or crater; into the realm of an "irrationality" that "leans toward" the empirical side and towards analysis, and whose ideals are physical and psychic regression and childishness; a realm that Kant would consider pathological and thus "morally repulsive."[16] From Gombrowicz's position, in fact, what is morally attractive for Kant—the categorical imperative and the cultural law—is also attractive, but what is morally repulsive for Kant—the pathological desire of the individual that follows the laws of desire—is similarly attractive, so that for Gombrowicz, it takes only a minute *clinamen* to push the subject into the force field of either one realm or the other.

The main difference between Gombrowicz and Kant is that in Kant (through the forces of practical rather than pure reason) one force field is completely repressed, whereas in Gombrowicz—and the conjunction of the mouths of Katasia and Lena in *Cosmos* is a case in point—the subject is always attracted by both forces, the "morally attractive" and the "morally repulsive." It is inevitably split into one part that is attempting to follow the law (what Lacan calls the symbolic subject) and one part that desires to transgress the law (what

Lacan calls the imaginary ego). These dynamics are staged in the opening scene of *Ferdydurke,* in which the symbolic, mature subject simply cannot believe and accept its own regression and fights against it—"the man must slay the youth and take wing like the butterfly, leaving the dead body of the chrysalis on the ground" (*F,* 15)—because, in a development that is comparable to the gradual hardening of honey, the libidinous ego, the chrysalis, has to move out of "the cloud, the chaos, from murky waters, from maelstroms, whirls, waves . . . into clear, crystalline forms."[17] On the other hand, the aggressive, polymorphously perverse, and infantile ego constantly disrupts order and attempts to loosen up and to soften up the hardened subject. This fight stakes a fluid, chaotic, and immature realm against a crystalline, mature order. As the narrator states, "[w]hat a curse it is that there is no permanent, stable order of things in our life on this planet, that everything in it is in perpetual motion, continual flux" (*F,* 16). In *Ferdydurke,* this split between the imaginary and the symbolic is continually operative in and defines the narrator. It denotes the moment when immaturity is honeycombed with maturity, and maturity with immaturity, "for it had seemed to me that the adult, the thirty-year-old who I am today, was apeing and mocking the adolescent that I was then, while the adolescent was mocking the adult; and that each of my two selves was thus taking the rise out of the other" (*F,* 13).

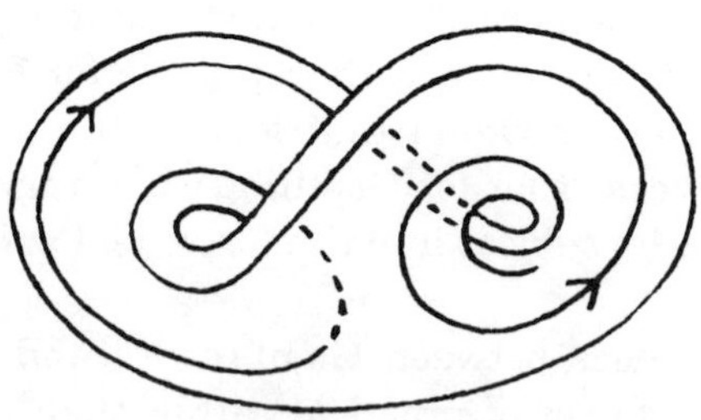

Figure 4.2 The Kantian antinomy about finitude and infinity is very elegantly solved in a strange attractor, because, although the expansion is infinite, it never leaves a finite envelope.

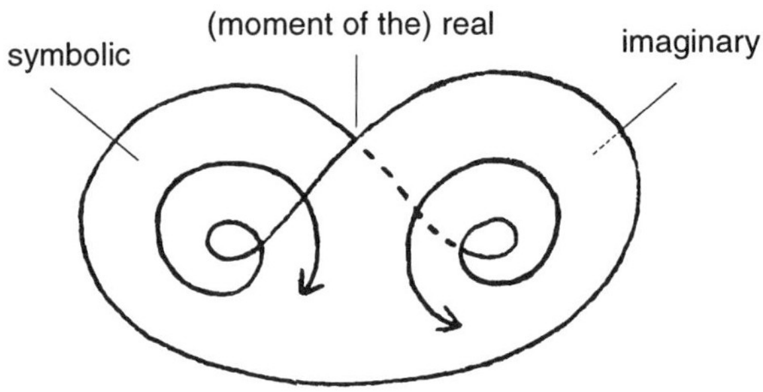

Figure 4.3 Diagram of a strange attractor applied to psychic parameters. The two attractive force-fields are those of the rational symbolic and the irrational imaginary respectively. The cusp-points represent the real.

In chaos theory, a dissipative system that is sensitive to two attractive force fields is defined by three forces: two attractive, centripetal ones and one centrifugal "line of flight." Its dynamics follow what has come to be called a "strange attractor," which visualizes a trajectory whose characteristics are that it shows a sensitive dependence on initial conditions, that it is unpredictable, and, finally, that it is fractal, because it is infinitely expanding yet constrained to a finite space and never repeats the same orbit (figs. 4.2 and 4.3). The interplay of the three forces brings about unpredictable and unaccountable catastrophic moments of bifurcation at which the system folds from one leaf, or crater, of the attractor onto the other one. These moments are crucial, because the forever expanding, centrifugal trajectory folds from the periphery of one leaf onto the center of the other one, from whence it once more expands, in an endless movement somewhat reminiscent of Escher's print *Ascending and Descending.* This seemingly paradoxical situation is made possible by the Möbial character of a "strange attractor," in which the moment of bifurcation denotes the twist in a one-sided topology—the movement through infinity that is marked by the "moment of the real" (fig. 4.4).

If the subject according to Gombrowicz is inscribed into a strangely attractive, Möbial topology, in Kant's case the topology of the system remains bilateral. The subject never leaves one side of the attractor: it follows either contractive or periodic dynamics. Attracted by the

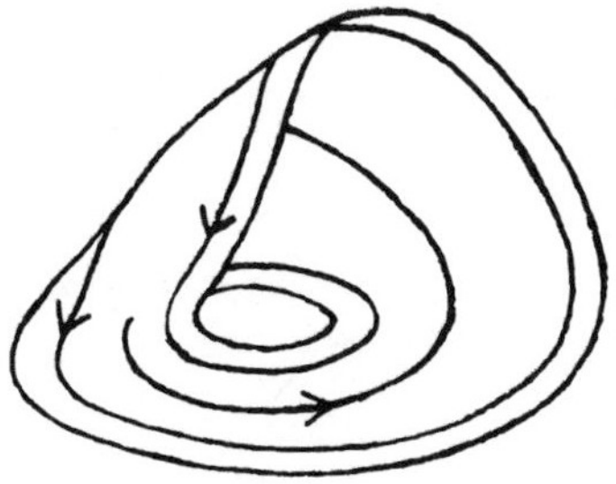

Figure 4.4 Diagram of the Möbial quality of the strange attractor.

force of reason, the subject topples over into the dogmatic, synthetical crater, where it remains indefinitely. In Kant's case, the regulative forces of rationality and symmetry draw the subject invariably into the dogmatic crater, in Gombrowicz's story, the forces of irrationality and asymmetry draw it first into the empirical, analytic one. At first, therefore, it seems that Gombrowicz's system is merely the opposite of the Kantian one. The end of the story, however, will show that ultimately (and this is what makes out its strangeness) the system will fold once more into its opposite. At one, itself undescribable, point, a *clinamen* will throw the system over onto "the other side."[18]

In the story, however, the fall is first into irrationality, because from the moment of deviation onward—the bullet strikes Mrs. Philifor's little finger—Philifor is forced to follow the sick, perverse, imaginary, and architectonically deconstructive symmetry of this asymmetry. As the narrator states, "[f]ascinated by his opponent's precision of aim, virtuosity and symmetry . . . he too diverged from the axis, fired . . . [and] hit Fiora Gente's little finger" (*F,* 99). Both go on shooting, and the result is the complete de-composition and subsequent death of both Mrs. Philifor and Fiora Gente, after which the fight becomes literally *meaning*less: "Strictly speaking, the analyst had won, but what difference did that make? None whatever. If the synthetist had won, it would have made no difference either" (100). At this, once more empty and a-temporal, moment the contestants experience a severe case of regression. They throw at or shoot at things, as children do to pass the time, and their greatest pleasure is an inherently chaotic one; "buying a red balloon and chasing it across country, waiting for the thrilling moment when it burst noisily as if struck by an invisible bullet" (101). Ultimately, both systems, as well as their representatives, disintegrate into a world of pure enjoyment—what Lacan calls *jouissance.* As Gombrowicz states in *A Kind of Testament,* "[i]n the end both the ideas of 'higher synthesis' and 'higher analysis' become mere pretexts for the *pure pleasure of action*" (*KT,* 70; emphasis added). At the end of the story, the trajectory has reached the catastrophic point of the real, after which the system will topple over once more into rationality (fig. 4.5).

At this very moment, however, the story ends. In this movement, it comes to recapitulate on a smaller scale a dynamics that defines Gombrowicz's work(s) in general. Such self-similarities are in fact one of the main characteristics of Gombrowicz's "fractal" poetics, according to which self-similar dynamics and structures can be traced from the micro- to the macro-level, from the most minute instances of shifts within the narrative voice to the overall dynamics of the plot.

In another sense as well, the internal structure of the narrative has at this point become analogous to the general structure of the

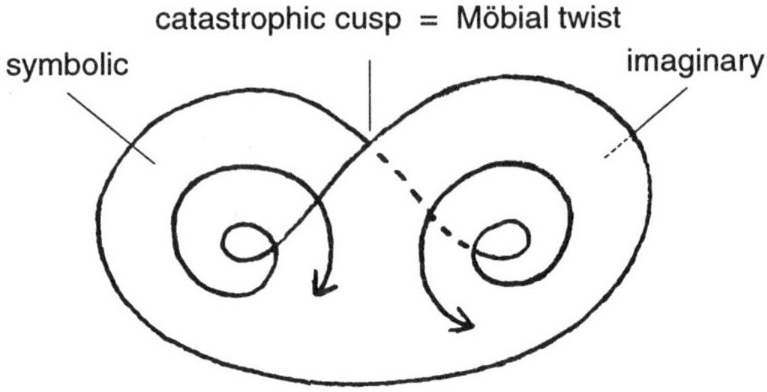

Figure 4.5 Diagram of the shift from one leaf of a strange attractor to the other, correlated with Thom's diagram of a cusp-catastrophe. The cusp denotes a shift from the inside to the outside—terms that are, of course, inapplicable in a unilateral topology.

book, because the figure of the deconstruction of the Kantian system is simultaneously the figure of the structure of *Ferdydurke.* Analogous to the concepts described by the narration, the book itself can never be a complete whole, serious and meaningful. Rather, it is a constant fight between form and chaos that defines the book, a fight that spans the whole range from the realms of art to those of life. In *A Thousand Plateaus,* Deleuze and Guattari evoke such a fragmented, "rhizomatic" book that is caught in the constant dynamics of assembly and disassembly—or, in their terminology, territorialization and deterritorialization—and which is, quite literally, a "machinic assemblage" that is caught in two movements simultaneously. It

> faces the strata, which doubtless make it a kind of organism, or signifying totality, or determination attributable to a subject; [yet] it also has a side facing a *body without organs,* which is continually dismantling the organism, causing asignifying particles or pure intensities to pass or circulate, and attributing to itself subjects that it leaves with nothing more than a name as the trace of an intensity. (*TP,* 4)

The important point is that Kant's rigorous abstractions and idealizations have to be supplemented by the chaos and chance of sensual life, because every consciousness is invariably a living consciousness. As Gombrowicz states in the *Diary,*

> To be consciousness, which walks around in pants and talks on the telephone. To be responsibility, which runs little shopping errands downtown. To bear the weight of significant being, to instill the world with meaning and then return the change from ten pesos. What do you want? I know how these contrasts come together in their theories. Slowly, gradually, from Descartes through German idealism, I grew accustomed to their structure, but laughter and shame toss me about at the sight of it with equal strength. . . . And even if you were to "convince" me a thousand times over, there would still always be some elementary, unbearable ridiculousness in this! . . . I could tolerate Cartesian or Kantian speculations because they were only the work of the mind. I, on the other hand, sensed that beyond consciousness is being. I felt elusive in being. (*D* I, 184)

The question is therefore once more that about the intermixing of psychic concepts and physical life. Against Kant's project to show a subject progressing from sensuality to pure reason and then back to practical reason, Gombrowicz is interested in how Kant himself has turned from immaturity to maturity and from an individual to an abstract idea(l), the mysterious "roads by which Kant-the-child and Kant-the-adolescent changed into Kant-the-philosopher" (*D* I, 185).[19]

Ultimately, Gombrowicz's and Kant's diverging ideas about the antinomies have to do with the position of the object as a stumbling block and as an obstacle within the flow of reality. As Jacques Lacan states in his essay "Kant with Sade," with Kant, the pure object—the thing-in-itself—is excluded because it remains in the "opacity of the transcendent."[20] It is only as a result of this fundamental opacity of the pure object—and this is what the chapter of Philifor and Anti-Philifor illustrated—that human(ized) objects can bifurcate into "pathological objects" and "objects of and according to the law" which is to say into irrational(ized) and rational(ized) objects.[21]

Within this antinomy, however, Kant's moral law favors the rational, mental side and eclipses the *objective,* irrational one. In fact, as Lacan states, Kant's moral law—the categorical imperative—represents desire "in the case where . . . the object . . . is *in default*" (*KS,* 67; emphasis added), because the categorical imperative negates the force of subjective desire and thus its relation to the "*object* of desire," over both of which it posits the cultural law. In fact, their respective exclusion of the object, Lacan argues, is the reason why, although they demarcate oppositional positions—Kant that of the neurotic and Sade that of the pervert—Kant and Sade mirror each other and why Kant can be tortured " 'with Sade,' that is to say with Sade filling the office, for our thought as in his sadism, of an instrument [of torture]" (63).

Lacan's ultimate criticism of the Kantian system concerns *not* the undecidability of the antinomies but the concept of a naively unproblematical confrontation of the subject with the categorical imperative, which means the unproblematical suppression of its own irrationality and desire. It is precisely this exclusion that allows for the subject to follow only one attractor (the law) and to behave as if the oppositional attractor could be sucessfully negated or, better, repressed. This, however, implies that also one half of the subject itself is negated; the bodily, *object*ive, empirical, and irrational one.

Only the Lacanian, phantasmatic "object *o*"—which functions as a hinge between a psychic and a physical object, and which shares characteristics of both realms—can ground "a new Critique of Reason" (KS, 63). In opposition to Kant's and Sade's exclusions, it is a *dynamic* term that inaugurates a reciprocal relation in which desire is "the desire of the Other" and in which the object's "vacillation complements that of the subject" (67). As Peter Widmer states, "the decisive thing is that the torn nature of man [*Zerrissenheit*] has to be neither acted out nor suppressed or repressed in the psychoanalytic process, but articulated and suffered."[22] Only in this mutual, reciprocal relation can the law and desire come to a meeting that "goes further than the *elusion* of their object, for the one as for the other" (67; emphasis added), a meeting in which the "Good" and the "Bad" become identical—that is, equally attractive—because "the *law* and repressed *desire* are one and the same thing" (68; emphasis added).

In chaos theory, the shift from one leaf of the strange attractor to the other one has been visualized as the "change of side" on a Möbius strip; and, in fact, the "object *o*," because it causes both the law and its transgression, instigates a Möbial topology. Both the morally attractive and the morally repulsive side are equally attractive, with the subject thrown from one and the other by an "*object*ive," real force—something that will become important in *Cosmos.* Human reality, according to Gombrowicz and Lacan, follows the dynamics of a strange attractor.

Symptomatically, the exclusions of the object in Kant and Sade are mirrored in the rigidity of their respective systems, a rigidity that has important poetological consequences, because it is precisely the scintillation and irridescence of the "object *o*" that introduces the realms of irony, humor, and, ultimately, literarity. Lacan's explicit statement that both Kant and Sade are specifically humorless and serious is the ultimate judgement on the poetic failure of their respective works. In fact, in his discussion of Kant, Lacan specifically mentions "the coldness of the man" (KS, 55) and the "lack of the least sense of the comic" (69). Ironically, Kant's seriousness is surpassed only by that of Sade, who is, as Lacan stresses, "someone who lacks it [the senes of the comic] . . . totally and absolutely" (69). Gombrowicz has also noted the coldness that results from the repression of the pathological object, stating that "[a]s for me, I can't believe that Socrates, Spinoza, or Kant were real people and completely serious ones at that. I claim that an excess of seriousness is conditioned by an excess of frivolity" (*D* I, 184). To do him honor, however, one must state that Kant himself realizes the unaesthetic and inhuman character of the ideal. In a passage that partly reconciles him with Gombrowicz, he grants, even while postulating the ideal, that

> to aim at realizing the ideal in an example in the world of experience—to describe, for instance, the character of the perfectly wise man in a romance, is impracticable. Nay more, there is something absurd in the attempt; and the result must be little edifying, as the natural limitations which are continually breaking in upon the perfection and completeness of the idea, destroy the illusion in the story, and throw an air of suspicion even on what is good in the idea, which hence appears fictitious and unreal. (*CP,* 335)

Unlike Kant's and Sade's works, then, Gombrowicz's work is defined by an interference pattern. It is neither the result of a neurotic nor that of a pervert. Because this work is produced by a neurotic who dreams up perversions which he then materializes in prose, in it Kant and Sade can be superimposed. In fact, by imagining Sadean heroes, *Gombrowicz becomes Kant dreaming of being Sade.*

The second part of *Ferdydurke* is also modeled on a deviation and an asymmetry, because Pimko's plan is to make Johnnie fall in love not only with the ideal of youth but also with *the ideal of youth as opposed to old age,* a juxtaposition in which Pimko himself willingly enters the position of victim. Accordingly, the amorous confrontation is not only that between Zutka and Johnnie, with Pimko functioning as a mere catalyst; it is that of the terrible combination of *Zutka with Pimko* and *Johnnie with Pimko*—the combination of the object of desire with the categorical imperative.

Already in Johnnie's first confrontation with Zutka, the antinomies of naturality and artificiality—which imply those of youth and adulthood—are chiastically conflated to form

the naturality of the artificial
X
and the artificiality of the natural.

Because Gombrowicz invariably temporalizes the Kantian antinomies—a temporalization that has once more to do with their immersion into the flow of life—the undecidable symmetry of these dynamics cannot be maintained indefinitely. In the confrontation of Johnnie and Zutka, therefore, "[w]ith each second that passed the artifice grew deeper, but so did the naturalness" (*F,* 123). As the situation is open to both sides, it can once more be thrown into either extreme by an ever so small *clinamen.* In this case, although Johnnie first feels that his consciousness has carried off the victory and that he has "conquered the girl *by the barbarous naturalness of my artifice,*" (emphasis added) it is suddenly thrown into utter artificiality when Zutka makes the terribly artificial, adult statement: "What can I do for you?" (123; emphasis added). Symptomatically, it seems as if her artificiality had somehow been grafted onto her *through* Johnnie's artificiality, because Zutka herself seems to be as astonished as Johnnie about what she has just said.

When it reaches the final, chaotic whirl or vortex, the situation, as with Philifor, has begun to blindly follow what the narrator calls a "law that might well be described as that of *deviation*" (*F,* 183; emphasis added). It is complete when Pimko, the former ideal, who has regressed to the state of a beaten animal—he "deliberately and of his own free will collapsed on to his back and raised his limbs in a gesture of complete subsidence" (*F,* 183)—enters the final melée by biting Mr. Youthful, "I think not far from the liver—and then he was carried off in *the maelstrom*" (184; emphasis added). At this moment, which is the chaotic whirl caused by the deflection of the logic of the antinomies, Johnnie experiences, for "a millionth of a second" (185), a complete "oblivion" (184) and a loss of self: "I was nothing at all, I was zero" (184). At this moment, he is precisely at the folding point between the two attractive forces at which, for the shortest of moments, the forces cancel each other out.

Before the story continues, therefore, the formal, unavoidable and "iron laws of symmetry and analogy" (*F,* 187) into which the story is suspended even while it deconstructs them, assert themselves. In fact, the

> law of symmetry . . . demands the insertion of *Philimor Honeycombed with Childishness* as balance and counterweight to *Philifor Honeycombed with Childishness;* and similarly the introduction to *Philifor Honeycombed with Childishness* must be balanced by an introduction to *Philimor Honeycombed with Childishness.* (187)

The "Introduction to Philimor Honeycombed with Childishness" deals with the impossibility of finding an origin for the genesis of the work. Although "the primary, the fundamental grief is purely and simply . . . the agony of bad outward form, defective appearance, the agony of phraseology, grimaces, faces" (*F,* 188), this statement is followed by a whole canon of reasons and tortures, all of which highlight other possible roots, so that at the end the discussion drowns, as with Philifor and Anti-Philifor, in childish echolalia: "with the most profound respect for the Word, and after the most scrupulous analysis, it must be admitted that we are no wiser than when we began, cluck! cluck! cluck! as the chicken said" (192). This impossibility of finding a cause and origin for the reality of life and art is subsequently illustrated in the story "Philimor Honeycombed with Childishness," with which Gombrowicz once more shows that the plot and the structure of the book originate in multiple instinctual and unforseeable, enigmatic reasons. The story relates a chain of events that originates in something completely mysterious and meaningless. In a scene that mirrors the deviation of the bullet in the chapter on Philifor, the straight line of the tennis ball is deflected because

> a certain colonel of Zouaves . . . started envying the brilliant and impeccable play of the two champions; and suddenly, to show the six thousand spectators what he was capable of—particularly as his girl-friend was seated by his side—he took out his pistol and fired at the ball as it flew between the two rackets. (193)

The chain of reactions originating from this deflection ends with the image of the Marquis de Philimor, who, because "at least thirty-six gentlemen, riding their thin-ankled, thoroughbred women bareback" charge towards his wife to insult her and cause her to have a miscarriage, is suddenly "doubled and completed by a baby," and, like Philifor and Anti-Philifor, is "honeycombed and riddled with childishness" (195).

In the third part of the book, finally, it is the Hegelian master-slave dichotomy that is being deconstructed. At the end of Mientus's attempts at fraternization, Albert, with a tremendous slap on Bert's face, re-creates order, and, subsequently, he and his father settle down to "break" (*F,* 261) Bert in through a veritable orgy of slaps, while they simultaneously gorge themselves with food. The objective is to restore order once and for all, "so that he should accept them as a thing in itself, a *Ding an sich*" (262). But when Mientus appears, and with him an anomymous mass of servants who watch the "orgy" from the outside and when Mientus "put[s] his arm round the lad and . . . [draws] him close to him," Edward and Albert try to attack Mientus, but Bert, "as if his courage in the face of his masters had been restored by Mientus's fra . . . ternization, suddenly fraternized on Uncle Edward's face" (263). With this reversal, the situation for a last time collapses into complete immaturity and chaos. At precisely this moment, the antinomy between outside and inside, which also figures that of nature and culture, is broken, and the thermodynamics of a sociohistorical entropy set in: With "the sound of broken glass. . . . The windows gave way, and the populace surged in" (263). What follows, as in the schoolyard or Zutka's bedroom, is once more a general chaos.

Trans-Atlantyk

The first moment in *Trans-Atlantyk* is also, as Zdravko Malić has remarked, a "« zero » point"[23] between two force fields. As its title suggests, *Trans-Atlantyk* begins in the free, as Deleuze and Guattari would say completely deterritorialized and smooth space, between the Fatherland and the country of exile. In between these two heavily striated cultural structures, the fluid expanse of the ocean symbolizes the utopia of a free, a-cultural, and formless "plane of consistency," or "body without organs," where the subject is quite literally dissolved. As the narrator says, "[e]xquisitely pleasurable the sail from Gdynia to Buenos Aires, and somewhat loathe was I to go ashore, for twenty days a man between Sky and water, *nothing remembered, bathed in air, melted in wave, through-blown with wind*" (*T,* 3; emphasis added). This erotic, utopian space, which is ruled over by the pleasure principle and which allows for the sociocultural subject to dissolve and for the libidinal one to come to the fore, will preside over the rest of the book. As the narrator says, almost losing his narrative thread, "[l]ikewise two Misses, pretty, Shapely, Willing, with whom in my spare moments I twaddled and dallied, turned their Heads, and so, I repeat, between Sky and Water, Tranquilly on and on . . ." (3–4).

If the geographic position—the catastrophic space between two stable structures—is mapped onto a literary one, therefore, the first scene is set in the central moment of what Kristeva calls a transposition; "the *passage from one sign system to another*" and the shift from an old thetic position to a new one. This shift entails the destruction of all former values and their subsequent reassembly within a different framework:

> It also involves an altering of the thetic *position*—the destruction of the old position and the formation of a new one. . . . In this connection we examined the formation of a specific signifying system—the novel—as the result of a redistribution of several different sign systems: carnival, courtly poetry, scholastic discourse. The term *inter-textuality* denotes this transposition of one (or several) sign system(s) into another.[24]

Within these dynamics, the passage on the ship denotes the moment when the old order is destroyed and the new one is not yet assembled. In this light, the trans-atlantic passage becomes analogous to a literary trans-position; the shift from *Pan Tadeusz* to "Pan Gombrowicz."

Yet already the first scene in the new country, which confronts Gombrowicz with the Baron, who offers to become his patron, and Pyckal, who wants to prevent the Baron from this, recapitulates "Philifor Honeycombed with Childishness," because it seems as if, according to an almost perverse logic, the positive side inevitably brings about its negative other. Pyckal immediately and categorically contradicts the Baron's offer: "Didye get dumped on your head to take on new Clerks for the Office without consulting me?! Are ye a Cretin? So for you I will drive out that clerk of yours, out, out, out!" (*T,* 19).

Fortunately, the aggressivity of the imaginary confrontation between the Baron and Pyckal is mediated by Ciumkała's arrival, which deflects the situation. Ciumkała, who is neither positive nor negative, is constantly ashamed because both the Baron and Pyckal—no doubt for oppositional reasons—despise him. In this position in between the Baron's yes and Pyckal's no, he represents precisely the split subject who is equally ashamed in front of each of the opponents. This shame, which figures the split, has surprising, and on the surface completely unforseeable, effects. Because of his shame, for instance, he puts his hands into his pockets, and, being even more ashamed because of this stupid, senseless gesture, he takes out, among other things "some small dried fishes" (*T,* 20). This stupid, seemingly irrelevant gesture figures how and why the split brings the two extremes into conflict, because the fishes are not Ciumkała's personal fishes. Unfortunately, they are metonymical reminders of the eternal fight between the three partners. When the ensuing quarrel stalls, Ciumkała intervenes once more through another seemingly senseless gesture. This time, he scratches his ear. Yet, fortunately for Gombrowicz, the senselessness and disgracefulness of this gesture is promptly taken up by the Baron and Pyckal:

> And so they stood, Stood until Ciumkała scratched himself behind the ear; and whilst he is scratching behind the ear, the Baron rubs his ankle and Pyckal his right shin.
>
> Says the Baron: "Scratch yourself not." Says Pyckal: "I'm not Scratching myself." Ciumkała said: "I have Scratched myself." Said Pyckal: "I'll Scratch you." Says the Baron: "Scratch, scratch away—this is what you are for." Says Pyckal: "I'll not Scratch you, let your Secretary scratch you." Says the Baron: "My secretary will Scratch me if I order him to." Said Pyckal: "I will engage your Secretary for Myself." (*T,* 21)

At the end of the disastrous duel with "Borges," the "Gran escritor, maestro" (31), the situation also threatens to stall, because Gombrowicz is, like a tennis ball, quite literally thrown back and forth between the poles of the (imaginary) ego and the (symbolic) subject. His choices are either to acknowledge the defeat of his ego and to accept the oedipal subjugation under the law of literature or to continue the impossible fight for the ego against the subject.

For a seemingly eternal moment, Gombrowicz remains caught in the dynamics of this ricocheting system. Like a caged tiger, he desperately turns round and round in its paralyzing motion:

> Yet when I had walked almost to the door, again I turned (for this Walking of mine is already transforming into just a walk

> across the Salon), and again through the salon I go . . . And more and more my walk strengthens, becomes Mightier . . . and so the Devil, the Devil, I Walk on and Walk forth and Walk, and so am Walking, Walking and Walking and Walking . . . (*T*, 34–35)

Because the others feel the terrible aggressivity of his walking "there by the walls as squirrels they crouched; this one or that crept under Upholstery, or guarded himself with a piece of Furniture." More and more, however, Gombrowicz becomes a victim of his own walking:

> The Devil, the Devil, and I know not what to do with this Walking of mine, for such a Walk, such a Walk, and I as if uphill Walk, am Walking, and hard, hard, uphill, uphill, oh what a Walk! Oh, what am I doing? Oh, now haply as a Madman I Walk and Walk and Walk . . . and the Devil, the Devil, Walk, Walk . . . (35).

At this moment, a deflection occurs. As if part of him had come to meet him from the outside, another person also begins to walk: "someone likewise goes walking, and Walks and Walks. And he so Walks and Walks that when I Walk he likewise Walks" (35). Unfortunately, Gonzalo, this "other," is a person whose allegiance can only mean an additional shame under the cultural gaze, because, as a homosexual, he is a cultural outcast. Through his walking, this other—who once more functions as a *clinamen* that makes a dialectical system deviate—draws Gombrowicz toward the imaginary:

> So think I, and what is't, and how and why has that man so adhered to me? . . . And more intently I look him over . . . I look him over and see a man of seemly height, very Dark, and of not at all dull, indeed quite noble visage . . . But red lips he has! Lips he has, I say, Red, made Red, Carmined! . . . And I as a Crab reddened! So as Boiled, Red, that Walk of mine, the Devil, the Devil, I directed to the door, and through that door—oh, now I'm not Walking on, Walking on but only Walking out . . . Walking—as if the Devil, as if Satan were chasing me—Out! (36).

The duel between Gonzalo and Tomasz once more follows a similar dynamics. It is only during the duel that Gombrowicz realizes their fateful mistake, because the "merciless" duel has to continue until blood is drawn: "we as if into a Trap had fallen and there can be no end here and this Duel can have no ending: viz. 'tis till blood and how is Blood to appear if with no bullets the pistols?" (76). As during the party, the situation is caught in a constant repetition from which there is no escape, and it is re-animated only through the freak deviation caused by the fact that "Pyckal's Stallion bit the rump of the Stallion on which the Baron sat" (77). As in "Philimor Honeycombed with Childishness," this freak accident causes a whole avalanche of silly and stupid events. First the riders begin to fight, then the horses go wild, some women fall to the ground, the dogs go mad and attack Ignacy, who has hidden himself in the bushes because of "Anxiety for his Father" (78). The scene ends in another one of Gombrowicz's infernal, "Dantesque symphon[ies]" (77).

The way a deviation is brought about can also be followed in the way that Gonzalo catches Ignacy in his scheme. Horatio, one of the waiters, functions as a kind of catalyst who seems somehow connected to Ignacy. As the narrator comments, his "moves were in sooth quite natural but also an Unnatural air they had . . . when Ignacy Moves, he moves . . . and indeed as if he were on Ignacy's string" (*T,* 84–85). In this way, Gonzalo connects Ignacy and Horatio: "And the Bajbak again stands and again at Ignac a bit, a bit Moves, and this as if he on a pipe with those Movements of his accompanied him" (94). This connection is created by letting Horatio echo Ignacy's actions during a game of baseball, a horseback ride, or a game of shooting. Each time, Ignacy's actions are repeated, but displaced into a slightly different context. His strikes during the baseball game, for instance, are underlayed by Horatio hitting a pole: "Ergo Ignac again bam. When he bam, at once likewise Horatio to match Boom with a picket upon a peg" (96). The objective of this counterpoint is to bind Ignacy to Horatio, who should subsequently function as the catalyst between Ignacy and Gonzalo: "Again Ignac bam upon the ball, Horatio boom upon a picket as if together against Gonzalo they did play." The game, then, is "a trap, that with this Boombam his Son is being charmed, that his Son is with this Boombam captivated" (96), the result of which is an "incessant blending, such that Bajbak's eternal, incessant, bothersome accompanying, companying in everything, bothering!" (97).

Before it reaches the ultimate climax, however, the situation once more drowns in senseless enjoyment and humor. The narration slows down, and, like a slow-motion movie it metamorphoses almost unperceptibly into the cacophony of a pure enjoyment:

> now he will that Father of his bam . . . But what's this, what's this? Oh, perchance Salvation! . . . Since, whilst he so at his Father Swoops, Swoops, Swoops, and yet Swoops, is Swooping, nigh, nigh Swooping down, upon him Laughter, oh, on him Laughter, Laughter, God, God, he into Laughter perchance, oh, he into Laughter and so he into Laughter, into Laughter is Swooping and aloft he Swoops! Ah, aloft Swoops! Laughter then, Laughter! The Minister his belly clutched, with laughter bammed! And Boom, Bam, Pyckal the Baron by the belly clutched, and the Accomptant Cieciszowski clutched, and with Laughter they boomed, bammed, Bam, Bam. (121)

Soon the whole congregation is laughing: "And so from Laughter into Laughter, they with laughter Boom, with laughter bam, boom, boom, bam Boom! . . ." (122). This laughter, like Johnnie's laughter, or the convulsive laughter of Zutka's father in *Ferdydurke,* is once more a purely corporeal, bodily, non-significant laughter in which the subject violently disintegrates, similar to the way in which it had dissolved peacefully during the ocean passage; a laughter that underlies and produces Gombrowicz's work, and which here makes the novel loop back onto itself. It is the universal, stupid laughter of the subject who forgets itself and, for short moments, has *jouissance* effects.

Pornografia

In *Pornografia,* Frederick brings the antinomies of empiricism and physics on the one hand and dogmatism and metaphysics on the other onto a collision course. In a manner similar to that in which his counsciousness forces physical nature to her knees—a victory that results in Frederick's tragic artificiality—it "murders" the other extreme; the psychic systems of religion and metaphysics. If he stakes the psychic aspect of human consciousness against (the ideal of) physical nature, he stakes its physical aspect against (the ideal of) metaphysics. In this way, his both physical and psychic—human—character, his *material consciousness,* undecides both realms.

The victory over metaphysics is staged in the scene in church and in Amelia's household, which is from the start defined within idealistic and religious registers. As Witold states, "a rigorous, *categorical force,* of a superior reason . . . of absolute reason . . . [a] metaphysical principle reigned here, a transcendental principle, in short, the Catholic God, liberated from all *corporal bounds* (*P,* 81; emphasis added). Within this veritable orgy of idealisms, Amelia's a-corporeal spirituality is confronted with "the eternal terror of the man who exists" (84). In the system of mutual reflection, in which Amelia tries to fathom "this alien depths next to her" (84), her ideal spirituality—once more according to the inevitability of a dialectical logic—only reinforces and heightens Frederick's "materiality" (85) and physical presence. In fact, it physicalizes him to monstrous proportions: "under the influence of this extreme spirituality, he affirmed himself physically and I saw his hand, for example, become very, very much a hand, more and more a hand" (85).

In a philosophical and metaphysical register, it is once more the inherent spirituality that is the target of Frederick's attack. During one of Gombrowicz's "strategic" walks Gombrowicz stresses that in contrast to the purely natural, physical immediacy of Henia's and Karol's relation to the natural world, Amelia's unmediated relation to the natural world is based on the metaphysical ideal of a divine, all-pervading spirituality. Against this logocentric, passive, and immediate experience of the world, Frederick stakes the human, active, and mediated experience; the fact that consciousness and the perceptual process itself forever separate man from nature.

Gombrowicz's discussion of this confrontation with the object is once more carried out in Kantian terms as the subject's confrontation with the thing-in-itself, which for Kant is categorically excluded from the human imagination because "[h]ow things may be in themselves, without regard to the representations through which they affect us, is utterly beyond the sphere of our cognition" (*CP,* 149). In fact, as Kant had stated quite categorically, the thing-in-itself is neither sensual nor mental but in-itself.

Gombrowicz deals with the difference between the thing-in-itself and its visual representation in a juxtaposition of the human imperfection of the representation and the inhuman perfection of nature-in-itself:

> I will not deny that in spite of everything, there is something in a painting, even if it is a faithful copy of nature, that

> disarms and attracts. What is it? A painted landscape undoubtedly says something else to us than does the same landscape in nature; its effect on our soul is different. But not because a painting is more beautiful than nature, no, a painting will always be incompetent beauty. . . . It is possible, though, that this is the reason behind the attraction. The picture shows us the beauty that was felt, seen by someone . . .
>
> If we consider that the contemplation of an object . . . fills us with the despair of *loneliness*—because then you find yourself alone with the *Thing* and the Thing crushes you—perhaps this fear of the thing, as such, would explain the paradoxical phenomenon that an imperfectly painted trunk is closer to us than a natural trunk in all of its perfection. *A painted tree trunk is a trunk filtered through man.* (*D* II, 41; emphases added)[25]

During the walk, Amelia tries to demonstrate to Frederick that the landscape is neither the lonely void of the real nor a landscape filtered through man but a landscape filtered through God. In seeing the landscape as a landscape suffused by a divine spirituality that permeates it like a divine light, Amelia successfully excludes the human element, and she sublates, in a Hegelian, synthetic move, the fear and loneliness felt in the confrontation with the thing-in-itself. In contrast, Witold's and Frederick's reactions highlight, in different contexts, that it is a landscape inevitably filtered through man. As such, they take up Kant's idea that nature-in-itself is excluded from the human realm and that every reality is inevitably human. Witold stresses the "humanity" of the landscape in his use of a simile that counters the divine eternity of the landscape with a human temporality whose perspective point is death: "the ground could be seen stretching in gentle hillocks down to the flat, almost invisible surface of the river, which lay there *like a corpse. It was pretty*" (*P*, 82; emphasis added). In his humanization, Witold evokes Gombrowicz's belief that a landscape filtered through man—even if the object of anxiety insists in its center—is more beautiful than a purely natural one. If Witold, however, still sees the landscape, Frederick's "punctum" is itself the negation of the landscape:

> But Frederick blurted out:
>
> "The barrel."

> And he was confused . . . because instead of admiring the *landscape* he had noticed something as insignificant and uninteresting as a barrel lying under a tree. He did not know how he could have said that, nor how to extricate himself. And Amelia repeated, like an echo:
>
> "The barrel" (*P,* 82–83; emphasis added).

Symptomatically, Frederick has zoomed in analytically on the only man-made object in the natural surroundings. By singling out this insignificant and rather repulsive detail, Frederick goes one step further than Witold, because through this reference, he does not only humanize the landscape—he literally obliterates it so that he can, in one sweep, actively "strangle" both the divine and the natural landscape.

Amelia's surprised echoing of Frederick ("The barrel") is a first clue to the fact that even a divine ideality is ultimately dependent on the approval of other human beings. In this context, the scene serves as Amelia's introduction into the realm of perception. It is her "fortuitous initiation . . . into a fortuitous object which extracts all its importance from the very importance you attach to it" (*P,* 83). This concrete, human object replaces the ideal, divine object of Catholicism, which Gombrowicz described in his *Diary* as "the subjective convicion that an objective world exists."[26]

The result of the implosion of these registers is ambivalence: If by attempting to mirror herself in(to) his universe Amelia gives up her ideal spirituality in favor of an intersubjective system, Frederick continually suffers from a consciousness that has him in its grip and that forever separates him from both an ideal naturality and an ideal metaphysics. For him, the world is forever "suffused with humanity."

The erosion of Amelia's belief in ideality is so massive that even her (sacrificial?) death is directed toward Frederick rather than Christ. In her death scene, "[t]he dying woman hardly glanced at the cross, turned her eyes to Frederick and would not take them off him" (*P,* 93). Frederick rather than God is "the *supreme arbiter* . . . she was dying for him" (96; emphasis added). Their imaginary capture is completed when, at the moment of her death, she actually tries to escape the ideal gaze of Christ in order to find Frederick's real one: "Maria held up the crucifix. Amelia searched desperately for Frederick and, gazing at him, she died" (97).

As in all of Gombrowicz's books, in *Pornografia* the antinomies of the human condition seem unproblematically clear:

consciousness	unconsciousness
maturity	immaturity
culture	nature
form	fluidity
artificiality	naturality
language	action
self-reflection	immediacy
thought	intuition
castration	polymorphous perversity
depravity	innocence
ugliness	beauty
knowledge	stupidity
age	youth
fragmentated body	body without organs
maturity	immaturity
seriousness	frivolity
logic	seduction
meaning	senselessness
death	life
rationality	irrationality
concentration	distraction

The problem is that the registers are mutually exclusive and irreconcilable.[27] In *Pornografia,* for instance, the old (conscious) cannot out of their own power negate their consciousness, while the young (unconscious) cannot by definition be conscious. Because of these basic antinomies, a dialectical reconciliation of the opposites cannot be thought of in terms of a Hegelian progression toward the ideal of the absolute spirit, nor by a regression toward a purely unconscious state, but only as a mutual perversion, distortion, and defilement of one term by the other. This means that the unconscious can be treated only by the conscious and vice versa. Accordingly, the field of human reality is neither that of a purely symbolic maturity nor that of a purely real immaturity, but the Möbial, "strangely attractive" field in which these two extremes are constantly folded onto each other. David Brodsky takes up these twofold dynamics when he states that there are "two basic spatial models which he [Gombrowicz] exploits in his art: on the one hand the model of irreconcilable polarities excluding a middle ground, and, on the other, that of dynamic balance achieved through joining contradictions."[28]

Cosmos

Like *Ferdydurke, Cosmos* opens up with a digression and a deviation, because Witold and Fuchs stray from their path—"It was sweltering . . . Trouser-legs. Heels. Sand. On we plodded. Earth. Ruts. The road was vile" (*C,* 9)—by entering the thicket where they find the hanged sparrow. In what follows, I will take my clue from Gombrowicz's own description of the structure of *Cosmos,* which describes the confluence of two currents:

> I am establishing two starting points, two anomalies, very distant from each other: (a) a hanged sparrow, (b) the association of Katasia's lips with Lena's.
>
> These two puzzles will begin to demand sense. One will permeate the other in striving to create a whole. A process of conjectures, associations, circumstantial evidence, something will begin to create itself but it is a rather monstrous embryo . . . and this murky, incomprehensible charade will call for its solution . . . it will search for an explanatory, ordering idea . . .
>
> What adventures, and what rows with reality during this tearing out of the fog!
>
> Internal and external logic.
>
> The stratagems of logic.
>
> Intellectual wilderness: analogues, oppositions, symmetries . . .
>
> Suddenly the growing dithyrambic rhythm of the furiously forming Reality. And its disintegration. Catastrophe. Shame.
>
> The sudden overflowing with excessive fact.
>
> The creation of backwater tributaries . . . dark caves . . . obstructions . . . impediments, whirlpools . . . twists . . .
>
> Etc., etc., etc. (*D* III, 160–61)

Throughout the book, these two images provide the parameters within which Witold's perception is structured. One image, the hanged sparrow, is an enigmatic external and physical one; the other, the phantasmatic conjunction of the two mouths, is an equally enigmatic—but this time internal and psychic—one. In the beginning of the novel, for Witold, these two obsessive images cannot be brought to overlap because he cannot find a common structural matrix. It is impossible for him "to place the sparrow on the same map as the mouth, it belonged to an entirely different one, a different area altogether" (*C,* 21). Instead of a logical connection, there is only an inexplicable *mise-en-abîme* of analogies, superimpositions, and associations:

> The meshwork reminded me of her leg on the springs of the bed, but I was distracted, what with one mouth over another mouth, the hanged sparrow and the hanged chicken, Lena's husband and Lena, the chimney *behind* the gutter, lips *behind* lips, mouth *behind* mouth, shrubs and paths, trees and road. (25; emphases added)

In *The Logic of Sense,* Deleuze relates these two series—which he also relates to "Lacan's paradox: two series being given, one signifying and the other signified" (*LS,* 48)—to the realm of the signifier (the symbolic) and the signified (the imaginary) respectively:

> Witold Gombrowicz established a *signifying* series of hanged animals (what do they signify?), and a *signified* series of feminine mouths (what is signifying them?); each series develops a system of signs, sometimes by excess, sometimes by default, and communicates with another (39; emphasis added).[29]

If the two series represent the symbolic and the imaginary respectively, the novel traces the gradual convergence and the subsequent folding of the registers onto each other. As Deleuze states, "Gombrowicz, in his fine novel *Cosmos,* shows how two series of heterogeneous differences (that of hangings and that of mouths) call forth their own communication."[30] This communication is made possible by what Deleuze calls "dark precursors" or the *"disparate"* (*DR,* 120). In a way similar to that in which the seemingly chaotic path of a thunderbolt (or, to use an image more evocative of chaos theory, the development of weather) is pre-determined by invisible and unaccountable forces, these "invisible, imperceptible *dark precursor[s],"* determine the relation of the series "in advance but in reverse, as though intagliated" (119). Through this temporal retroaction, these dark precursors bring about—somewhat like the unaccountable fixation—a resonance between two series.[31]

The dark precursors ensure that heterogeneous series can be related without recourse to an earlier or more fundamental identity. Accordingly, the literary project consists of drawing together

> a maximum of disparate series . . . by bringing into operation linguistic dark precursors (here [in the case of *Alice in Wonderland*], esoteric words, portmanteau words) which rely upon no prior identity, which are above all not "identifiable" in principle, but which induce a maximum of resemblance and identity into the system as a whole. (*DR,* 121)

These communicators function somewhat as puns do in the logic of dreams, because they are both *affective* and *aleatory.* As Deleuze and Guattari state in *Kafka: Toward a Minor Literature*, "[t]he points of connection between series or segments, the remarkable points . . . are often sensible qualities, odors, lights, sounds, contacts. . . . They are connected to chance."[32] According to Deleuze, in *Cosmos,* the series communicate with each other both on the level of content and of the language material; "by means of strange interfering objects [such as the hanged cat] and by means of the esoteric words pronounced by Léon" (*LS,* 39).[33]

From the very beginning, *Cosmos* highlights the enigmatic communication between the series and the problem of creating order and imposing order onto a fundamentally chaotic reality. During a night walk after the ominous dinner, for instance, Witold connects the constellations of the night sky and the inevitable "shapes and relationships" (*C,* 19) one sees in it with the "oral constellation" (24) of the two mouths:

> there was really nothing whatever in common between Katasia's dissolute perverseness, that indecent, gliding mouth movement, and Lena's fresh, virginal, half-open lips, except that they were "related" to each other as on a map. . . . In reality there was no link whatever between those two mouths, I had merely seen one in relation to the other, it had been *an accident of distance, angle and position.* (19–20; emphasis added)

These analogies on the level of content, are parallel to the two series on the level of form, in which slight deviations, inclinations, and bifurcations are also operative. Throughout, in fact, the connection between the series is also operative on the level of the signifier, with words related through formal as well as semantic similarities. Such puns and acoustic similarities—for instance, that between *kulka,* (little ball), *kurka* (chicken) and *kurwa* (whore) or Fuchs's referring Katasia's "facial affliction" (*C,* 38) back to the sparrow's beak by calling it a "mannered little beak"—always denote communicative bridges between the two series.[34] Yet this communication and convergence happens within a diverging, chaotic field: "[e]ach series tells a story. . . . The basic series are . . . absolutely divergent in the sense that the point or horizon of convergence lies in a chaos or is constantly displaced within that chaos" (*DR,* 123). This chaos ensures the possibility of an endless number of series, and, as such,

> [t]his chaos is itself the most positive, just as the divergence is the object of affirmation. . . . Each series explicates or develops itself, but *in* its difference from the other series which it implicates and which implicate it, which it envelops and which envelop it; *in* this chaos which complicates everything. (*DR,* 123–24)

The communication between the infinitely plural series are precisely the criminalistic, deductive problem, and it is the plurality of the series that causes the impossibility of a solution. As Deleuze states, "the totality of the system, the unity of the divergent series as such, corresponds to the objectivity of a 'problem' . . . The essential point is the simultaneity and contemporaneity of all the divergent series, the fact that all coexist." While the universal, positive and all-encompassing chaos is that of the real, reality is the realm of what Deleuze calls the "chaosmos" in which the "problem of resonance between two series" is posed (*DR,* 124). Because every order is enveloped by the universal chaos, however, in whose "divergent series and incompossible totalities" the subjects are "pushed apart, kept open . . . instead of being closed upon the compossible and convergent world that they express from within," every order will be chaotic and every subject will be a split one.[35]

The moment when Witold hangs Lena's cat is the moment at which the two series fold onto each other for a first time, the moment of complication that superimposes the signifier and the signified and thus inside and outside.[36] As a dark precursor or disparate, the hanged cat produces—and is, in turn, produced by—the Möbial topology of the phantasm, which "has the property of bringing in contact with each other the inner and the outer and uniting them on a single side" (*LS,* 220). In fact, at this point, the *signifying* series (the hangings) has been crossed with the *signified* series (the obsession with the mouths). This moment of suture is a central moment for Gombrowicz's poetics, because quite simply, *this folding of the signifier onto the signified series denotes precisely the moment when knowledge establishes itself as paranoiac.* Symptomatically, after the murder, Witold feels: "I belonged to both configurations . . . had I not in a way myself constructed a bridge connecting the whole?" (*C,* 101). It is the problem that the outside causes the inside, while it is on the other hand its mirror image, which fundamentally problematizes Witold's relation to himself. As he notes, "[h]idden somewhere in all these places and things, in the totality of these places and things, lay the path that had led me to strangle the cat" (86).[37] It is precisely this hidden path that leads back from the figure to the moment of fixation. Symptomatically, however, the way to the fixation is discernible only belatedly, from within the figure, and never directly. Furthermore, as the paranoiac system itself is the creative agent, Witold's own action is so detached from himself as a subject that, although he himself has hanged the cat, he can speculate "that in spite of everything she [Kulka] *could* have done it" (*C,* 79). The final merging of the two series is of course once more the whirls and eddies that end the novel, which is another moment of a real chaos that terminates Gombrowicz's plots.

Conclusion

As I have argued, Gombrowicz's works are defined by a number of formal and thematic constants. Invariably, and the momentum of *Cosmos* from a *clinamen* to its fluid, chaotic, and turbulent ending is probably the best example, their overall movement is from a *clinamen* to the production of a realm defined by chaotic dynamics that follow the logic of a strange attractor and further toward a completely turbulent chaos. In the time between a laminar flow and this turbulent chaos, which is defined by the laws of deterministic chaos and which is also the one that is writable, the chaotic twists from one attractive physical force field to the other figure psychic twists from the symbolic to the imaginary and vice versa. These twists, which denote a shift of sides and of perspective, cause the protagonists' inevitable shame—the shame of the ego before the agency of the law and the shame of the subject before the agency of the ego—and their constant flights.

If they are mapped onto the plane of a strange attractor, in *Trans-Atlantyk, Pornografia,* and *Cosmos,* the subjects' movements start in the center of the symbolic, that is, at the point at which the attractive force of the symbolic is strongest. In *Ferdydurke,* it is the moment of the intervention of Pimko as the formal imperative; in *Pornografia,* it is the order of Hippolyte's household; finally, in *Cosmos,* it is the moment before Witold's and Fuchs's flight from the paternal order into the country. Gradually, as the stories develop, however, the subjects follow an excentric line of flight from the symbolic pole until they fold catastrophically onto the imaginary side at a real point when, for an infinitesimally short moment, the forces cancel each other out and the subjects, as in the beginning of *Ferdydurke* or during the melée in Zutka's room, are "nothing at all." Immediately, however, this opening is closed up again because, in both physical and psychic terms, the attraction of the symbolic is replaced by that of the imaginary: The initially symbolic protagonists are more and more attracted by the aggressive—in the case of *Pornografia* and *Cosmos* actually murderous—forces of the imaginary. Even after they have folded over onto the center of the imaginary plane, however, they still remain attracted by the symbolic one. This ambivalence is figured by their split into an ego and an alter-ego at the moment of the folding: in *Ferdydurke,* these are Johnnie and Mientus; in *Trans-Atlantyk,* Gombrowicz and Gonzalo; in *Pornografia,* Witold and Frederick; and, less rigorously, in *Cosmos,* Witold and Fuchs. Even while they are attracted by the imaginary force, therefore, the subjects remain on a line of flight toward another real point. Tragically, this line of flight leads not only to such a point of dispersal that is figured by the turbulence of a bodily or—in the case of *Cosmos* cosmic and atmospheric—melée, which denotes, in Lacan's terms, a "fragmented body" and in Deleuze and Guattari's ones a "body without organs," it also leads to a renewed folding onto the symbolic plane. Although at every position the subject is on a line of flight, it remains caught in a "molar" envelope.

It is invariably at the moment of the second "real twist" back onto the symbolic plane that the novels end. In this context, *Ferdydurke* differs from the other novels only in that this movement is played out three times—according to its three scenes whose trajectories go from the symbolic through the imaginary to the moment of the real twist—while the overall movement leads, like a counterpoint, from the imaginary to the symbolic.

In *Possessed,* the movement also starts within the symbolic, a symbolic that is transferred to an almost forgotten past; it folds onto the imaginary plane and moves toward the moment of the twist, where, once more, the novel terminates. Uncannily, however, the lost, true ending of *Possessed* describes precisely the moment of the renewed folding onto the symbolic plane. The fact that the ending was missing figures uncannily that this moment actually lies outside of the text. Generally, this "moment of the real" describes the time from the ending of one story to the beginning of the next one; the line of flight from book to book that Gombrowicz had announced at the end of *Ferdydurke.* As in a "strange attractor," in this unwritable moment, the trajectory folds from the imaginary *through the real* (as the "movement through infinity") to the symbolic, from where the telling of another adventure starts up again.

Possessed figures this unwritten moment, because the final pages—which describe how the protagonists spend the night in the "Old Kitchen" up to the moment that the fireplace breaks open and Handrycz scrambles out, saying, "I've been here before,"[38] and which end with them leaving the "Old Kitchen" through the hole in the wall caused by the breaking-up of the fireplace—are not the final pages, and thus the *real* ending of the story. In one of those cases in which the fictional and the real world seem to suddenly map, it has been superceeded by a real ending that was discovered only in 1984. In this ending, almost all of these mysteries are solved. The reader learns that Francis has not died at all but has fallen through the fireplace and escaped; that Handrycz is in fact Francis, and that Walchak and Maya have escaped by the same route and are now happily united, although Walchak's hair has turned white when he threw the towel out of the window during the night. As such, the lost ending of *Possessed* figures precisely the story's re-folding onto the symbolic plane: If the fragmented novel ended at the threshold between the imaginary and the real, the final chapter is situated fully within the symbolic. It describes not only Henia and Karol's newly mature, symbolic relationship but also the rational explanations of the seemingly fantastic happenings. As Molowicz had stated, the evil force possessing Maya may be, as the first ending implies, of the devil; but, and the real ending implies this possibility, it may also be human.

Notes

1. See for instance Kazimierz Bartoszyński, "Kosmos i antynomie" in *Gombrowicz i krytycy: Wybór i opracowanie,* ed. Zdzisław Łapiński (Kraków: Wydawnictwo Literackie, 1984).

2. For an application of chaos theory to literary studies see the work of Katherine N. Hayles, especially *Chaos Bound: Orderly Disorder in Contemporary Literature and Science* (Ithaca: Cornell UP, 1990).

3. Michel Serres, *La naissance de la physique dans le texte de Lucrece: Fleuves et turbulences* (Paris: Minuit, 1977), 13. Subsequent references to this text will appear parenthetically as *N.*

4. See Gilles Deleuze, *The Logic of Sense,* trans. Mark Lester (New York: Columbia UP, 1990). Subsequent references to this text will appear parenthetically as *LS.*

5. For an early image of such vortices and eddies, see Leonardo da Vinci, "Studies of Water Passing Obstacles and Falling into a Pool," 298 × 207 mm, Windsor Leoni volume (12660v).

6. For such a flow-chart, see René Thom, *Semio Physics: A Sketch,* Addison-Wesley, Reading, 1990, 45.

7. On the relation between the theory of turbulence and chaos theory see David Ruelle, *Chance and Chaos* (Harmondsworth: Penguin, 1993), and Tom Mullin, "Turbulent Times for Fluids," in *The New Scientist Guide to Chaos,* ed. Nina Hall (Harmondsworth: Penguin, 1992), 59–68.

8. As Serres states, "theorem of the world: neither nothingness nor eternity. Neither straight line nor circle [*cercle*]. . . . Nature, which is to say birth, which is to say death, is the straight line inclinced by an angle that produces a cycle [*cycle*], which is a cycle inclined by the angle, that produces a global vortex, which the wear and tear of time returns to a straight line" (*N,* 74).

9. Gilles Deleuze and Félix Guattari, *A Thousand Plateaus: Capitalism and Schizophrenia* (Minneapolis: U of Minnesota P, 1987), 371. Subsequent references to this text will be marked parenthetically as *TP.*

10. Serres also relates the *clinamen* to the production of meaning: "on the white noise a signal appears, in the laminar flow there is a *bifurcation.* Meaning is a bifurcation in the univocality" (*N,* 179).

11. Refer: Dante, *The Divine Comedy,* trans. H. R. Huse (New York: Holt, 1965).

12. Immanuel Kant, *Critique of Pure Reason,* trans. J. M. D. Meiklejohn (London: Dent, 1988), 471. Subsequent references to this text will be marked parenthetically as *CP.*

13. Immanuel Kant, *Prolegomena to any Future Metaphysics,* trans. James W. Ellington (Indianapolis: Hackett, 1977), 80. See especially the "inclination" of the antitheses to a view that sees the world as an open, self-regulatory system that shows "a sensitive dependence on initial conditions."

14. See also Tadeusz Kępiński, who has noted that "the names of the characters in the two philosophical tales were derived from *Analyse du Jeu des Echecks* by the eighteenth-century French chess player Philidor. Gombrowicz's early interest in philosophy (he read Kant at the age of sixteen) accounts for the topic of the first tale" (quoted in Ewa M. Thompson, *Witold Gombrowicz* [Boston: Twayne, 1979], 71).

15. Witold Gombrowicz, "Guide de la philosophie en six heures un quart" in *Gombrowicz,* ed. Constantin Jelenski and Dominique de Roux (Paris: l'Herne, 1971), 390–417. Gombrowicz attaches "the greatest importance to the *antinomy in art*" (398). He relates this antinomy to the theories of Einstein and Planck, in analogy with which the human spirit appears to be something formed through "two different elements which never acknowledge [*recontrent*] themselves" (400).

16. In this context see also Gombrowicz's story "Memoirs of Stefan Czarniecki" (*Pamiętnik Stefana Czarnieckiego*), in which the protagonist states that "wherever I find some kind of mysterious feeling, be it virtue, or family, belief or Fatherland, I always have to do something mean." Witold Gombrowicz, *Bacacay,* trans. Walter Tiel and Olaf Kuhl (München: Hanser, 1984), 36. Already in this story, the "forever lost time" is that of childhood. As the narrator states, "full of emotion I run towards you, you my childhood, in my thoughts" (19).

17. Witold Gombrowicz, *Ferdydurke,* trans. Walter Tiel (München: Hanser, 1983), 9–10. The passage is missing from the English translation.

18. As Ruelle argues, because the system shows a sensitive dependence on initial conditions, if the initial situation were only slightly different, "[t]he general aspect would remain the same, but the number of successive turns around the right and left ears would be quite different. . . . The number of successive turns around the left and right ears is . . . erratic, apparently random, and difficult to predict" (*Chance and Chaos,* 63). In the case of the Lorenz attractor and the Rössler attractor, the systems are defined by three forces, and, accordingly, the visualization is embedded in three-dimensional space. There are, of course, strange attractors that are defined by an interplay of more than three forces. In *A User's Guide to Capitalism and Schizophrenia: Deviations from Deleuze and Guattari* (Cambridge: MIT P, 1992), Brian Massumi argues that only the open structure of such a "monstrous *fractal attractor*" (64) can figurize or diagram life and that *"whole attractors"* (64) are superimposed upon this nomadic life (64). In fact, in Massumi's discussion, oedipalization is the prime movement by which a "fractal attractor is eclipsed by a whole attractor" (74). I am using an attractor defined by three forces because it is the most "abstract" one and because it can be mapped onto a psychic force field that is also defined by three forces.

19. As Gombrowicz writes, "Because all of his Critique is an superhuman effort in order to end in a wisdom that is the aim, not the point of departure. Kant was somebody who was 'immature' and who wanted himself mature." Gombrowicz, *Varia,* vol. 1, trans. Allan Kosko (Paris: Bourgois, 1978), 194.

20. Jacques Lacan, "Kant with Sade," trans. James B. Swenson, Jr., *October* 51 (1989): 55–75, 60. (This was originally published as "Kant avec Sade," *Écrits* (Paris: Seuil, 1966), 765–90. Further references to this text will appear parenthetically as KS.

21. See also Slavoj Žižek, *Enjoy Your Symptom: Jacques Lacan in Hollywood and Out* (New York: Routledge, 1992).

22. Peter Widmer, "Einleitung: Ethik und Psychoanalyse," *Ethik und Psychoanalyse: Vom kategorischen Imperativ zum Gesetz des Begehrens: Kant und Lacan,* ed. Peter Widmer and Hans-Dieter Gondek (Frankfurt a. M: Fischer, 1994), 7–23, 23.

23. Zdravko Malić, "La construction du *Trans-Atlantique* de Witold Gombrowicz," *Zagadnienia Rodzajów Literackich* 13 (1970), 95–112, 96.

24. Julia Kristeva, *Revolution in Poetic Language,* trans. Margaret Waller (New York: Columbia UP, 1984), 59–60.

25. On Gombrowicz's polemics on painting see also Witold Gombrowicz, "Correspondance Gombrowicz Dubuffet" in *Gombrowicz,* 337–54. See

also my essay "The Visual and the Gaze in the Works of Witold Gombrowicz: The 'Evil Eye' of Painting," in *Reading Seminar XI: Lacan's Four Fundamental Concepts of Psychoanalysis,* ed. R. Feldstein (Albany: State U of New York P, 1995), 175–82. In this context, Gombrowicz's use of *tableaux vivants* in *Pornografia* is especially apt, because they dramatize the complex relation between nature and art. If painting is the attempt to copy life and nature while simultaneously giving it a higher existence in the realm of artistic ideality, *tableaux vivants* partly reverse this process by re-translating artificial, artistic representations into life and nature. Yet they retain the framework of artistic composition. If in a painting art copies nature, in a *tableau vivant* nature copies art. As such, it can be read as an attempt to return life to itself via the detour of art.

26. Witold Gombrowicz, *Tagebuch,* trans. Olaf Kühl (München: Hanser, 1988), 985. On Gombrowicz's relation to Catholicism, see also the interview "Gombrowicz et le catholicisme," in *Gombrowicz,* 56–57.

27. On the oppositional pairs in Gombrowicz see also Jan van der Meer, *Form vs. Anti-Form: Das semantische Universum von Witold Gombrowicz* (Amsterdam: Rodopi, 1992).

28. David Brodsky, "Gombrowicz's Spatial Poetics," in *Proceedings of the XIIth Congress of the International Comparative Literature Association,* vol. II, ed. R. Bauer and D. Fokkema (München: Iudicium, 1990), 277–82: 277.

29. See also: "[o]n the constitution of divergent series and the manner in which they resonate and communicate at the heart of a chaos, see the profound comments made by W. Gombrowicz in the preface to his novel *Cosmos*" (*LS,* 361–62).

30. Gilles Deleuze, *Difference and Repetition,* trans. Paul Patton (London: Athlone, 1994), 123. Subsequent references to this text will appear parenthetically as *DR.*

31. In this context, see Deleuze's discussion of sense: "sense, in its organization of aleatory and singular points, problems and questions, series and displacement, is doubly generative: not only does it engender the logical proposition . . . it engenders also the objective correlates of this proposition which were themselves first produced as ontological propositions" (*LS,* 120).

32. Gilles Deleuze and Félix Guattari, *Kafka: Toward a Minor Literature,* trans. Dana Polan (Minneapolis: U of Minnesota P, 1986), 69.

33. On Gombrowicz and the concept of a "minor literature," see also Ewa Płonowska Ziarek, *The Rhetoric of Failure: Deconstruction of Skepticism, Reinvention of Modernism* (Albany: State U of New York P, 1995).

34. See also Wilkiewicz's discussion of the series *wbicia-wbijanie-dobijanie* in Zbigniew R. Wilkiewicz, *Personendarstellung und Menschenbild im Kosmos Witold Gombrowiczs* (Mainz: Liber, 1986), 26. *Dobijać się*, furthermore can denote two things: "to hammer" as well as "to get nearer to something or someone." In this context, see also Raymond Roussel, *How I Wrote Certain of My Books* (Boston: Exact Change, 1995). On the other hand, see Gombrowicz's essay in the magazine *Aurora—Revista de la Resistencia,* reprinted in Witold Gombrowicz, *Argentinische Streifzüge* (München: Hanser, 1991), 172–81, in which he makes fun of a writer who is all too faithful to words, and who changes a story just because he cannot bring himself to erase punning typos (*pero,* "but," for instance, becomes *perro,* "dog," so that the sentence that should have been "and she answered, but . . ." turns into "but she answers, dog," a change that has decisive consequences for the rest of the story. Symptomatically, Gombrowicz's own piece ends in an orgy of typos. Note also the phonological similarity of *cat* and *Katasia* in the English version.

35. Gilles Deleuze, *The Fold: Leibniz and the Baroque,* trans. Tom Conley (Minneapolis: U of Minnesota P, 1993), 81.

36. See also Gombrowicz's statement in *A Kind of Testament* that hanging the cat "is a treacherous and perverse act, because it overflows from the inner world to the outer world" (*KT,* 70).

37. In the case of Gombrowicz, the hieroglyphic motifs are libidinally structured and defined by desire and guilt. After Witold has become guilty—after he has killed the cat—he feels that from now on he is on "the obverse side of the medal and I was now in a realm of hieroglyphics, where occult and mysterious things took place" (*C,* 72).

38. Witold Gombrowicz, *Possessed; or, The Secret of Myslotch,* trans. J. A. Underwood (London: Boyars, 1980), 221.

PART TWO

Modernity and the Trajectories of Exile

Marzena Grzegorczyk

5

Formed Lives, Formless Traditions:

The Argentinean Legacy of Witold Gombrowicz

In one of his essays, the philosophical scientist Loren Eiseley relates the following legend. A famous scientist persisted in wearing huge padded boots, much too large for him. He had developed an irrational fear of falling through the interstices of the largely empty molecular space that common men refer to as "the world." As a consequence, "a stroll across his living-room floor had become, for him, something as dizzily horrendous as the activities of a window washer on the Empire State Building. Indeed, with equal reason he could have passed a ghostly hand through his own ribs." The network of his nerves, the movement of his thought, had become a vague cloud of electrons. The world that this man had helped to create, Eiseley observes, became the world in which he found himself a lonely and imprisoned occupant.[1] This disturbing anecdote could be a twisted fantasy from one of Witold Gombrowicz's protagonists, whereby the imposition of form extends itself over the character and eventually leads to his self-destruction. Gombrowicz himself would be Eiseley, the storyteller; that is, somebody who is able to keep a healthy distance from form, avoiding the elderly scientist's problem: confusing *thinking about* the world with *living in* the world. Obsessed with the fearful majesty of structure, the scientist does not have a way of breaking out of the recognition that stifled his life: since atoms are more space than matter, he may fall through the holes. The paradox is that he created the system—nature as science—in which he eventually became enclosed.

Many of Witold Gombrowicz's protagonists struggle with similar problems, which might be summed up as the question of how to live and create *in between*—not between particles but between styles and stereotypes, between forms imposed by others and by forces of the past. Whereas Eiseley's protagonist is a victim of solipsistic aggression—he became the slave of the form he helped create—Gombrowicz's protagonists usually are submitted to form imposed by others. They avoid self-destruction by remaining in constant suspension between competing ideals. While outwardly striving for maturity and fulfillment, they respect their secret desire: the temptation to inhabit the subaltern world of supposed immaturity and imperfection. The result is a complicated struggle between the imposed stasis of form and the emancipatory energy of the formless.

Gombrowicz's reflection on the tension between form and formlessness and his protest against the fetishization of received forms are particularly attractive today when categories such as "plurality," "experience," and "hybridity" govern the realm of cultural criticism. This essay, focused on Gombrowicz's notion of Form and its Latin American permutations, is a reflection on Witold Gombrowicz as a sort of found proponent of alternative cultural theory. The first part is a brief genealogy of Gombrowicz's notion of Form as an aesthetic and cultural category. In the context of numerous mis-encounters between Gombrowicz and "philosophizing, aestheticizing Argentina" (as he used to say), I discuss the ways in which Gombrowicz's call to decompose oppressive discourses—especially discourses of the nation—has been interpreted and translated by intellectuals of Buenos Aires, a city in which Gombrowicz carried out a twenty-four year battle for literary prominence. During the military dictatorship of 1976 to 1983, an Argentine version of Gombrowicz's "garbage aesthetics" became a vehicle for creating an alternative Argentine intellectual tradition, one celebrating hybridity rather than the deformed purity propagated by the military government. In the final part of the essay, I place Gombrowicz's dialectic of form and formlessness in the context of other theories of cultural mediation that emerge from Latin America. Gombrowicz's international sense of cultural conventions underscores the pragmatics of Form (that is, what Form does) in the postcolonial context. With its predilection for evolution, change, and transformation, his "garbage aesthetics" is a useful tool in the complex process of cultural self-construction in postcolonial cultures.

Confrontations

The opposition between form and formlessness is perhaps the single most important and most commented on figure in Gombrowicz's work. In a 1956 letter to Artur Sandauer, a prominent Polish critic, Gombrowicz writes: "My views form an organic unity . . . My relation to art, nation, and other similar issues is basically a bifurcation of a tree whose root is my concept of form."[2] In his reviews and articles published in the Polish press as early as 1935, he uses this term with reference to linguistic form (dialect) and also as a synonym for literary style and composition. With time Gombrowicz's concept of Form undergoes considerable transformation; its meaning becomes more complex. The anecdote that begins this essay—the story of a mad scientist—captures the nature of Gombrowicz's more mature interest in this concept. Form interests him not in the Aristotelian sense, with pure reference to object, but as a subjective category (that is, in the Kantian sense, as an a priori attribute of the human mind, constitutive of our whole experience of the world) and as a social category (as means of expression and communication with others). Gombrowicz's notion of Form denotes a kind of cosmos, a private reality that people are compelled to formulate and express. The oscillation between competing ideals, that of form and that of formlessness, often presents itself in Gombrowicz's texts as the result of an ontological conflict: the imperative to describe oneself and the world is competing against the simultaneous desire to throw oneself into unreflective, spontaneous existence. Trying to reconcile, in the neo-Kantian fashion, the critique of reason with that of culture, Gombrowicz presents a choice between the world that is understood yet falsified because of a priori categories, or authentic existence based on the spontaneous eruption of imagination. Although this tension remains insoluble, the key for Gombrowicz is to maintain the dynamism of the process, that is, to produce form for social use but to avoid identifying with it.[3]

While Gombrowicz was initially interested in the individual on whom form (cultural, pedagogical, and national) is imposed (e.g., *Ferdydurke,* 1937), the main protagonists of his later works are the ones who impose form on others, directing their desires and shaping the world. His last novel, *Kosmos* (1965) is, among other things, a narrative about the process of creating a private reality. Sexual and criminal intrigue is often interrupted by the investigations of its narrator, who, assuming the position of "detective of the world," reflects on the mechanisms of meaning making, its self-constitution and self-destruction. In his plays, however, Gombrowicz was interested not so much in the sphere of human interaction or individual cognition as in portraying "drama of the self" as an unconscious battle with form.

Yet form interests Gombrowicz not only as aesthetic, psychological, and social categories but also in relation to the nation. He makes this connection explicit in remarking that his own relation to Poland is a consequence of his attitude toward form (*D* I, 36). In *Imagined Communities,* Benedict Anderson underscores the importance of invention in the process of nation formation by shifting the weight from historical acts to imaginative visions of national communities. Gombrowicz, on the other hand, chooses to focus on the pitfalls of this process. Full of disdain for heroism, always trying to rescue the individual from the unconsciously formed life, the Polish writer calls for breaking the collective inertia based on old patterns of behavior and myths forged by Polish romanticism. In the national sphere Gombrowicz is fascinated by the same basic rules of the workings of form that take place in the interpersonal realm: its fundamental, albeit denied, instability (the fact that form imposes, destroys, and only rarely maintains stability) and its tendency to produce hierarchies. In criticizing the "national longing for form," to use Timothy Brennan's phrase, Gombrowicz underscores the fact that nationalism bases itself on a false return to pure uncontested origin. While doing this it erases all that threatens a notion of integrity and purity. In Gombrowicz's work the homogeneity of the tradition assumed by the nationalistic discourse becomes a point of contention. Through strategies of de/transformation, he enters into debate with major figures of the Polish tradition. Instead of following nineteenth-century romantic discourse—the ideological and aesthetic base of Polish nationalism—Gombrowicz decides to be outside, to understand and articulate his relationship to his native culture from discursive gaps. Always underlining the uniqueness and spontaneity of position, he articulates his vision of Polish culture through those who speak from illegitimate spaces: homosexuals, the insane, traitors. With "the strategy of the deviant," to borrow Leonard Neuger's concept,[4] Gombrowicz manages to create the category of national Form and consequently decompose it.

Gombrowicz's notion of "national form," besides criticizing the conscious forgetfulness of cultural tradition, opens up another perspective on cultural production and reception in the world system. In his view, the battle between the "formal imperative" and the tendency to preserve authenticity, spontaneity, and immaturity becomes the basis for cultural classification. This almost taxonomic exercise begins with *Ferdydurke* and intensifies after his arrival to Argentina. Without ever defining it precisely, the sphere of the universal for Gombrowicz encompasses cultures that have well-defined forms, that is, forms of expressions that have been developed for centuries, such as the French, Italian, German, and English. The so-called secondary cultures include Argentina, Canada, and other "secondary European cultures" (*KT,* 53). Within this problematic model, his native Poland, "the country of weakened form," is placed on the frontier between East and West where the Form and its degradation achieve equilibrium. It is a place condemned to imperfection and a minor role because of its geographic position and historical development.

Combining a critique of reason with a critique of culture, Gombrowicz refers to his native culture by pointing out the following contradiction: while wanting to protect their authenticity and independence, Poles are constantly competing against other nations. The lack of form, on one side, tortures and, on the other hand, liberates them (*KT,* 56). Yet, the desire to "have form" is ultimately damaging. Gombrowicz remarked that in Poland's case the workings of Form are very strong and profits for the individual and national culture fairly weak. Trying to join the "universal" world, the nation becomes infected with a rigidity it imposed on itself, sacrificing in this way its authenticity. Thus, Gombrowicz believed that his compatriots had more reason than the French or English not to identify themselves with the national form. This inherent critical distance, a sort of disregard of their own achievements, is for him the only guarantee of any original Polish contribution to world culture.

The opposition between form and formlessness is not only the central theme of Gombrowicz's work, but the preoccupation that changed the course of his life. Justifying his earlier decision to leave his native land—or perhaps just shifting the weight from mere chance to a more conscious choice—Gombrowicz sees his life in Argentina as a continuation of his adventures into the abyss of formlessness. Despite the fact that, as he admits in his *Dziennik* (Diary), at times he "confuses Paris with the world,"[5] he admires the spontaneity and lack of dogmatism that he sees as characterizing Argentine culture. He realizes that the *latinidad* in some way complements his Polishness. Seduced, on the one hand, by the youth of his new country and, on the other hand, by the forms that "grew lazy under the southern sun,"[6] Gombrowicz reflects on the redemptive composition of a new cultural foundation made of forms that are perhaps melted but not totally decomposed.

"I live here, in Buenos Aires, a little bit as if on the moon."

Invited by a naval company to visit Argentina on their ship's maiden voyage, Gombrowicz left Poland in 1939. He did not suspect that he would spend the balance of his life in that country.[7] After Germany invaded Poland, however, Gombrowicz decided not to return. In 1947, having exhausted the modest economic help offered by the Polish Embassy, he began working for the Banco Polaco in Buenos Aires. As Gombrowicz himself suggested, his life in Argentina could be divided into three parts, each one lasting approximately eight years: the first, marked by poverty, bohemia, and light-heartedness; the second spent, in the Polish Bank; and the third, of modest life and growing literary prestige.[8]

While Gombrowicz's 1927 visit to Paris was crucial for his vision of form, his idea of the formless was shaped by the Argentine experience. In terms of his notion of form, Gombrowicz's arrival to Argentina did not represent radical change. Being a "specular border intellectual," as Abdul JanMohamed defines it, Gombrowicz situated himself on the frontier between his native culture and the rest of Europe before leaving Poland: even there he was using other cultures to see the structure and functions of his own.[9] Looking back on his first novel *Ferdydurke,* written while still in Poland, Gombrowicz comments: it is a text in which "two loves fight with each other, two strivings: the striving for maturity and the striving for eternally rejuvenating immaturity" (*D* I, 140). It is not surprising, then, that Gombrowicz would develop and use his expertise in immaturity on

American soil. Argentine literature, to a higher degree than any other Latin American literature, has been the site of tension between the "immature" and the "overtly mature." As Gombrowicz suggests, the conflict produced by the oppositions between maturity and immaturity or form and chaos that defines Polish culture could be projected on Argentine culture as well. This conviction, together with the fascination that the writer felt for Argentina and its inhabitants, produced diverse texts.

By 1947, when Gombrowicz began to work in the Banco Polaco, he was quite poor, although very well liked, and often aided by his numerous Argentine and Polish friends. Having learned Spanish from his interlocutors, he spent two years translating *Ferdydurke* with their generous help, playing chess, and taking pleasure in discussing whatever there was to be discussed.[10] Although he had published articles in *La Nación* and *Océano,* he did not write much. While working for the bank, he tried to use his cultural insights productively on behalf of its clients. He was not a Wallace Stevens who worked as an insurance executive during the day and wrote poetry at night, for part of his job was to use his abilities as a cultural critic, as an analyst of national forms. The result was various texts written for *Biuletyn Banco Polaco S. A.* in which he analyzes the conditions of understanding between Polish and Argentine cultures.[11] Treating lack of understanding between the two nations as the point of departure, Gombrowicz writes with humor, sometimes with anger. He challenges cultural stereotypes, questions and tries to explain their origin in order to define the essence of the Argentine. In one example, Gombrowicz complains about the belittling notion that Argentines have of Poland. They believe, he writes with reference to the commentaries on the Polish political situation, that "we are a mass amassed by others."[12] In the course of the article, his annoyance with his second homeland continues to grow. At the end, with a gesture of a person deeply surprised and scandalized by what he sees, Gombrowicz offers a definition of Argentina that is a mixture of ignorance and arrogance:

> Argentina, along with Mexico, is the most civilized of Latin American countries . . . Buenos Aires determines the hierarchy of nations and tells Latin America: you should respect this; you should not pay any attention to that. Argentina is the head of Latin America and Buenos Aires is the brain of this head. One

> ought to lament, with regard to us Poles, that emptiness and obscurity watered in the salsa of old legends reign in this brain.[13]

In this passage, Gombrowicz, somewhat irritated by the formlessness of his own position (what does it mean to be a Pole in Argentina?), defines Argentina as a secondary culture that does not recognize itself as such. In *Wędrówki po Argentynie* (Wandering through Argentina) Gombrowicz decides to focus on the affinities of the two countries rather than on the differences that separate them. Argentine culture, Gombrowicz notices, suffers from the same illness as the Polish one: both are marginal in their relation to "European culture" and, in the case of Poland, to "Western culture." Having surrendered to the dictatorship of "General Forma" they both get tired and bored under his iron discipline.[14] To escape this gridlock, both cultures should transform the secondary conditions into creative potential: instead of hiding the inferiority, they should expose it.

Garbage Aesthetics

Gombrowicz's arrival in Argentina was, as the Argentine novelist, Juan José Saer eloquently puts it, "a lucky disgrace," because "thanks to the atypical character of his destiny as an exile, an excessive one when compared to other emigrants who fully integrated themselves into Western culture, Gombrowicz became, from a dry leaf taken by the wind of contingence, a notorious sign, paradigm and emblem."[15] Although Gombrowicz had a significant effect on Argentine culture, the legacy he left behind has a peculiar character, for it has not formed a clear corpus of academic and critical inquiry. Instead of a plethora of critical articles and aesthetic treatises about his work, he left numerous friendships, a personal fable, and just a few filmic, oral, and written commentaries.[16]

The reason for this clandestine fascination with and official ignorance of Gombrowicz common in Buenos Aires's intellectual circles lies, perhaps, in the fact that Gombrowicz was interested more in the "silent youth" of Argentina than in the literary establishment:

> What fascinated me in that country were the masses, while I was being received by high society. I fell under the spell

> of the nights in the Retiro while the others were under that of Paris, the city of lights. For me the silently sinful youth of that country were the vibrant confirmation of the sentimental state in which I found myself.[17]

The distance that separated Gombrowicz from the literary world of Buenos Aires was, as Laura Ayerza de Castillo and Odilde Felgine note, "an opposition between two conceptions of literature: one centered around life, the other around culture."[18] The journal *Sur,* for instance, represented everything that Gombrowicz detested: an elitist conception of art, excessive fascination with European literature, and strict social conventions.[19] In the period of military dictatorship euphemistically called "the Process of National Reorganization" (1976–83), however, the space between high and low culture was reduced.[20] What once seemed to be an inappropriate combination of Gombrowicz's own distance and his celebration of the formless became a locus from which the dictatorship (an excess of form) and its self-legitimizing rhetoric could be questioned. The literary production of this period is held together by an interest in historical reevaluation, questioning of social structure from the marginal positions, and the recovery of the values shattered by the authoritarian regime. For example, Ricardo Piglia's 1982 novel, *Respiración artificial,*[21] questions the authenticity of official versions of history and indicates possibilities of resistance. This engaging novel is, among other things, the most complex attempt to assess Gombrowicz's legacy in Argentina.

The novel is in some ways a parody of a detective novel. It begins with a letter from Marcelo Maggi to his nephew Emilio Renzi. Renzi has written an amateurish novel, a family saga, that misrepresents the details of a scandalous affair Maggi had years ago with an exotic dancer. Maggi, who has lived in obscurity since the events, writes Renzi in order to set the record straight. The family saga, however, is only a pretext for establishing correspondence between these two failed intellectuals who, albeit relatives, have never met. In the second half of the text, when Renzi arrives to Entre Rios to finally meet his uncle, Maggi has disappeared, having appointed his friend, Tardewski—a Polish exile and ex-student of Wittgenstein—to meet Renzi.

Gombrowiczian themes run throughout the novel: the idea of a duel, criticism of narrow cultural nationalism, the philosophy of "anti-form," and the importance of "remains" in cultural tradition. They intensify in the second part of the novel, which is of most interest for the discussion here. While the first part is composed exclusively of letters, the second part of the text is essentially one night-long conversation between Renzi and Tardewski in which others occasionally intervene. The investigation of the mysterious life of Renzi's Uncle Maggi is displaced from the material plane onto the speculative one: Maggi's presence is evoked through the discussion of his ideas. Although his disappearance is a generative formula for the conversation—and also a poignant reminder of the disappearances of so many during this period of brutal dictatorship—the conversation soon becomes an unsettling mixture of philosophical and literary commentary. The reader overhears controversial discussion of the Argentine tradition. Playing off their peripheral perspective, Renzi and Tardewski discuss issues that are central to Argentine literature and its various components: tradition, style, creativity, and originality.

Tardewski, an intelligent yet frustrated émigré from Poland openly modeled on Gombrowicz, narrates various episodes from his life during that long, elliptical conversation: his arrival in Buenos Aires after Germany's invasion of Poland, the curious destiny of an article speculating on a meeting between Kafka and Hitler. Tardewski transforms his "secondary" condition of exile, dispossession, and a lack of cultural goods into creative potential. His fantasy is to construct a work whose prototype—with its Benjaminian resonance—could be called a "workshop of quotes." Piglia's protagonist is a transculturated subject similar to Gombrowicz. Both reflect on the secondary condition of Argentine culture, which, according to Tardewski, shares its complex with Polish culture. While Gombrowicz was obsessed with the contribution of so-called secondary cultures (that is, cultures that have not developed perfect, mature forms) to universal culture, the protagonists of Piglia's novel discuss the reverse of this interaction: the role of Europeans in Argentine culture. They start with a perspective imposed by Domingo Faustino Sarmiento[22] and developed by Europeans residing in Argentina such as R. Cunningham Graham, Paul Groussac, Pedro de Angelis, Waldo Frank, and, at a different level, by Gombrowicz himself. They—the Europeans, "the dictators" and "cultural arbiters"—are responsible for having created an inferiority complex among Argentines. Although the European represented by Tardewski does not appear as a model that others would desire to emulate (just the contrary!), he is depicted as necessary for Argentine culture. For Gombrowicz, the extra-European position is imperative for the revision and critique of European Form (*KT*, 63). In the same way, Maggi needs Tardewski, who with his peculiar combination of intimacy and distance helps the Argentine intellectual interpret his own culture. In this process of re-evaluation, critical distance not only appears as privileged but is actually valued higher than knowledge itself. Tardewski discusses Argentine tradition from his peripheral position. He is a dispossessed exile from a "homeland erased from the map, without money, without future, without friends."[23] Although he does not lose his pragmatic attitude, Tardewski is fascinated by the intellectual dimension of his failure. In fact, failure is his strength. The condition of marginality grants him the privileged place of the eternal "tourist-philosopher" who is able to see reality from the other side.

The process of redefining the attitude toward European culture coincides with the need to construct a new authenticity. What would its constitutive elements be? Both Gombrowicz and Piglia propose to build it with ingredients of tradition. But, as Raymond Williams suggests, tradition is a process of a deliberate continuity: it is made up of selection and reselection of elements of the past that represent not a necessary unity but a desired one.[24] Thus, the components of national tradition that drifted into obscurity now emerge into prominence. In his *Diary* Gombrowicz outlines an alternative aesthetics, which might be called "garbage aesthetics":

> The Rubbish heap. The point is exactly that I come from our rubbish heap. All that you cast off through the centuries as refuse is now speaking out through me. If my form is a parody of form, then my spirit is a parody of spirit and my person a parody of a person . . . It is not a coincidence that precisely at the moment when we desperately need a hero, up pops a clown—a conscious and, thereby, serious clown. You were too literal for too long . . . You forgot that man not only is himself but also pretends to be himself. You threw everything that was acting and theater in you into the trash can and you tried to forget about it. Now, when you look out the window, you see that a tree has sprung up on that trash heap that is a parody of a tree. (*D* I, 36)

In this passage Gombrowicz comes back to the issue of national form by criticizing the existential invisibility of acting. According to Gombrowicz, the Polish complex is the fact that the Poles have forgotten about their form, about the fact that "acting as a Pole" is an essential part of "being a Pole." He is aware of the transformation and fecundity that rubbish entails: once relegated to invisibility, this particular national characteristic gave life to a new form. Rubbish—the main element in Gombrowicz's new aesthetics—is a fundamentally dynamic category. Rubbish is not self-evident, nor is it stable: it has transient characteristics. As Michael Thompson argues, its commonsense definition as something that has no value or is of negative value is inadequate: "Something which *is* of value can be seen as rubbish if it is placed in the wrong place."[25] By recovering what has been disposed, Gombrowicz ensures the survival of particular components of the Polish tradition and the system of values that they represent.

Next to acting, another element that Polish tradition put into the trash is the baroque. Bothered by heroism, Gombrowicz criticized the influence that the Polish romantic poets (Adam Mickiewicz and Juliusz Słowacki) as well as their followers (Henryk Sienkiewicz, Stefan Żeromski, Stanisław Wyspiański, Stanisław Przybyszewski, and Jan Kasprowicz) had on Polish culture.[26] In *Trans-Atlantyk,* a novel written in Argentina yet directed to the Polish reader, Gombrowicz attacks romantic pathos, melancholy, and other stereotypes of Polish culture. This attack on the spirit of Polishness is carried out through a kind of linguistic transvestitism. Parodying Polish national epic—Adam Mickiewicz's *Pan Tadeusz* (1834) and *Trylogia* (1888) by Henryk Sienkiewicz—Gombrowicz brings forth the latent baroque elements in Polish phraseology and syntax. In effect, his baroque language comes close to the twentieth-century peasant dialect. In this way Gombrowicz criticizes the intellectuals' ignorance of the baroque heritage in Polish culture.[27] The fascination that Gombrowicz feels for the baroque is organically linked to his "philosophy of immaturity" because the baroque, as Heinrich Wölfflin observes, never offers perfection, plenitude, or the static quietness of being. On the contrary, it brings change, tension, proliferation, ultimately depriving the privileged systems of authority.[28]

Gombrowicz's interest in the subaltern elements of culture and his predilection for a fundamentally fluid system of semiotic renovation has political potential. Leonard Neuger suggests that the natural context for Gombrowicz's thought are cultures that "tend to close themselves and produce ideologies of closure"; that is, cultures that have in their memory or reality repression and oppression or cultures that in their way of functioning produce repressive elements such as provincialism, totalitarianism, or anarchism.[29] In Argentina during the period of military dictatorship, Gombrowicz's iconoclastic and parodic attitude toward the cultural tradition appears as a possible locus of resistance, for it contradicts the notion of linear history promoted by the military. In *Artificial Respiration* history and tradition appear as something that can be redone, rebuilt, or reassembled. Piglia places particular importance on style, reading, and chance in constituting the new tradition. The discussion of language within this novel, which is sometimes written in purposefully misspelled Spanish legitimizes the immigrant origins of Argentine literature while exploring the dynamic of linguistic purity and corruption. With this gesture Piglia converts the writing of Roberto Arlt—who allegedly represents bad, perverse, immature writing, the complex of Argentine literature—into the true beginning of Argentine literature.

In the immature world of Gombrowicz, to escape the existing form means to be creative. At the level of artistic creation, to evade the already elaborated form means an opening of narrative structure; thus, his sympathy for the avant-garde. While Gombrowicz focuses on writing, Piglia broadens the creative space by displacing the problem of writing to the level of reading, if one accepts the conventional distinction between the two. Piglia opens up the text by introducing a density of intertextual references, privileging parody and foregrounding the fragmentation of discourse. Reading conceived as creative manipulation has an important role in the constitution of the literary tradition, which appears in Piglia's novel as a history of readings. Tardewski reads the pre-Socratics from Heidegger, suggests reading Kafka from his precursors; Piglia-the novelist (and Piglia-the critic) reads Sarmiento from Borges. Borges appears in the novel as a reader of Paul Groussac, Arlt as a reader of bad translations. Given the impurity of the act of communication, mistake and misunderstanding are implicitly present in the process of reading. Paul Groussac, for instance, contributes to the art of reading with his "technique of anachronism" and "erroneous attributions." Tardewski himself writes his own book inspired by a marginal annotation in Joachim Kluge's edition of Hitler's *Mein Kampf.* He proposes reading philosophy as novels, a gesture that undermines the very foundation of the philosophical tradition.

The techniques and functions of the intertextual references present in the novel are quite varied, opening to an almost infinite number of possible texts. In the context of the novel, the processes of writing and reading appear as a dynamic series of displacement and constant revision. Piglia uses different pre-texts in varied ways. The presence of some of them is explicit: there is a considerable number of names of authors and thematization of their works. In other cases, the novelist transgresses the limits of marked intertextuality. Undoubtedly, he is playing with the reader's competence, testing the limits of his/her ignorance: "in order to read . . . one should know how to associate."[30] Piglia counts on a sophisticated reader, a well-read and educated one.[31] The intrigue, set forth at the narrative level, has its metacommunicative projection: the reader is witness to the investigation conducted by Emilio Renzi, and, at the same time, the text converts the reader into a detective or spy. Piglia suggests that criticism is a modality of detective fiction in which the critic is "the detective: the reader of the law. And the writer is often a criminal, the transgressor. One could think that the detective novel is a big fictional form of literary criticism."[32] Through his emphasis on reading, Piglia underlines an essential phenomenon in the Argentine tradition that thus far had been considered secondary, namely, chance. He knows that there is no chance that every reader will catch every intertextual reference. A Polish reader is more likely to know, for instance, that when Tardewski mentions his compatriot Korzeniowski, he is referring to the writer who is much better known internationally by the name of Joseph Conrad. Even more coded is a reference to Malcolm Lowry. At a certain moment, another member of Entre Rios society, Count Tokray, notifies Tardewski about the death of Malcolm Firmin, a man who broke his neck in the bathroom, perhaps because he had too many drinks. A little bit later the count asks Renzi for money in order to go to the "dark grave wherein my friend is laid." Geoffrey Firmin is one of the protagonists of Malcolm Lowry's *Under the Volcano* and the conditions of the supposed death of the (probably fictitious) friend of Count Tokray allude to the death of Lowry himself. In order to complete the sequence of associations, one should add that the phrase quoted above is the title of another Lowry novel, *Dark as the Grave Wherein my Friend is Laid.*[33]

Chance has an important role in the creation of tradition, for it destabilizes the notion of form. It seems that Piglia's interest in the pragmatics of chance is a variation on Gombrowicz's affection for rubbish. Contingency is one of the primary characteristics of rubbish: we never know why particular elements are in the heap, and we are not quite sure what will spring from them. Rubbish has to be excluded, for, just like chance, it is a threat to the work of reason. Chance is addressed in the novel not only through emphasis on how reading creates rival, unpredictable and even conflicting meanings but also at the narrative level. Working against the superior condition of European rationalism, Tardewski suggests that chance—not rationality—is the constitutive moment of creative consciousness. Chance has marked all his life: his arrival to Argentina, his move to Concordia, everything. His entire creative activity has been submitted to the order of the accidental as well. As soon as they published his article on a chance encounter between Kafka and Hitler, he is robbed of all the materials and notes. He is left holding a copy of *La prensa,* a newspaper that has a translation of his own writing. Since he does not know Spanish, he cannot even read it. This baroque narrative of how his own text became alien to him establishes dialogue with the poststructuralist postulate according to which every text, in the moment of being published, ceases to belong to the author and becomes instead a robbed text, snatched by the readers and critics, who, with their own readings, construct multiple meanings. The stripping of Tardewski is further symbolized in the novel through the error in his authorial name. Instead of Tardewski, his name is printed as Tard*o*wski. Although he recognizes contingency as the main element of his creativity, this makes him doubt for a moment his own originality. Despite that, the philosopher concludes that the idea expressed in his work on Kafka and Hitler is still his own. Although Tardewski eventually changes his strategy—he decides to write nothing of his own and maintains his diary of quotes—he does not stop being creative. This concession seems an extreme version of dropping the pretense of authenticity. He finally accepts that "being" and "writing" are not co-equal.

The episodes described above are examples of the complex cultural and political texture of a concrete historical moment. Both Piglia and Gombrowicz work with the material offered by their cultures. Gombrowicz does it despite his constant protests against equating human identity with the national one; Piglia, despite (or perhaps *because of*) the trivialization of the concept of the national during the dictatorship. Both writers look critically at cultural heritage, and oppose artistic colonialism and servility. While Gombrowicz's attitude is based mainly on the "aesthetic imperative," Piglia, by creating a productive tension between text and metatext, puts in evidence the need for sociopolitical discourse in Argentine society. It is necessary, he points out, that the revalorization of history encompass the literary tradition, too. For Piglia, there is not solely one history because there is no reality except for our conception of it. Similarly, more than literature itself and the literary tradition, what counts is our perception of them—or our different perceptions. More than history and tradition, the *attitude* toward history, literature, and the cultural patrimony should be at the center. Following Gombrowicz, Piglia constructs a retrospective vision of Argentina, liberating it from the rigid categories of perfection and stylistic purity, placing the imperfect above the perfect yet stiff.

Gombrowicz, trying to escape cultural hierarchies, removes the forgotten elements of his culture from the rubbish heap and tries to find a useful place for them. This gesture locates him among those who participate today in the negotiation of cultural space with the purpose of recuperating heterogeneous traditions suppressed by one national hegemonic ideology. Piglia, with his insistence on a similar recuperation, underlines the fact that an important part of all negotiation is the alteration of perspectives. That is why he values hybrid genres so highly. With Walter Benjamin's "workshop of quotes" as prototype, they allow for spaces of negotiation. In them, people discuss, reflect, and question national formation. As a result, Piglia successfully constructs a notion of civic ethos based on the individual's rejection of the ideal of aesthetic truth and its ethical and political dimension. In the period of so-called national reorganization, when the military sought to homogenize and unify the nation, Gombrowicz's legacy provided a powerful model for mapping out a space far from the all-embracing and imprisoning notion of a purified "we."

Within the Latin American context, where the main stake in cultural transactions lies in the preservation of difference and the avoidance of forced homogenization, Gombrowicz's fluid energetic system of semiotic renovation is particularly appealing and perhaps in the near future will be placed next to Oswald de Andrade's *antropofagía,* Angel Rama's notion of *transculturation,* or Gloria

Anzaldúa's concept of *borderlands*. Once placed in this company, however, Gombrowicz, the self-proclaimed iconoclast, appears traditional, for he continues the dominant tradition of assuming the subaltern to be formless. In his proposition to exchange a "man who has form" for a "man who produces form" (to use Jan Kott's formulation), he suggests a modification of the system of aesthetic preferences whereby the cultural complex should become the cultural value. What is superior for Gombrowicz is the formless and its transformative energy, which tends to create form that then needs to be constantly questioned, decomposed, deconstructed. Aware of the fundamentally unequal and antidemocratic character of Form, Gombrowicz, himself a victim of cultural colonialism (or, perhaps, enriched by experiencing it), questions the colonial schema of cultural subordination. Although the category of race, central to the colonial dynamic, is practically absent from Gombrowicz's work, he responds to the imperative produced by the tension between universal civilization and "national culture," "between the involuntary mutual awareness and dependency of every people and region made possible (and inevitable) by 'civilization.'"[34] Gombrowicz articulates dependency theory without calling it so. Dependency, according to Neil Larsen, is "more than the misfortune of the neocolonial status"; it is "the very logic of a historical subject that never catches up, that never 'makes History' except in the image of an already-made."[35] Gombrowicz's celebration of the immature and formless and his belief in their positional superiority removes the process of national form production from its teleological axis and locates it in the position of autonomy vis-à-vis the hegemony of Western cultures of mature forms. Gombrowicz represents the transcultural model, which, as Larsen observes, through initial prohibition of the consumption of imported cultural products, transfers the locus of production to the regional site, removing it from the authoritative cultural aura.[36] Gombrowicz's implied methodology leads to questioning any received Form—including his own. His insistence on the artful oscillation between particles is especially relevant today with the value of hybridity being aggressively questioned around the world. With hybridity comes what may seem to be the random arrangement of particles, a threat to unity or assumed purity. Rereading Gombrowicz can aid us in negotiating hybrid cultures—that is, all cultures—without the lockstep of the military mindset, so that facing the chaos of everyday life we are still able to resist resorting to the action of Eiseley's fearful scientist; that is, to avoid putting on big boots.

Notes

1. Loren Eiseley, "How Natural is 'Natural'?" *The Star Thrower* (New York: Harcourt, 1978), 280.

2. Quoted in Jerzy Jarzębski, "Pojęcie 'formy' u Gombrowicza," *Gombrowicz i krytycy: Wybór i opracowanie,* ed. Zdzisław Łapiński (Kraków: Wydawnictwo Literackie, 1984), 313. Unless otherwise stated, all translations from Polish and Spanish sources are mine. In summarizing the genesis and transformations of Gombrowicz's concept of Form, I rely primarily on the following: Jan Błoński, *Forma, Śmiech i rzeczy ostateczne* (Kraków: Znak, 1994) and Jarzębski, "Pojęcie 'formy' u Gombrowicza," 313–46. See also Konstanty A. Jeleński, "Bohaterskie niebohaterstwo Gombrowicza," *Gombrowicz filozof,* ed. Francesco M. Cataluccio and Jerzy Illg (Kraków: Znak, 1991), 155–67; and György Gömöri, "Formateremtő küzldelem formákkal: Witold Gombrowiczról," *Nuyagtról nézve* (Budapest: Szépirodalmi Könyvkiadó, 1990), 210–13.

3. Given the fact that the primary source of our experience of form is vision, it is not surprising that Gombrowicz, as he often proclaimed, was not interested in painting. On the link between form and vision see Martin Jay, "Modernism and the Retreat from Form," *Force Fields: Between Intellectual History and Cultural Critique* (New York: Routledge, 1993), 147–57.

4. Leonard Neuger, "Polskość jako cel," *Teksty Drugie* 1/2 (1991): 15.

5. Witold Gombrowicz, *Dziennik (1961–1966)* (Paris: Instytut Literacki, 1966), 113.

6. Gombrowicz, *Dziennik (1961–1966),* 83.

7. Gombrowicz explains the circumstances of his arrival in Buenos Aires in *A Kind of Testament,* 83. This reflection on living in Buenos Aires "as if on the moon" comes from Gombrowicz, "Risum teneatis," *Listy 1950–1969* (Warszawa: Czytelnik, 1993), 455.

8. Gombrowicz, *Dziennik (1961–1966),* 82.

9. JanMohamed offers a brief typology of border intellectuals. The basis of distinction is the "intentionality of their intellectual orientation." While the syncretic intellectual is at home in both cultures and "is able to combine elements of the two cultures in order to articulate new syncretic

forms and experiences" (e.g. Chinua Achebe, Wole Soyinka, Salman Rushdie), the specular (e.g., Zora Neale Hurston, Edward W. Said, W. E. B. DuBois, Richard Wright), while being familiar with the two cultures, "is unable or unwilling to be at 'home' in these societies." Rather than combining cultures, such an intellectual subjects them to intellectual scrutiny. See Abdul JanMohamed, "Worldliness-without-World, Homelessness-as-Home: Toward a Definition of the Specular Border Intellectual," *Edward Said: A Critical Reader*, ed. Michael Sprinkler (Oxford: Blackwell, 1992), 96–120.

10. Traces of Gombrowicz's influence are visible in the work of Cuban writer and member of the "translation committee," Virgilio Piñera. On Piñera and Gombrowicz, see Daniel Balderston "Estética de la deformación en Gombrowicz y Piñera," *Explicación de textos literarios* 12 (1990/1991): 1–7.

11. *Biuletyn* was a quarterly first published in 1947 and devoted to the discussion of issues related to the services that El Banco Polaco provided to the Slav emigrants in Argentina. In order to attract their clients, El Banco first tried to appeal to their hearts, becoming in this way a kind of bridge between Argentine and Polish mentalities. Gombrowicz was in charge of this subtle mediation. See Jerzy Jarzębski, " 'Bankowe' " teksty Gombrowicza?" *Teksty Drugie* 5, (1991): 145–47.

12. Witold Gombrowicz, "Jak sobie wyobrażają Polskę Argentyńczycy?," *Teksty Drugie* 5 (1991): 152.

13. Gombrowicz, "Jak sobie wyobrażają Polskę Argentyńczycy?" 153.

14. Witold Gombrowicz, *Wspomnienia polskie Wędrówki po Argentynie.* (Warszawa: Res Publica, 1990*)*, 143.

15. Juan José Saer, "La perspectiva exterior: Gombrowicz en Argentina," *Punto de Vista* 35 (1989): 14.

16. Rita Gombrowicz's collection *Gombrowicz w Argentynie* (Gombrowicz in Argentina; Wrocław: Ossolineum, 1991) contains reflections from Gombrowicz's friends, their correspondence, and numerous pictures. In Alberto Fisherman's 1986 film *Gombrowicz o la seducción* (16 mm film; Buenos Aires, 1986), the Polish writer is evoked as a great *orientador* of the Argentine youth. Four of his friends, Mariano Betelú, Juan Carlos Gómez, Alejandro Rússovich, and Jorge di Paola discuss their relation to Gombrowicz in a highly stylized way, imitating him, impersonating him, or identifying with him. Germán Leopoldo García's *Gombrowicz: El estilo y la heráldica* (Buenos Aires: Atuel, 1992) is the only book-length critical piece on Gombrowicz. Touchingly chaotic, it is a suggestive piece, an act of Argentine invention of Gombrowicz. The book includes the most extensive bibliography of articles about Gombrowicz published in the Argentine press.

17. Quoted in Laura Ayerza de Castillo and Odilde Felgine, *Victoria Ocampo* (Barcelona: CIRCE, 1993), 247.

18. De Castillo and Felgine, *Victoria Ocampo,* 230.

19. Borges's response to this tension, for instance, produced proverbial, though somewhat surprising, hatred between the two writers. Gombrowicz's aversion to Borges lies in the supposed desire that Borges had to bring all the maturity of European culture to Argentina instead of choosing the productive immaturity of his native culture as a literary subject. Ricardo Piglia, however, suggests links between Gombrowicz and Borges (Piglia, "¿Existe la novela argentina? Borges y Gombrowicz," *Espacios de crítica y producción* 6 [1987]: 13–15). Both writers, he observes, share an interest in secondary literatures. Both ask—Borges in his essay "El escritor argentino y la tradición," *Obras completas,* vol. I (Buenos Aires: Emecé Editores, 1989), 267–74, Gombrowicz in *Ferdydurke, Trans-Atlantyk,* and *Diary*—similar questions: How to become universal living in the world's suburbs? How to free oneself from nationalism without ceasing to be "Argentine" or "Polish"? Should one be Polish (or "Argentine") or resign oneself to being "an European exile"?

20. For an overview of narrative during the military dictatorship see the following: Edna Aizenberg, "Kafka, Moyano, Piglia and the Semiotics of Antiauthoritarianism," *Discurso Literario* 2, (1985): 421–30; Francine Masiello, "La Argentina durante el Proceso: Las multiples resistencias," *Ficción y política: La narrativa argentina durante el proceso militar,* ed. Daniel Balderston et al. (Minneapolis: Institute for the Study of Ideologies and Literature/Alianza Editorial, 1987), 11–29; Masiello, "Cuerpo/presencia: Mujer y estado social en la narrativa argentina durante el proceso militar," *Nuevo Texto Crítico* 2, (1989): 155–72; Marta Morello-Frosch, "Ficción e historia en *Respiración artificial* de Ricardo Piglia," *Discurso Literario* 1, (1984): 243–55; Kathleen Newman, "The Argentine Political Novel: Determination in Discourse" diss., Stanford U, 1983; Johnny Payne, *Conquest of the New Word: Experimental Fiction and Translation in the Americas* (Austin: U of Texas P, 1993); Saúl Sosnowski, *Represión y reconstrucción de una cultura: El caso argentino* (Buenos Aires: Eudeba, 1988).

21. Ricardo Piglia (1941–) is an Argentine intellectual. His short story collection *La invasión* (1967) received the prestigious Casa de las Américas prize. In 1975, he published another collection of stories, *Nombre falso;* his novel *Respiración artificial* came out in 1982. As critic and essayist he has published numerous articles on Argentine writers (among others Domingo F. Sarmiento, Roberto Arlt, Jorge Luis Borges and Macedonio Fernández). In 1986, *Crítica y ficción* (a compilation of interviews and texts

about the poetics of narration) appeared (Santa Fe: Universidad Nacional del Litoral, 1986); in 1990, *Prisión perpetua,* a collection of stories (Buenos Aires: Editorial Sudamericana, 1990). His last novel, *La ciudad ausente,* was published in 1992 (Buenos Aires: Sudamericana, 1992).

22. Domingo Faustino Sarmiento (1811–88), president of the Argentine Republic (1868–74), was one of the most prominent Latin American nineteenth-century intellectuals. He was a comitted journalist, tireless autodidact, strong supporter of educational reforms, and a prolific writer. He kept up the promise of democracy by advocating the leadership of Buenos Aires' liberals in a representative government. He also linked together the possibility of democracy in Argentina with increased foreign investment and a reliance on European models that included arguing for immigration as a way of resolving demographic and economic problems. Echoing some of the principles of the Generation '37, he believed in the existence of a national elite endowed with superior qualities—racial and educational as well as economic—who rightfully direct the destiny of the nation.

23. Ricardo Piglia, *Artificial Respiration,* trans. Daniel Balderston (Durham: Duke UP, 1994), 238.

24. Raymond Williams, *The Sociology of Culture* (New York: Schocken, 1982), 187.

25. Michael Thompson, *Rubbish Theory: The Creation and Destruction of Value* (Oxford: Oxford UP, 1979), 116.

26. See Gombrowicz, *Dziennik (1953–1956),* 199–207. On the attitude of Gombrowicz toward Polish culture, see also Ewa M. Thompson, *Witold Gombrowicz* (Boston: Twayne, 1979), chapters 9–10.

27. Thompson, *Witold Gombrowicz,* 81.

28. Heinrich Wölfflin, *Renaissance and Baroque,* trans. Kathrin Simon (London: Collins, 1964), 14.

29. Neuger, "Polskość jako cel," 22–23.

30. Piglia, *Artificial Respiration,* 260.

31. Part of Argentine literary criticism's mission during this period was the preoccupation with educating the reader "how to read." Reader-response criticism was particualarly relevant, as explained in Masiello, "La Argentina durante el Proceso: Las multiples resistencias," 22.

32. Quoted in Analia Roffo, "Piglia y la reflexión literaria," *Redacción* 9 (1981): 70–71.

33. For an extended study of intertextual relations between Piglia's text and the works of Argentine novelists Juan Carlos Onetti and Roberto Arlt see José Sazbón, "La reflexión literaria," *Punto de vista* 4 (1981): 37–44.

34. Timothy Brennan, "The National Longing for Form," *Nation and Narration,* ed. Homi K. Bhabha (London: Routledge, 1990), 46.

35. Neil Larsen, *Modernism and Hegemony* (Minneapolis: U of Minnesota P, 1990), 79.

36. Larsen, *Modernism and Hegemony,* 81.

Piotr Parlej

6

Gombrowicz, Dialectically Speaking:

Of Lyricisms, Dissidents, and Politics

In the opening pages of *Ferdydurke,* the protagonist finds himself in the nightmare of being back in school in his thirties. During the Polish literature class, he witnesses a scene between a visiting school superintendent and a student by the name of Gałkiewicz, in which the latter is asked to explain to other students why he admires the great Polish romantic poet Juliusz Słowacki. Perplexed, angry, and inarticulate because of the gush of powerful but renegade emotion, Gałkiewicz exclaims, to the collective shock of the class: "But I do not admire! I cannot admire! I cannot!"[1]

The scene has gained considerable notoriety in the wide reception of Witold Gombrowicz as the destroyer of Polish national idols, icons, creeds, and myths; it has become the mantra—in popular perception—of open rebellion against and attack on a certain tradition of Polish literature as a servant of patriotism. However, besides offering the reader an original perspective on patriotic feeling, and besides tantalizing him with its provocative eloquence, this passage also points to a systematic direction in Gombrowicz's general views on (Polish) literature. Even a casual reading of his *Diary* will reveal that Gombrowicz is skeptical and suspicious of poets and of poetry; hence it is not only Słowacki, and Polish romanticism, that gets short shrift, but a certain idea of poetry in general.[2]

What comes under attack in this systematic posture, I want to argue, is the predominant understanding of poetry as the domain of lyricism, as pure sentiment, or, more precisely, as a lyricism purged of dialectic. Gombrowicz has caused controversy among his compatriots not only because he frequently attacks and sometimes overturns national idols and offends patriotic sensibilities, but also because he adopts the dialectical method as his method of practicing art. This choice has proved controversial to many: to the general reading public, partly because it smelled of anachronism, of a musty Hegelianism, and partly because dialectic has been discredited in principle as the discourse of choice of Poland's Marxist politicians and intellectuals; to Polish dissident writers, because they sought to counteract official art by resorting to pure lyricism, by understanding authenticity independently of dialectic; and, finally, to the Communist Party officials, not only because the dialectic that Gombrowicz developed was deviant from the point of view of Marxist dialectical materialism, but also because it allowed the artist to forge an avant-garde art with a method supposedly destined to promote the goals of a proletarian revolution. In a word, if Gombrowicz managed to offend practically everybody, it was because of a deplorable programmatic distrust of dialectic in Polish culture.

Gombrowicz is able to cause stir in virtually all quarters because he remains a remarkable exception to the national anti-dialectical sentiment; and his work is all the more remarkable in that the original interpretation of dialectic as a creative method, developed at the time of *Ferdydurke* to accommodate the demands—and cut through the flabby surface—of Polish modernist aesthetics, has preserved its sharp edge when confronted with the stiff, simplistic aesthetics of official communist art in postwar Poland. Gombrowicz's dialectic could accomplish this difficult task perhaps because—whether on the right or on the left—modernism tended to politics, according to the mechanism systematized so eloquently by Walter Benjamin. In order to discuss the case of Gombrowicz, we must sketch the historical contexts of this relation in more detail.

One of modernism's distinguishing traits is that it has discovered a close affinity between art and (radical) politics—and, more often than not, has put this affinity into practice. Certainly, earlier ages were aware of this relationship, but modernism seems to be the first to have explicitly argued for a certain *necessity* of this transaction. The affinity between the aesthetic and the political posture—and we can observe its inauspicious but symptomatic origins in Italian futurism, for example—arises from the desire for authenticity.

But here the issue becomes complicated. Whether a "true" discourse or, as Theodor Adorno puts it, a mere "jargon," authenticity as a vehicle of art has seduced, or attracted, to politics such otherwise diverse thinkers as—on the left—Benjamin, Brecht, Bataille, Malraux, and Sartre and—on the right—Hamsun, Benn, Pound, Blanchot, and Céline.[3] Whence derives the powerful force of this attraction, one responsible for what Frank Kermode has called "the modern apocalypse"?[4] One way to account for the source of this attraction would be to speculate that art and politics share a common component by virtue of which an artist can become a politician and vice versa. To use Plato's model, both the poet and the statesman claim the right to rule the Republic; the very fact that the statesman controls the state, and excludes the poet from the public realm, proves that he considers the poet a legitimate, and very dangerous, rival. At this point we confront one of the central problems of modern philosophy, the problem of how these two metaphysical *offices* are related to each other. Here the historical modernism has remained faithful to the legacy of speculative philosophy, including its classical origins in Plato's dialectic: the dialectical requirement that identity become its opposite in order to come into its own. Underlying the question of truth (politics) and beauty (art) is the status, form, and efficacy of the dialectical method. Let us examine one pertinent example from this tradition.

Truth stands over untruth—truth is dialectical. Just because of this dialectical moment, however, untruth resides in truth; such is the case, for instance, when something only appears to be true—this is the case of ideology. The task of convincingly demonstrating the difference between true philosophy (critical philosophy) and mere ideology (a philosophy that appeals to truth rather than accounting for it) has preoccupied Immanuel Kant. As Paul de Man argues, however, the difference remains, in Kant, what it had already been for Socrates—an infinite division without term. Moreover, the appeal to a "critical" philosophy itself presupposes a true moment, which either begs the question or else repeats the initial fallacy.[5] To avoid this deadlock an *untrue* moment must be assumed as a necessary component of this infinite process.

In other words, the problem with dialectic is that it necessitates a further distinction into good and bad dialectic in what amounts to an infinite regress or, in Kantian terms, to an asymptotic striving without resolution. When practiced in this fashion, dialectic can offer fascinating avenues and lead to intriguing, if radically new and unexpected, constructions (for example, Hegel's distinction between good and bad infinity, which claims to have gone beyond Kant's asymptotic irresolution; or Martin Heidegger's distinction, in *Being and Time,* between authenticity and inauthenticity in which the two terms coexist in a complex mutual genealogy and interdependence). It is possible and tempting, however, to resolve this endless process and bring it to a halt; here the bid to validate true philosophy deliberately ignores the circularity of "critique" described by Paul de Man and brings the interminable process to an arbitrary conclusion: the dialectical process is rescued by what I want to call a "lyrical" gesture (by no means restricted to the poet). And it is this attempt to escape from infinite regress, I would like to propose, that defines the distinctive trait of modernism. Faithful to Shelley's claim that poets are "the unacknowledged legislators of the world," modernist authors assume the office of the politician; bent on achieving "authenticity," they attempt either to resolve dialectic lyrically (W. B. Yeats, D. H. Lawrence) or else to impose a dialectical interpretation on lyricism (Ezra Pound, T. S. Eliot). The discovery—but also the trap—of modernism is its belief that dialectic can be supplemented with emotion, and emotion with dialectic, and that, consequently, authenticity is a stable concept that supervises and organizes these building blocks into a condition of suitable equilibrium.

The thought of Witold Gombrowicz offers an engaging, creative, and instructive treatment of the modernist dilemma, and this for two reasons. First, during his modernist phase, beginning with *Ferdydurke,* Gombrowicz registers the vagaries of authenticity in the specific case of the "modern apocalypse" in Poland; second, in his later writings, most notably in his *Diary,* Gombrowicz develops an original model of dialectic that underlies his model of authenticity, a particularly delicate task to undertake when the opponent is official dialectical doctrine and the threat a socialist realist Polish art based on it.

In what follows I would like to examine several well-known "concepts" from Gombrowicz's vocabulary—*młodość* (youth), *heraldyka* (heraldry), *brzydota* (ugliness), *forma* (form), and *gęba* (mug)—on the assumption that for these and other terms Gombrowicz undertakes to reinterpret their dialectical structure and to bring out their postdialectical implications. In the second place, I want to describe the role this reinterpretation played in Gombrowicz's polemic with state Marxism in Poland and with Polish dissident writers: more specifically, I will present some possibilities of critique that Gombrowicz's dialectic creates when it is used to scrutinize the predominant tendency among Polish writers to resist a monolithic dialectic with an equally monolithic lyricism (the Juliusz Słowacki syndrome).

After a period of considerable popularity in the modernist episode, dialectic receded as a dominant force in Polish letters, to re-appear only after the Second World War. When it did return, however, it did so with official state encouragement, which later—in the early 1950s—turned into obligation and coercion. It is in this context that one should place the fate of dialectics in Polish art, especially the choice in favor of the lyrical option among the majority of Polish poets confronted with the politicized aesthetics of socialist realism. Polish postwar poetry furnishes ample testimony of this encounter with the treacherous dissimulation between dialectic and totalitarianism, and the record tells a story of an agonizing, convoluted, and often confused battle to sort the two out.

To resist the seduction, Zbigniew Herbert, for instance, finds it enough to appeal to "good taste," a reaction consistent with Herbert's classicism as expressed in the praise of the symbols of the Enlightenment in "An Elegy on the Departure of Pen, Ink and Lamp."[6] In the poem "The Power of Taste," dedicated to Professor Izydora Dąmbska, Herbert praises the dignity with which renowned Polish scientists refused to sponsor the party doctrine. When Herbert explains that, simply put, "it was a matter of taste" to see through the crudeness of Communist discourse, firstly, he is asserting a vast, although subtle, qualitative superiority of those who have a modicum of taste over those who have none (Communism, Herbert explains, expresses itself in a grammar that would surely manage to offend the Latin masters of oratory, style, and linguistic purity); secondly, he believes that all that is necessary to unmask the sham of the totalitarian system is this minimal aesthetic, or even social, refinement and grace; finally, Herbert claims, taste is sufficient to evaluate the quality of the idea that propelled the Communist project.[7]

In another poem, however, Herbert himself considerably undermines the ability of "taste" and the "beauty of the subjunctive" to resist the totalitarian opponent. In "Livy's Metamorphoses" (*Elegia na odejście*) he meditates about his grandfather studying, as a young boy in the Austro-Hungarian empire, the beauty of Latin syntax. Herbert reflects that as he learned Latin, the grandfather might have been inhaling poisonous vapors as much as stylistic elegance. For the purpose of classical education is ostensibly to educate in taste and refinement, especially in the realm of linguistic finesse. Herbert intimates, however, that the texts used for this purpose subtly promote the ideological interests of the Empire. In other words, "the beauty of the subjunctive" delights the mind even as it legitimizes official doctrine. The "good taste" which founds the classicist unity of form and content at the same time proves Herbert's undoing, because in itself taste is indifferent: form and content can be separated, and stylistically beautiful grammar can be attached to ethically questionable political designs. Caught in this trap, Herbert's Mr. Cogito assumes the sublime vantage point of self-objectification ("Mr. Cogito's Calendars")[8] from which the past appears as nothing more than a collection of themes and lessons for posterity, and which refines physical reality out of existence: "The most beautiful is the object / which does not exist."[9]

Let us look briefly at the case of Adam Zagajewski. In contrast to Herbert, Zagajewski admits to a short period of active participation in political life, an activism which he attributes to the tendency of youth to mix art with politics, to "(seek)/justice, confusing it with beauty."[10] In "Fire," for example, he speaks with horror of the creative impulse that has the combined potential to inspire us to write books and to burn them (*Tremor*). Despite this difference, Zagajewski, like Herbert, relies on lyricism when faced with official art, in a reaction canonized by Adam Ważyk's classic of political disillusionment, "Poem for Adults" (*Poemat dla dorosłych,* 1956), in which he speaks of a "naked poem," not affected (*obrośnięty,* "overgrown") by the complexities of life.[11] (The case of Ważyk is perhaps the paradigmatic instance of the process that forms the background for the present argument. A poet who lyrically supported Marxism now resorts to lyricism to reject it. The hidden dialectical complicity—and possibility—remains unacknowledged and unexplored.) Herbert finds authenticity in "the garden of childhood" ("Elegy" [*Elegia na odejście*]) and in the "Clouds over Ferrara" (*Rovigo*), symbols of truth sheltered from dialectical corruption in a cocoon of lyrical immediacy. In a similar fashion, Zagajewski in his manifesto, *Reality Not Represented* (1974), calls for a return to the simple reality outside the official party language of "Plans, Reports";[12] like Herbert, he places his trust in direct experiences—"fresh morning, trees,"[13] the innocence of "children and cats."[14]

These examples may help bring the point of the argument into sharper focus. It seems that the lyrical option carries within it the potential to trivialize a poet's encounter with a politicized aesthetics precisely because it tends to trivialize dialectic itself. One may well be led to doubt the validity of a lyricism used, if ever so slightly, for extrinsic ends (here, against totalitarian discourse) and to suspect that this lyricism will neither successfully oppose the enemy nor attain to pure lyricism. Such poetry runs the risk of paying the highest price for its magisterial stance: the risk of repressing creative ferment, externalizing inner tension, and filling the resulting vacuum with imaginary tokens of immediacy. One has reasons to worry about the strength of the "tower of classicism" in which lyrical poets are "barricaded" (as Gombrowicz puts it speaking of the Polish poet Jan Lechoń) (*Dz* VII, 155).

The frailty of this tower emerges with alarming urgency in Herbert's poem "Three Studies on the Subject of Realism."[15] In this poem Herbert helplessly watches socialist realism assume equal status in painting along British landscape painting and Dutch naturalism, and he is forced to concede a high degree of resemblance—if not essential identity—between classicist realism and the crude realism of official ideology (or at least to admit his inability adequately to explain the relevant—*the capital*—difference). Still, he opts for classicism even if it means accepting this repulsive affinity, for he finds the alternative, that is, revolutionary, nonrepresentational art, in principle unacceptable, on the erroneous assumption that revolutionary art is *necessarily* totalitarian, collective, or else empty and formalistic. Gombrowicz's impatience with poetry as lyricism would be inflamed in the face of such carefully calculated—or desperately transacted—accommodations, maneuvers, and, perhaps, resignations.

Zagajewski is more flexible when faced with this confusing proximity of art and politics, possibly because he has tasted a bit of the seduction. In a short essay "Everything" (*Solidarność i samotność*) he reminisces how, as a young poet, he used to meet with other young poets to dream about a "poetry of everything." Here and elsewhere Zagajewski recognizes and concedes the revolutionary and total ("everything") claim of art, when he speaks of a "force" that moves the world of plants, that animates Napoleon's conquering armies, and that impels the world of the poem. In the last case, however, the case of poetry, Zagajewski makes a telling exception—in poetry the "force" is "very still" ("That Force," *Tremor*). Not only is the efficacy of poems comparable to that of military might, and not only is the difference one of mere degree, but also—and here art and politics mix beyond distinction—the poet treats the poem as a site of *power,* both in the sense of art's creativity and in that of sheer physicality.

However, having confronted art's dialectical exigency, Zagajewski does not take the final step and, instead, attempts to delimit art's dangerous ambivalence by retreating into classicist objectivity. In the poem "A River" Zagajewski firmly and decisively separates the creative fruitfulness of art's own self-engendering from its "secular," or "instrumental" counterpart, the creativity of the self-manifestation of power as power ("A River," *Tremor*). The two worlds, of art and of war, are securely separated by "an indifferent wave" of a stream of water, a buffer zone that precludes the commingling and the confusion of the two distinct realms. The classicist moment of this solution lies in the assumption that one can bend dialectic to one's will, that one can have both ironic distance and lyrical immediacy: "A poem grows on contradiction but it can't cover it" ("Ode to Plurality," *Tremor;* instead of rendering *"jej nie zarasta"* as "it can't cover it," one can also translate this—with a possibly significant change in meaning—as "does not cover it"). The passage is ambiguous in that it recognizes the potential of dialectic ("a poem grows on contradiction") and even allows dialectic to retain a measure of autonomy (the poem "can't cover it"); at the same time, however, in a complex moment, it is unclear whether the lyrical sensibility leaves dialectic behind as an inferior stage, or whether dialectic is recognized as an equal partner in a process of creation composed of two sources, one lyrical, the other dialectical. At any rate, the phrase confirms Kierkegaard's lesson for modernity: our essence dominates us as much as we dominate it—thinking thinks us, and feeling feels us, as much as we think and feel them.[16]

Czesław Miłosz recognizes the profound measure of this complexity in his reflections on the nature of poetry.[17] In an early fragment of his C. E. Norton lectures that has not, perhaps, received sufficient attention, Miłosz discusses an episode of his political activism, his involvement in the leftist poetic movement "Żagary." The significance of this episode lies in the contradiction between poetic and revolutionary hope, or the mystical and historical concerns of the poet. At one point in the argument Miłosz identifies poetic hope with the dynamics of history and revolution, while at another point he passionately protests his classicist affiliation. The conflict between the dialectical and the lyrical option is presented in the poem "No More," which, in the author's own exegesis, attempts shrewdly to evade the issue in a series of ironic positionings that mediate the desire to achieve realism and the impossibility of achieving it. Miłosz experiences the conflicting demands of lyricism and dialectic under the emblems of classicism and romanticism, in an impossible attempt to mediate history (dialectic) with form (lyricism) that ends in a stalemate of formalism ("No More"). Miłosz stops short of making a definitive breakthrough in a brief digression about a possibility of open-ended dialectic that makes room for lyricism in the "noneschatological" poetry of ancient China. But, he skeptically observes, this poetry is, at best, an inaccurate, historically filtered, and distorted conjecture.[18]

Here we arrive at the decisive crossroads in the argument. The lyrical quality invoked by many Polish writers in their rejection of politicized aesthetics stands in sharp contrast to the aesthetic value invoked by Gombrowicz. The difference between Herbert/Zagajewski/Miłosz and Gombrowicz reflects the contrast between an aesthetics that controls, delimits, resists, or otherwise qualifies the dialectical dimension, and an aesthetics that recognizes the formative power of this dimension, one that surrenders all possibility of complete objectification, adequate representation, or exhaustive accounting. The significance of this difference as the defining "fault line" in modern Polish literature is acknowledged in Zagajewski's concept of hierarchical and anarchic currents, with Herbert representing the former and Miron Białoszewski the latter.[19] Gombrowicz captures the difference with his *terminus technicus "młodość"* (youth). Youth is a postdialectical formation able to cultivate art's dialectical roots without degenerating into rigid doctrine and without collapsing into stagnant lyricism.

What is youth according to Gombrowicz? Youth is not an idealistic stage destined for transition to adult disillusionment; the dialectic in question does not bring forth the adult out of the youth but inverts this derivation and leaves it structurally open-ended, exacerbating the adult's eternal dependence on the youth: maturity is "podszyta"—[padded with] immaturity. In other words, there are two possible relations between youth and maturity, and two accounts of creative experience. On the one hand, when youth "supplements the Incomplete with Completion" (*D* II, 200) [młodość uzupełnia Pełnię Niepełnią] (*Dz* VII, 208), in a "dialectic Completion-Incompletion, Value-Nonvalue" (*D* II, 206) [dialektyka Pełnia-Niepełnia, Wartość-Niedowartość] (*Dz* VII, 214), life regains its full vibrancy and authenticity.[20] "There where the child ends and the adult does not yet begin, there, from the fourteenth to twenty-fourth year, man is given his time to blossom. This is the only time of complete beauty in man. There is in humanity a refuge of immortal beauty and grace, but—too bad, too bad!—it is tied to youth" (*D* III, 150).

On the other hand, when youth is subordinated to maturity, the relation to life and values is falsified. And it is here that Gombrowicz's critique of youth bears on socialist realism and its feeble dialectic with greatest impact. Gombrowicz clarifies this relation in the notorious essay "Sienkiewicz" (*D* I, 223–30; *Dz* VI, 292–301). The essay criticizes Polish literature for falsifying, beginning with mid-eighteenth century, its relation to youth. Polish literature is a project in "producing beauty" [wytwarzanie urody], that is, hastily "equating" it with virtue (*D* I, 223–24; *Dz* VI, 293). The tendency to base beauty exclusively on virtue was solidified by Mickiewicz, whose "Ode to Youth" (Oda do młodości), seemingly a praise of spontaneity, in fact subordinated youthful beauty to adult beauty. "[O]ne could say that this is still a literature of the fathers and it is not the young man that fascinates Mickiewicz, it is the man or a young man having the requirements for a man" (*D* I, 226). Sienkiewicz's novels inherit and reinforce the theory of the "likable sin, decent sin, charming sin, 'pure' sin" (*D* I, 227), they perpetuate the ideal of the robust, rosy-cheeked Polish youth vulnerable only to the most innocent of vices. As a result of this national mystification, Polish spirit, "not being saturated enough with sin" (*D* I, 224), has "blurred . . . all the antinomies with which a serious literature bleeds" (*D* I, 227). This is why "a more real, more authentic Polish beauty does not exist. Neither beauty, nor form, nor style" (*D* I, 229) [prawdziwej, autentycznej piękności polskiej dotąd nie ma. Ani piękności, ani formy, ani stylu] (*Dz* VI, 300). Poles can "settle down to themselves" only if they "dare reveal Polish sins and Polish ugliness" (*D* I, 229).

It is generally accepted that in this provocative, if not devastating and merciless, critique of Polish sensibility Gombrowicz targets a certain national cult, fetish, or idol (emotional partriotism, myth of national innocence, a naive idealism that constitutes Poland's collective existence). If this is so, however, the interpretation risks a certain hypocrisy. Put differently, while most commentators accept Gombrowicz's critique of national idealism, they are reluctant to apply it to an idealism employed in the laudable, noble task of resisting a materialist, crude, and antispiritual ideological system. It is necessary, I would like to propose, to recognize that Gombrowicz's essay calls into question not only a certain idealism from the past but also this idealism's contemporary manifestation. The essay on Sienkiewicz not only exposes a historically established syndrome of false national sensibility; it also, firstly, establishes a connection between false virtue and the relative popularity (or *draw*) of inauthentic aesthetics of socialist realism, and, secondly and most pertinently for Poland's modern history, it establishes a sobering connection between this false sensibility and the rejection of socialist realism in the name of lyricism by Polish dissident writers. In other words, Gombrowicz is telling us that both the limited *popularity* of socialist realism among Polish poets (Gałczyński, Szymborska, Woroszylski, Ważyk, and many others) and the predominant strategy of its *rejection in the lyrical option* are symptoms of the same national malaise. All countries, without exception, are affected by a false moment; and everywhere in the world bad dialectic (ideology) seeks out such falsities with the intention to implant itself on them. In the case of Poland—Gombrowicz says, concluding his essay on Sienkiewicz—socialist realism found friendly ground in the cult of the soft sin, because socialist realism itself is a system of false beauty and feeble virtue: "In Poland today, more than ever, the Polish masses are choking in the muzzle of an artificial aesthetics imposed on them in the name of proletarian virtue" (*D* I, 230). Moreover, ideology finds ever more subtle ways to adjust to the native falsity: *even when it is rejected,* it allows itself to be rejected in the name of values that do not directly invalidate ideological dissimulation. As such an impotent weapon, these noble values may remain harmless and ineffective. In sum, socialist realism enters with an unexpectedly but also disturbingly snug fit a systematic history of inauthentic experience of values that has determined Polish culture since the period of Saxon kings (*D* I, 224; *Dz* VI, 294).

This is why—we may observe parenthetically—according to Gombrowicz rigorous avoidance of falsity, while indispensable for both good art and ethical life, must first occur in the domain of art. It is instructive that, writing from Argentina to his fellow intellectuals tested by the totalitarian challenge, Gombrowicz was less busy attacking the system than chastising the artists and admonishing them to preserve the purity of art. At one point he charges dissident artists with four errors: (1) they exaggerate the demon of communism—it is trivial compared to the terror of existence; (2) by reducing the problem to the antinomy between the East and the West, they simplify and schematize—a capital sin for an artist; (3) they are tempted by communism to assume the collective voice (in defense of values) and this is already its triumph; (4) they analyze the present, but since art is by nature future-oriented and prophetic, even precise analyses of today's world are essentially incompatible with art's long-term mission (cf. *D* I, 17–18; *Dz* VI, 28).

But here, at the heart of Gombrowicz's enterprise, where authenticity meets dialectics, we reach a potential impasse. At this point it is easy to accuse Gombrowicz of being inconsistent. How can he appeal to a solid core of authenticity when he has said that the self is constructed on a divergence between man and form, that it is "deformed" (*D* II, 226; *Dz* VII, 234) into a "mug" "beyond [which one] has no face" (*D* II, 4) [poza nią nie ma żadnej twarzy] (*Dz* VII, 10–11)? How can he speak of authenticity when he maintains that the only authenticity available to us is "the admission that honesty is inaccessible to me" (*D* II, 4)? How can he demystify national inauthenticity if his own philosophy denies authenticity? How can he criticize the artificiality of Polish sensibility and of communist doctrine in the name of deeply personal and individual nature of art when he himself maintains that "thought and feeling entirely 'my own' do not exist for me. There is artificiality in even the most intimate reflexes" (*D* I, 192)? What are we to make of this contradiction?

One can interrogate Gombrowicz even further, by expanding the problem from the field of literature to the problem of the relation between Gombrowicz's dialectical conception of Form and politics. If I claim that life is intrinsically inauthentic, why then am I offended by the inauthentic communist aesthetics? Gombrowicz writes: "In that case, why does the falsity and artificiality of man, submitted to Communism, disturb me? What interferes with my acknowledging that this is exactly how it should be?" (*D* I, 192). Unlike dissident writers in Poland (although a recently published correspondence between Czesław Miłosz and Melchior Wańkowicz reveals the intellectual and emotional agonies over dialectic of a rare order), Gombrowicz has repeatedly confronted this perplexing question openly: If art is revolutionary, what stops me from joining the party? For, I agree with communism that man is socially conditioned, that the individual is but a product of interhuman mediation, a mere toy of Form. In short, what is the difference between revolution in politics and revolution in art?

To address this inconsistency Gombrowicz gives the following example. If, one morning, we were to grow a second head "out of our rear," both heads would insist on being authentic (*D* II, 226). In other words, authenticity is not a constituted and stable fund of identifying features but a process of perpetual insistence, constant litigation by the self *that it be* a self. The self is authentic only in being dominated, tormented, and defined (de-formed) by Form. The model presents "an elusive man who is a play of contradictions, a fountain of gushing antinomies and a system of infinite compensation" (*D* I, 30).

Both the role of authenticity in the constitution of the artistic and ethical self in Gombrowicz and the contradictions that his concept of authenticity provokes must be examined as part of Gombrowicz's original reinterpretation of dialectic. It may be of help to cast a quick glance at Gombrowicz's use of heraldry. Another *terminus technicus,* heraldry is for him the concrete symbol of the in itself pure and empty chain which conditions the self, erases its autonomy, and prevents it from recuperating itself in simple reflection. In confrontation with this ominous force all names fail, all language crumbles: "Socrealism? Surrealism? The avant-garde? The proletariat? Poetry? Art? No. A forest of genealogical trees and we under them, sitting in their shade" (*D* I, 47).

Modeled on the French tradition of Rabelais and Montaigne (*Dz* VI, 41), Gombrowicz's art is open to the tradition's modern and postmodern continuators—Rousseau, Foucault, and Lacan. When he exclaims: "O human being—be a human being!" [*Człowieku, bądź człowiekiem!*], or when he states that "man does not have form—man makes form," Gombrowicz sets in motion a mechanism of supplementation and of sliding of the familiar substances, terms, and ontologies.[21] Such summons resemble the movement of self-constitution and self-surpassment found in Kant (the self-constitution of the subject in "I think"), and in Nietzsche ("the art of becoming what we already are"). When he summons each and every "human being" to be "a human being," Gombrowicz invokes a tradition of humanism inaugurated by Kant's critical philosophy. This humanism originates in Kant's notion of pure space: if man makes form, what is there anterior to the form in which the human (form) might properly appear? The anterior emptiness invites a transcendental inquiry into the concrete system of completion, supplementation, and compensation that might bring this formative process to a conclusion (for example, the romantic solution of Fichte and Friedrich Schlegel). Like Martin Heidegger's *Dasein* from *Being and Time,* this humanism seeks to circumvent the familiar notions of the subject in the anthropological sense: the new subject always already exists in excess of whatever cognitive forms are available to it in its conscious modality.[22] In other words, Gombrowicz's appeal to authenticity does not invoke a preexisting fund of value; rather, authenticity comes into being in and as this appeal, in the "play of contradictions" that unfolds indefinitely and unpredictably. Most importantly, the self that emerges out of this "play" is always something more and/or less than authentic, it creates the authentic/inauthentic matrix on which it, as its original creator, leaves only an elusive trace. Anterior to the (in)authentic self is the "mug," *pure, form-less form.*

"Youth" supplies the framework for art based on the "play of contradictions." Youth is "a value in itself, that is, a destroyer of all other values, which are not necessary to it because it is self-sufficient" (*D* I, 130). As self-sufficient, not referable to other markers, youth denotes the condition, or moment, anterior to any act of valuation, constitution, self-presence, or systematic interrelation. In this "transvaluation of all values" Gombrowicz realizes a unique possibility first opened up by Nietzsche's attempt to separate the notion of value from equivalence and exchange, and to develop a new concept, standing outside of metaphysics, that would be an absolute, that is, a value-in-itself. Gombrowicz finds the historical instances of this absolute value (youth) in the art of Greece—and while this appeal to (neo)classicism may seem inconsistent, it invokes not the Apollonian clarity so dear to Herbert but the Dionysian aspect of Greece (*D* I, 183); Gombrowicz also finds it in Renaissance painting and in the image of youth in *Romeo and Juliet* (*D* I, 226). The distinctive characteristic of an art based on the irreducible power of youth is that it is produced instinctively: "[Rabelais] wrote the way a child pees against a tree, in order to relieve himself" (*D* I, 57). It is precisely this artistic abandon that makes art revolutionary: "How does one resist a revolution if it endows us with meaning, our own meaning?" (*D* I, 191) [Jak opierać się rewolucji, gdy ona nadaje nam sens, nasz własny sens]? (*Dz* VI, 250).

It is in this sense that Gombrowicz accepts what Herbert fears and rejects—the program of revolution for, and as, art. And it is in this sense that revolutionary, or, as Zagajewski says, "elastic" art[23] has the authority to reproach both doctrine and lyricism with overlooking the power of dialectic. This is not to say that Gombrowicz underestimates communism and treats it as mere ideology. On the contrary, he calls on Polish literature to enter into a debate with existentialism and with what he termed "theoretical Marxism," for such a debate offers an excellent opportunity for (Polish) art to purge itself of superficiality and mobilize its inner resources (*D* I, 167–68; *Dz* VII, 175). In the final analysis, however, this vigilant supervision of dialectic must be cultivated, not for the sake of maintaining a *"dialog"* with Marxism or strengthening the nation's moral fiber, but for the sake of preserving artistic integrity against traps that come from all directions: on the one hand, communism constantly threatens to convert the artist's open-ended dialectic into rigid dogma, to convert the problematic conscience of the artist into the categorical conscience of the party functionary (*Dz* VI, 254); on the other hand, lyricism—that is, the belief that one can do without mediation—is always susceptible to the seduction, as in the case of Herbert's grandfather, by "the charms of the subjunctive," and it can always begin to ring as false as bad dialectic itself.[24]

It is this neglect of dialectic that accounts for the unfortunate collusion, exposed by the essay on Sienkiewicz, between Poland's infantile avoidance of negative values and the naive optimism of communist ideology. Equally disastrously, if more subtly, the programmatic choice of the lyric over dialectic perpetuates, and perhaps encourages, this intriguing complicity between a national and a utopian falsification of virtue that comes close to turning, in a Polish fashion, the modernist dream of authenticity into the nationalistic/ideological fascination. As for Gombrowicz, he cannot become fascinated with realism, socialist or otherwise, because he treats dialectic, and the authenticity based on it, far more seriously than any party line would allow.[25]

But the price of this freedom is the inability to be infatuated pure and simple—a resistance to both dialectical closure and lyrical transport. Gombrowicz's conceptions of dialectic and of art exhibit a structure similar to the inversions we have identified in his discussion of authenticity and inauthenticity, of youth as the absolute value, and of completion and incompletion. Dialectic and lyricism supplement each other, always guarding their respective place in the totality claimed by the other exclusively for itself. Because dialectic lacks lyricism, lyricism remains within—but outside—dialectic to guarantee the latter's meaning; it remains neither here nor there, and this u-topian placement is articulated as lyricism. Conversely, what is missing from lyricism can only come to surface dialectically. In either case, something always speaks as the index of the constant externality that orchestrates each saying.

According to Frank Kermode, of the major representatives of high modernism only James Joyce managed to avoid the modernist trap of politicized aesthetics. Beginning with *Ulysses,* Joyce persistently refused to subject the empirical world to an ordering paradigm, to sacrifice the phenomena at the altar of an ideal construct. In *Ulysses* Joyce patiently records the entire empirical universe, resisting a narrative, philosophical, linguistic, symbolic, allegorical, or perspectival synthesis. The patient using up of dialectic (if it is dialectic) does not yield a cumulative result but only calls up an aggregate of examples of empirical reality; these instances of the mundane are no longer random, but they do not yet constitute a systematic "world" either. In a model of local universality, Joyce "shows us fiction fitting where it touches."[26] Gombrowicz belongs to the tradition of such resistance to dialectical closure; together with Joyce, Adorno ("negative dialectic"), Bataille ("eroticism"), Blanchot ("neuter"), he labors to fashion a place of otherness out of the seemingly unproblematic calculus of the negative and the positive. Up to a point, his endless dialectic operates in terms of and within the symbolic order of language, sign, and meaning. Up to a point, for example, it operates in the matrix of youth and adulthood, but within this structure, "there where the child ends and the adult does not yet begin," Gombrowicz finds a moment absolutely anterior and irreducible to the binary framework. Similarly, Gombrowicz works, up to a point, with the system of heraldic reference, with "the forest of genealogical trees." But on the periphery of this "forest," under the trees, "in their shade," he finds a hidden "place" of respite and toil, origin and disappearance, creation and loss. This moment of non-dialectical occurrence is a divergence, a loophole, or a "miss," "all that 'goes by,' including that which is the ultimate secret of art" [rozminięcie, które jest ostatecznym sekretem sztuki] (*D* III, 30; *Dz* VIII, 37). It is one of the consequences of this "miss" that Gombrowicz can be dialectical, lyrical, authentic, Polish—only by not being so, or at least by not being *completely* dialectical, lyrical, authentic, or Polish—and that in this *not-completely-being* consists his art, that is, his mug, his coat of arms, and his youth.

Notes

1. The text is a paraphrase of a longer section, which can be found in *F*, 46.

2. For the English version of the *Diary* I will refer to the text as edited by Jan Kott and translated by Lillian Valee in 3 vols. (Evanston: Northwestern UP, 1988–93). For the Polish version of the *Diary*, I will refer to *Dziennik* in the Paris edition of Gombrowicz's collected works, vol. VI, (1953–56), 1971; vol. VII (1957–61), 1962; and vol. VIII (1961–66), 1966 (Paryż: Instytut Literacki). References to the Polish version will be marked as *Dz*.

3. Philippe Lacoue-Labarthe, *Heidegger: Art and Politics*, trans. Chris Turner (Cambridge: Blackwell, 1990), 22.

4. Frank Kermode, *The Sense of an Ending* (New York: Oxford UP, 1967), 93–124.

5. Paul de Man, "Phenomenality and Materiality in Kant," in *Hermeneutics: Questions and Prospects*, ed. Gary Shapiro and Alan Sica (Amherst: U of Massachusetts P, 1984), 121–44; 122–24.

6. Zbigniew Herbert, *Elegia na odejście* (Paryż: Instytut Literacki, 1990).

7. Zbigniew Herbert, *Report from the Besieged City and Other Poems*, trans. John Carpenter and Bogdana Carpenter (New York: Ecco, 1983), 69–70; 69.

8. Zbigniew Herbert, *Rovigo* (Wrocław: Wydawnictwo Dolnośląskie, 1992).

9. Zbigniew Herbert, "Study of the Object," *Postwar Polish Poetry: An Anthology*, ed. Czesław Miłosz (Berkeley: U of California P, 1983), 134.

10. Adam Zagajewski, "Lightning," *Tremor: Selected Poems*, trans. Renata Gorczynski (New York: Farrar, 1985).

11. Adam Ważyk, *Poemat dla dorosłych i inne wiersze* (1956). In *Introduction to Modern Polish Literature: An Anthology of Fiction and Poetry,* ed. Adam Gillon and Ludwik Krzyzanowski (New York: Twayne, 1964), 463 (trans. Paul Mayewski).

12. Adam Zagajewski, *Oda do wielości* (Paryż: Instytut Literacki, 1983), 12 (trans. mine).

13. Adam Zagajewski, *Solidarność i samotność* (Paryż: Zeszyty Literackie, 1986), 60 (trans. mine).

14. Adam Zagajewski, *Dwa miasta* (Kraków: Oficyna Literacka, 1991), 22 (trans. mine).

15. Zbigniew Herbert, *Hermes, pies, i gwiazda* (Warsaw, 1957).

16. The insistence of the word *rosnąć* (to grow), here and in Ważyk's poem, points to a certain domination of dialectic in poetic thought. Indicating both passive and active stance (to grow, to be grown), implying a spread that is both that of a weed and a plant, and, finally, imposing a controlled and an uncontrolled expansion, growing feeds what is to grow and is the thing that does the growing; effectively, growth is pure activity that can neither *obrosnąć* (grow into—Ważyk) nor *zarosnąć* (cover—Zagajewski) itself or the plant. Put simply, growing grows on you.

17. Czesław Miłosz, *The Witness of Poetry: The Charles Eliot Norton Lectures 1981–82* (Cambridge: Harvard UP, 1983).

18. Miłosz, *The Witness of Poetry,* 37.

19. Zagajewski, *Dwa Miasta,* 41.

20. A comparison of the Polish and the English versions of this passage reveals a glaring imprecision, simple in its reversal and revealing about the power of sheer habit. The translator has retreated before the vertiginous logic of Gombrowicz's thought: "młodość uzupełnia Pełnię Niepełnią" [youth *supplements* Completion *with Incompletion* (italics mine)], and not "supplements the Incomplete with Completion." The incompletion of youth "supplements" Completion (Polish: *uzupełnia,* where *pełnia* is the root that pervades all three words caught up in this game/thought); put differently, lack fills in what is complete and makes it truly full by adding that which was missing from completion, namely, incompletion. This thought echoes Maurice Blanchot's thesis about Hegel's system: while complete and all-encompassing in its explanatory triumph, the system is unable to include within its apparatus the possibility (the thought-possibility) of its success or its failure. That which makes it work (or fail) lies outside it, unaccounted for.

21. "To be a man is to recite humanity," writes Gombrowicz (*D* II, 4). Expression is recitation, quotation, a belonging to a pre-established order; authenticity is intertwined with inauthenticity.

22. Gombrowicz emphatically exhorts his readers to read Heidegger and Jaspers on this point (*D* I, 182).

23. Zagajewski, *Solidarność i samotność*, 78.

24. The task, the risks, and the rewards, are enormous. In the conclusion to the essay on Sienkiewicz Gombrowicz writes about the challenges posed by the submission of Poland to another version of false (i.e., proletarian) virtue in the context of the situation in Europe: "What is more, never have we been more torn between East and West. These two worlds, destroying each other right before our eyes, create an emptiness in us which we will be able to fill only with our own contents. Sooner or later, the real devil will appear to us and only then will we know which God we must worship" (*D* I, 230). For the traps that await unsuspecting opponents of dialectic, see *D* I, 165–66.

25. Gombrowicz writes:

> The poet Broniewski said to me: "What are you doing? What kind of diversion is this? You have infected even the Communists with your coats of arms." (*D* I, 47)

26. Kermode, *The Sense of an Ending,* 113–14.

Katarzyna Jerzak

7

Defamation in Exile:

Witold Gombrowicz and E. M. Cioran

> *C'est à tort qu'on se fait de l'exilé l'image de quelqu'un qui abdique, se retire et s'efface, résigné à ses misères, à sa condition de déchet. A l'observer, on découvre en lui un ambitieux, un déçu agressif, un aigri doublé d'un conquérant.*
>
> E. M. Cioran, "Avantages de l'exil"

> I wander in the world, I sail this abyss of incomprehensible idiosyncracies, and wherever I see a mysterious feeling, be it virtue or family, faith or fatherland, there I must commit a vile act. This is my mystery, which I in turn impose on the great mystery of being.
>
> Witold Gombrowicz, "Pamiętnik Stefana Czarnieckiego"

In 1952, the Paris magazine *Kultura* published a Polish translation of E. M. Cioran's "Avantages de l'exil" with a "Commentary" by Witold Gombrowicz.[1] In his essay, written in French, the Romanian writer Cioran depicts an exile who calls to mind a Gombrowiczian figure: "un aigri doublé d'un conquérant"[2] (the Polish translation of that phrase, "zgorzknialec podszyty zdobywcą," reads like something straight out of Gombrowicz's *Diary*), or, in Richard Howard's translation, the one whose "very acrimony [is] qualified by his belligerence" (*TTE,* 74), a disinherited loser eager to impose himself, his misfortune driving him to a megalomania characteristic of those whose countries have not been "so childish as to make up a past for themselves" (*TTE,* 76). An exile as described, or rather decried, by Cioran in "Avantages de l'exil" necessarily represents the "second" Europe and adds to the fate of being an expatriate the malediction of representing a minor literature and a lesser language, "a language of which the cultivated are either ignorant or contemptuous" (*TTE,* 74). Representing the experience of the European periphery entails antagonism: Cioran rejects any imitation of the "central" models (Germany, France), proposing their critique and even radical dismissal justified by the marginal perspective. Poetry, this "prerogative of troglodytes and aesthetes . . . always on the margin of civilization,"[3] is in Cioran's assessment the exilic genre par excellence. Lyrical and barbaric, it flourishes in young nations which lack the literary tradition necessary for the formation of prose, and it naturally proliferates in exile, requiring no discipline, only a lyrical overflow. This condemnation of the lyrical marks the French Cioran's disavowal of his Romanian writings, which, though never in verse, were intensely lyrical and poetic. In his defamatory fervor Cioran turns against himself as well as against others, in accordance with his motto, which to borrow one of his titles might be "To Think Against Oneself" ("Penser contre soi"). To think against oneself as Nietzsche, Baudelaire, Dostoevsky—and before and after them, that other exile, the devil—have taught us.

In his "Commentary," published immediately following Cioran's text in the same issue of *Kultura,* Gombrowicz purports to quarrel with the picture presented by Cioran. He opens his remarks by effecting a degrading displacement: he accuses Cioran of speaking, as it were, from a cellar, or a grave—from the underground, we are tempted to add. Quibbling with Cioran's imprecise definition of "the writer in exile" he puts forth an unlikely—or perhaps only perverse—comparison between Adam Mickiewicz and Mr. X, between, on the one hand, Poland's Great National Poet, the epitome of patriotic convulsions (whom Gombrowicz discredits elsewhere as the Lithuanian bard), and, on the other, the Unknown Exile of literature, the anonymous martyr who wrote and wrote but did not make it. Thus, Gombrowicz questions the validity of Cioran's arguments by pointing out that the issues confronting an artist in exile are not so different form the issues confronting an artist *tout court.* But Cioran is well aware of that: he bids us think of Rilke, that "expatriate *de luxe,* and of the number of solitudes he had to accumulate in order to liquidate his connections, in order to establish a foothold in the invisible" (*TTE,* 76). Like religious mystics, who gain their deprivation by "monstrous efforts," Rilke had to exert himself to achieve the distance that others owe to exile or disease.

This paramount analogy, reverberating with Nietzschean echoes, that links the exile with a sick person is equally dear to Cioran and to Gombrowicz. Both note that malady, like expatriation, puts one further from the point where one coincides superficially with oneself, forces one to inhabit a more distant realm. Cioran presents disease as a means of extension into unknown territory, an invitation to detachment from the mechanical character of life: "[The expatriate] resembles the sick person who, like him, installs himself in metaphysics or in poetry without personal merit, by the force of circumstances, by the good offices of disease" (*TTE,* 77; with my emendations).[4] Writing in his *Diary* some years later, Gombrowicz concurs:

> For it is well known that progress and development are not the work of people who are of average health, . . . but are worked out by deformed persons, exiled from decent 'normality.' A sick man is better able to grasp the absolute essence of health . . . Those who because of personal flaws cannot join the herd and who wander the peripheries see the path of the herd more clearly and know the surrounding forest better (*D* II, 17).

Cioran warns, however, that the vertigo of exile cannot be transformed into a cheap source of perpetual creative energy. Suffering and nostalgia wear out with time, and then the writer in exile has two paths of salvation: faith or sarcasm. Having opted for the latter, Cioran remains "un réprouvé convenable" (*TE,* 68) [a fitting outcast], a paradoxical icon for modern times. Rejected and rejecting, damned and yet dispensing anathemas left and right, the Cioranesque spirit of vituperation thrives in the "situation limite," of which exile is emblematic.

Thus the dialogue of the Romanian and the Polish exile is a dialogue between two men unwilling to hear each other and, above all, unwilling to recognize the unison of their voices. Gombrowicz pointedly dispenses advice to Cioran, but he does it in what Cioran deems to be a "barbaric" language and, moreover, in an émigré magazine—which, according to Cioran, exiles put together "to get up subscriptions, to bleed each other white in order to publish their regrets, their cries, their echoless appeals" (*TTE,* 75). But even though Gombrowicz growls and froths at the mouth, he in fact is in emphatic agreement with Cioran's assessment of the dangers inherent in both the exilic and the artistic predicament: exile as such does not offer a facile substitute for the discipline of style. In fact, exile may lead to a futile establishment in the "Cité du Rien, patrie à rebours" (*TE,* 67) [City of Nothingness, homeland in reverse] with no readers, no support, and, worst of all, no inspiration. Despite its ostensible contentiousness, Gombrowicz's text makes clear not only that the two authors are in the same boat but also that they are engaged in a project of redefining exile.

I analyze here the redefinition of exile proposed by these two authors. Both treat any form of exile as a painful but potentially rewarding kick in the pants, equally effective whether it comes from outside or whether one is obliged to bend over backwards to give it to oneself. Estranged from and disgusted by their native environments, Gombrowicz and Cioran greet the outbreak of the Second World War as the catastrophe that furnishes them with an excuse to make a final break with their homelands: they become exiles "with the cooperation—i.e. the hostility—of history" (*TTE,* 76) but not at all unwillingly. Not only do they not want to be sacrificed at the national altar, they do not even wish to be citizens of their respective countries. Both die without ever returning home.

Rejecting nationalism, patriotism, religion—all traditional ways of belonging in and despite exile—Gombrowicz and Cioran adopt a mode of intensified confrontation, a strategy oscillating between calumny and accusation that I call defamation. This strategy forms part of Gombrowicz's and Cioran's conscious engagement in a redefinition of exile which opposes the twin modernist topoi of, on the one hand, the nostalgia for the lost sense of belonging or, on the other, the glorification of homelessness. In their struggle with the centripetal pull of attachment, Gombrowicz and Cioran cunningly exploit the power of disgust: both cultivate the Cioranesque "horreur de chez soi," feeding the forces of abjection in order to release them against such fossilized forms as the nation, the literary tradition, and the unified subject.

Cioran, or Double Disenchantment

Cioran's defamatory strategies take shape early—in his last Romanian book, *Îndreptar Pătimaş* (*Passionate Corrigenda,* written in France between 1940 and 1944, translated into French as *Bréviaire des vaincus* only in 1993) he posits Job's vituperations as a model of his future blasphemous practices. Throughout his oeuvre Cioran finds time and again a certain consolation as well as much inspiration in various forms of heresy with which he identifies (e.g., the medieval sect of Bogomiles[5]). But his most basic reaction is against the homeland as a soporific—and, more specifically, against the Romanian peasant's apathy—and it is this reaction which prompts his defamatory outcries.

Cioran is equally eager to liberate Romanians from the attachment to their homeland as Gombrowicz is to free his fellow Poles from the bonds of their provincial Polishness. "The paradox of being a Persian (or as the case would have it, a Romanian) is a torment one must know how to exploit, a defect by which one must profit" (*TTE,* 70)—such is Cioran's precept for those born into small nations. The destiny contained in being Romanian is, in Cioran's words, "un salut négatif" (*TE,* 55) [negative salvation] consisting in resignation which is to be overcome. Cioran's relationship with his country began as his vehement reaction against its national lethargy: "Hating my people, my country, its timeless peasants enamored of their own torpor and almost bursting with hebetude, I blushed to be descended from them, repudiated them, rejected their sub-eternity, their certainties of petrified larvae, their geologic reverie" (*TTE,* 70; with my emendations).[6] This in-bred soil-bound apathy provoked his propensity for revolt and an attitude of defiance: "To deprecate your own kind, to vilify and pulverize them, to attack their foundations, to undermine your very basis, to destroy your point of departure, to punish your origins . . . , to curse all those non-elect, lesser breeds, torn between imposture and elegy, whose sole mission is not to have one . . ."[7] This hatred directed toward his own origins does not, however, make Cioran embrace his adopted homeland, which in his opinion is tainted by a complacency common to all great nations. Cioran fouls his own nest without remorse and yet with equal consistency bites the hand that feeds him, or, to be more accurate, rejects the fare as decadent and indigestible. His critique of the West which, after all, he chose as his dwelling, renders him doubly alone. The rule he follows permits him no habit, no "stationary beatitude":

> I have never been attracted by minds confined to a single form of culture. *Not to take root, not to belong to any community:* such has been and is my motto. Oriented towards other horizons,

> I have always wanted to know what was happening elsewhere; by the time I was twenty, the Balkans had nothing more to offer me. This is the drama, and also the advantage, of being born into a minor "cultural" space. *The foreigner* had become my god. Whence that thirst to travel through literatures and philosophies, to devour them with a sickly ardor. What is happening in Eastern Europe must inevitably happen in the countries of Latin America, and I have noticed that its representatives are infinitely better informed, more "cultivated," than the incurably provincial Westerners.[8]

Here Cioran effects a reversal worthy of Gombrowicz: it is the Westerners who are provincials, so entrenched in their civilized comfort that they have lost all trace of their nomadic vigor: "The crusaders, turned gardeners, vanished into that home-loving posterity in which no trace of nomadism subsists. But history is a nostalgia for space, a horror of home, a vagabond dream and a need to die far away." (*TTE*, 60–61).[9] Thus, in the same motion, Cioran denounces the Romanians and the French, effectively depriving himself of the native and the foster spaces.

Cioran's credo of non-adherence is aimed at a certain freedom—by virtue of defaming all, including himself, the subject is delivered from the illusions of belonging: "In the past, you were defined by the values to which you subscribed; today, by those you repudiate" (*TTE*, 121). For Cioran, then, defamation is not a function of power,[10] but a means of filling the void with one's outcries. More concretely, it offers a linguistic shelter, a zone of withdrawal from conformity in which the author maneuvers freely, but not in a void. Cioran's is an individual notation of dissent uttered from the periphery.

Gombrowicz: From Abomination to Profanation

Gombrowicz, like Cioran, draws attention to the early formulation of his defamatory tactics. At their source lay, above all, an unspecified but nonetheless acute sense of stigmatizing difference which, beginning in his childhood, separated him from his peers, his family, and even his friends. This awareness of abnormality, thematized by Gombrowicz in the short stories published in 1933 as *Pamiętnik z okresu dojrzewania* (Memoir from the time of adolescence), prompted a state of internal exile even before Gombrowicz faced actual physical displacement. The other, related element at the source of Gombrowicz's defamatory tactics is the feeling of disgust. A central and persistent theme, disgust can both prompt and explicate exile in Gombrowicz's writing. By focusing on the individual's inner response of disgust to his or her environment, rather than on exile as the society's act of revulsion toward the offending individual, Gombrowicz redefines the traditional notion of exile. It is by virtue of disgust that Gombrowicz's characters are misfits, outsiders, and exiles. They are as much expulsed by their environment, as they experience revulsion toward it—and toward themselves.

The categories of spatial heterogeneity have determined the character of exile's historical forms. In antiquity exile occurred in the context of a spatial duality of the contemporary world: being forced *extra solum* signified being expelled from civilization into barbarian territory, or into wilderness, the *ager incertus.* The punishment consisted of cultural dislocation, of separation from the source of civilized life as the exile had known it, and of simple annihilation of the familiar. Modern exile is a more complex phenomenon: an individual is expelled from a society because this society cannot accept him or her, it cannot function with the given individual in its midst, but the feeling of abhorrence may also lie at the core of an individual decision to take distance from a group—whether by leaving it physically, or by removing oneself into an internal exile. In the twentieth century, exile has, on the one hand, lost some of its pathos and, on the other, acquired a new dimension. The masses of people displaced during the Second World War took away the romanticized nimbus from the idea and drew attention to the social and cultural significance of exile. Simultaneously, the modern aspect of exile was defined by the repudiation and abandonment of Nazi Germany by its foremost intellectuals, writers, and artists. The physical forced separation from the homeland, conventionally identified with the image of expulsion from paradise, from the protective familiar milieu, was belied by the sudden reality of exile defined as liberation from a suffocating, repressive atmosphere, as an escape from terror and authoritarianism. While until the end of the nineteenth century exile was by and large characterized in terms of forced banishment (by a decree or enactment), nowadays we ascribe to it two essentially opposed meanings: one stresses the forced nature of the removal from one's country or home and the other focuses on the possibility of a voluntary absence. It is in this grey area of the concept of exile that Gombrowicz and Cioran meet and through the implementation of the practices of defamation conspire to redraft it as an instrument of modern ascesis.

Exile and the Abject

Julia Kristeva's concept of the abject and the role of abjection in the formation of identity that she discusses in *Pouvoirs de l'horreur* would find uncanny material in Gombrowicz's fiction as well as in his *Diary* and, above all, in *A Kind of Testament,* Gombrowicz's self-revealing "auto-interview" presented as a series of supposed conversations with Dominique de Roux. Shame, being ill at ease, the sense of unexplainable ambiguity at one's core—all these signs of abjection, which, according to Kristeva, provoke a violent revolt *against,* are Gombrowicz's own, especially during his adolescent years in Poland. Drawing on Lacan and Bataille, Kristeva posits the existence of a formative pre-linguistic phase in which one's sense of self develops as a reaction to what she calls the abject substances: filth, bodily fluids, other "borderline" substances which arouse both disgust and fascination. By an act of separation from the source of the abject (often embodied by the mother), the self constitutes itself as a deject or stray. This violent separation involves rejection—in Gombrowicz's case the rejected mother is above all "Matka Polka," the figure of Poland as a nurturing mother, a commonplace in Polish literature.

In his early fiction Gombrowicz links the abject and exile in the same manner in which Kristeva connects them in her study: in "Stefan Czarniecki's Memoir" he presents a half-Polish half-Jewish youth who experiences himself as a "neutral rat," a raceless, colorless being, incapable of belonging in the society which surrounds him; in "Feast at Countess Kotłubaj's"—a petit bourgeois out of place at an aristocratic vegetarian dinner during which the guests devour a cauliflower which may or may not be the body of a peasant boy whose last name is Cauliflower; in "Adventures"—a white Negro pursuing his victim, who at the same time is his alter ego, across continents and oceans in order to subject him to elaborate forms of imprisonment, exile, and torture; in "The Rat"—a vagabond giant with an intense phobia of rats who witnesses his persecutor's sudden death in the mouth of his beloved. These examples from Gombrowicz's early collection of short stories *Bakakaj*[11] are emblematic of a persistent motif which marks the Polish author's oeuvre. The impossibility of achieving a fixed and secure identity propels the hero along the road of exile, either in search of completion or in escape from a driving fear—such is the synoptic plot which appears regularly in Gombrowicz's writings.

In "Stefan Czarniecki's Memoir" (written in 1928, published in 1933),[12] the main character's mixed racial origin renders his existence marginalized and superfluous. What Gombrowicz will later define in terms of an essential incompatibility of the individual human being with both nature and social environment is dramatized in this story as a specific, concrete case of unassimilability which results from a misalliance of races, from an "unnatural" coupling. Like his contemporary American counterpart, Faulkner's Joe Christmas in *Light in August,* Stefan is an unwitting victim of the elements which clash within him, he is the site of what his father prophetically calls an "inner pogrom." It is as if instead of cutting the individual from the social body, a figurative scalpel were thrown inside that individual, cutting and wounding from within. This painful process often prompts an external form of exile: a tormented, divided being searches for the means of ending the inner struggle by leaving the environment which seems to perpetuate his or her misery. Whenever internal exile stems from issues of inner strife and incompatibility, escape is futile, because the internalized conflict resides within the hero who carries it along. The ever-resurging discomfort pushes him or her on, without hope for settlement or stability.

Precluded from enjoying an inherited "simple" identity and stigmatized by his split origin, Stefan escapes into the most intense form of Polishness he can envisage: he joins the Polish Army and becomes an uhlan.[13] This figure is fraught with irony. Considered to be the epitome of militant bravery, the uhlan stands for Polishness itself, and yet the origin of the formation is doubly foreign, as the uhlans were modeled after a Tartar troop which served in the Lithuanian army. The word itself is derived from the Turkish word *oglan,* meaning "boy," "brave one." It is important to note here that the investment of otherness with positive qualities, and its subsequent assimilation, characterize the Polish mentality as seen by Gombrowicz. Poles to him exemplify a more general human attitude of ambivalence toward the foreign: their contempt is intertwined with jealousy and desire. As Gombrowicz remarks in his *Diary:* "nothing that is really your own can impress you. If, therefore, our greatness or our past impresses us, it is proof that it has not yet entered our bloodstream" (*D* I, 8).

The elevation and transformation of the uhlan figure to the pedestal of highest national sentiments resembles the trajectory of the Sarmatian image, parodied by Gombrowicz in his novel *Trans-Atlantyk,* from its inception as the paragon of bellicose horsemen of the steppes to the fantastic glorification of the Sarmatians as the noble ancestors of the Polish gentry. Stefan's nostalgia for wholeness translated as the desire to belong prompts his attempt at active and somewhat showy patriotism. *Pro patria* in this case signifies also *pro pater,* as it is Stefan's pure-blooded Polish father who encourages him to repudiate the stain of his improper origin. For his converted Jewish mother, on the other hand, Stefan's military involvement embodies a vague revenge on the world which does not accept her. She tells him: "You are the tool of wrath, of disgust, of loathing and hate."[14]

Rejected and rejecting, Stefan is Kristeva's "exile who asks 'where?' ":

> a *deject* who places (himself), *separates* (himself), situates (himself), and therefore *strays* instead of getting his bearings, desiring, belonging, or refusing. Situationist in a sense, and not without laughter—since laughing is a way of placing or displacing abjection.[15]

Many years later, in South America, Gombrowicz himself will ask "where?" The sense of estrangement mixes with an uncanny feeling of belonging and familiarity as Gombrowicz adopts as his own an empty shell of somebody else's house, a house to which he is linked by a "largely arbitrary bond" and which he does not even enter:

> I know that I am not supposed to be here! Where then? Where is my place? What am I supposed to do? Where am I supposed to be? My native land is not my place nor is the house of my parents, no thought, no word, no, the truth is that I have no other home except that one, yes, unfortunately, unfortunately, the only house I have is that uninhabited, that white Pueyrredon house! (*D* I, 108)

For Kristeva, as for Gombrowicz, the exile is concerned with space and territory, someone who forms an identity through a confrontation with the outside, who attempts to locate the frontier between the "I" and the other in order to establish the self:

> Instead of sounding himself as to his "being," he does so concerning his place: "*Where* am I?" instead of "*Who* am I?" For the space that engrosses the deject, the excluded, is never *one,* nor *homogeneous,* nor *totalizable,* but essentially divisible, foldable, and catastrophic. A deviser of territories, languages, works, the *deject* never stops demarcating his universe whose fluid confines—for they are constituted of a non-object, the abject—constantly question his solidity and impel him to start afresh.[16]

The exile's preoccupation with placement and place, as well as the insistence and dependence on the perception of all space as the divisible "espace strié" [striated space] rather than the soothing a-political and a-geographical "espace lisse"[17] [smooth space] evident in the above passage can be seen in the following fragment from Gombrowicz's *Diary:*

> Here I am. Why here? If someone had told me years ago in Małoszyce that I would one day be in Goya . . . If I am in Goya, then by equal right I could be anywhere else and suddenly all the places in the world begin to weigh heavily on me, demanding that I be there. (*D* I, 203)

An overwhelming sense of contingency renders the otherwise unremarkable Argentinean town the locus of fate's scenario. There is nothing special about Goya, but for Gombrowicz to find himself there smacks of a ploy of destiny. Suddenly, he feels doubly estranged: as a tourist, and also as one who is perceived as foreign, thus experiencing a split self, a doubling:

> I stroll along Plaza Sarmiento in a bluish evening. An exotic foreigner to them. Finally through them, I become a stranger to myself: here I lead myself around Goya as a person unknown to myself. I stand him on a corner, I sit him down on a chair in a café. I order him to exchange meaningless words with an incidental interlocutor and I listen to my voice.[18]

Contingency and estrangement which so often appear to be Gombrowicz's natural elements, here strain his sensibility prompting his wish for a more architectonic kind of fate:

> Everything was happening as if on the bottom—of a deep silence—on the bottom of my sojourning here, in Goya, in the peripheries, a place on the globe which for unknown reasons became mine. This silencing . . . Goya, why have I never dreamt of you, why didn't I then, once, ever sense that you lay in my destiny, on my route?[19]

The lack of an identifiable continuity between the old self—the self who did not anticipate Goya—and the present one constitutes the crux of the Gombrowiczian definition of the self. The fluid inner core which Gombrowicz and his characters try to protect from deformation is never at one with itself. As Gombrowicz says, "I don't know who I really am, but I suffer when I am deformed. So at least I know what I am not. My 'self' is nothing but my will to be myself" (*KT,* 77). The only relevant territory in the Gombrowiczian scheme is then the space delineated by the amorphous self, an ever-changing narcissistic sphere. There can be no true home, because there is no firm identification with a place or a person.

The Language of Disgust

Thus, if Gombrowicz's hero is an exile, he does not share Ulysses' certainty of where Ithaca lies. Stefan, like most Gombrowiczian characters, is a homeless outcast, a living incarnation of the impossibility of uniting one's individual fate with anything greater than oneself. He embodies the tragedy of striving to defend an identity which is not known, stable, or secure, and which seems to rely on an acute sense of alterity. That the trial of abjection in Gombrowicz brings about a crisis of consciousness, rather than a formation and solidification of identity, is clear also from the autobiographical insight offered by Gombrowicz's *A Kind of Testament:*

> I don't think it was so much that I felt abnormal as that I *knew* myself to be abnormal, and this knowledge persisted despite all the signs of my healthy normality: a young man, apparently

> perfectly average (except for a few inoffensive eccentricities) and yet under no illusion about being a black sheep, outside the herd, on a road that led nowhere—a young man who knew himself to be open to all possibilities, even the most grotesque, like those plasticine figurines which can be modeled indefinitely and turned into the most hideous monsters. I knew: alone, out on a limb, like this or like something else, dissolute and uncontrolled. That was the source of my relationship with all that is repugnant, disgusting, horrible—for, though it disgusted me, yet I felt drawn to it, not to say attached to it. But this sensation plunged me into still greater disgust . . . So I oscillated between disgust and an inner attachment to all that was disgusting. (*KT,* 39)

Normality and alterity, attraction and repugnance: these antinomies inform the hero's struggle in "Stefan Czarniecki's Memoir" and will reverberate in Gombrowicz's oeuvre, coming to a head in his last novel, *Kosmos.* In the "Memoir," any illusion of self-definition through belonging is swept away when Stefan witnesses a scene of ultimate battlefield violence *in vivo.* A bullet tears open his fellow uhlan, turning his stomach into a fountain of blood. Holding his bursting insides the dying young man laughs a long, hysterical laughter. This image is clearly reminiscent of numerous trauma-filled accounts of World War I, as well as of their surrealist expression. The echo of the laughter and the memory of the grotesque scene will pursue Stefan, annihilating all hope and initiating him to eternal wandering. The graphic disintegration of the body accompanied by the victim's absurd laughter marks a turning point in Stefan's understanding of life. This ambiguous laughter, which according to Kristeva may accompany the experience of the abject, constitutes also the pivot of the story and returns to introduce a linguistic twist in the metaphysical theme of meaning and alterity. When Stefan's beloved refuses to repeat after him a series of gibberish words—"Ciam—bam—biu, minu—mniu, ba—bi, ba—be—no—zar"[20]—words which he introduces as an example of his mystery, of his singularity, Stefan threatens to punish her by putting a toad under her blouse. Constrained by an inexplicable sense of shame, Jadwisia persists in her refusal: "I can't, I can't—she repeated, sobbing—I'm embarrassed, how could I . . . such senseless words!"[21] The absurdity of meaningless sounds is a menace to her integrity and, in an implied sense, to her decency.[22] Stefan fulfills his threat and as Jadwisia rolls on the ground with the toad next to her body, he compares the sound she emits to the laughter heard in the battlefield. Then he comments: "Perhaps this comparison as well as the practical joke with the frog are distasteful, but please keep in mind that I, a colorless rat, a neutral rat, neither white nor black, I also am distasteful to most people."[23] Just like Kristeva's abject self, Stefan ultimately accepts the impossibility of recognizing himself outside of himself: "weary of fruitless attempts to identify with something on the outside, [he] finds the impossible within: when [he] finds that the impossible constitutes [his] very *being,* that it *is* none other than abject."[24] For Kristeva, the "abjection of self" is symptomatic of "the inaugural loss" or lack, while for Gombrowicz, if lack there be, it is filled by language, by the language of disgust which formulates our inadequacy. Thus, if Gombrowicz appears to be intransigent, it is not because his self is one and stable but because to him the sense of self only comes into being momentarily, through the dynamics of confrontation. This confrontation necessarily involves all the matrices of societal support and identification: family, religion, political ideology. "For abjection is the other side of religious, moral, and ideological codes on which the sleep of individuals and the appeasement of societies rest."[25] It is against the soporific aspect of belonging that the insomniac Cioran and the odd man out Gombrowicz speak.

But can language, or form, rescue exiles from alienation? It seems that at least on one level the answer is affirmative. Gombrowicz, who consistently rebels against the stilting effects of form on life, nevertheless gives full recognition to the metamorphosis offered by the linguistic feat: "Let us also admit that these revolting elements lose their repugnance when they turn into elements of Form. They serve Form, their role is functional, they follow a superior aim: artistic creation" (*KT,* 40–41). Cioran agrees, but displaces the focus to a private auto-soteriology: "To formulate is to save oneself, even if one only scribbles insanities, even if one doesn't have any talent."[26] If one does have talent, then the potential of this secular salvation will extend also to the reader, providing a mold which can hold what may be otherwise inexpressible. And yet the danger inherent in considering form as an escape from the alienation of exile is a real one: to project oneself into the word, to inhabit it, as it were, is necessarily a reductive and limiting enterprise, haunted by irony. And so when Cioran declares: "One does not inhabit a country; one inhabits a language. That is our country, our fatherland—and no other,"[27] it is as much an admission of hubris as of helplessness. Thus Cioran's abandonment of Romanian is also a proclamation of the radical nature of his own exile.

While language as such can offer only a temporary and whimsical shelter against the reality of exile, it nevertheless makes possible a simulacrum of the exilic experience to those who have not lived it. In Gombrowicz's case, the more his linguistic form serves to discomfort the reader, the more effective his representation of exile becomes. Gombrowicz's project, then, is the opposite of Mickiewicz's or Sienkiewicz's: instead of transporting our "homesick soul" to the native land and making us feel at home there again, he unsettles us even further, ensuring that expatriation coincide with ex-patriotism.

Avant-garde, particularly surrealist, modes of writing and art come close to, and ultimately are at the bottom of, Gombrowicz's method; yet he is not merely an epigone of surrealism or a practitioner of estrangement. His style, though it may be designed to jolt the reader out of passive digestion of an unrebellious material, nevertheless strives to sustain a communication with the real. The shuttle never quite ventures into outer space; we are never submerged in a world which is thoroughly alien. Instead, Gombrowicz cultivates a certain representational and stylistic disjointedness which has as its aim to encourage the reader's overcoming of the Form. In this Gombrowicz's strategy is unlike Cioran's, whose even and polished, almost classical style contrasts with the anarchistic and sacrilegious content. For no matter how fragmentary it may seem, Cioran's use of aphorism is not disruptive but rather contrapuntal, each fragment elegantly resounding the original sense of disenchantment.

Against the Lure of the Native Realm

In "Stefan Czarniecki's Memoir," the title character abandons his quest for a unified identity and turns to the subversion of unity instead. The confrontational aspect so dear to Gombrowicz is at work here: the outcast as a paradoxical fanatic of patriotism or even nationalism changes sides and allies himself with the forces of disruption, discontinuity, perhaps anarchy, and most assuredly the forces of individual dissent. Like his character, Gombrowicz will remain forever suspicious of any feeling other than pain. He sets no store by the love of one's country or one's family; all his credibility goes out to the experience of suffering.

Cioran, who in his youth has himself experienced the lure of national fanaticism, later comes to share the Gombrowiczian distrust of nationalism. Both writers see fit to unmask patriotism as a sentiment petty or fanatical. Their opinions earn them a place on the black list of censorship in their home countries[28] and an ambivalent attitude on the part of those fellow exiles who are more attracted to the conventional mode of exilic lament or idealization of the lost homeland. Cioran and Gombrowicz reject not only the farcical implementation of communist ideas but any form of collective ideology which, in pursuit of an abstraction, ignores, or worse yet, tramples the human person. Traditionally, in countries bereft of political autonomy, literature serves as a medium for honing the national consciousness. For exiles poetry especially is that which offers a connection to home—it is not for nothing that Sienkiewicz's lighthouse keeper reads *Pan Tadeusz.* But both Cioran and Gombrowicz are inspired to speak against literature as the bulwark of national identity. Gombrowicz attacks and parodies Mickiewicz's epic poem *Pan Tadeusz* in his novel *Trans-Atlantyk*, while Cioran simply but radically breaks with his native tongue. Both also speak against poetry: Cioran dismisses it as "verbal demiurgy [that] develops at the expense of lucidity"[29] while Gombrowicz denounces poetry as pure, chemical form, and poets as priests in a church of mutual adoration.

Gombrowicz's strategy of defamation is, among other things, about the rending of the fathers. Gombrowicz's lucid and, to some extent, prophetic vision of worship sessions in which literary critics and dilettanti chew on the holy wafer of his body, that is, his texts, projects a macabre outcome for those who dare speak of him in terms reasonable and boring: "I punish them cruelly. I die on their lips and they remain with a mouthful of my corpse."[30] Rather than gnaw at the dry bones of our forefathers, or pick at them, we must get at their flesh where there is flesh still—as Gombrowicz does in his essay on that archetypal exile, Dante—and if we incorporate them, flesh become word shall live again.

But Gombrowicz and Cioran mistrust the very medium they cultivate and in which they clothe their defamatory tactics. The struggle for power takes place also between the writer and language:

> A contemporary stylist must have a feeling for language as something infinite and dynamic that does not allow itself to be mastered. He will emphasize his struggle with form rather than form itself. His attitude towards the word, as something that eludes him, is one of distrust. This loosening of the bond between the writer and the word ensures a greater boldness in using words. (*D* I, 68)

Cioran, who often eulogizes the word, nevertheless sees fit to defame it as well. In "Le style comme aventure" he writes: "In the life of the mind, there occurs a moment when writing, transforming itself into an autonomous principle, becomes destiny. It is then that the Word, as much in philosophical speculations as in literary productions, reveals both its vigor and its void" (*TTE,* 127; with my emendations).[31]

Before Cioran's experiment with language can end in silence, he must expunge his native tongue not only from his writing but also from his dreams. This enterprise, which became Cioran's exercise of choice and which remained foreign to Gombrowicz, is what Cioran calls the "heroic betrayal," the abandonment of his native tongue. Cioran not only migrates into the French language but also chooses prose—albeit poetic—perfecting the process of linguistic crystallization, so alien to his disowned idiom of "dung and blood," the Romanian language, that embodiment of "génie barbare" (*TE,* 61) [barbaric genius] lacking in form. French to him is devoid of life, its expressions no longer retain a connection with the body and the soul: "not a trace of soil, of blood, of soul is left in them."[32] To choose a form of expression alien to himself fits well with Cioran's ascetic practices; moreover, to opt to write in French is to distance himself even further from the motherland and, by the same token, to repudiate it:

> And there is also this: I should have chosen any other language than French, for I have little in common with its distinguished vaunt; it is at the antipodes of my nature, of my outbursts, of my true self and my kind of wretchedness. In its rigidity, in the quantity of elegant constraints that it represents, French

> seems to me an exercise in ascesis or, rather, the combination of a straitjacket and a salon. Yet it is precisely on account of this incompatibility that I have attached myself to this language.[33]

To some extent Gombrowicz shares Cioran's feelings toward the French language. According to Rita Gombrowicz's account, the Polish writer "felt ill at ease in this language, the French cramped him like a corset. 'I feel that I'm becoming Marquise de Sévigné!' He was angry that while writing in French he could not find in it 'the juiciness, the taste, the concreteness, the brutality, and the infinite sweetness' of the Polish."[34] So while Cioran chooses to give the world a bad name in an unnatural tongue, Gombrowicz maligns it in his own juicy idiom.

Provincial Letters

Exile presents the writer with distance, offers him a relativized center, deterritorializes as it displaces. The external perspective, as defined in Gombrowicz's case by Juan José Saer,[35] is rendered more acute by the fact that Gombrowicz's exilic fate brought him to Argentina, the spacious "suburb of the West," which reinforced the effects of removal from Poland by adding the transatlantic point of view. The "good air" of Buenos Aires was no more than an ironic anachronism to the Polish exile. Nevertheless, that is why he claims he "existed more": "I thank Almighty God that he got me out of Poland when my literary situation began to improve and cast me onto American soil, into a foreign tongue, into isolation, into the freshness of anonymity, into a country richer in cows than in art" (*D* II, 180–81). In his essay on Borges, Cioran presents an equivalent vision of Latin America: "It is the South American void that makes the writers of an entire continent more open, more alive, and more diverse than those of Western Europe, paralyzed by their traditions and incapable of shaking off their prestigious sclerosis."[36] Exile sharpens rather than dulls Gombrowicz's vision, thus prompting defamatory practices: "There is the distance, the chilling distance of years and kilometers. I watch Poland as if through a telescope and can see only the most general contours of their existence, and this invites ruthlessness" (*D* II, 9). Writing in the *Diary* about the interwar period in Polish literature, Gombrowicz admits that his aim is to undercut the literary figures of the time:

> My present dire predicament demands this. If I agree inwardly that they were the way they were supposed to be—blossoming, healthy plants on fertile soil while I am something dying in a desert, a cripple cast onto an alien shore, without a homeland, etc., . . . an exile, astray, lost . . . what would be left except to resign from all meaning? Therefore: I have to mobilize the strong points of my situation thereby showing that I can live better and more authentically. (*D* I, 159)

Cioran, too, relishes an external perspective, even though he has placed himself in what to all appearances is one of the centers of European culture. In his view, the human being cannot help but act "as profaner, traitor, agent of dissolution; always on the side of, or outside of, things."[37]

Against Religion

Julia Kristeva envisions the "artistic experience, rooted in the abject it utters and by the same token purifies," to be the "essential component of religiosity" and as such, she suggests, capable of surviving "the collapse of historical forms of religion."[38] If Gombrowicz's and Cioran's strategies of defamation share a religious aspect, it is because these two atheistic thinkers are deeply preoccupied with faith and ritual. Cioran's *dictum acerbum*—"We exert our minds to demolish reputations, above all that of God"[39]—could serve as their motto. God may have died, but for Cioran he remains the sole worthy, even if absurd, interlocutor. Gombrowicz, on the other hand, keeps his distance from the old God, while tracing the human persistence in resuscitating familiar gestures of religious worship. Cioran never ceases to calumniate God, perhaps outdoing that old slanderer and spirit of contradiction, the devil: "I am not pessimistic, but violent . . . and it is that which makes my negation enlivening . . . I am like the devil, who is an active individual, a negator who shakes things up."[40] At the same time, his penchant for the apocalyptic points to the grandiose scale on which his defamation wants to operate in order to *uncover*—as if true hell were defined by concealment. According to Cioran, a single cry of human suffering compromises the music of the spheres, supplying sufficient proof of the universe's imperfection and denying all divine wisdom and order. For Gombrowicz, the fossilized forms of religious—above all Catholic—worship remain a valid currency in the rituals of what he calls the interhuman church. With perverse delight, Gombrowicz records and unmasks every form of mass, be it black or pagan, pointing to the glorification of the human in place of the absent divine. A peculiar prophet, he announces not the coming of any savior but, rather, the advent of a democratic religion in which each will be a perpetual creator and celebrator. Cioran, notorious for perpetrating every codified form of heresy, admits to being a hopeless believer in rebellion: "Bluntly: my rebellion is a faith to which I subscribe without believing in it" (*TTE,* 42). He excels at depriving us of our various props as well. He asserts that we remember the suffering of Christ, not because he suffered for us, but because he suffered for no reason at all and is therefore one of our own kind. When Cioran feels particularly benevolent towards God, he grants him the status of an exile and allows humans to model themselves after the divine "Apatride," ironically misplaced in Nothingness by his last apologist.

Self-mortification and Disillusionment

Gombrowicz's and Cioran's strategy is to take away from any potential critics the pleasure of applying their own game to their work—so they exceed at stabbing themselves in the spirit of self-mockery and self-irony. But the most far-reaching category of defamatory practices, one in which Cioran excels, is aimed at the metaphysical. The author of *De l'inconvénient d'être né* vituperates against being as such, while Gombrowicz accompanies him with his proclamations of ontological shame. Cioran professes that one must not grow accustomed to anything, not even to despair. The principle of individuation out of original chaos has worked to separate us from one another and from all; and yet, paradoxically, we ought to strive for further non-coincidence. To act as agents of revelation is the goal which Cioran and Gombrowicz present as their duty and ultimate responsibility to the rest of humankind. The author of *Aveux et anathèmes* wants to compromise existence, to bare it once and for all in an effort to bereave human beings of their illusions. He comes as a revealer who removes, one by one, the veils which humanity stubbornly places over its own eyes. Gombrowicz, too, believes in a naked man, pitting the concreteness of the body against the abstraction of aesthetic theories.[41] And he does not unmask music, painting, or art in general just for the perverse pleasure of iconoclasm. Instead, he uses defamation to uncover the authentic being who has been hidden by the props of so-called culture. Like Cioran, he believes that humans are "indirect animals," but he begrudges them their unmediated relationship to their paraphernalia. Gombrowicz does not expect humans to stand unsupported and unfalsified, but he would like them to become conscious of their screens and scales, shields and armors. Unlike Cioran, Gombrowicz does not pretend to envy animals their animality. Rather, he deplores the fact that human beings have not gone far enough from their animalistic stage: "The means of our interaction with people are still minimal. The horrible isolation of animals which can barely communicate . . . but man? We have not yet grown so remote from animals and we haven't the least notion of what it means to have another human being tear into your locked self" (*D* I, 176). Cioran, on the other hand, sees humans as animals who refuse to stay in their original condition, escaping into perfectibility. "Always different, we are not ourselves except to the extent that we deviate from our definition, because as Nietzsche said, man is *das noch nicht festgestellte Tier,* the animal whose type has not yet been determined, fixed."[42] Consciousness interferes with what we perceive as the enviable unity of the animal, but by the same token it allows us the satisfaction of an existential revelation, the pleasure of self-torture.

The Serious Clown and the Ironic Subject

Gombrowicz and Cioran use paradox, negation, parodic laughter, and irony as chief vehicles of their defamatory tactics. All these means serve to introduce separation and distance and yet precisely for that reason they cannot function without a firm background of tradition from which to spring. Just as the notion of exile would be unthinkable in a political context devoid of nations and borders, the idea of defamation could not subsist without a set of established values and concepts against which one may speak. Neither Gombrowicz nor Cioran utters defamatory cries *in deserto;* rather, they both rely on the buildup of ideological residue against which they can assert themselves. In going against the *doxa,* against the commonly accepted opinion, both thinkers strive for the disclosure of something that perhaps is not even there. The author of *La tentation d'exister* favors terse, oxymoronic paradoxes, while the Polish writer, though not averse to the baroque charm of conceit and oxymoron, puts forth a methodology of reintegrated antinomy. Contradiction and negation occupy a prominent place for both writers, but Gombrowicz places too much importance on imperfection to be comfortable with modes of captivating the human factor which elegantly encapsulate the messiness of being human. That is why he often employs parody, another formal means of achieving distance from tradition and from the reader. Just as paradox does, parody points to the side of reality that is not commonly seen; it inverts and reveals the underside and, by the same token, provokes. As a model of the Gombrowiczian defamating subject, the clown combines the powers of gesture, laughter, and the deflating, parodistic word:

> The rubbish heap. The point is exactly that I come from your rubbish heap. All that you cast off through centuries as refuse is now speaking through me. If my form is a parody of form, then my spirit is a parody of spirit and my person a parody of a person. Isn't it true that one cannot undermine form by opposing it with another form, but only by laxity in one's very attitude toward it? No, it is not a coincidence that precisely at the moment when we need a hero, up pops a clown—a conscious and, thereby, serious clown. (*D* I, 36)

Gombrowicz himself was not averse to playing the role of the serious clown in life, not merely in literature. His aim was to stand out, even if that meant exposing himself to ridicule: "Gombrowicz is not reducible to an image. Always unlike the expected character. Quite consciously an aristocrat among the petits bourgeois, a commoner among the aristocrats, country bumpkin in the city, an urbanite in the countryside, always unstable, always in contradiction."[43] Gombrowicz then emerges as an anti-chameleon, who instead of blending into the surrounding reality is out to be radically, antinomically different, out to provoke and to stimulate.

For Cioran and Gombrowicz laughter may seem absurd, but it is the only answer, if not the antidote, to the absurd character of existence. Cioran offers the following advice to a friend disenchanted with life: "when you won't be able to laugh any more, only then should you kill yourself. But as long as you are able to laugh, wait a little longer. Laughter is a victory, the true, the only victory over life and death."[44] That is why Gombrowicz administers laughter as a panacea to his compatriots. In 1954, he writes in his *Diary:*

> in moments when devastating conditions force us to a complete inner transformation, laughter is our last resort. It draws us out of ourselves and allows our humanity to survive independently of the painful changes in our shell.
>
> No nation has needed laughter more than we do today. And never has a nation *understood* laughter's liberating role less. (*D* I, 101)

His own understanding projects laughter as a form of violence that is instrumental in procuring distance.[45] Such laughter, directed against others, but mainly against oneself, becomes a key element of Gombrowicz's defamation, his strategy in exile:

> Our laughter today, however, can no longer be an elemental, that is, automatic laughter. It must be premeditated laughter, humor applied coldly and with gravity, it must be a serious *application* of laughter to our tragedy. . . . That laughter, dictated by awful necessities, should encompass not only the world of enemies, but above all us ourselves and that which is dearest to us. (*D* I, 101–2).

This all-inclusive character of the Gombrowiczian laughter corresponds to Cioran's radical albeit subtle handling and application of irony. Kierkegaard's understanding of irony as that which is "no longer directed against this or that particular phenomenon, against a particular existing thing, but that [in which] the whole of existence had become alien to the ironic subject and the ironic subject in turn alien to existence,"[46] not only holds valid for the essence of Cioran's outlook but provides a useful conceptual framework in which to interpret his notion of negation as well as his method of implementing this notion by means of defamation.

Irony, Kierkegaard tells us, "denotes the subjective pleasure as the subject frees himself by means of irony from the restraint in which the continuity of life's conditions holds him."[47] When Cioran states, "Solitude: so fulfilling that the merest rendezvous is a crucifixion,"[48] or declares, "The only significant events in a life are the ruptures,"[49] the hyperbole of these affirmations momentarily lifts the ironic subject out of life's predicament. Meiosis is another ironic figure cultivated by Cioran. In the aphorism "Man is free save for his depths,"[50] the derogatory understatement serves as its author's ally in the rhetorical proceedings against the misery of the human condition. As Kierkegaard observes: "In irony, the subject is continually retreating, talking every phenomenon out of its reality in order to save itself—that is, in order to preserve itself in negative independence of everything."[51] Such is indeed Cioran's enterprise and method:

> The self converts the world into nothingness, for irony only procures feelings of power when everything is abolished. The ironic perspective: a subterfuge of the delusion of grandeur. To console itself for its inexistence, the self becomes *all.* Irony attains to the serious when it raises itself to the implacable vision of nothingness. The tragic is the ultimate stage of irony.[52]

For Cioran then, irony is an imperative of the self too conscious of its own lack.

If the self is macerated in irony, or filled with abject disgust, then in the name of what do Gombrowicz and Cioran defame? If both authors favor dynamic processes which always continue or recommence *da capo senza fine,* it is because the inner core they want simultaneously to disclose and to protect is constantly in motion: "The 'self' is the privilege of those only who have not gone to the limits of themselves,"[53] states Cioran. Or, as he asserts in "Rages et résignations": "The self: a label. Parallel to my face, I preen myself in my glances. Each thing is other, everything is other. Somewhere, an eye. Who is watching me? I am frightened and then I am outside my fear" (*TTE,* 198–99). Gombrowicz's preferred mythic icon, and one with which he readily identifies, is Proteus. This god, known for his ability to change shape at will, when caught and bound would appear in his true form (whatever that might be) and foretell the future. Gombrowicz, when taking digs at his readers, does not hope that they will begin to speak in tongues, nor even indeed that they will be made aware of their truth at that moment. On the contrary, his aim is to make them more aware of falseness; defamation is to aid them in the transformations which will lessen the hold of imposed and imposing form. At stake is not some stable, set essence or self but, rather, dynamic personal energies. To borrow an analogy from Diderot's *Paradoxe sur le comédien,* the paradox of Gombrowicz's man is that he must become connected to the theatricality of everyday life: "You were too literal for too long, too naive in your game with fate. You forgot that man not only is himself but also pretends to be himself. You threw everything that was acting and theater in you into the trash-can and you tried to forget about it" (*D* I, 36). Just as Diderot's actor has to dissociate himself as well as he can from the character he represents because any affective identification with the role would harm the actor's power of unity, and consequently of expression, so the modern man, in an effort to be as authentic as possible, cannot but accept the actor in himself, rejecting the dream of spontaneous life unmediated by form: "An eternal actor, but a natural one, because his artificiality is inborn, it makes up a feature of his humanity—to be a man means to be an actor— . . . to be a man is to recite humanity" (*D* II, 4). Thus, to combat inauthenticity, one must act more, but in doing so one has to take care to spoil others' and above all one's own play, so as not to become too entrenched in any particular shape.

Defamation with a Loophole

Gombrowicz's tactics of defamation participate in a struggle for power, power whose realization takes place in a very limited sphere: it is the power to protect oneself, one's amorphous but sensitive core, for a short moment from being deformed by others. Gombrowicz's proposed dynamics of style, then, include programmatic defamation whose role is to inoculate the subject against deformation. The process is rarely a simple one; Gombrowicz's strategy could be called defamation with a loophole, since it operates much like the dialogic tactics Bakhtin identifies in Dostoevsky's Underground Man. Every attack or accusation, every act of demystification which purports to be final, turns out—if challenged—to have been the penultimate one. The loophole provides the subject with a certain security zone; it procures sufficient room for spontaneous changes, necessitated by external pressure, or by internal contradiction. In Gombrowicz, defamation does not require verbal expression—it fulfills its aim and is perhaps more pronounced when it relies on gesture (e.g., the pointing finger which becomes the paramount tool for "deflating the other" in Gombrowicz's plays, especially in *Ślub* [*The Marriage*], where to touch someone means to bare their pretenses). Gesture is both more to the point and more immediate because it involves the body at its most basic level. Words and gestures can be engaged in a veritable contest: speech can contradict gestures, gestures can belie words with irony as the by-product. Communication as strife persists in the Gombrowiczian universe because, unlike Bakhtin, Gombrowicz not only sees through the authoritative discourse's claims on the individual, but also is aware of the treacherous potential of language as such. The primal sphere of human interaction is space, and it is in the interhuman space that the processes of deformation and defamation occur.

Defamation's Last Word

A writer in exile often retreats into the most subjective of territories, that of the "I." When Gombrowicz and Cioran retreat, it is to come out again with a vengeance and in the same motion to question the solidity of the subject. Cioran's style, as all style in his opinion, is simultaneously "un masque et un aveu" (*TE,* 138) [a mask and an avowal]—it dissimulates as it confesses. His strategy of defamation is at once an avowal of helplessness or, rather, of helpless rebellion and a disguised profession of faith in the exorcizing powers of the word. Both Gombrowicz and Cioran speak against the "spirit of Seriousness," understood as the stiffening effect of Form which must be loosened by defamatory confrontation, or as "ce péché que rien ne rachète" (*TE,* 117) [this sin that nothing can redeem], the fatal lack of distance which can be remedied only by the proclamation of absolute discord. The general uprootedness proposed by both Cioran and Gombrowicz makes one exception: the body. If defamation as practiced by the two thinkers can be said to be rooted, its soil is human physicality. The body teaches us about suffering, and suffering is the only emotion exempt from defamation.

For Cioran defamation is a modern form of ascesis: rather than mortify his flesh by deprivation and abstinence, he chooses to deprive his soul—his inner body—of any support, any rest, any delight. His physical body thus becomes the sole *point d'appui*. In the process of calumniating everything around him he leaves himself a diminutive territory from which to deliver his anathemas. His body is equivalent to the island of Patmos from which, as Saint Cioran, he fashions the modern apocalypse of irony. For Gombrowicz, defamation is an imperative in the struggle with deformation. The modern human being, imprisoned by ideological constructions and structures, takes recourse to the only source of certitude: the body twisted in a grimace of pain. Gombrowicz strives to recuperate the body's status as perpetual regeneration, a status, however, that entails the foregoing of the attachment to an individual body—that which gets unavoidably older and stiffer until its ultimate form of rigor mortis—in favor of the supple literary corpus. The body as answerable to the word, the word as traceable to the body.

Defamation is not a result of exile: for both Gombrowicz and Cioran it is a conscious strategy which they adopt before they leave their homelands. Both writers are motivated by a consciousness of their provincial roots, of their allegiances to the minor, of their perverse preferences. Defamation is their response to the stifling effect of patriotism, to the danger of fanaticism, to the inflexibility of Form but also to the formlessness of self. Defamation in language, aware of its own illusion, is nonetheless our sole empowerment.

Notes

1. Cioran's essay appeared—in Gombrowicz's translation but at his request without credit—under the title "Dogodności i niedogodności wygnania" (Advantages and disadvantages of exile). This blatant addition to the original title has done Cioran a great disservice in the eyes of the Polish readers. Cioran's text is a celebration of exile, but ever since the title's mistranslation, and Gombrowicz's polemical response, Cioran's supposed pessimism in face of exile has been juxtaposed to Gombrowicz's verve and optimism. Hence Cioran has been doing penance in the world of Polish letters as "the moaning Romanian émigré writer Cioran, a personified Apocalypse for private use" (Gustaw Herling-Grudziński, *Dziennik pisany nocą 1989–1992* (Warszawa: Czytelnik, 1993), 225; trans. mine).

2. E. M. Cioran, *La tentation d'exister* (Paris: Gallimard, 1956), 63. Subsequent references to this text will appear parenthetically as *TE*. References to the English translation, *The Temptation to Exist,* trans. Richard Howard (Chicago: Quadrangle, 1968), will be marked parenthetically as *TTE*.

3. ". . . apanage des troglodytes et des raffinés, . . . toujours en marge de la civilisation" (*TE,* 65; trans. mine).

4. "[L'apatride] ressemble au malade, lequel, comme lui, s'installe dans la métaphysique ou la poésie sans mérite personnel, par la force des choses, par les bons offices de la maladie" (*TE,* 66).

5. "Thraces et Bogomiles—je ne puis oublier que j'ai hanté les mêmes parages qu'eux, ni que les uns pleuraient sur les nouveau-nés et que les autres, pour innocenter Dieu, rendaient Satan responsable de l'infamie de la Création." E. M. Cioran, *De l'inconvénient d'être né* (Paris: Gallimard, 1973), 29.

6. "Haïssant les miens, mon pays, ses paysans intemporels, épris de leur torpeur, et comme éclatants d'hébétude, je rougissais d'en descendre, les reniais, me refusais à leur sous-éternité, à leurs certitudes de larves pétrifiées, à leur songerie géologique" (*TE,* 54). Kristeva's comment on the sentiment of hatred which accompanies the stranger without and within ("[La haine] fait résonner à l'*extérieur* cette autre haine, secrète et inavouable, honteuse au point de s'éteindre, que l'étranger porte *en lui* contre tous, contre personne, contre lui-même. . . ." *Étrangers à nous-mêmes* [Paris: Fayard, 1988], 24) characterizes well the double bind of an exile's fate, but her claim that this hatred is not admissible applies neither to Cioran nor to Gombrowicz, who both exteriorize their disagreements, hatreds, and, above all, shame.

7. E. M. Cioran, *The Trouble with Being Born,* trans. Richard Howard (New York: Seaver, 1976), 183. "Rabaisser les siens, les villipender, les pulvériser, s'en prendre aux fondations, se frapper soi-même à la base, ruiner son point de depart, se punir de ses origines . . . , maudire tous ces non-élus, engeance mineure, quelconque, tiraillé entre l'imposture et l'élégie, et dont la seule mission est de ne pas en avoir . . ." Cioran, *De l'inconvénient d'être né,* 211.

8. E. M. Cioran, *Anathemas and Admirations,* trans. Richard Howard (London: Quartet, 1992), 224–25; with my emendations. (This is a joint translation of Cioran's *Aveux et anathèmes* and *Exercises d'admiration.*) "Je n'ai jamais été attiré par des esprits confinés dans une seule forme de culture. *Ne pas s'enraciner, n'appartenir à aucune communauté,*—telle a été et telle est ma devise. Tourné vers d'autres horizons, j'ai toujours cherché à

savoir ce qui se passait ailleurs. A vingt ans, le Balkan ne pouvait plus rien m'offrir. C'est le drame, l'avantage aussi, d'être né dans un espace «culturel» mineur, quelconque. *L'étranger* est devenu mon dieu. D'où cette soif de pérégriner à travers les littératures et les philosophies, de les dévorer avec une ardeur maladive. Ce qui se passe à l'Est de l'Europe doit nécessairement se passer dans le pays de l'Amérique latine, et j'ai remarqué que ses représentants sont infiniment plus informés, plus «cultivés» que ne le sont les Occidentaux, incurablement provinciaux." Cioran, *Exercices d'admiration* (Paris: Gallimard, 1986), 162.

9. "Les croisés, devenus jardiniers, se sont évanouis en cette postérité casanière où ne subsiste plus aucune trace de nomadisme. Mais l'histoire est nostalgie de l'espace et horreur de chez soi, rêve vagabond et besoin de mourir au loin" (*TE,* 42).

10. The subjective, inflated sense of abstract dominion over the world comes, in Cioran's scheme, not through defamation, which, oddly enough, links one to the objects one has maligned, but through renunciation: "On a autant plus de prise sur ce monde qu'on s'en éloigne, qu'on n'y adhère pas. Le renoncement confère un pouvoir infini." Cioran, *De l'inconvénient d'être né,* 44.

11. The original 1933 title of the collection published in Warsaw was *Pamiętnik z okresu dojrzewania,* that is, *Memoir from the Times of Adolescence.* In 1957 Gombrowicz added several short stories and re-published the collection under the title *Bakakaj,* after the name of the street in Buenos Aires where he lived—thus enacting yet another displacement typical of the Gombrowiczian universe. Argentina as a mirror image of Poland functions as an underlying matrix in most of Gombrowicz's works written in exile.

12. The original title of the story was "Jakub Czarniecki's Memoir"; the name Jakub (Jacob) revealed the Jewish heritage of the boy. In the second edition Gombrowicz renamed the protagonist, opening another interpretative possibility: Stefan Czarniecki was a seventeenth-century Polish patriot who fought against the Swedish invasion (1626–29), the Chmielnicki insurgents (1648), the Swedish "flood" of 1655, and Moscow (1660). One of Gombrowicz's favorite authors, Jan Chryzostom Pasek, who served in Czarniecki's army, documented Czarniecki's campaigns in detail in his *Memoirs* (1690–95, published 1836).

13. Uhlans were a formation of light cavalry, armed with sabres and lances and, later, with carbines. Uhlan regiments were first organized in Poland in the eighteenth century after the fashion of Tartar formations in the Grand Duchy of Lithuania. One of Gombrowicz's cousins, Bebuś Rosset, was an officer in the First Regiment of Uhlans during the Polish-Russian

war of 1920. It was because of Gombrowicz's mother's strong resistance to what she called "drafting children" and despite the father's attempt to force his son to "fulfill his duty" that the sixteen-year-old Witold, instead of serving in the army, was employed in its civilian quarters. "The year 1920 made me into a being 'different from everybody else,' separated, living on the margin of the society. I continue to live this marginalized life to this day," Gombrowicz wrote in the 1950s in what was to be a broadcast by Radio Free Europe, but was never aired. Witold Gombrowicz, *Wspomnienia polskie. Wędrówki po Argentynie* (Warszawa: Res Publica, 1990), 31.

14. Gombrowicz, "Pamiętnik Stefana Czarnieckiego," 25 (trans. mine).

15. Julia Kristeva, *Powers of Horror: An Essay on Abjection,* trans. Leon S. Roudiez (New York: Columbia UP, 1982), 8.

16. Kristeva, *Powers of Horror,* 8.

17. The fundamental conceptual framework developed by Deleuze and Guattari in *Mille plateaux* relies on the opposition between two kinds of space: the smooth and the striated. "L'espace lisse est un champ sans conduit ni canaux," such as that of the sea, the desert, or the steppe. "L'espace sédentaire est strié, par des murs, des clôtures et des chemins entre des clôtures, tandis que l'espace nomade est lisse, seulement marqué par des «traits» qui s'effacent et se déplacent avec le trajet." Gilles Deleuze and Félix Guattari, *Capitalisme et schizophrénie: Mille plateaux* (Paris: Minuit, 1980), 459, 472.

18. Witold Gombrowicz, *Dziennik 1953–1956* (Kraków: Wydawnictwo Literackie, 1988), 319–20 (trans. mine).

19. Gombrowicz, *Dziennik 1953–1956,* 320 (trans. mine).

20. Gombrowicz, "Pamiętnik Stefana Czarnieckiego," 28.

21. Gombrowicz, "Pamiętnik Stefana Czarnieckiego," 29.

22. Jadwisia is perhaps right to perceive the curious words as implicitly indecent—the language used by Stefan will come back in Gombrowicz's last novel, *Kosmos,* as a tool of self-erotic practices of the main character, Leon.

23. Gombrowicz, "Pamiętnik Stefana Czarnieckiego," 29.

24. Kristeva, *Powers of Horror,* 4.

25. "Car l'abjection est en somme l'autre côté des codes religieux, moraux, idéologiques, sur lesquels reposent le sommeil des individus et les accalmies des sociétés." Julia Kristeva, *Pouvoirs de l'horreur,* (Paris: Seuil, 1980), 246.

26. "Formuler, c'est se sauver, même si on ne gribouille que des insanités, même si on n'a aucun talent." E.M. Cioran, *Entretien à Tübingen* (Paris: l'Herne, 1988), 102.

27. Cioran, *Anathemas and Admirations,* 12. "On n'habite pas un pays, on habite une langue. Une patrie, c'est cela et rien d'autre." Cioran, *Aveux et anathèmes,* 21.

28. It is only after 1989 that both Gombrowicz's and Cioran's works are once again published freely in Poland and in Romania.

29. ". . . démiurgie verbale [qui] se développe aux dépens de la lucidité" (*TE,* 205). He does, however, admit that poetry can also function as "the absolute of our *negative hours* . . . which derive from our malaise in the verbal universe" (*TTE,* 189) ["l'absolu de nos *heures négatives* . . . qui dérivent de notre malaise dans l'univers verbal"] (*TE,* 205).

30. Gombrowicz, *Dziennik 1953—1956,* 116 (trans. mine).

31. "Dans la vie de l'esprit il arrive un moment ou l'écriture, s'érigeant en principe autonome, devient destin. C'est alors que le Verbe, tant dans les spéculations philosophiques que dans les productions littéraires, dévoile et sa vigeur, et son néant" (*TE,* 128).

32. ". . . plus aucune trace de terre, de sang, d'âme en eux." E. M. Cioran, *Histoire et utopie* (Paris: Gallimard, 1960), 10.

33. Cioran, *Anathemas and Admirations,* 255–56.

34. Rita Gombrowicz, *Gombrowicz w Europie: Świadectwa i dokumenty 1963–1969* (Kraków: Wydawnictwo Literackie, 1993), 339 (trans. mine).

35. Juan José Saer, "La perspective extérieure," *Witold Gombrowicz, vingt ans après, suivi de correspondances et une jeunesse* (Paris: Bourgois, 1989), 130–39.

36. Cioran, *Anathemas and Admirations,* 225.

37. ". . . en profanateur, en traître, en agent de dissolution; toujours à côté, ou en dehors des choses." E. M. Cioran, *La chute dans le temps* (Paris: Gallimard, 1964), 13.

38. Kristeva, *Powers of Horror,* 17.

39. "Nous nous ingénions à démolir des réputations, celle de Dieu en tout premier lieu." Cioran, *La chute dans le temps,* 64.

40. "Je ne suis pas pessimiste, mais violent . . . c'est ce qui rend ma négation vivifiante . . . Je suis pareil au diable, qui est un individu actif, un

négateur qui met les choses en branle . . ." Cioran, *Œuvres* (Paris: Gallimard, 1995), 1791.

41. There is something vaguely pagan in Gombrowicz's appeal to the beauty of the "naked man." At the same time, while he proposes that the beauty of the world be apprehended through human beauty, he insists that the meaning of existence is to be derived from the physical anguish and pain that the bodily aspect of existence entails. In this way Gombrowicz's attitude goes beyond the concept of the body in antiquity when, in Bakhtin's account, "Everything corporeal was consecrated by the category of the *other*, and was experienced as something immediately valuable and significant" (Mikhail Bakhtin, *Art and Answerability* [Austin: U of Texas P, 1990], 53) and moves toward the Christian ideal in which the only acceptable body is the martyrized body of the man-God.

42. Cioran, *La chute dans le temps,* 22.

43. "Gombrowicz est irréductible à une image. Toujours autre que le personnage attendu. Très consciemment aristocrate chez les petits-bourgeois, peuple chez les aristocrates, hobereau en ville, citadin à la campagne, toujours en porte-à-faux, toujours en contradiction." Michel Nuridsany, "L'art de déplaire," *Magazine littéraire* (April 1991): 56.

44. Cioran, *Entretien à Tübingen,* 103.

45. For Gombrowicz laughter is never a carefree expression of joy or good cheer. Luba Jurgenson characterizes the peculiar nature of Gombrowiczian laughter as follows: "Tel le son d'une cloche qui annonce la venue d'un lépreux, le rire peut être le dernier rempart avant le fait pur et insupportable de l'être, avant le scandale que constitue l'homme avec sa peau moite, ses organes, son agitation inutile, et son âme qui suinte l'horreur, reflet déformé de choses innommables." "Un rire charnel et ambigu," *Magazine littéraire* (April 1991): 56.

46. Søren Kierkegaard, *The Concept of Irony, with Continual Reference to Socrates,* ed. and trans. Howard V. Hong and Edna H. Hong (Princeton: Princeton UP, 1989), 259.

47. Kierkegaard, *The Concept of Irony,* 255–56.

48. Cioran, *Anathemas and Admirations,* 4. "Tant la solitude me comble que le moindre rendez-vous m'est une crucifiction." E. M. Cioran, *Aveux et anathèmes* (Paris: Gallimard, 1987), 10.

49. "Les seuls événements notables d'une vie sont les ruptures." Cioran, *Aveux et anathèmes,* 47.

50. Cioran, *Anathemas and Admirations,* 4.

51. Kierkegaard, *The Concept of Irony,* 257.

52. “Le moi convertit le monde en néant, car l’ironie ne procure des sensations de puissance que lorsque tout est aboli. La perspective ironique, un subterfuge du délire des grandeurs. Pour se consoler de son inexistence, le moi devient *tout.* L’ironie atteint au sérieux lorsqu’elle s’élève à la vision implacable du rien. Le tragique est le stade ultime de l’ironie.” Cioran, *Des larmes et des saints* (Paris: l’Herne, 1986), 64.

53. “Le ‘moi’ constitue le privilège de ceux-là seuls qui ne vont pas jusqu’au bout d’eux-mêmes” (*TE,* 136).

PART THREE

Gombrowicz's Provocations: National Forms, Queer Sexualities

Ewa Płonowska Ziarek

8

The Scar of the Foreigner and the Fold of the Baroque:

National Affiliations and Homosexuality in Gombrowicz's Trans-Atlantyk

Gombrowicz has never been particularly shy in appropriating the most incredible postures for the purposes of provoking or irritating his readers. On the occasion of the publication of *Trans-Atlantyk,* he claimed, with a note of parody that could only recall his quarrels with the socially engaged Polish writers such as Stefan Żeromski (1864–1925), that the experimental writer is in fact a "social reformer," by which he meant a "re-former of form."[1] Despite its provocative ring, the title of a social "re-former" reopens the question of the social function of the literary form in the aftermath of the avant-garde legacy. This question is all the more complex in Gombrowicz's case, because his career seems to be characterized by a strange bifurcation between aesthetico-philosophical and socio-cultural interests, nowhere more apparent than in the contrast between his "Guide to Philosophy in Six Hours and a Quarter" (a series of lectures tracing the history of form in Western philosophy and aesthetics from Kant to structuralism) and his essay "Sienkiewicz" (where Gombrowicz proposes a history of aesthetics and popular literature in the formation of national culture).[2] Kant, the creator of one of the most rigorous philosophical systems, and Sienkiewicz, the Polish popular historical writer ("this first-rate second-rate" genius, as Gombrowicz calls him [*D* I, 223]), might seem to be rather strange bedfellows; yet, Gombrowicz finds it indispensable to think through the relation between philosophy and popular culture in order to diagnose the social complexity of literary form.

By calling himself a social re-former of form, Gombrowicz wants to oppose what he sees as the twin "pathologies" of modernism: the quite different but equally irritating pieties of "pure poetry" and "national literature," both of which share the "ostrich politics in relation to reality" and the cult of beauty (*D* I, 218). Despite an apparent opposition between "pure" and "national" art perpetuated in many discussions of modernism, the cult of beauty in both of these cultural formations consolidates, in the last resort, national affiliations. As Gombrowicz writes sardonically, "beauty is . . . necessary to be able to fall in love with oneself and that which is one's own—and it is in the name of this love that one is able to resist the world. Therefore, nations turn to their artists in order to extract beauty from them and this is where French, English, Polish, or Russian beauty comes from" (*D* I, 223). This love of beauty favored by national communities is, at the same time, asexual and deeply homophobic; as Gombrowicz writes with all the intended ambiguities, it is the paternal love and not the love of/among young men, a safe love avoiding forbidden temptations and "the beauty of iniquity."

By locating the unacknowledged similarity between "pure poetry" and national literature in the concept of 'love,' Gombrowicz traces a rather complicated configuration of aesthetics, sexuality, and nationalism. As he repeatedly argues, the sublimated union of love and beauty, or the complicity of sexuality, aesthetics, and politics, promises a shallow "harmonizing of life with spirit" and eventually covers over all the antinomies in collective affiliations (*D* I, 227). It is this aspect of his work, often unexplored or simplified, that bears closest resemblance to queer theory, focused likewise on the paradoxical cultural work that the constructions of homosexuality and heterosexuality perform in various domains of social life. One of the most productive encounters between Gombrowicz and queer theory can occur in the context of the recent discussions of transgressive aesthetics and sexual/political dissidence. For instance, Jonathan Dollimore's reading of Wilde's work can illuminate the often ignored role of sexual dissidence in Gombrowicz's project of the cultural reform of form: "Wilde's transgressive aesthetic . . . facilitate(s) the development for cultural politics of the concept of the perverse dynamic . . . Provisionally then, this concept of the perverse dynamic denotes certain instabilities and contradictions within dominant structures which exist by virtue of exactly what those structures simultaneously contain and exclude."[3]

In *Trans-Atlantyk,* published for the first time in Paris in 1952 and recently translated into English, Gombrowicz intensifies the "instabilities and contradictions" within the "national form" in order to create a space for alternative collectivity. Directed against the spirit of reconciliation, Gombrowicz's devastating critique of nationalism proceeds by juxtaposing the modern experience of queer eroticism in exile with the obsolete aesthetics of the Baroque. In order to escape the "Polish legend" of national martyrdom, Gombrowicz explodes the shallow unity of the national form by uncovering "dangerous" tropes this form cannot reconcile: the obsolescence of the Baroque, on the one hand, and the "exotic novelty" of gay eroticism, on the other. Either too outmoded or too proleptic, these two interrelated liminal figures—the aesthetic and the erotic significations of marginality—are perpetually excluded from the historical narrative of the nation and yet re-emerge as the fractures within national identity. In the first part of this essay, I will explore Gombrowicz's understanding of aesthetics' role in national culture by thinking through the disjunction between the philosophical and cultural implications of the Baroque style in *Trans-Atlantyk.* In the second part, I will focus on the ambivalent role of "love" in national affiliations by engaging Kristeva's analysis of the foreigner and Gombrowicz's figuration of homosexuality.

"A little trumpet tossed onto the rubbish of unexploited Polish possibilities": Nationality as Form

> My attitude to Poland is a consequence of my attitude to form: I would like to elude Poland as I elude style . . .
>
> Witold Gombrowicz, *Diaries*

> Communities are to be distinguished, not by their falsity/genuineness, but by the style in which they are imagined.
>
> Benedict Anderson, *Imagined Communities*

One of the most striking features of *Trans-Atlantyk* is the jarring juxtaposition of the modern experience of the foreigner in exile with the anachronism of its Baroque style—a juxtaposition that, in itself, evokes the dissonances and the heterogeneity of Baroque aesthetics.[4] It is as if Gombrowicz envelops "the national beauty" in the extravagant and overflowing drapes of Baroque prose in order to escape all the more effectively its tenacious and mesmerizing hold: "I was loathe to reveal the whole truth to this man, to this Fellow Countryman, or to other Fellow Countrymen, Kinsmen . . . as I would haply be burnt alive at the stake, pulled apart by horses or tongs, deprived of good fame or credit" (*T*, 6). Why this turn toward the Baroque style in a seemingly autobiographical text describing Gombrowicz's own experience of being a refugee, when his short literary mission to Argentina turned unexpectedly at the outset of the Second World War into permanent exile? Why this peculiar mediation of the foreigner's experience through the obsolete aesthetics of the Baroque?

One of the most important functions of the excessive Baroque style in *Trans-Atlantyk* is to suggest that nationality requires a specific signifying economy and, therefore, that it has to be considered as a cultural formation similar to literature, religion, or morality. Gombrowicz's analysis of the "national form" anticipates in this respect the influential argument of Benedict Anderson, who proposes to treat nation as "an imagined political community," where the adjective *imagined* does not merely refer to ideological fabrication, or false consciousness, but rather poses the problem of signification at the very center of political analysis. Hence Anderson's famous claim that the imaginary character of national identifications does not bespeak falsity or delusion, as many analysts (including Gellner[5]) suggest, but underscores the constructed character of all communities: "in fact, all communities larger than primordial villages of face-to face contact (*and perhaps even these*) are imagined."[6] With the erasure of the opposition between fabrication and authenticity in social relations, the distinctions among different types of communities is carried by the mode of signification or, as Gombrowicz would say, the form of their affiliations: "Communities are to be distinguished, not by their falsity/genuineness, but by the style in which they are imagined."[7] For Anderson, the specificity of national communities is captured by "the idea of a sociological organism moving calendrically through homogenous, empty time."[8] This provocative insight into the relation between nationality and style, politics and aesthetics, historical narratives and temporality, although left largely undeveloped in Anderson's work, is central to Gombrowicz's preoccupation with the "national form."

Gombrowicz's recycling of the Baroque style in *Trans-Atlantyk* stresses not only the interdependence of nationality and form but also the crucial difference between the signifying economy of the nation and the mode of signification operating in the Baroque aesthetics. To articulate this difference more clearly, let us turn for a moment to Gilles Deleuze's analysis of the philosophical stakes of the Baroque in his influential study *The Fold: Leibniz and the Baroque.* In contrast to the "sociological solidity" and historical continuity of the nation, the Baroque's economy of signification, according to Deleuze, can be characterized by the figure of the fold; that is, by the dynamic principle of difference that operates not through rigid demarcations or binary oppositions but through infinite variations displaying the fluidity of matter and the elasticity of bodies. Without establishing a common measure or producing discrete units, such as culture/nature, subject/object, matter/form, body/soul, this mode of signification both distinguishes and connects the severed terms and is, in turn, differentiated by them. In his study, Deleuze refers to Gombrowicz's work as one of the striking examples of the neo-Baroque strain within modernism. By radicalizing the operation of the fold, the neo-Baroque art liberates even further its power of dissonance. If the Baroque attempts to deal with social and linguistic incongruity by dividing divergences into incompatible worlds, modern art intensifies discords from within and treats them as enabling conditions of social change: "in the same chaotic world divergent series are endlessly tracing bifurcating paths. It is a 'chaosmos' of the type found in Joyce, but also . . . in Borges, or Gombrowicz . . . The play of the world has changed in a unique way, because now it has become the play that diverges. Beings are pushed apart, kept open through divergent series that . . . pull them outside, instead of being closed upon the . . . convergent world that they express from within."[9]

Gombrowicz offers a striking allegory of such a divergent play of signification in his representation of Gonzalo's estate, a representation that violates not only the coherence of aesthetic taste but also the order of nature and the logic of desire:

> A hall large with divers things filled but one upon the other, one with the other, there a Triptych under a Vase, yonder a

> Carpet upon a Candelabra, an Armchair upon a Chair, a Goblin, a Madonna . . . and Brothel, Brothel, Brothel, and with no shame one with the other couples as it goes . . . instead of a Dog after a Bitch, a Dog perchance with a Cat or with a Wolverine, with a Goose, a hen, perchance with a rat . . . and so, epithalamium, Brothel, Brothel and Epithalamium. (*T,* 91)

In Gonzalo's fabulous household, where a Madonna coexists with a Goblin, and where a dog mates with a rat, neither conventional nor natural boundaries are able to contain the dispersed world. With the erosion of classifying reason and the destruction of aesthetic taste, Gonzalo's world erupts into the proliferating series put in motion by the "denatured" desire violating the divisions between the species and, as we shall see, the gender arrangements within the same species. It is a world in which nature itself, no longer capable of guaranteeing moral order, rational unity, or beauty, is turned into a "brothel." In Gonzalo's fantastic estate the stylistic dissonances are pitted not only against the fabrication of the organic unity of the nation but also against the attempts to fix the meaning of sexuality by reference to nature. It is only fitting that this signifying space, where both nature and culture are debased and reconfigured, becomes in Gombrowicz's text a location of the final carnivalesque performance, announcing an alternative community.[10]

In the context of social modernity, the intensification of dissonance "from within" corresponds, according to Deleuze, to the changed way of living in the modern world, where the closed Baroque monads are turned into "wandering nomads."[11] This analysis of the Baroque aesthetics—in particular, the emphasis on the diverging play of signification that destroys both the metaphysical unity of Being and the political unity of the nation—is helpful for understanding the overall strategy of *Trans-Atlantyk,* where the excessive style of the Baroque is pitted against the imaginary unity of the nation and the "reconciliation of life and spirit" it promises. Deleuze's brilliant insights, which illuminate the relation between avant-garde aesthetics and the search for the alternative modes of collectivity, come nonetheless short of explaining Gombrowicz's strategy of parodic recycling of the obsolete popular forms. Because Deleuze centers his analysis of the Baroque on the philosophical model provided by Leibniz, he fails to take into account the fact that in *Trans-Atlantyk*

Gombrowicz deliberately avoids the Western models of Baroque art and philosophy, which, within Polish culture are connected with the cosmopolitan life of the courts and the sophisticated work of the court poets, like Andrzej Morsztyn, deploying instead the provincial, and verging almost on the disreputable, aspects of the Polish Baroque—the so-called Sarmatian model.[12] In *Trans-Atlantyk* the emphasis falls, therefore, not on the production of the modern neo-Baroque aesthetics but on the parodic repetition of an obsolete and degraded cultural formation, no longer in service of the preservation of national identity. This strategy allows Gombrowicz to produce stylistic dissonance in the form of carnivalesque laughter, which clears the space for alternative forms of community.

Let us move then from the Leibnizean portrait of Gombrowicz, offered us by Deleuze, to the Sarmatian caricature drawn in *Trans-Atlantyk.*[13] In order to do so, we will have to understand the basic features of the Sarmatian Baroque, especially, its relation to the political ideology of the seventeenth century and its status as the popular literary form. As Andrzej Walicki suggests, the Sarmatian ideology of the Polish gentry in the seventeenth century combined the idea of the democratic political system, regarded as "infinitely superior to Western monarchies," with the agrarian ideal of the country.[14] Opposed to the strong royal power, the gentry attempted to assure its political freedom through the infamous *liberum veto,* a vote of protest, through which any single member of the Diet (Parliament) could at any time oppose and effectively cancel the work of the entire assembly. For both of these reasons—the commitment to the agrarian ideal and the sense of political superiority—the self-righteous gentry was opposed to anything Western, in fact, to any foreign influence. Despite their own self-congratulatory portrait as the defenders of "the golden" freedom, democracy, and patriotism, the Sarmatian gentry, so frequently ridiculed by the subsequent generations of Polish intellectuals, became the stereotype of anarchy, drunkenness, religiosity, narrow-mindedness, and unruliness.

This anachronistic and degraded stereotype of the Sarmatian gentry resonates in Gombrowicz's satirical portrayal of the figures of the Baron, Ciumkała, and Pyckal—the grotesque inseparable trio locked in endless personal wars with one another. Their responses, actions, and words automatically repeat the invincible logic of the obsolete Sarmatian stereotype, which proves to be stronger than any individual motivation of the character:

> The inveterate quarrel between the Baron, Pyckal and Ciumkała had its beginning in a Mill, the which fell to them in equal parts from the Liquidation . . . Ergo one would drown the other in a spoon of water, but in the continuous sequence of Trials, summonses, quarrels, in that ceaseless Gnawing communion, so one with the other as bigos, as Hodgepodge mixed, stewed, that perchance one cannot live without the other . . . And they have forgotten God's world, with themselves only, amongst themselves, self-selved; and from the old days so many Relicks have piled up . . . so that . . . a word heedlessly thrown out at once reminds them of something Older and Baked In, and moves them as a weathercock on a Church tower. (*T,* 24–25)

As the figure of "a weathercock on a Church tower" suggests, the Baron, Ciumkała, and Pyckal are hideous marionettes, blindly repeating the same ritual, the same movement, as if steered by the invisible strings of some monstrous performance beyond their control. In this grotesque resurrection of the Sarmatian gentry, Gombrowicz deploys anachronistic modes of national identification—or what he calls the interhuman church—where the very obsolescence of intersubjective relations exposes the blind compulsion of form behind "organic" national identity.

Gombrowicz is particularly interested in the oral and popular character of the Sarmatian Baroque because these features display the "anomalous" formation of Polish national consciousness in the seventeenth century. In contrast to the usual stress on the pivotal role of print capitalism in the spread of nationalism in the West, the Sarmatian Baroque confronts us with the first mass cultural phenomenon in Polish literature that does not depend on print culture.[15] Unlike its elite courtly counterpart, this Baroque is associated with the flood of memoirs of the half-educated country squires, describing either their military exploits in numerous wars or their exotic travels. Most of these writers were educated in the parochial Jesuit schools, where they learned nothing more beyond Latin, the models of exalted and pompous speeches, and the art of composing "poems" for special occasions. Their stories were disseminated orally first, or, when written down, they circulated in the manuscript form among family members, neighbors, and friends. It is this orality, associated with the parochial and already anachronistic "intimate" community of neighbors, that *Trans-Atlantyk,* written in the style of *gawęda* (oral tale), so brilliantly parodies: "I feel a need to relate here for Family, kin and friends of mine the beginning of these my adventures, now ten years old, in the Argentinian capital. Not that I ask anyone to have these old Noodles of mine, this Turnip (haply even raw), for in the Pewter bowl Thin, Wretched they are and, what is more, likewise Shaming, in the oil of my Sins, my Shames, these Groats of mine, heavy, Dark with this black kasha of mine" (*T,* 3).

The Baroque period lasted in Polish literature for a long time—depending on the mode of periodization, for one and one-half or almost two centuries, ending with the conservative poetry of the Confederation of Bar (1768–72). It is its last phase, the late seventeenth and eighteenth centuries, frequently called by the historians of Polish literature the "Saxon or Sarmatian night," that has been submitted to most devastating criticism by subsequent generations, especially by the writers of the Enlightenment. Despite more complex recent reassessments of the heritage of the Sarmatian Baroque by literary scholars, one would still be hard pressed to find a more narrow-minded and parochial literary example in the history of Polish letters. The very opposite of any national aspiration to the rich literary heritage, this fallen Baroque—a legacy of ravaging seventeenth century wars, Counter-Reformation, anarchy, the weakening of the state, as well as of the decline of education and urban life—is associated in Polish history with the overwhelming cultural and political crisis which prefigures the impending loss of national independence in the eighteenth century.

As this detour through the basic features of the Sarmatian Baroque suggests, the specific inflection of the Baroque style in *Trans-Atlantyk* creates dissonance within national identity by parodic repetition of a degraded popular cultural formation—a formation that puts the very status and cultural value of literature into question. In the composition of the novel, the imaginary unity of the nation is pulled apart by the temporal fold of *obsolescence,* on the one hand, and by the axiological fold of cultural *inferiority,* on the other. Gombrowicz's fascination with cultural obsolescence excavates those forgotten social forms of significations that no longer produce intersubjective identifications. Obsolescence is thus one of Gombrowicz's strategies to denaturalize collective identities, to expose their historical and constructed character, and especially to interrupt the linear temporal progression associated with national narratives. As Gombrowicz explains in *Polish Recollections,* "when certain customs are about to be finished, they become afflicted with a kind of sclerosis—the living content escapes from them and only the rigidity of 'pure form' remains, as Witkiewicz would put it. I was fascinated by this formalism, it irritated and captivated me artistically—in my work there are plenty of such dying forms."[16] One cannot fail to notice the originality of Gombrowicz's definition of formalism here—it does not denote, as Peter Bürger suggests, the interest in form for its own sake but rather enables the exploration of the signifying economy within which social identities are produced and reproduced.[17] By excavating the remnants of social forms that no longer participate in the "living essence" of national memory or tradition, Gombrowicz exposes not only the force and the rigidity of their constructed character but also the historical discontinuities in national narratives.

Gombrowicz's artificial resuscitation of the oral but already "dead forms" of the parochial Baroque memoirs and their juxtaposition with the "living" form of national identity perpetuated by print culture is a striking example not only of his interest in obsolete cultural formations but also of his ongoing preoccupation with cultural inferiority—with the discarded refuse and remnants of national culture. Thus, we might say that the other fissure in the national identity in *Trans-Atlantyk* is created by the fold of aesthetic valuation; that is, by the dissonance between cultural refuse and the dominant norms of aesthetic taste, regardless of whether these norms favor traditional beauty or the avant-garde break with tradition. In one sense, Gombrowicz's preoccupation with cultural inferiority contests the main premise of the Kantian aesthetics, namely, the understanding of beauty as disinterested pleasure. Thus, if Gombrowicz's strategy of obsolescence is pitted against the imaginary unity of national history, his preoccupation with degraded cultural formations exposes the unacknowledged cultural value of beauty and the spirit of collective reconciliation it promises. In another sense, however, Gombrowicz's strategic use of Eastern-European "provincialism" and its "second rate" cultural productions frustrates in an equal measure the self-congratulatory revolutionary claims of the Western avant-garde: "Think of my diary as the intrusion into European culture of a villager, of a Polish country gentleman, with all the mistrust, the common-sense and the realism of a peasant . . . Despite so many years of exile and urban life, I still remain a Polish yokel" (*KT,* 118). This self-professed Eastern-European provincialism allows Gombrowicz to expose the cultural levels of "undervalue" or, what Artur Sandauer calls "the degraded reality."[18] Instead of being one step ahead of his times, Gombrowicz recycles what is forgotten or left behind by the modern culture obsessed with the value of contemporaneity.

By presenting himself as a scavenger sifting through cultural refuse, Gombrowicz looks for the new configurations of collective, artistic, and sexual identities not in the practice of the avant-garde but in the "garbage" of Polish and European culture:

> The rubbish heap. The point is exactly that I come from your rubbish heap. All that you cast off through the centuries as refuse is now speaking out through me . . . You threw everything that was acting and theater in you into the trash can and you tried to forget about it." (*D* I, 36)

What is characteristic about this passage is that the "cast off" refuse is associated with acting and theater—the tropes Gombrowicz so frequently deploys to figure his own performance of homosexuality. As he confesses in the conversation with Dominique de Roux, "Erotic impulses dragged me down . . . I was 'between.' And I was an actor" (*KT,* 38). Thus, the parodic recycling of the obsolete and degraded cultural forms parallels Gombrowicz's trans-valuation of homosexuality—in particular, his contestation of the homophobic representations of queer eroticism as "regression" or "degeneration." In both cases, Gombrowicz retrieves what is deemed by culture as shameful, inassimilable, obsolete, or regressive and reinterprets it as a hope for a different future.

Gombrowicz's retrieval of the remnants and refuse of national culture is intertwined with a rethinking of the social value of literature itself. Can there be a collective dimension of literature beyond, or apart from, the spirit of reconciliation promised by national culture? Gombrowicz's scavenger mode of writing provides an answer to this question that is remarkably similar, on the one hand, to the concept of minor literature elaborated by Deleuze and Guattari and, on the other, to Mary Russo's rethinking of the carnivalesque modernism. In particular, Gombrowicz's use of the discarded and discredited elements of culture evokes the strategy "to make use of the polylingualism of one's own language, to make a minor or intensive use of it, to oppose the oppressed quality of this language to its oppressive quality, to find points of nonculture or underdevelopment."[19] Such a strategic use of the forgotten layers of "nonculture," which certainly dramatizes the deterritorializing effects of writing itself, does not separate literature from the collective conditions of enunciation but intensifies instead the dissonances within collectivity—the antinomies covered over by the imagined unity of the national identity. Yet, the sheer hilarity and the Rabelaisian laughter that accompanies Gombrowicz's debasement of the Baroque turns the deterritorializing effects of writing into a carnivalesque performance, which, as Mary Russo argues, "suggests a redeployment or counterproduction of culture, knowledge, pleasure . . . In this sense, carnival can be seen, above all, as a site of insurgency."[20]

When Gombrowicz turns, then, to the provincial and parochial prose of seventeenth-century memoirs, he intends not to lend them a new veneer of nobility or nostalgia in the manner of Mickiewicz (1798–1855) or Sienkiewicz (1846–1916) but, on the contrary, to intensify their ugliness—to turn them into the unworkable caricature of national literature:[21]

> This is the source of our incredible, . . . almost brilliant crisis of Polish beauty, which put us face-to-face with our Ugliness . . . a century of sclerotic, senile old stiffening and at the same time, a dull unruliness . . . Never before or since have we been closer to rubbing up against hell and any thought about Poland and the Poles is not worth much if it bypasses the period of Saxon scurrility . . . What happened was that the Pole suddenly felt himself the caricature of a Pole . . . desperate with a tormenting sense of our own awfulness and ridiculousness, we tottered into sclerosis and farce. (*D* I, 224)

Not merely parodying the Baroque style, Gombrowicz takes it upon himself to carry the Baroque "burlesque . . . to its ultimate conclusion"—to intensify the inferiority of cultural formations up to a point where the affective identifications at work in national community explode, as the ending of *Trans-Atlantyk* suggests, into carnivalesque laughter. Conceived as the antinomy, or as "the brilliant crisis" of national beauty, the stylistic dissonances of the Baroque debase the collectivity of the "interhuman church" and turn it into a carnivalesque "counterproduction" of culture. By creating the "incurable disharmony" between the ideal of "national beauty" and the degraded language of the Baroque, Gombrowicz thus hopes to change nothing less than a world-view created by national culture—and to open an imaginary space for a different collectivity.

Trans-Atlantyk pits carnivalesque hilarity against the "Polish legend," against the traumas of national martyrdom; that is, against the very essence of the nostalgic romanticism, exemplified in Mickiewicz's national epic, *Pan Tadeusz* (1834).[22] Unlike the opening invocation (memorized by all Polish schoolchildren) of *Pan Tadeusz* in which the lost country is nostalgically extolled as the source of life, Gombrowicz's novel opens with a mockingly blasphemous curse of the nation and with the betrayal of the patriotic ethos:[23]

> Sail, sail, you Compatriots, to your People! Sail to that holy Nation of yours haply Cursed! . . . Sail to your St. Freak, cursed by all Nature, ever being born and still Unborn! Sail, sail, so he will not suffer you to Live or Die but keep you for ever between Being and Non-being. (*T,* 6)

Although Gombrowicz claims that he is interested in refiguring the contemporary attitudes to nationality as such ("I would like to propose a similar revision to peoples of other nations, since the issue [in *Trans-Atlantyk*] does refer not to the Pole's attitude to Poland but to the subject's attitude to the nation as such"; trans. mine[24]), the audacity of this sacrilegious gesture can be better appreciated in the specific context of Polish history. After all, what Gombrowicz attacks is not the triumphant history of nationalism associated with the West but the Polish legend of "national martyrdom" at the moment when the historical catastrophe of the Second World War not only outdoes the pathos of this legend but perpetuates it as the very means of survival and hope for the future. The irony of destroying the "national form" of the already destroyed nation at a time when nationality functions as the only form of political legitimation for any collective claim to independence is certainly not lost on Gombrowicz. In his numerous prefaces to different editions of *Trans-Atlantyk,* in his *Diaries,* and autobiographical recollections, he raises the question whether his critique is not "out of place, inadmissible in the circumstances in which we found ourselves, at the depth of the catastrophe" (*KT,* 104). He does not hesitate to compare the provocation of *Trans-Atlantyk* to an indecent "burst of laughter at a funeral . . . At the darkest hour of our history, when we would have done better to sing a Requiem mass . . . a bold laugh in the face of tragedy" (*KT,* 105). The initial fury over *Trans-Atlantyk* was not so much fueled by the undoing of the national ethos but by turning the national requiem mass—the melancholy beauty of a ceremonial lamentation over the lost independence—into a farce.

"This panic-stricken masculinity": Homophobia and National Identifications

> Whole nations threw themselves like bulls onto the sword of the toreador in paroxysms, in the mad fear that the audience might attribute something of the *Ewig-Weibliche* to them . . . So I had no doubt that the magnified bull might charge me, too, if he scented my attack on his priceless genitalia.
>
> Witold Gombrowicz, *Diary,* I, vol. 1

> The problem is not so much homosexual desire as the fear of homosexuality.
>
> Guy Hocquenghem, *Homosexual Desire*

If Gombrowicz bursts into laughter in the face of national tragedy and turns a requiem mass into a carnivalesque performance, it is because he wishes to call attention to the dangers that nationalism itself represents. As he writes in his preface to the 1953 edition of *Trans-Atlantyk,* "it is quite possible to have such an attitude to the nation, in which our natural attachment to it, what is more, our inescapable and from our will independent bond with it, will be supplemented by an acknowledgment that nation is a dangerous force" (trans. mine)."[25] To acknowledge nationality as a dangerous force, one has to take into account another aspect of national form, namely, the specific logic of intersubjectivity and affect operating in a national community. Gombrowicz exposes the contradictions and antinomies generated by this logic by focusing on two marginal figures barred from the ideal of national community and yet indispensable for the formation of its identity: the foreigner and the homosexual. Perpetually excluded from the historical narrative of the nation, these two interrelated figures—the foreigner and the homosexual—contest the imaginary unity of national community just as the tropes of obsolescence and degradation disrupt the cultural unity of the national form. Thus, the figuration of homosexuality and foreignness repeats on the level of collectivity the effects of the Baroque style generated on the level of form.

Gombrowicz's strategy of rethinking national affiliations from the borderline and excluded positions parallels in this respect the project of Julia Kristeva to interpret the narrative of the nation from the perspective of the foreigner. Associated with French psychoanalysis and feminism, Kristeva is hardly ever considered, especially in the American academy, as an Eastern-European intellectual. Yet, her 1989 *Étrangers à nous-mêmes,* translated into English as *Strangers to Ourselves* might be read as a peculiar testimony to her own position as a foreigner in French culture just as Gombrowicz's *Trans-Atlantyk* is a fictional account of his. In both works—*Strangers to Ourselves* and *Trans-Atlantyk*—the figure of the foreigner is treated as the generalized mark of various oppositional terms against which national community attempts to define and consolidate its identity.[26] As a reminder of the oppositional and differential logic of national identity, the appearance of the foreigner invariably provokes "the prickly passions aroused by the intrusion of the *other* in the homogeneity of a group" (*ST,* 41).

For Kristeva as for Gombrowicz, the foreigner is a figure of the ambivalence characterizing national affiliations: it provides the best exemplification of the logic of nationality and its most vertiginous aberration: "The difficulty engendered by the matter of foreigners would be completely contained in the deadlock caused by the distinction that sets the *citizen* apart from *man* . . . The process means . . . that one can be more or less a man to the extent that one is more or less a citizen, that he who is not a citizen is not fully a man. Between the man and a citizen there is a scar: the foreigner" (*ST,* 97–98). Signifying an always already failed attempt to subsume the differential identity of the nation into an organic unity, the figure of the scar suggests a double meaning of the foreigner in Kristeva's text—not merely the external border of the nation, the foreigner signifies otherness disrupting national identity from within: "psychologically he signifies the difficulty we have of living as an *other* and with others; politically, he underscores the limits of nation-states and of the national political conscience" (*ST,* 103). Yet, the scar is not only a signifying trace—its materiality also evokes the disfiguring marks on the body imprinted by national identifications.

Since in this account the foreigner becomes the uncanny double of the political rationality of the nation, Kristeva, like Homi Bhabha, turns to Freud's concept of uncanny in order to diagnose the instability of the inside/outside opposition characteristic of national affiliations.[27] In the political sense, the psychoanalytical concept of the uncanny is used to describe both the ambivalent logic of national identifications and the alternative concept of community. Instead of occupying the position of the other against which the nation defines its identity, the uncanny appearance of the foreigner disrupts the homogeneity of social identity from within. This emphasis on the liminality fissuring the unity of the nation from the inside serves as a corrective to those accounts of nationality that either presuppose the imaginary unity of the people or, as Eve Kosofsky Sedgwick suggests, explain the national identity by using the simple oppositional logic of scapegoating.[28]

In the "psychological" sense, however, the affect of the uncanny—that is, the anxiety associated with the return of the repressed—allows Kristeva to diagnose the "fascinated rejection of the foreigner" as a defensive projection: "when we flee from or struggle against the foreigner, we are fighting our unconscious—that improper facet of our impossible 'own and proper' " (*ST,* 191). Projected outside as something foreign to the self, the strangeness manifesting itself in the uncanny is, in the last resort, is a defense against the other within the self. By unraveling these defensive projections, psychoanalysis not only shatters the imaginary unity of the self but also initiates a different logic of the community, far removed from the fraternity or brotherhood characteristic of national affiliations. By setting "the difference within us in its most bewildering shape" and presenting "it as the ultimate conditions of being *with* others" (*ST,* 192), Kristeva elaborates a paradoxical logic of community, one that respects the differences within and among the subjects rather than seeking their reconciliation in a common essence.

Although Gombrowicz concurs with Kristeva's analysis of the uncanny and ambivalent logic of national affiliations, he suspects that the figure of the foreigner does not quite explain how this ambivalence is implicated in the politics of sexuality. Consequently, as the peculiar friendship between the narrator of *Trans-Atlantyk* (the Sarmatian alter ego of Gombrowicz) and the homosexual Gonzalo (the Argentinean "double" of Gombrowicz[29]) suggests, the figure of the foreigner is redoubled and disrupted by a more "dangerous" fold of homoeroticism—a proliferation of doubling that itself might be seen as uncanny. In fact, Gonzalo occupies both of these positions at the same time: the other characters perceive him as a person of mixed national lineage—Turkish mother, Portuguese father—and as a rather stereotypical representation of the homosexual—effeminate and decadent aristocrat attempting to seduce a Polish youth away from his patriotic duty. This structural redoubling suggests the mutually constitutive role of sexuality and national identity—the entwinement also implied, but not pursued, in Kristeva's interpretation of the uncanny and its relation to "an erotic, death-bearing unconscious" (*ST,* 192). What Gombrowicz suggests in *Trans-Atlantyk* is that the formation of national identity depends upon the rigid distinction between heterosexual and homosexual masculinity—a distinction that is consistently unraveled by the Baroque style and composition of the text. Put in a different way, between "a man" and "a citizen" there is another, much deeper scar, marked by the specter of homosexuality: within the homophobic logic of nationality, one can be a citizen only to the extent one is a heterosexual man.

Gombrowicz's diagnosis of the ambivalent logic of sexuality underlying national identifications becomes the very principle of the narrative of *Trans-Atlantyk.* The novel moves back and forth between two opposite narrative planes: on the one hand, the revolt against nationality is intertwined with the sexualization of male bonds, on the other hand, the mobilization of the national pride and patriotic spirit in exile is fueled by paranoid suspicion and persecution of homosexuality. The novel is thus split between the national plot, in which the main protagonist, the retired Major, endeavors to dispatch his son to Europe to defend Poland against the Nazi invasion, and the homoerotic "revolutionary" intrigue, in which Gonzalo attempts to seduce young Ignacy and to liberate him from his obedience to the regime of the Father and patriotic duty. The narrator, "Gombrowicz," endlessly vacillates between these two narrative poles, repeatedly betraying all the characters and their causes. It is in response to this vacillation and the erasure of difference between the national ties and homoeroticism that the other characters, driven by panic, constitute a grotesque, paranoid Order of the Chevaliers of the Spur, in which everyone watches everyone else and punishes the slightest transgression of the fellow comrades with a thrust of the spur into the flesh.

Gombrowicz's figuration of homoeroticism as a rupture within national identity presents the most stunning reversal of Polish romantic epic, Mickiewicz's *Pan Tadeusz*—a national epic, let us add, also written in exile in the aftermath of lost national independence.[30] In *Pan Tadeusz,* the patriotic motif of the political struggle for national independence is so fully harmonized with the heterosexual romance that the heterosexual couple, Tadeusz and Zosia, embodies the spirit of national union and the promise of national freedom. The happiness of the couple becomes the figure of hope for the future independence of the partitioned nation. By contrast, Gombrowicz not only removes any traces of heterosexual romance from *Trans-Atlantyk* (to the effect that the female characters are conspicuously absent in the narrative) but also coordinates the struggle against the dangers of nationality with the sexualization of male bonds. Thus, the narrator's curse against the monstrous nation and his blind compatriots at the beginning of the text opens a possibility of his participation in Gonzalo's erotic plot, just as Gonzalo's help during the confrontation with the Argentinean poet prevents the narrator, "Gombrowicz," from being seduced by the title of "national genius." Throughout the text, Gombrowicz suggests that one of the greatest antinomies generated by the national form inheres in the concept of love itself: although the national identity privileges the idealized love among men "after thirty," it, at the same time, cannot withstand the possible eroticization of this love.[31]

For Gombrowicz, the emergence of gay eroticism presents the most radical demystification of national unity because this unity rests on the imperative—all the more stringently prescribed as it is impossible to be fulfilled—to exclude homoeroticism from the homosocial ties forming the national community. As Gombrowicz writes in his essay "Sienkiewicz," "the young man . . . was destined only for the role and function of the 'virtuous son of Poland.' If, therefore, carried away by instinct and temperament, he made his way into a jungle of those forbidden charms [which were to find their expression in Baudelaire, Wilde, Ruskin . . .], it was always on his own, without a guide, left to his own unsophisticated, murky instincts" (*D* I, 226). Gombrowicz's reference to Wilde leaves little doubt about the specific character of the charms forbidden to the "virtuous son of Poland."[32] We must ask at this point why national communities forbid so stringently homosexuality to their "virtuous sons." As the editors of the recent volume *Nationalisms and Sexualities* suggest, the intolerance of homosexuality is not incidental but rather a structural counterpart of the widespread representation of national community as an idealized fraternity—or, in Benedict Anderson's words, as "a deep, horizontal comradeship." While explicitly privileging the male homosocial bonding, this conception of nationhood demands a separation of idealized fraternity from the erotic relations among men: "nationalism favors a distinctly homosocial form of male bonding . . . Typically represented as a passionate brotherhood, the nation finds itself compelled to distinguish its 'proper' homosociality from more explicitly sexualized male-male relations, a compulsion that requires the identification, isolation, and containment of male homosexuality."[33]

One of the pervasive mechanisms of containment and exclusion of homosexuality from the "proper" homosocial relations can be illuminated, as Guy Hocquenghem suggests, by the psychoanalytic account of sublimation. From his 1911 analysis of the Schreber case to his 1922 essay "Certain Neurotic Mechanisms in Jealousy, Paranoia and Homosexuality," Freud consistently regards social instincts, in particular friendship and comradeship, as the sublimation of "homosexual tendencies": "In the light of psychanalysis we are accustomed to regard social feeling as a sublimation of homosexual attitudes toward objects."[34] As Hocquenghem argues, sublimation becomes thus the name for a "proper" social investment of homosexuality, for the containment of the homosexual desire within the homosocial feelings of fraternity—a containment all the more "necessary" since the Freudian theory of bisexuality makes the possibility of homosexuality ubiquitous.[35]

It is this "proper" social utility of homosexuality that is perpetually undone in *Trans-Atlantyk*. The breakdown of the mechanism of sublimation, and the subsequent emergence of queer eroticism within the structures of homosocial exchange, in turn exposes the rivalry and psychological blackmail underlying national affiliations. It is deeply symptomatic, for instance, that Gonzalo's first appearance in the text disrupts the bizarre confrontation between the Polish and the Argentinean national geniuses. Surrounded by his aggressive compatriots and the patronizing literary elites of Argentina, the narrator, "Gombrowicz," is forced to fight a verbal duel with the

Argentinean poet in order to assure the foreigners of the strength of Polish national spirit in the face of the Nazi invasion: "'Sick him, else Shame for he is their most Famous Author and it cannot be that they Celebrate him when the Great Polish Author, Genius is in the room! Bite him, you chitsh.t, you genius, bite him for if not, we will bite you!' . . . Now behind me stand all my Brood . . . I perceived there is no other Remedy but that I must bite him else my Countrymen will give me no peace" (*T,* 32). Trapped without an exit by this patriotic blackmail ("bite him for if not, we will bite you!"), the fictional alter ego of Gombrowicz finds a possibility of an escape only after Gonzalo joins him in his defiant walking and thus turns the very ritual of male rivalry into parody: "But red lips he has! Lips he has, I say, Red, made Red, Carmined! And so with Lips Red he walks forth, is Walking, Walking! And 'tis as if someone gave me a whack in the Chops! . . . So as Boiled, Red, that Walk of mine, the Devil, the Devil, I directed to the door, and through that door—oh, now I'm not Walking on, Walking on but only Walking out" (*T,* 36).

If Gonzalo's first intrusion creates an ambivalent effect of panic, shame, and welcomed relief, his second intervention evacuates the very structure of masculine rivalry through its parodic repetition. In the climax of the narrative, the retired Major, Ignacy's father, challenges Gonzalo to a duel in order to force him to become "a Man" and thus deny his possible erotic interest in his son: "Ergo, I must challenge him. I will duel with him so that this matter in manly manner betwixt Men is settled; to be sure, I will make a Man of him that it cannot be said that a Puto is after my Son! Ergo, if he does not stand up to me, I will shoot him as a Dog" (*T,* 54). Obsessed with the preservation of his "panic stricken" masculinity, Ignacy's father attempts to restore the heterosexual identity of his son and to save national honor by reinscribing male eroticism within the ritualized, and already obsolete, structures of aggressive rivalry. This enforced restoration of straight masculinity compounds the previous patriotic blackmail with a homophobic terrorism: Gonzalo is given an option of either being killed as a manly man (if he stands the duel with the military man) or else being shot as a gay man. Whatever his choice, the terms of the blackmail do not allow him the luxury of being both a gay man and staying alive. This point in the text discloses the precise meaning of Gombrowicz's warning that nationality is a dangerous, and, let us add, homophobic force.

Although the narrator again feels entrapped without an exit or "a remedy" in Major's machinations, Gonzalo, the masterful actor pretending in his erotic adventures to be his own servant, and a figure for the aesthetic transgression of the text itself, responds to the recurring patriotic/homophobic blackmail with a parodic evasion. Apparently consenting to the terms of the duel, he secretly empties the pistols of their bullets. Gonzalo's gesture of parodic disarmament reverberates thought the text, depriving all the ritualized forms of hierarchies between men of their substance and power: "Here heavy Fright seized me, but completely Empty. Ergo, the strangest feeling I experienced since perchance not Fear but the Emptiness of my fear is frightening me; and not the Fear itself but, indeed, Fear caused by the lack of Fear" (*T,* 86). In vain does the narrator attempt to submit to the punishment and the authority of the father to cover over this overwhelming emptiness—even the threat of castration no longer works: "Oh, why can I not at the Father's wrathful legs, and on my knees, Attrition, Anguish, Terror feel . . . Ergo I trembled, Stiffened, but in vain did I Tremble, Stiffen, since Void, Void, Empty Barrel and Pistol Empty!" (*T,* 88). This void dissolving the national and masculine identity reminds us, as Lee Edelman argues, of the homophobic representation of homosexuality as "an epistemological gap, a space, a void, in maleness itself—a gap in which, in the end, as it were, there is nothing to be seen, and no assurance, therefore, that the visual display of masculinity's phallic ensign can suffice as evidence of the heterosexuality."[36]

The fear of emptiness within masculinity itself, paradoxically represented in the text as fear of "the lack of Fear," or the threat of effeminization, provokes the most fierce mobilization of the national spirit. Gombrowicz's diagnosis of the homophobic nature of this mobilization in *Trans-Atlantyk* points to the constitutive role of paranoia in maintaining the national and sexual identity. Struggling against the "fear of the absence of fear"—against the fatal void at the heart of the masculine and national identity—the panic-stricken characters respond to the threat of homosexuality by creating the paranoid society, the "redemptive" Order of the Chevaliers of the Spur. As the Accomptant instructs the narrator, the organizing principle of the punitive order is watching and being watched: "Do not attempt an escape or any betrayal as with a Spur they will prod you, and if you notice the faintest wish to Betray . . . in any of your

Comrades, into him a Spur you must shove . . . Keep an eye on yourself then, and on those others keep an eye, and mind the slightest Movement" (*T,* 100).

The visual display of the heterosexual masculine identity and its submission to collective surveillance is directed against the feared confusion of the boundaries between heterosexuality and homosexuality. Even though Gonzalo is the only openly gay figure in the entire text and even though he is separated from the other characters by his status as a foreigner, his very appearance is enough to create the homophobic panic as if homosexuality, like pestilence, could infect the entire social body. The strange effects generated by Gonzalo's appearance might be read as a sign of incoherence of the homo/heterosexual opposition, diagnosed by Sedgwick in *Epistemology of the Closet:* "modern homo/heterosexual definition has become so exacerbated a cultural site because of an enduring incoherence about whether it is to be thought as an issue only for a minority (distinctly lesbian or gay) individuals, or instead as an issue that cuts across every locus of agency and subjectivity in the culture."[37] The genealogy of the Order of the Chevaliers of the Spur is instructive in this respect—Ciumkała can accuse his companions of their "secret" homosexuality on the basis of the mere accidental association with Gonzalo:

> Then says the Accomptant: "Spurs I have, the which have a point sharply twisted, so if you would with these Flails beat each other, haply better with these Spurs . . . yet these are Spurs not for Mares but perchance only for Stallions! . . ." And Ciumkała: "Mares, mares!" "Stallion!" they cry, and ask to have these spurs affixed and will anon stab each other to death with them! (*T,* 102)

Armed with spurs, the characters police their identities and discipline their bodies in order to liberate themselves from what they perceive as the overwhelming emptiness created by the slightest suspicion of their own homosexuality. Yet this act of collective discipline, performing the rigid separation of the homosexual from homosocial bonds, is itself inseparable from the gruesome dismemberment of the individual and collective bodies. This image of the wounded bodies recalls and gives a precise meaning to Kristeva's figure of the scar between the man and the citizen: the scar in this context is both a trace of the impossible and yet strictly enforced homo/heterosexual distinction and the disfiguring mark left on the body by the disciplinary regime of national identifications. It is perhaps one of Gombrowicz's morbid jokes that straight masculinity can be "affixed" only with "sharply twisted" spurs.

The twisted spur is a means of defense not only against the suspicion of homosexuality but also against the national weakness this suspicion exacerbates. Like Ignacy's father, the Accomptant attempts to convert his companions, the "degraded Mares," first into "Stallions" and eventually into the military cavalry: "The Accomptant told me that when War surged and the Clap of Firing, Thunder of canons, and Moaning and Crying and Killing, Cracking, his own gentlessness and likewise the Weakness, Smallness of all compatriots became so loathsome to him that he wished to found an Order Anguish and Suffering, Agony and Awe, viz. that these flames might sear redemptively!" (*T,* 103). As this condensation of surveillance and military training suggests, Gombrowicz deploys paranoia not as a psychological delusion but as a social disciplinary mechanism producing and sustaining national affiliations. The figure of "redemption" is crucial here as it implies that this paranoid mechanism produces sublimation itself—sublimation that disciplines desire "to soar redemptively."

Gombrowicz's diagnosis of the disciplinary and social function of paranoia in sustaining national affiliations is similar, I would argue, to Guy Hocquenghem's "reversed" reading of Freud. Freud, let us recall, defines paranoia as a psychic struggle of the individual with "the homosexual wish-fantasy." In the outcome of this defensive mechanism, the internal sexual feelings are suppressed, distorted, and projected outward as the persecution coming from the loved object. According to Freud, the paranoid delusions projected upon the object of love are thus both a misrecognition and a defense against homosexual "tendencies"—in the last resort, they are a defense against the undoing of sublimation and the subsequent sexualization of social bonds. For Hocquenghem, the Freudian theory of paranoia demonstrates the inescapable failure in the social mechanisms of sublimation and, at the same time, contains the effects of this failure "by attributing to the individual the paranoiac discourse." As Hocquenghem suggests, however, this theory can be reread as an amazing diagnosis of the *social* role of paranoia in maintaining collective identity: "The attitude of what is commonly called 'society' is, in this respect, paranoiac: it suffers from an interpretative delusion which leads it to discover all around it the signs of homosexual conspiracy . . . So it is society as a whole that defends itself against the sexualization of its investments . . . and struggles with all its might against homosexual desublimation."[38] Since Freud's insistence on the "necessary" connection between paranoid delusions and homosexuality points to the "constitutive" rejection of homoeroticism from the social ties of fraternity, Hocquenghem proposes to read paranoia as social (rather than individual) defense mechanism against the possible re-sexualization of these bonds: "the repression of homosexuality is directly related to the jealousy paranoia that constitutes the daily fabric of society, and to the ideology of an integral social whole, the 'human community.' "[39]

Gombrowicz contrasts these pervasive paranoid delusions, which constitute homosexuality as threatening, unlivable, and thus deprived of future, with a utopian representation of homoeroticism as a hope for different collective identities. If the paranoid characters blame homosexuality for the dissolution of the very principle of sociality, Gonzalo affirms homosexual desire as the possibility of an alternative mode of being in common. Indeed, what others experience as the overwhelming emptiness he reinterprets as a rupture liberating future from the blind repetition of the past:

> Would you not become something Else, something New? Would you have all these Boys of yours but just repeat everything forever after Fathers? Oh, release Boys from the paternal cage. Let them veer off the path, let them peer into the Unknown! . . . To the Devil with Pater and Patria! . . . Is not Filistria better? (*T,* 57)

Gonzalo's rhetoric of temporality performing a radical break in the continuity of tradition can only recall the disruptive temporal effects of the Baroque style, discussed in the first part of this essay. Specifically, this rhetoric of temporality performs the most stunning reversal of the homophobic representations of homosexuality as "regression" or "degeneration," that is, as a non-reproductive sexuality threatening the future of the species and the nation. Although, as Lee Edelman has argued, homosexuality comes to represent for the homophobic imagination "futurity imperilled, . . . history as apocalypse, by gesturing toward the precariousness of familial and national survival,"[40] in *Trans-Atlantyk* it is the patriarchal filiation and reproduction that is deprived of future because it functions as the deadly repetition of the past. Significantly, this diagnosis of patriarchy mirrors the narrator's earlier condemnation of ghostly temporality of national history, perpetually suspended between being and non-being: "[that Holy Nation of yours haply Cursed] will not suffer you to Live or Die but keep you for ever between Being and Non-being!" (*T,* 6). In both cases the temporal structures of national and patriarchal narratives are demystified as deadly and regressive: instead of effecting the linear progress along "the empty homogenous time," they are figured as the monotonous repetition of the empty forms from the past. Indeed, Ignacy's father's resolution first to send his son to the army and then to murder him in order to restore the masculine and national honor is the most striking indication of the foreclosure of collective and individual future. What is being rehearsed in all of these textual examples is the disruption of the ideological fiction that the coordination of filiation and national history represents the linear temporal progression holding the monopoly for the collective future.

The sense of futurity proclaimed by Gonzalo cannot be confused, however, with the outcome of the dialectical struggle against the order of the father. This is precisely an error committed even by the narrator, "the shriveled genius Gombrowicz" himself. Faced with the transgressive movement of desire, the narrator is tempted to subsume all the conflicts in the text—the tensions between patriotism and homosexual love, fidelity to tradition and the cult of novelty, past and future, father and son—into the dialectical opposition between patria and filistria. Although the rhetoric of sexual liberation from the dependence on the past, nationality, and the regime of the father is incredibly seductive, it predictably ends in the dialectical struggle to death and reinscribes the structure of masculine rivalry it attempts to overcome: in this scenario, the father and the son can only conspire to kill each other.

However, the novel does not subscribe to this dialectical outcome. Instead of ending with the murderous resolution of the conflict between patriarchal tyranny and erotic freedom, instead of ending with a murder that looms as the logical and inevitable solution of the national plot, the novel ends with an uncontrollable outburst of laughter, which makes the entire edifice of national identity tremble and burst at its seams. In a spectacular collapse of the disciplinary mechanisms sustaining national identifications, this carnivalesque ending clears a different space for a sociality to come—a utopian vision of the polyphonic "chaosmos" in place of the catastrophic undoing of history:

> Laughter then Boomed . . . And by the wall they Gasp, well-nigh Piss, and there again Stifle, and now perchance Can no more; here again one from laughter a Stitch so in Stitches, or Chokes and indeed through his ears sprays, there again on the floor another sat, his legs stretched out, and Soars, Roars with laughter shaking . . . And so from Laughter into Laughter, they with laughter Boom, with laughter bam, boom, boom, bam Boom! . . . (*T,* 121–22)

Functioning more as an opening toward the unknown future rather than as a closure, the unexpected ending of the text suggests that the contestation of homophobia and national identity does not follow the model of dialectical conflict (which only mirrors the structure of male rivalry) but rather that of the parodic repetition and carnivalesque laughter. The political logic of such a performance, as Mary Russo argues, "sets carnival apart from merely oppositional and reactive." In place of the dialectical struggle, "the masks and voices of carnival resist, exaggerate, and destabilize the distinctions and boundaries that mark and maintain high culture and organized society."[41]

Since this sense of an ending privileges the logic of the Baroque style rather than the logic of national plot, we have to return to the function of the Baroque aesthetics, this time, in the context of the novel's figuration of homosexuality. That this relation is absolutely crucial for our understanding of *Trans-Atlantyk* can be intimated from the fact that Gonzalo, the doubled figure of the homosexual and the foreigner, is also, as we have seen, an embodiment of the Baroque style of the text. Such a correlation of the revision of homosexuality with the carnivalesque recycling of obsolete forms suggests, first of all, that both disclose a similar mode of signification: unlike the main agonistic confrontations of the national plot, pitting the past against the future, father against the son, homoeroticism against patriotism, national literature against aestheticism, and so forth, the specific mode of differentiation in *Trans-Atlantyk* perpetually erodes and reinscribes the discrete categories presupposed by the logic of binary opposition. This mode of signification, characteristic of both male-male desire and style, not only reinforces the cultural character of this desire but also, as Jonathan Dollimore suggests, "facilitates one of the most disturbing of all forms of transgression: the outlaw turns as inlaw; more specifically, that which society forbids . . . [is reinstated] through and within some of its most cherished and central cultural categories—art, the aesthetic, art criticism . . ."[42] The transgression Jonathan Dollimore describes here is characteristic of the logic of the carnival itself, which, by allowing for the return of the outlaw as the inlaw, contest the value of "the most cherished cultural categories." We have to add, however, that if the outlaw desire is thus reinscribed in *Trans-Atlantyk* as the integral part of culture, it, at the same time, displaces art itself from its cultural pedestal and divorces aesthetics from the reproduction of national identity. This is in the end the double movement, the double crossing, that the text appropriately called *Trans-Atlantyk* incessantly performs and presents as the condition of the social re-form of form.

In *Trans-Atlantyk,* where action takes place at the outset of the Second World War and where the local rivalries among men function as a synecdoche of global military aggression, the dissolution of national identity ends with the "bam boom" of carnivalesque laughter rather than with the trumpet of apocalypse, with the opening of future rather than a threat to national survival, and, finally, with a certain affirmation of style. It would be yet another error, however, to confuse—as many readers of this text have done—this "gay art" of *Trans-Atlantyk* with an expression of Gombrowicz's cynicism, aestheticism, or indifference to historical disaster.[43] We have to be aware of the fact that confusions of this sort might be themselves an expression of "patriotic blackmail," safeguarding the national past from any critical assessments. By refusing the terms of patriotic blackmail, Gombrowicz's "bold laugh" in the face of national tragedy does not forget the history he himself was spared but prevents the appropriation of the memory of the historical catastrophe for nationalistic or homophobic ends. Rather than a manifestation of cynicism or betrayal, Gombrowicz's parodic contestation of the dangerous force of nationality confronts us with an ethical imperative to imagine alternative collectivities that would no longer reproduce the same deadly logic of homophobia.

Notes

I am grateful to my colleagues Barbara Green and Graham Hammill for their careful reading of this essay and for their useful suggestions. In particular, I would like to thank Barbara for pointing out the analogy between my argument about the Baroque and Mary Russo's reading of the carnivalesque. I would also like to thank Marjorie Perloff for inviting me to give an earlier version of this paper at the MLA convention.

1. Witold Gombrowicz, "Przedmowa do *Trans-Atlantyku*" [1953], reprinted in *Trans-Atlantyk, Dzieła,* vol. III, ed. Jan Błoński (Kraków: Wydawnictwo Literackie, 1988), 137. In addition to reprinting the 1953 "Preface," this edition of *Trans-Atlantyk* also reprints Gombrowicz's prefaces to the 1951 and 1957 editions. For Gombrowicz's polemics with the Polish writers of the twenties, see Witold Gombrowicz, *Wspomnienia polskie: Wędrówki po Argentynie* (Warszawa: Res Publica, 1990) 40–45, 70–84, 88–100. For an illuminating discussion of Gombrowicz's place in the literature of the twenties in Poland, see Jan Błoński, *Forma, śmiech i rzeczy ostateczne* (Kraków: Znak, 1994), 259–69.

2. Witold Gombrowicz, "Przewodnik po filozofii w sześć godzin i kwadrans" *Gombrowicz filozof* ed. Francesco M. Cataluccio and Jerzy Illg (Kraków: Znak, 1991), 71–128. The essays "Sienkiewicz" and "Against the Poets" are included in *Diary,* vol. I.

3. Jonathan Dollimore, *Sexual Dissidence: Augustine to Wilde, Freud to Foucault* (Oxford: Clarendon P, 1991), 33.

4. For a discussion of the Baroque in *Trans-Atlantyk,* see, among others, Zdravko Malić, "*Trans-Atlantyk* Witolda Gombrowicza" *Gombrowicz i krytycy: Wybór i opracowanie,* ed. Zdzisław Łapinski (Kraków: Wydawnictwo Literackie, 1984), 250–53.

5. Ernest Gellner, *Thought and Change* (London: Weidenfeld, 1964), 169. Gellner's critique of nationalism is contested by Benedict Anderson in his *Imagined Communities: Reflections on the Origin and Spread of Nationalism* (London: Verso, 1991), 6.

6. Anderson, *Imagined Communities,* 6.

7. Anderson, *Imagined Communities,* 6.

8. Anderson, *Imagined Communities,* 26.

9. Gilles Deleuze, *The Fold: Leibniz and the Baroque,* trans. Tom Conley, (Minneapolis: U of Minnesota P, 1993), 81.

10. As Mary Russo argues in a creative revision of Bakhtin, "carnival and carnival laughter remain on the horizon with a new social subjectivity." *The Female Grotesque: Risk, Excess and Modernity* (New York: Routledge, 1994), 75. For a notion of the carnival as the enabling condition of social change, see Mikhail Bakhtin, *Rabelais and His World,* trans. Helene Iswolsky (Bloomington: Indiana UP, 1984), 30–44.

11. Deleuze, *The Fold: Leibniz and the Baroque,* 137.

12. For a discussion of the Baroque in Polish literary history, see Czesław Miłosz, *Historia literatury polskiej* (Kraków: Znak, 1993), 137–89. See also Julian Krzyżanowski, *Dzieje literatury polskiej* (Warszawa: PWN, 1979), 114–70, and Wiktor Weintraub *Od Reja do Boya* (Warszawa: PIW, 1977), 103–54.

13. For a discussion of the Sarmatian influence in Gombrowicz's texts, see Stanisław Barańczak, "Introduction to *Trans-Atlantyk,*" trans. Carolyn French and Nina Karsov (New Haven: Yale UP, 1994), xvi–xix; Jan Błoński, "Sarmatyzm u Gombrowicza" *Tradycje szlacheckie w literaturze polskiej,* ed. Z. Stefanowska (Warszawa, 1976), 137–53; and Błoński, *Forma, śmiech i rzeczy ostateczne,* 229–51. See also François Bondy, "Witold Gombrowicz czyli szlachcica polskiego pojedynki cieniów," 129–45; and Czesław Miłosz, "Kim jest Gombrowicz?" 185–200; both are in *Gombrowicz i krytycy.*

14. See Andrzej Walicki, *Poland between East and West: The Controversies over Self-Definition and Modernization in Partitioned Poland,* Harvard Papers in Ukrainian Studies (Cambridge: Harvard Ukrainian Research Institute, 1994), 11.

15. It is a famous thesis of Benedict Anderson that "nothing precipitated" the spread of nationalism more "than print-capitalism." *Imagined Communities,* 36.

16. Gombrowicz, *Wspomnienia polskie,* 38 (trans. mine).

17. For a discussion of Gombrowicz's Form, see Błoński, *Forma, śmiech i rzeczy ostateczne.* See also Jarzębski, "Pojęcie 'formy' u Gombrowicza," *Gombrowicz i krytycy,* 313–46.

18. Artur Sandauer, "Witold Gombrowicz—człowiek i pisarz" *Gombrowicz i krytycy,* 103–28. See also *Zebrane pisma krytyczne* (Warszawa: PIW, 1981), 557–79.

19. Gilles Deleuze and Félix Guattari, *Kafka: Toward a Minor Literature,* trans. Dana Polan (Minnesota: U of Minnesota P, 1986), 26–27.

20. Russo, *The Female Grotesque,* 62.

21. For a discussion of Gombrowicz's often conflicting relation to Polish literature, in particular to Mickiewicz, see Jeleński, "Tajny ładunek korsarskiego okrętu," 21–32; and Czesław Miłosz, *The History of Polish Literature* (London: Macmillan, 1969), 432–37.

22. For a representative discussion of Mickiewicz's career and its place in Polish literature, see Mieczysław Jastrun, *Mickiewicz* (Warszawa: PIW, 1974).

23. For a discussion of Mickiewicz and Gombrowicz, see, for instance, Konstanty Jeleński, "Tajny ładunek korsarskiego okrętu," 21–32 and Stanisław Gębala, "Odczynianie uroków—czyli *Trans-Atlantyk* contra *Pan Tadeusz," Poezja* 11/12 (1984): 87–94.

24. "To samo zaproponowałbym ludziom innych narodów, bo problem dotyczy nie stosunku Polaka do Polski, ale człowieka do narodu" "Przedmowa do *Trans-Atlantyku"* [1957], 6.

25. "Sądze że jest zupełnie możliwy taki stosunek do narodu, w którym naturalne nasze do niego przywiązanie, ba, nieunikniony i od naszej woli niezależny z nim związek, zostałyby uzupełnione odczuciem narodu jako siły niebezpiecznej . . ." "Przedmowa do *Trans-Atlantyku"* (1953), 140.

26. Julia Kristeva, *Strangers to Ourselves,* trans. Leon S. Roudiez (New York: Columbia UP, 1991), 96. Subsequent references to this edition will be marked parenthetically in the text as *ST.*

27. Similarly, Homi K. Bhabha reassesses the logic of national narratives from "the perspective of the nation's margin and the migrants' exile." Homi K. Bhabha, "DissemiNation: Time, Narrative, and the Margins of the Modern Nation," *Nation and Narration,* ed. Homi K. Bhabha (New York: Routledge, 1990), 291.

28. As Sedgwick observes, "the topos of the creation, reification, and expulsion of the Other . . . in the emergence of the modern European state, has become a central tool of liberal analysis." *Tendencies* (Durham: Duke UP, 1993), 147.

29. Alejandro Rússovich suggests that the figure of Gonzalo could be influenced by the homosexual lifestyle of the Cuban dancers, the friends of Virgilio Piñera, or by Piñera himself. "Rússovich o Gombrowiczu," *Teatr* 9 (1995): 10–12. I am tempted, however, to read Gonzalo as the distorted mirror image of Gombrowicz's own Argentinean homosexual experiences: here

the rich Gonzalo attempting to seduce a Polish youth would be a reversed figure of the impoverished Gombrowicz cruising after Argentinean boys.

30. The issue of homosexuality is usually ignored in the frequent comparisons of these two texts. Stanisław Gębala, for instance, explicitly claims that the focus on the homosexual desire produces "trivial interpretations." "Odczynianie uroków—czyli *Trans-Atlantyk* contra *Pan Tadeusz,"* 94.

31. Zdravko Malić, among other Gombrowicz's interpreters, sees the equation between patriotism and sexual love as the "key" to understanding *Trans-Atlantyk, "Trans-Atlantyk* Witolda Gombrowicza," 242.

32. One can observe here certain similarities between Gombrowicz and Wilde: for both homosexuality is associated with transgressive aesthetics and with the destruction of the illusory inner self. For a discussion of Wilde's aesthetics, see Jonathan Dollimore, "Different Desires: Subjectivity and Transgression in Wilde and Gide," *The Lesbian and Gay Studies Reader,* ed. Henry Abelove, Michèle Aina Barale, and David M. Halperin (New York: Routledge, 1993), 626–41. For a longer version of this argument see his *Sexual Dissidence : Augustine to Wilde, Freud to Foucault,* 64–74, 307–20.

33. Andrew Parker, Mary Russo, Doris Sommer, and Patricia Yaeger, "Introduction," *Nationalisms and Sexualities,* ed. Andrew Parker et al. (New York: Routledge, 1992), 6.

34. Sigmund Freud, "Certain Neurotic Mechanisms in Jealousy, Paranoia and Homosexuality," *Sexuality and the Psychology of Love* (New York: Collier, 1963), 170.

35. Guy Hocquenghem, *Homosexual Desire,* trans. Daniella Dangoor (Durham: Duke UP, 1993), 58–61.

36. Lee Edelman, "Tearooms and Sympathy, or, The Epistemology of the Water Closet," *Nationalisms and Sexualities,* 279.

37. Sedgwick, *Tendencies,* xii. For a more extensive discussion of this incoherence, see her *Epistemology of the Closet* (Berkeley: U of California P, 1990), 67–91. As she writes, "the now chronic modern crisis of homo/heterosexual definition has affected our culture through its ineffaceable marking particularly of the categories of secrecy/disclosure, knowledge/ignorance, private/public, masculine/feminine, majority/minority, . . . natural/artificial, new/old . . ." (11).

38. Hocquenghem, *Homosexual Desire,* 55, 60.

39. Hocquenghem, *Homosexual Desire,* 105–6. As Eve Kosofsky Sedgwick similarly remarks, the logic of the paranoid rejection of homosexuality aims to institute a radical break between male homosocial and homosexual

bonds, but, at the same time, it also marks the instability of the very division that is supposed be constitutive of sociality itself. See her *Between Men: English Literature and Male Homosocial Desire* (New York: Columbia UP, 1985), 1–5, 83–94.

40. Edelman, "Tearooms and Sympathy," 277.

41. Russo, *The Female Grotesque,* 62.

42. Dollimore, "Different Desires: Subjectivity and Transgression in Wilde and Gide," 633–34.

43. See for instance, Tadeusz Kępiński, *Witold Gombrowicz: Studium portretowe* (Kraków: Wydawnictwo Literackie, 1988), 339–87.

Agnieszka M. Sołtysik

9

Witold Gombrowicz's Struggle with Heterosexual Form:

From a National to a Performative Self

Witold Gombrowicz's reputation as a radically innovative writer has been established largely on the basis of his stylistically experimental novels and avant-guard plays. Yet it was in his Argentine literary journal, spanning thirteen years and three volumes, that he undertook some of his most acute and comprehensive interrogations of traditional epistemological and aesthetic concepts. The *Diary* was also the work in which he felt the most personal and creative agency as a writer. Unlike his novels and plays, which Gombrowicz describes as almost writing themselves, it was only when he began to write the *Diary* that he felt that he was really "wielding [his] pen," an experience that he also describes in the following way: "It was as if I were accompanying my art all the way to the point where it dropped into another person's existence and became hostile to me" (*D* II, 181). This is an odd way to characterize the most explicitly autobiographical of his works, but paradox is Gombrowicz's preferred rhetorical gesture, often accommodating insights which are not easily figured by conventional language and conceptual forms.

Though paradox constitutes a particularly clear instance of this rhetorical move, the expository and the performative overlap in Gombrowicz's work in a variety of ways and to a degree that has often been overlooked. Thus, the *Diary* is not only the text where he develops his model of fluid and multiple subjectivity most thoroughly—it is also one of its most vital instances. Accordingly, one of the concerns of this paper will be to map out the ways Gombrowicz theorizes and constructs identity (particularly his own) in the *Diary,* focusing on the rhetorical strategies deployed in the text as well as the explicit narratives it contains. But this is actually the pretext for another, more specific project, namely, bringing the hermeneutic concerns of what is loosely called "queer theory" to bear on the *Diary* in order to read its highly elusive and uniquely charged discourses of sexuality and gender. The imperative for this reading arises not only from the fact that sexuality and gender issues permeate Gombrowicz's *oeuvre* but also from the fact that they have long been neglected, largely due to the scarcity of responsible critical tools for dealing with gender and sexuality prior to the research yields of feminism and gender studies.

Anyone who has ever read anything about Gombrowicz knows that no discussion of his work fails to address the question of his national and cultural identity as a point of departure. During his lifetime, most of the criticism generated by his work focused contentiously on his alleged obsession with Poland and/or lack of reverence for her; and consequently much of the *Diary* discusses, defends, attacks and attempts to transcend certain constants of this debate about his Polishness and status as exile writer. From a cultural studies point of view, the problem begins with the word *exile* itself, as it tends to collapse the difference between the displaced individual and the state of loss itself, thereby overdetermining the exiled writer as a mere function of his political status.

Also problematic is the fact that exile is frequently understood to bear on artistic production in one of the following two ways: either as a space which transcends national categories and instead communes with the universal or as a metaphysical dimension of national identity (also transcending the geopolitical entity), wherein the exiled writer becomes the special guardian of the nation as it exists in the hearts and minds of its patriots. Both the universalist and nationalist prongs of this exile debate tend to assume a unified and self-transparent (essentially humanist) subject who is a coherent product of his cultural home and invested in an unproblematic way with its values, remaining a national of his home country no matter how long he remains abroad. If the exile is influenced by his host culture at all, this influence is at best figured in terms of a hybridity which attributes to the host culture the coherence and stability it assumes in the home culture.[1]

One of the most useful interventions into this tradition has emerged from postcolonial theory. Abdul R. JanMohamed has proposed the notion of the "specular border intellectual," who differs from the exile writer, nursing the wounds of his past; the immigrant, rushing to embrace the host culture; and the "syncretic border intellectual," combining elements from one or more cultures into new syncretic forms, in that s/he maintains a critical stance toward both (or all) the cultures s/he intersects.[2] JanMohamed explains: "Caught between several cultures or groups, none of which are deemed sufficiently enabling or productive, the specular border intellectual subjects the cultures to analytical scrutiny rather than combining them; s/he utilized her/his cultural interstitial space as a vantage point from which to define, implicitly or explicitly, other utopian possibilities or group formations."[3]

In other words, the specular border intellectual does not merely sit on the border and opine critically about the two cultures; this idea denies the writer any agency in the cultures as well as sealing him/her off from influence from both. Rather, specular border intellectuals are "forced to constitute themselves as the border, to coalesce around it as a point of infinite regression."[4] In short, they must invent themselves as something entirely different and concretely individual, constructing their personal, cultural, and literary identities through an endless series of self-founding performances.

This model of intellectual identity is an invaluable aid in understanding Gombrowicz's resistance to recuperation by both the universalist and nationalist agendas of exile criticism. Struggling not to be overdetermined by Poland, Gombrowicz always insisted on the concretely individual nature of his creativity. For example, defending himself against claims that he was obsessed by Poland in *Trans-Atlantyk,* he explains in the *Diary* that it was a story "in which, among other things, Poland appears. But Poland is not the subject; the subject, as always, is I, I alone, these are my adventures, not Poland's. Except that I happen to be a Pole" (*D* II, 19–20).

Since Gombrowicz thought that all such collective identities dwarf and infantalize the self, the defense of the subject as an individual against the totalizing tendencies of collective identities can be seen as one of his principal political and artistic tasks. He discusses this question in linguistic rather than psychological terms and diagnoses the problem of nationalism as beginning with the tendency to think and speak in the first-person plural rather than the singular. Having to operate from within this obvious fiction results in both creative and intellectual impairment: "this foggy, abstract and arbitrary 'we,' therefore deprives them [Argentineans] of their concreteness, that is, their sanguineness; it ruins their directness, almost knocks them off their feet and puts them in a haze" (*D* II, 129). He insists instead on the need to think and write as individuals; in effect, he would like everyone to assume the responsibility of inventing him/herself as a unique and critical subject.

What this requires is the understanding and acknowledgment of the power of what he calls Forms, which are the ideas, identities, behaviors, and discourses (based on and including nationality, culture, class, gender, occupation, age, etc.) available to the subject, by which the self is circumscribed and through which it constructs and expresses an identity. Although this process is ineluctable, Gombrowicz nevertheless insists on the need to resist complacency in accepting these Forms: "try to set yourself against form, to shake free of it . . . Mistrust your opinions. Mistrust your beliefs, and defend yourself against your feelings" (*F,* 85). Paradoxically, Gombrowicz proposes that the subject distance itself from precisely the cognitive functions, that is, conscious intellectual positions and affective allegiances, by which the subject has been defined as a subject (unique, autonomous, rational, and responsible) in Western modernity.

In short, Gombrowicz denies the possibility of unmediated subjectivity, and the way he proposes one should acknowledge this mediation is again linguistic. This time, the grammatical shift is from a personal to an impersonal verb construction, a more circumspect style which foregrounds the role of language in creating the illusion of a coherent and self-transparent subject: "instead of shouting and bellowing: I believe this, I feel that, I am this, I stand for that, we shall say more humbly: In me there is a belief, a feeling, a thought, I am the vehicle for such-and-such an action, production, or whatever it may be" (*F,* 86). There is also an important critique of traditional notions of agency in this injunction; but the point is not to deny the subject agency so much as to sensitize the subject to its historical, cultural, and ideological embeddedness.

Although Gombrowicz has been called a determinist, and his ideas may appear at times to merely instantiate the determinist cliché that we are products of society and its norms, this is far from the case. On the contrary, Gombrowicz insists on the need to recognize that the subject must constantly grow, change, shift positions, and struggle to resist Forms that tend to limit or stabilize its identity into some illusion of organically complete personhood. In other words, the process of self-invention and self-performance is constant, involving a high degree of self-consciousness and critical thought (a project clearly more indebted to, if anything, humanism than to determinist principles).

Another easily overlooked aspect of social identity for Gombrowicz is that this process of externally contingent "formation" occurs even on the most concrete and specific interpersonal level, that is, a single interlocutor is enough to influence and (de)form us. Gombrowicz calls this process the "Interhuman" and it amounts to a dramaturgical model of social behavior and identity that is best understood through a reading of sociologist Erving Goffman's work. For example, in *The Presentation of Self in Everyday Life* (1959), Goffman describes in dramaturgical terms how people perform themselves, acting out their personalities, social roles, gender, class, profession, and every other temporary or "permanent" aspect of their identity for others, who function as audiences and for whom they adapt their performance according to the rules or conventions governing the situation.

Much of this behavior is not necessarily conscious, and the degree to which the actor regards his behavior as "inauthentic" depends on many factors. For example, when a young middle-class American girl plays "dumb" for the benefit of her boyfriend, Goffman points out that we are quick to see the contrivance of her behavior (which, by the way, is not really considered deceitful as much as adaptive), but, he argues, "like herself and her boyfriend, we accept as an unperformed fact that this performer IS a young American middle-class girl. But surely here we neglect the greater part of the performance."[5] Though the girl herself may remain unconscious of the degree to which her identity is socially constructed, she is nevertheless the product of a lifetime of training (sometimes subtle and sometimes quite coercive) in behavior appropriate to her gender, class, country, region, and age, among other things. It is crucial to keep in mind that this model does not posit a "real self" underneath the performances which would then exist merely as masks. While not denying the validity of other factors—internal or external—determining behavior, Goffman's theory served as a much needed corrective to the tendency to see human psychology exclusively in terms of deep-seated drives and unconscious forces which needed to be "uncovered." Such "depth" models, including psychoanalysis, tend to define normality in terms of existing gender and cultural norms, thereby producing enormous varieties of pathologies to diagnose and treat.

In contrast, Goffman's theory lends itself well to social analysis that aims to denaturalize (in order to delegitimize) the status quo, and it is not surprising, therefore, that his model has been appropriated most recently by Judith Butler, who describes gender as "the impression of a real and coherent sex" created through a series of "sustained social performances" compelled by "social sanction and taboo."[6] Playing on the double sense of the word *performance,* she argues that instead of being understood as a role being acted out, gender must be understood as an "act" which constructs the "reality" of gender entirely through its performance, as in a performative speech act.[7] Although Goffman and Butler agree that performance is an inevitable and intrinsic fact of social life, Butler regards this process of social interpellation with more alarm than does Goffman.

Although self-performance and mutual (de)formation can assume a tragicomic complexion in Gombrowicz's fictions, his general attitude toward this process has more affinity to Butler's position than to Goffman's, and for largely the same reasons. For Butler, the problem is that subjects are forced to perform roles that perpetuate the illusion of complementary gender within a misogynist and heterosexist cultural economy, with particularly destructive results for women. Similarly, Gombrowicz is concerned about the constraining and controlling aspect of social Forms, and he is especially conscious of the psychic violence produced by traditional sex roles. In fact, one of the arguments of this essay will be that a resistance to the dominant heterosexist regime fuels a tremendous amount of Gombrowicz's thinking, beginning with his critique of Form and extending into many other topics.

One should note that Gombrowicz does not dismiss the experiential reality of social identities. Although one must "struggle with the mug" (his facetious term for the social persona or face presented to others), it is impossible to divest one's self entirely of artifice—"for behind it he has no face—here one can only demand that he be conscious of his artificiality and confess it" (*D* II, 4). This is an interesting imperative, since it exacts a confession of a lack of authenticity and sincerity, and posits this lack as universal, that is, the secret in everyone's closet. By taking a category of experience which has been paradigmatic of the way homosexuality is understood in our culture, that is, masquerade and artifice, and making it axiomatic of modern subjectivity, Gombrowicz undermines the facile logic of "natural" versus "unnatural" identities/behaviors that sustains all homophobic discourses. This is only one way in which what I call a "queer problematic" informs virtually all aspects of Gombrowicz's thinking and work.

Although "queer theory" is really not precise or developed enough yet to constitute a specific methodology within literary criticism, nor should it necessarily strive to be, it is an approach based on certain insights and assumptions and goals. One of these goals is to better understand the textual inscription and production of sexualities, especially since homosexuality exists in a curious and paradoxical relationship to textuality. On the one hand, as everyone knows, homosexuality is often excluded from official discourse and representation; it has long been the "love that dare not speak its name." On the other hand, homosexuality, by virtue of the fact that it exists as an "excess" to the dominant heterosexual economy, necessarily becomes textual; being forced to exist as an excess of signification, a double meaning or instability in the sexual signifier, homosexuality is the figure of textuality par excellence.[8]

Most importantly, homosexuality has been forced to inhabit other issues or problematics, in a relationship analogous to the rhetorical figure called catachresis.[9] Catachresis is defined as "the improper use of a word or phrase," even "an abuse of language," and has always been considered the most scandalous of tropes. Yet, sometimes a word simply must be borrowed—stolen, really—by a thing which has no other name, such as the "leg" of a table, or the "face" of a mountain. Homosexuality, sometimes known as a range of acts, other times regarded as an inflection (or a corruption) of identity, but always linguistically and conceptually disenfranchised from cultural legitimacy, has often resorted to such thefts. One of the tasks of queer theory is to identify and map this discursive terrain, this booty. Unfortunately, most of our critical terminology figures criticism itself as "discovery" or "revelation," which assumes a paradigm of hermeneutic activity analogous to the homophobic logic of the "closet," as defined by Eve Kosofsky Sedgwick.[10] In other words, a queer reading does not propose to "out" a queer content of an otherwise straight discourse in order to prove that a "really" queer meaning has been illegitimately masquerading as something innocent and "normal." This would be tantamount to immediate recuperation by a homophobic logic, not to mention a kind of literary voyeurism. Instead, what queer theory does is permit the gender and sexuality-inflected meaning of a text to be read at all, not displacing so much as supplementing other readings.

I should also say that I use the word *queer* in accordance to the distinction between "gay studies," which grew out of the identity politics of the 1970s and assumed a shared and coherent category of identity for gays and lesbians, and "queer theory," which emerged from poststructuralist insights and defines queerness as an ontologically unstable, desire-affirming subject-position rather than a clear and fixed "identity." Though the emergence of the latter would probably not have been possible without the groundbreaking work of the former discipline, the superiority of the latter lies in its greater versatility and subtlety with regard to the semiotically overcharged field of gender identity, its construction, performance, and subversion.

The point of a "queer" reading of Gombrowicz is twofold: first, it throws into relief his engagement with the problematics of gender identity and sexual desire, and second, it accommodates the fluid and performative aspects of his thinking on subjectivity, which is especially important for reading a text as complex and nuanced as the *Diary.* One of the principal advantages of queer criticism over a gay studies approach is the ability to avoid both the need to fix the subject within a binary hetero/homosexual field and to even establish what the subject biographically did and with whom. After all, Gombrowicz explicitly denies in the *Diary* that he was "a homosexual" (though he "confesses" to a few "sporadic incidents" in adolescence). But he does admit that his attraction to the men of the Retiro area of Buenos Aires might have been symptomatic of certain "tendencies" and then actually credits these tendencies with giving him a stabilizing weight of "reality" against which he describes an affair with a woman as making him feel like a "fraud" (*D* I, 132–38). The difference between his relations with young men and that with a female lover consists in the fact that the latter requires from him only that he be a "man," while the former demand something much more important and personal: his youth and attractiveness. The alienation he feels from the type of manhood exacted by a woman—a stereotypical, sexually dominating, egotistical, and inherently violent manhood—is paradigmatic of the alienation he postulates as necessary from all other kinds of social forms. It is also significant that he regards his youth as the most unaffected and fundamental part of himself, where he can be "simply a living being, nothing else" (*D* I, 138). The language in which he figures this youthfulness borders on the language of authenticity but avoids making a full commitment to its essentialist implications.

It is worth noting that the rhetorical category of an authentic inner self does not play any significant role in the *Diary* except at these highly anxious moments when Gombrowicz deals with his thoughts on sexuality and gender. In any case, a literary journal is a genre that necessarily raises the question of authenticity and veracity, since it consists of an odd coupling of personal and aesthetic agendas. Furthermore, as a fusion of creative and critical work it often completely collapses the distinction between the two. The subject, or "I," of the literary journal is a particularly curious phenomenon: neither the "real" author assumed (however naively or erroneously) in autobiographies nor a truly fictional character. Nevertheless, the question of "authentic" identity often occupies the foreground of the writer's attempts to invent, define, and "express" himself.

Given that Gombrowicz held complex and self-conscious theories about identity and expression, it is not surprising that his attitude toward "authenticity" in writing the journal is a good deal more complicated than merely trying to stabilize and authorize his narrative voice. In fact, his strategy could be described as just the reverse: his use of different tones, personae, and narrator positions serve to constantly undermine and parody the conventions of literary authority and narrator identity. His attitude toward the reader is both seductive and aggressive, intimate and insincere, persuasive and exaggerated, encouraging and shocking. He occasionally strikes arrogant, deliberately provocative poses just to nettle the reader, and his attitude toward truth and fiction is playful, irreverent, and deeply indebted to Nietzsche and Oscar Wilde.[11] However, whenever he explicitly addresses his homosexuality/sociality, his authorial voice loses most of its assertiveness and poise, and his writing assumes instead an urgent and earnest loquaciousness, thickly layered density, and, above all, a striking evasiveness.

Perhaps the most obvious place to begin a gender-inflected reading of Gombrowicz is with his remarks about women, since he has often been accused of misogyny in his representation of and comments about women. Actually, his attitude is not unlike that of the Anglo-American male modernists, who defined themselves and their work against what they saw as a hypocritical, sentimental, stultifying, and, above all, feminized miasma of mass culture.[12] Similarly, Gombrowicz sees himself as struggling against the hypocritical and sentimental "Literary Aunts" who control literary criticism and whom he sees as the prudish guardians of a high culture he would like to both artistically deflate and elevate.[13]

Gombrowicz differs most from other male modernists in his ability to self-consciously acknowledge his hostility toward women and explain it on a theoretical level with a critique of gender socialization. In brief, they represent to him not only culture its most judgmental and inflexible form but artifice in its most stifling aspect, that is, of "deforming" youthful energy and sexuality. But Gombrowicz makes a crucial distinction between women as actual people and femininity as a social Form, and it is to this latter that he objects. In effect, it is the mutual definition and formation of male and female social identity within the context of what Adrienne Rich called "compulsory heterosexuality" that Gombrowicz wants to attack.[14] In a passage that anticipates contemporary feminist theory, Gombrowicz describes the way in which gender is constructed and reified within a binary system of heterosexual complementarity. Masculinity is produced "mechanically" as a function of the drama of seduction and the passive and active roles it imposes on the players. What begins as a performance, the acting out of social conventions, quickly acquires a momentum and the players lose all sense of "reality" and perspective. He describes his own task as an intervention with the goal of "unburdening" Man as well as Woman. He sees himself as the uninvited guest at the ball of mutual gender validation, the outsider who wants to "ruin the game" and "liberate Man from the yoke of his masculinity" (*D* I, 118–19). His goal, he says, is to expose the game for what it is, that is, a "show" performed for others.

It is in the light of both the modernist and socially critical dimensions of Gombrowicz's work that we should read his perception that it is mostly women readers against whom he must defend himself and his work, especially in the *Diary*. For example, he writes: "Once again a certain woman (because it is always a woman, but this one is a woman-enemy who does battle with me) accuses me of egotism." And he quotes from her letter: "To me, sir, you are not eccentric, but egocentric. This is simply a stage in your development (*vide* Byron, Wilde, Gide). Some pass from this to the next phase which may be even more extreme but others don't go anywhere at all and remain fixed in their egos. This is a tragedy but a private one. It enters neither the Pantheon nor history" (qtd. in *D* I, 113). Gombrowicz's response is framed in typically modernist terms: accusing her of aesthetic and intellectual naiveté, he defends himself against her apparent attack on his autonomy as a writer by insisting upon his freedom to choose to write about whatever he pleases, including the private, the trivial, and personally significant.

This leads into a discussion of the importance and sovereignty of the "I" and the inevitable centrality of Gombrowicz in his own journal, with the interesting move of calling himself his favorite "hero" or character in his writing, as if to stress his distance from his narrative voice. This gesture allows him to insist on the personal nature of the *Diary*, as distinguished from a critical review or fictional story, while simultaneously suggesting that the "I" of the *Diary* is possibly no more accountable to autobiographical fact than any other fictional character. The effect is to create as much ambiguity and instability around the pronoun "I" as possible, without ever renouncing its ability to signify autobiographical truth.

But the most interesting thing about this letter is the fact that he does not explicitly address its obvious import. By comparing Gombrowicz to three of the most famous gay writers, the letter writer has "found him out," as it were.[15] The fact that she accuses him of self-absorption, narcissism, and an excess of personal self-revelation is precisely the problematic that Eve Sedgwick calls the "double-bind" of the homosexual, who is caught between social pressure to both disclose and conceal the "difference" of their desire. Any revelation which might not seem unusual if the speaker is heterosexual can be received as unwelcome and "excessive" (or narcissistic, even exhibitionist) if the speaker is gay. Another dimension of the double-bind is that the standard heterosexist discourse of homosexuality creates a possibility that a subject may not be "aware" of his/her own sexuality and, therefore, will not be in control over that "knowledge." Perhaps Gombrowicz edited the letter for inclusion in the *Diary,* but it is significant that neither the letter writer nor Gombrowicz ever addresses the issue by name. Homosexuality is tactfully or shamefully allowed to remain at the margins of signification, as an anxious force field of unacknowledged meaning exceeding the purported issue of authorial egotism.

Nevertheless, this letter marks the beginning of a series of chapters which address homosexuality either explicitly or again indirectly "through" another issue. The question of Gombrowicz's desire and identity keeps erupting in the next section and leads to an articulation of his attitude toward his entire project as a writer and thinker. He ostensibly begins the 1955 section with the intention of reviewing the period of his arrival in Argentina. This was a difficult period, since he felt isolated and anonymous both personally and as a writer. Though he knew that he should try to establish friendly contacts with Argentine literati, he found it difficult to get along with other writers and intellectuals, partly because of what he saw as their pretentiousness and inferiority complex vis à vis European belles lettres, and partly because of his indecision about how to present himself, that is, who to be with them (and for them).

What eventually happened was that he immersed himself in the gay subculture of the Buenos Aires area called the Retiro. Just as the nocturnal Retiro life seduced him away from the stuffy literary circles of his new city, in the *Diary,* digressions on issues related to the Retiro displace and overpower his attempts to describe that era in any other terms than those related to homosexuality. Moreover, these passages contain unprecedented apologies for subjecting his readers to his "confessions." And he explains that he mentions his sexual adventures only in order to "delineate the limits" of his experience, in order to reassure readers that he's not "really" gay. Yet, the "limits" he describes are not the furthest points from his "real" and central self but the place where he habitually, if furtively, resided. He confesses that he could not leave this "dangerous periphery" that obsessed him, but he also could not reveal it to anyone, not even his closest literary friend, and not even as "merely" the source of his inspiration (*D* I, 133).

After a passage in which he attempts to convince his readers and himself that the charm of the Retiro lies in the fact that young men are "life incarnate," he pauses and promises to "put an end to these confessions." But he cannot, since, as he admits, nothing in him has been "resolved" since those days at the Retiro. He simply was drawn away from that life by pressing concerns with what he calls his "other homeland," Poland, and had to suspend the questions that had been raised in those early days (*D* I, 144). Here is another border that casts an intriguing new light on the very concept of cultural identity. The fact that Gombrowicz felt a mutually opposing pull from the Retiro, which represented a certain sexual and gender territory, on the one hand, and Poland, which represented a certain national and social problematic, on the other hand, is symptomatic of the way that national identities are themselves gendered. The degree to which national identity (or allegiance) imposes a gendered worldview has been only recently interrogated by feminist and postcolonial critics. It would be useful to examine Gombrowicz's struggle with his Polishness not only in terms of his American or exilic context but also in terms of his critique of gender. To put it crudely, there is no viable subject-position in Polish culture for a gay male (or lesbian, for that matter). This is not to imply that Argentina or America offered an acceptable cultural space for homosexuality either. Nevertheless, Gombrowicz was able to find a social niche there which enabled him to construct an identity that he could not have in the older and more traditional context of Poland, and this is why he refers to the Retiro as "another, painful homeland . . . from which I would not know how to tear myself away today" (*D* I, 146).

The above passage about Poland immediately leads into a discussion of masculinity in general. He says that the Retiro gave him two tasks: firstly, to elevate the Boy, and by extension, the human body to its properly divine level; and secondly, a prerequisite for the first task, to rid himself of masculinity, and the fear of his femininity. This was a task of the first order, since it had to be done in order for him to be able to speak or write. The explanation that follows is truly radical in the scope of its critique of masculinity as a social construct. He describes masculinity as something that men "[fabricate] among themselves, goading each other into it, mutually forcing themselves to it in a panick-stricken fear of the woman in themselves" (*D* I, 145). This masculinity—which is acted out as a brutal, aggressive excess—robbed a man not only of his perspective, but "of all intuition in dealing with the world: where he needed to be flexible, he inflicted himself, pushing and flaying noisily with his whole being. Everything became excessive: heroism, severity, might, virtue. Whole nations threw themselves like bulls onto the sword of the torreador in paroxysms, in the mad fear that the audience might attribute something of the *Ewig-Weibliche* to them" (*D* I, 145).

Gombrowicz then writes that he would like to find for himself "a different position for myself—beyond man and woman—which would nevertheless not have anything to do with a 'third sex'—an asexual and purely human position (*D* I, 145). However, the point of finding such a space, in which he could be a human being before being a man, is not just to be a better or more neutral person. What is so significant about Gombrowicz's struggle with gender and sexuality is that he sees these issues as fundamental to his task and efficacy as a writer. What escaping masculinity would entail is the ability to say much about many "inexpressible things." But the problem is not merely of freedom of expression or shame; it is the ability to discursively figure the world in a different and more "accurate" way than permitted within the discursive system delimited by heterosexual binarism, and he diagnoses an urgent need to find a language for what he calls the most mystified and clouded topic of all (i.e., gender and sexuality, especially homosexual attraction). It is something about which one can't speak, let alone write, and about which "no one desires to be or can be objective" (*D* I, 142). It represented for him the very frontier of discursive terrain, and his task as a writer would be to map the border and the territory beyond.

Moreover, the social control surrounding homosexuality cannot be characterized simply as repression. As Foucault suggests, hegemonic social power produces as well as represses discourse. Thus, one consequence of the heterosexual paradigm is that everything that falls outside of it must be seen as a pathology. In fact, Gombrowicz himself often ends up "admitting" that homosexuality is a deviation and an "illness." There is even a passage in which he falls into such contortions of shame and self-consciousness that he calls his attraction to homosexual circles a "descent into baseness and depravity." Yet, even when he allows heterosexuality to be "healthy," he demands of his audience, "Don't you feel that here even your health becomes hysterical? You are inhibited, gagged unconfessed" (*D* I, 146). In this way, he subverts the most paradigmatic and pernicious effect of the closet (by which I mean the homosexual's double bind regarding sexual information) by transferring the onus of silence and concealment onto the heterosexual. This move is not a simple inversion. Instead, it points to a gap in heterosexual Form that is not so much a secret as an unmapped frontier, to continue the figure used earlier. Heterosexual Form passes itself off as stable and self-evident and complete, but Gombrowicz diagnoses it as a site of masquerade, restriction, and insincerity.

It is essential not to underestimate the degree to which a related critique of social norms and definitions informs every aspect of Gombrowicz's artistic work. This is the border between the private and the public, a border that Gombrowicz navigates and reinvents at every step. For example, he defends the *Diary* against a reader who complains that he preaches and critiques too much by asking, "What is a diary if not this especially: private writing done for one's own private use?" (*D* I, 149). Yet, several pages away he justifies his long discourse on the Retiro by saying, "it is important for a man speaking publicly—a man of letters—to lead his reader beyond the facade of form, into the boiling cauldron of his private history" (*D* I, 144). These two quotes diverge not on the point of subject matter, but on the role of the author and his relationship to his reader. This is a role that Gombrowicz addresses specifically at the end of the long Retiro section, where he claims that his strategy as a writer has been to assume roles and postures and that "everything is dependent—why should I conceal this?—on the effect it has." In other words, he tells his readers that it is they who partly determine what he says and how he says it, thereby making them as responsible for his indiscretions as for his obfuscations.

The problematic of the closet is equally pertinent to any stylistic analysis of his writing. For example, he describes the prose of the *Diary* as a "concession" when he recounts the ultimate postponement of his project (to transcend his gender and say all the things that he could not say as a "man"). Conversely, he describes his rhetorically most exceptional novel, *Trans-Atlantyk,* as his final effort to tackle the issue. The correlation between the gender project and his inventiveness as an avant-guard writer is explicit and profound. Although he alludes at one point to an almost organic connection between his "grotesque" writing style and his "incapacity" to love and his "grotesque" interior life, this correlation is much more difficult to explain than to note. For this reason, I prefer to figure the issue strictly in terms of rhetorical strategies. Thus, in *Trans-Atlantyk,* written in an antiquated oral style based on former Polish manorhouse culture (the *gawęda*), the final effect is both a Brechtian distancing and the most compelling intimacy. Evidence of the latter effect is the startling number of critics who take this outlandish and hallucinatory novel as autobiographically true, conflating the narrator with Gombrowicz himself and completely overlooking how much of what the caricatured gay character, the *puto,* says could be ascribed to Gombrowicz himself. In fact, these two characters, the narrator and the *puto,* are best understood as two voices within Gombrowicz's polyphonic debate with himself over this vexing but unavoidable issue.

Another strategy of mediated self-revelation in the *Diary* is the use of the third person, which appears almost always in connection to issues related to the gay problematic. The first time this happens is early in the first volume, when he attempts to recount an episode from the period of his arrival in Buenos Aires, and he feels so altered from the person he was then that he feels he can only narrate his past behavior and feelings in the third person. Later in the second volume, he explains the adoption of this strategy in typically Wildean terms:[16] the third person pronoun "was, in his [Gombrowicz's own] opinion, an important discovery, intensifying the immeasurably cold artificiality of his admissions, which also allowed for greater honesty and passion . . . In addition, this division into voices was justified by the very structure of style and firmly grounded in reality. But beyond this—what wealth to be able to speak about oneself in the first and third persons simultaneously! For he who speaks of himself with 'I' must, of necessity, lie a lot and leave much unsaid—while he who speaks of himself with 'he' and tries to describe himself from the outside will also be wielding only a partial truth" (*D* II, 126). This passage throws a very curious and destabilizing light on the first-person narrator, who appears throughout the rest of the *Diary,* unabashedly implying that he can (even "must") lie, but without replacing him with any reliable substitute, since a third-person narrator sounds even less "authentically" autobiographical than the first. The reader is obliged to read critically, suspiciously, and actively, regardless of what form the narrator temporarily adopts.

Earlier in this passage Gombrowicz describes the problem of his "I" becoming inflated with the increasingly frequent appearance of his name in international journals. He debates what pose to adopt toward this growing fame and proposes Thomas Mann as the most admirable candidate for emulation, since he had been able "to link, better than anyone else, greatness to illness, genius to decadence, superiority to degradation, distinction to shame." He feels that he could even surpass Mann dialectically to create a new sort of greatness on an even higher level of consciousness and the reason he could do this was because he had "a new honesty at his disposal, and even a new shamelessness—resulting from his slogans that pronounced an eternal breach between man and his form" (*D* II, 122–23). He suggests describing his own "coming into prominence . . . as if it weren't about him, as if this triumph were merely the imposition of a new and not very comfortable 'form'—'made for him,' and even warping him." In fact, this is exactly what the passage is doing, so that in fact Gombrowicz simultaneously proposes and exposes the attitude that he also acts out at that moment.

The passage continues with the admission of some sort of resistance or block to writing about himself so much, a resistance which he does not quite understand. All he can say is that "something very personal, lyrical, intimate, stood in the way, something connected with—watch out!—youth and something almost as shameful as love" (*D* II, 125). This passage circles around this unknown or unspoken material in an elliptical and allusive way both thematically, invoking Freud and love and religion, and stylistically, freely employing ellipses, breaks, and interrogations, before finally ending with the enigmatic, "what was it that had remained unsaid?" Although Gombrowicz is speaking about fame and literary reputation, the discussion is always permeated with questions of public and private knowledge that always finally arrive back at the core problematic of homosexuality and the questions he implicitly associated with it. For example, later in the passage, he decides that "he who in the sphere of collective life succumbed to being elevated always had to be below . . . and it is here that greatness, distinction, dignity, and mastery became insufficient, immature . . . secretly affiliated with everything young . . . Mastery therefore was eternal tawdriness!" The itinerary of this discussion of literary fame, arriving at youth and immaturity via Proust and disease, can be followed on a strictly literal level, but it makes much more sense when read with an awareness of the substrata that link these heterogeneous topics in Gombrowicz's mind.

The third person appears also another time in the second volume, in which it is used unambiguously to distance the narrator from an explicitly sexual revelation, and that is when he travels to Santiago and succumbs *"to a wave of belated eroticism, the same as before, years ago"* (*D* II, 101). The most extraordinary thing about this passage is that after explaining his sexual fixations there in the usual way, as I discussed above, in terms of a project *"of* linking *old age to youth, so that a generation that was nearing its end could, in its twilight, draw new substance from youth, and experience the beginning once again . . . ,"* he then admits that this is merely a rationalization, even a boldfaced lie! In fact, he claims that the lie is not really a lie because of *"its naive and disarming obviousness,"* thereby virtually warning the reader that failing to see through the smoke screen of rationalization constitutes a willful misreading of the text. In other words, he gives the reader a singularly unequivocal mandate to read the Youth/Age problematic not in a literal and transparent way, but as a "code" for his queerness.

The nexus of values he identifies with Youth, all of which are derived from sexual desire and specifically homosexual desire, serve as an indispensable vantage point from which he launches his critiques and interventions in culture and art. This is not merely a source of "inspiration," although he explicitly uses that word when describing the passions aroused by the Retiro evenings. It is really another culture, whose values he uses to deflate and qualify the values of "straight" European high culture: "It was enough for me to bind myself emotionally to Retiro for one second for the language of culture to begin to sound false and empty" (*D* I, 144). But he cannot abandon himself completely to the pursuit of pleasure and youth, and "had to impose the semblance of reasoning onto that which was my passion in reality and this led me into the fathomless constructs, which were really a matter of indifference to me . . . but isn't this the way thought is born: as an indifferent surrogate of blind strivings, needs, passions, for which we are unable to establish the right to exist among people" (*D* I, 133).

Like the specular border intellectual mentioned earlier, Gombrowicz expresses dissatisfaction with and mistrust of both the heterosexual norm, and the culturally available homosexual opposite (more or less a function of the former) prompts him to keep constructing the border that he occupies. I have tried to suggest that this project functions paradigmatically for every critique and strategy of the *Diary*. He is inventing himself as a border subject, as a writer, as a Polish-European-American-Argentinean, and as countless other things. Between the meaning he gives himself and the meaning imposed on him by others "arises a third meaning, which delineates me" (*D* I, 146). This third meaning is precisely what needs to be cultivated in the gap between every subject and the Forms imposed on him/her. But it is no accident that the primary and most charged faultline lies along the sexual polarity, since it is this "difference," according to feminist theory, that precedes and naturalizes all other differences and hierarchies in patriarchal systems of meaning.

Finally, I would like to acknowledge what might appear as a contradiction between the argument that human subjectivity has no depth and essential nature on the one hand, and the claim that queer desires erupt irrepressibly, like weeds in concrete, around and in spite of the available cultural forms. This is a weakness inherent in constructivist theories. I can only suggest that although sexuality is produced, defined, judged, and channeled by social systems, as Foucault has demonstrated, it must also always either exceed or fall short (or both) of social categories and meanings. Without resorting to essentialist claims about instinct and nature, we should nevertheless be wary of believing that any theory will wholly account for and contain human sexuality, or any other human activity or faculty, for that matter. On the other hand, sexuality has been elided from critical discourse far too often, much to the latter's impoverishment. One thing Gombrowicz makes clear is that no philosophy or theory can afford to ignore the body. Throughout his work, he insists on the body and its physical existence as a carnivalesque anchor against the tendency of the intellect to drift off into severe, joyless, and pompous irrelevance.

Notes

1. John H. Spalek and Robert F. Bell, *Exile: The Writer's Experience,* University of North Carolina Studies in the Germanic Languages and Literatures 99 (Chapel Hill: U of North Carolina P, 1982).

2. See Abdul R. JanMohamed, "Wordliness-without-World, Homelessness-as-Home: Toward a Definition of the Specular Border Intellectual,"

Edward Said: A Critical Reader, ed. Michael Sprinkler (Oxford: Blackwell, 1992), 96–120.

3. JanMohamed, "Worldliness-without-World, Homelessness-as-Home," 97.

4. JanMohamed, "Wordliness-without-World, Homelessness-as-Home," 97.

5. Erving Goffman, *The Presentation of Self in Everyday Life* (New York: Doubleday, 1959), 75.

6. Judith Butler, "Performative Acts and Gender Constitution: An Essay in Phenomenology and Feminist Theory," *Performing Feminisms: Feminist Critical Theory and Performance Theory,* ed. Sue Ellen Case (Baltimore: Johns Hopkins UP, 1990), 271.

7. J. Hillis Miller uses this term in this sense when he states that any critical or artistic act can be considered a "performative political act" because the "work, whether of art, popular culture, or criticism, changes the society into which it enters, makes it, in however minute a way, begin again." In *Impressions* (London: Reaktion, 1992), 56. Yet, this appropriation of the term *perfomative* needs to be re-examined and employed with circumspection, since even the way that Austin uses the term attributes more power to the linguistic utterance than it necessarily possesses, given how much a perfomative speech act actually depends on non-linguistic factors for its "success" or efficacy.

8. This notion is based on Lee Edelman's discussion in *Homographesis: Essays in Gay Literary and Cultural Theory* (New York: Routledge, 1994).

9. For my purpose, what matters is that catachresis describes the way in which something which does not have a name of its own occupies a word that "properly" belongs to something else, e.g., the "leg" of a chair. Paul de Man argues that catachresis is paradigmatic of the way language functions in general, in "The Epistemology of Metaphor" *Critical Inquiry* 5 (1978): 13–30.

10. Eve Kosofsky Sedgwick, *Epistemology of the Closet* (Berkeley: U of California P, 1990).

11. Particularly Wilde's *Decay of Lying.*

12. See Andreas Huyssen, *After the Great Divide: Modernism, Mass Culture, Postmodernism* (Bloomington: Indiana UP, 1986), for a variation of this proposition.

13. The fact that Anglo-American modernists saw popular culture as their enemy, while Gombrowicz directs his resentment and attacks against high literary culture is a function of which field of cultural production claimed the most power during this epoque. Since it was the market that ruled artistic production and distribution in the West, modernists like Pound and Eliot railed against the commercialization of art. In Poland, however, the postromantic hegemony of high culture (especially of a nationalistic and tendentious nature) was never seriously challenged by any other artistic or cultural activity. The important point is that both Gombrowicz and the Anglo-American modernists felt they needed to "save" art from the sentimental, feminine forces that were unmanning it, whether from above or below, by injecting a brutal new honesty, virility, and a razor-sharp precision into it.

14. Having made this claim, I wish to acknowledge that Gombrowicz's misogyny is neither justifiable nor entirely acountable through my reading of it.

15. Moreover, all these writers have been widely known to be gay long before it became fashionable—in the 1970s—to retroactively "discover" the suppressed homosexuality of important writers, e.g. Shakespeare, Herman Melville, Tennesee Williams, etc.

16. An excellent discussion of Wilde's theory of subjectivity and the politics of social identity can be found in Jonathan Dollimore's "Different Desires: Subjectivity and Transgression in Wilde and Gide," *The Lesbian and Gay Studies Reader*, ed. Henry Abelove, Michèle Aina Barale, and David M. Halperin (New York: Routledge, 1993).

Allen Kuharski

10

Witold, Witold, and Witold:

Performing Gombrowicz

> Before the 1970s, when direct professions of homosexuality were taboo, writers from Oscar Wilde to Cocteau and Genet made their mark with works that were often theatrical, oblique, florid and artificial . . . Wit and paradox became more important than sincerity, since sincerity meant self-acceptance (which could be difficult) and self-exposure (which could be dangerous); style, baroque fantasy and sensuous detail were disguises that suited them far better than verisimilitude or realism. Oscar Wilde built a whole Nietzschean esthetic on "lying," and only devolved into plain speaking (in "De Profundis") when his whole life had gone to pieces.
>
> Morris Dickstein, "Intimations of Mortality"

Though written in a review of Edmund White's *Skinned Alive,* Morris Dickstein's words capture both the opportunity and the challenge of discussing Witold Gombrowicz as a queer voice in Polish literature and contemporary theater. Gombrowicz's writing is indeed theatrical, oblique, florid, artificial, witty, and paradoxical. Like Wilde, he confessed to homosexual experiences in the first volume of his *Diary,* published in the early 1950s in the wake of years of poverty and obscurity as a result of his decision to remain in Argentina at the outbreak of World War II—years in which it seemed he had nothing left to lose. Gombrowicz's confessions of homosexuality—or more precisely bisexuality—from the *Diary* through *A Kind of Testament* (written just before his death in 1969) were not apologies, however, and were accompanied by two works with openly homosexual elements: the novel *Trans-Atlantyk* (published in 1953) and the unfinished play *History* (written in 1951, published posthumously in 1975). Gombrowicz's other plays and novels better fit Dickstein's description, their queer erotics usually expressed indirectly. Czesław Miłosz, in his essay "Who Is Gombrowicz?" describes the playwright's writing as "unique in the twentieth century, because there is not a single description of copulation in it."[1] Yet Gombrowicz declared in his *Diary:* "I do not believe in a nonerotic philosophy. I do not trust thought that liberates itself from sex" (*D* II, 201). No one has ever charged Gombrowicz with "plain speaking," and he is nothing if not baroque in style and sensibility, with disguise (if not lying) central to his aesthetic. In fact, even his apparent candor in the *Diary* is often a performance and a disguise—its representation of sincerity, self-acceptance, and self-exposure a rehearsed and designed theatrical turn. In spite of its title, the *Diary* has long been known for its singular unreliability as autobiography.

One of the anomalies of the stage history of Gombrowicz's plays is their acceptance as modern classics in the continental European theater together with their lack of significant professional performance in English—this in spite of their promotion by critics such as Martin Esslin, Czesław Miłosz, and Jan Kott over the years. As a result of the fall of the Berlin Wall, Gombrowicz's place in European theater is in flux. After decades of selective censorship of his writings in Poland, he has been officially enshrined in the country's literary and theatrical canon, with a biannual International Gombrowicz Theatre Festival established in his honor in 1993. The first wave of productions of his plays in Western Europe in the 1960s linked his work with that of Beckett, Ionesco, and Genet—comparisons which Gombrowicz always found odious. A new wave of European productions of Gombrowicz's work on both sides of the former Berlin Wall began in 1990, suggesting the playwright's paradoxical potential as a canonical writer for a "united" Europe.

However, such a canonization of Gombrowicz in and out of Poland must somehow address the issues of sexuality raised by the author's person and work. In Polish literary and theatrical circles there still exists considerable discomfort and denial regarding the playwright's sexuality and its significance in his writing. Ironically, it is precisely the performed nature of the *Diary*'s confessions that perpetuates the denial of his homo- or bisexuality—a line of reasoning that fails to consider the possibility that his accounts of heterosexual experiences might also be a form of provocation, or that one life might in truth contain both forms of desire. More importantly, such responses tend to deny the significant and complex erotic dimension of his works. With the arrival of lesbian and gay studies and queer theory in the English-speaking world over the last decade, it seems that the best environment for the theatrical and critical exploration of sexuality in Gombrowicz's work may now be found in Great Britain, the United States, or Australia—as well as a newly receptive critical and theatrical audience for his work. For the theater, foregrounding sexuality in Gombrowicz's life and work moves him away from Ionesco and Beckett and toward Wilde, Genet, Orton, Mishima, and Ludlam. It is no surprise, on this score, that among the small cult of American admirers of Gombrowicz can be counted John Waters and Gary Indiana, and that British director Ken Russell is currently planning a film adaptation of Gombrowicz's novel *The Possessed.*

My focus here will be Gombrowicz's performance of queer sexuality both in and around his works, and its integral role in understanding his artistic, political, and philosophical choices throughout his career. I will also consider his work in light of recent queer theory, in particular that of the philosopher Judith Butler. Not only does Butler provide a useful critical vocabulary and theoretical paradigm for the analysis of sexuality in Gombrowicz's writing, but indeed Gombrowicz in retrospect can be seen as anticipating in literary and theatrical form much of Butler's theory of "performativity" and, in certain respects, augmenting her arguments.

As a writer, Gombrowicz fabricated a variety of authorial *personae,* often but not always named after himself, and consistently placed them at the center of his plays, novels, and diaries. In the playwright's own words:

> Everything is hypothetical. Everything is dependent—why should I conceal this?—on the effect it has.
>
> That characteristic defines everything that I have produced as a writer. I have tried various roles. I assume various postures. I impose various meanings on my experiences and if one of these meanings is accepted by people, I live on in it. (*D* I, 146)

Gombrowicz's quest for such a performative effect anticipates Butler's essay "From Parody to Politics," in which she writes:

> Paradoxically, the reconceptionalization of identity as *effect,* that is, as *produced* or *generated,* opens up possibilities of "agency" that are insidiously foreclosed by positions that take identity categories as foundational and fixed. For an identity to be an effect means that it is neither fatally determined nor fully artificial and arbitrary.[2]

Gombrowicz thus became an "actor" in and around his work, in a project of both literary and existential self-definition—and self-liberation—through such significant "effects." Though varied, these *personae* are almost always openly or tacitly queer in character. Thus the dance of concealment and self-exposure performed by Gombrowicz the author is inseparable from that of the various "Witolds" that populate his works. I will limit my discussion to three such "Witolds": the narrator of the *Diary* and the protagonists of *Trans-Atlantyk* and *History.*

Though neither the *Diary* nor *Trans-Atlantyk* is written in dramatic form, both fully embody the performative principles that pervade Gombrowicz's writing—a quality reflected in their growing history of performance in various theatrical adaptations. *Trans-Atlantyk* is the playwright's most thoroughly queer work and has been frequently adapted for the stage in Poland since the early 1970s, with these adaptations at times also broadcast on Polish television. The early stage adaptations of the novel also represented a breakthrough in the sympathetic treatment of homosexual subjects in the Polish theater. In spite of its unfinished form, *History* has been professionally produced in Germany, Austria, and Poland, with more than a dozen stage and television productions in Polish since 1981. In each of these works, the taboo embrace and performance of "queerness" is also a rejection of the "form" (to use Gombrowicz's own term) of heterosexual courtship and desire, or what lesbian critic Adrienne Rich has dubbed "compulsory heterosexuality." The playwright's position on this score in the *Diary, Trans-Atlantyk,* and *History* is inseparable from at least two others: emigration to Argentina (the rejection of the mythologies of Polish romantic nationalism and European cultural "superiority") and pacifism (the rejection of the interlocking mythologies of heterosexual machismo and militarism).

The "Witold" that speaks in the *Diary* in 1955 is very conscious of the risks that his "confessions" may entail:

> I broach this subject reluctantly. Much time will pass before it will be possible to talk, let alone write about this. There is no other area that is so distorted and muddled with passion. Here no one desires to be or can be objective. [. . .] . . . The fury of "manly" men, contorted with revulsion—manified, mutually nurturing and strengthening the masculinity in themselves—the curses of morality, all the ironies, sarcasms, and angers of culture, guarding the primacy of womanly charm—fall on the ephebe sneaking along the the border of our official existence. (*D* I, 142)

"Witold" struggles in the *Diary* to disassociate himself from being labeled homosexual even as he confesses to being obsessively drawn both to the Retiro in Buenos Aires, a park known as the city's center of homosexual cruising (especially by and for sailors), and to a circle of highly sexed gay male ballet dancers living in the same boarding house in the city.

It was at this time that Gombrowicz shared living quarters with Alejandro Rússovich, a young Argentinean who later became a professor of philosophy, and befriended Virgilio Piñera, an exiled gay Cuban writer who was later imprisoned in Cuba by Castro's regime on account of his homosexuality. Both Rússovich and Piñera collaborated with Gombrowicz on the first Spanish translations of the playwright's work published in Argentina in the late 1940s. Addressing the Second International Gombrowicz Festival in 1995, Rússovich not only confirmed many details of the largely homosexual milieu described in the *Diary* that both he and the playwright inhabited but also revealed the complex ways the facts of their lives were transformed in Gombrowicz's writing. Rússovich saw himself, for example, as the model for the somewhat bland and colorless "Witold" that narrates Gombrowicz's novel *Pornografia,* with Gombrowicz's true self-portrait being the novel's Mephistophelean theater director Frederick—an interpretation shared by Gombrowicz himself in his *Diary* (*D* III, 168). Rússovich also cited Piñera as the likely inspiration for Gonzalo, the flamboyant gay character at the center of the action of *Trans-Atlantyk.* How carefully Gombrowicz was hedging his bets in his "confessions" in the *Diary* is suggested by Piñera's accounts of their life together, retold by the gay Cuban novelist Reinaldo Arenas in his 1992 memoir, *Before Night Falls:*

> [Virgilio] emigrated to Argentina, where he lived for more than ten years, working at minor bureaucratic jobs, as sort of a Kafka of underdevelopment. There he met the Polish writer Witold Gombrowicz. Both émigrés, they became friends and buddies in cruising and erotic adventures. Gombrowicz, as Virgilio used to say, was very handsome then; to survive he became a male prostitute at the Buenos Aires baths, letting himself be fucked for a few coins . . .
>
> I think this friendship influenced Virgilio considerably, making him more daring, more irreverent. Or perhaps they influenced each other. Their lives were uprooted and grim; they did not believe in institutionalized culture, or in taking culture too seriously, in contrast to Jorge Luis Borges who, even then, was already the most important Argentine writer . . . When Gombrowicz finally left Argentina to settle in Europe, someone asked him what advice he would give to the Argentines. He answered, "Kill Borges."[3]

Does Piñera here provide a glimpse of the elided scene of copulation noted by Miłosz? While Miłosz aptly observes the surface effect of Gombrowicz's work, he does so without addressing the cause or significant motive behind the artistic choice. Copulation—heterosexual or homosexual—is always kept offstage in Gombrowicz's theater—it is *obscene* in the original Greek sense of the word. Arenas's memoir was posthumously published in Spain in 1992, and the passage regarding Gombrowicz and Piñera predictably proved a bombshell. The reliability of Arenas's secondhand account has been sharply questioned by Rússovich and others, particularly given Piñera's willingness to sacrifice the truth in the service of the outrageous in conversation. Rússovich's accounts of his own involvement with Gombrowicz are in contrast remarkable for their candor and lack of sensationalism, and he has confirmed the abject destitution in which the playwright lived for years after the outbreak of the war. The difficulties in either proving or disproving Arenas's account reflect Gombrowicz's own determination to control any discussion of his sexual life—a pattern confirmed by several of his closest Argentine friends in Rita Gombrowicz's *Gombrowicz en Argentine: 1939–1963.*

"Witold's" struggles with sexuality articulated in the *Diary* ultimately led to questions of gender identification, as well. In the culminating passage of the section dealing with his homosexual experiences in volume one of the *Diary,* Gombrowicz wrote:

> Two clear and important tasks emerged from the fog of the Retiro: deciding whether or not I would be able to express myself more honestly in the future or whether I would be forced to hide myself . . . But here emerged yet another task, because even touching this subject with the tip of my pen was impossible without a prior liberation from "manliness" and, in order to be able to talk or write about this, I had first to overcome my own fear of insufficiency in this regard, fear of femininity. Ah! I knew the masculinity that they, men, fabricated among themselves, goading each other into it, mutually forcing themselves to it in a panic-striken fear at the woman in themselves . . . Whole nations threw themselves like bulls onto the sword of the toreador in paroxysms, in the mad fear that the audience might attribute something of the *Ewig-Weibliche* to them . . . So I had no doubt that the magnified bull might charge me, too, if he scented my attack on his priceless genitalia.
>
> In order to prevent this, I had to find a different position for myself—beyond man and woman—which would nevertheless not have anything to do with a "third sex"—an asexual and purely human position from which I could begin airing these stuffy and sexually flawed areas. So as not to be a man, but a human being who just happens to be a man. Not to identify with masculinity, not to want it. If I could get out of this masculinity openly and decisively, its judgement of me would lose its bite and I could then say much about certain inexpressible things. (*D* I, 145)

Thus "Witold" aspires to a seemingly androgynous identification in consciousness and the world. In this and other passages in the *Diary* "Witold" provides a critique of conventional gender constructions that informs the portrayal of gender and sexuality throughout Gombrowicz's work. It is here that Gombrowicz's consistent, though generally tacit, rejection of compulsory heterosexuality finds its voice. The language of the passage also raises questions of the interconnectedness of the issues of gender, and specifically machismo, with those of nationalism and militarism—a relationship I will consider at greater length below.

Gombrowicz and Butler overlap in their proposed strategic responses to received gender roles. Again in volume one of the *Diary,* Gombrowicz writes:

> Here, as in all my writing, my goal—one of my goals—is to spoil the game, for as soon as the music dies and the couples break up, an invasion of reality is possible and only then does it become clear to us that the game is not reality but a game. To bring uninvited guests to that ball of yours; to bind you differently to one another; to ruin your dance. (*D* I, 119)

In "Subversive Bodily Acts," Butler unknowingly echoes not only Gombrowicz's point in the passage above but also his idiosyncratic vocabulary of "form" and "anti-form":

> The possibilities of gender transformation are to be found precisely in the arbitrary relation between such acts, in the possibility of a failure to repeat, a de-formity, or a parodic repetition that exposes the phantasmatic effect of abiding identity as a politically tenuous construction. (*GT,* 141)

The implications of these passages fan out over Gombrowicz's plays and novels: to Prince Philip's mysteriously motivated and utterly inappropriate pursuit of the sickly and lowborn Ivona as a fiancée, to the conspicuous breakdown of the carefully stage-managed courtship of Józio and Zosia at the end of *Ferdydurke,* to the mechanical and passionless seductions of Charmant and Firulet in *Operetta,* and so forth. In each instance, the characters either pointedly depart from a conventionalized scenario of heterosexual courtship and seduction or play it through until the underlying lack of sexual desire (at least in the male characters) reveals the lack of essential identification with the roles being enacted. In these and other scenarios, the playwright dramatizes the disjunction between desire and its conventionalized performance, resulting in either a parody of the scenario or a break in its prescibed repetition.

The complexities of Gombrowicz's manipulations of the persona of "Witold" in the *Diary* are perhaps most fully manifested in its third and final volume. Gombrowicz here makes one of his most telling statements regarding his own sexuality in response to an essay on the subject by Polish critic Artur Sandauer:

> Sandauer's reflections in this essay in regard to my purported sexual deviations? By all means! As long as this is done with tact and solemnity . . . I know very well that the right to pride is paid for with humility and I am not avoiding analyses that I myself provoke with my half-hearted confidences. (And why are the confidences half-hearted? Because one is and is not a homosexual; because one is at a certain point in one's life or in certain circumstances; that—this is my opinion—there is practically no man who could swear under oath that he never had the temptation. It is difficult to demand too-categorical a confession on the subject). (*D* III, 166)

Gombrowicz thus acknowledged the critical discussion of sexuality his work had begun to inspire in Poland and France by 1965, ultimately taking Sandauer to task but praising Konstanty Jeleński, who would later write at length on the significance of homosexuality in Gombrowicz in his introduction to the posthumous first edition of *History* in 1975.[4] Yet the ambivalence and artifice of Gombrowicz's performance of his own sexuality was dramatically reasserted in the last passages of volume three, where "Witold" gives a fragmented account of the appearance of an alleged illegitimate son from Brazil in the midst of the author's newly won European fame and rapidly declining physical health. The arrival of the bastard son gives the *Diary* a striking sense of narrative closure, not to mention the seductive breath of scandal, subtly invoking a Faustian pattern to the playwright's life.[5] The only problem with the story, still at times invoked as evidence against Gombrowicz's confessions of homosexuality, is that according to the playwright's widow the entire incident was, in fact, itself a fiction.[6]

The first narrator/protagonist that Gombrowicz named after himself was "Witold" in *Trans-Atlantyk*. The novel was his first new work published in Polish in fifteen years. The autobiographical inspiration of the work was obvious, telling the story of "Witold's" first months in emigration in Argentina immediately following the German invasion of Poland in September 1939. The novel's action begins with the narrator's decision not to return to Europe and enlist in the defense of his homeland. Thereafter the story concerns the curious friendship that develops between the destitute narrator with the wealthy Argentinian homosexual Gonzalo—who is quite promiscuous and has an occasional taste for drag. While Witold's reputation is repeatedly compromised in public by his association with the flamboyant *puto,* their relationship is a Platonic one. Gonzalo bluntly states early on that Witold is simply not his type, and, in spite of the leering notoriety Witold must now endure among his compatriots, he grudgingly admits that the Argentinian is his only friend in this new country. The initial basis for their friendship is Gonzalo's willingness to share Witold's public shame in the wake of a disastrous first encounter with "a great Argentinian writer," a figure clearly inspired by Borges.

A crisis arises in Witold's friendship with Gonzalo when the *puto* becomes infatuated with Ignacy, the teenage son of a member of the Polish émigré community in Buenos Aires, and asks the narrator to aid in his efforts to befriend and seduce the boy. Unlike Witold, Ignacy is being prepared by his upright father for military service. Witold, who himself starts feeling flashes of desire for Ignacy, is in effect placed in the role of procurer for his friend. In the course of a plot of baroque complexity, Ignacy becomes the object of a bizarre murder plot by a group of émigrés seeking his death as a symbol of Polish resistance after the fall of the country—an act suggested by Witold himself in a moment of despair. Realizing too late the true nature of Gonzalo and Ignacy's developing relationship, the father formulates his own plan to kill his son in the name of family and national honor. Meanwhile, under Gonzalo's heady influence, Ignacy is subtly prompted with the idea of killing his father rather than leaving Gonzalo's estate and going off to war.

The novel's language and action thus sets up an opposition between *patria* (in the original Polish *ojczyzna,* or fatherland) and *filistria* (*synczyzna,* or "sonland," a neologism coined by Gombrowicz), with both Ignacy and the equivocating Witold having to choose between them. Witold resolves his dilemma in the following words while gazing apprehensively—and appreciatively—at the nude body of the sleeping Ignacy. The English translation here gives its version of Witold's Falstaffian voice in the original Polish—one of Gombrowicz's most baroque stylistic devices:

> . . . enough of that Old! May there be something New! Give then some free-rein to the boy! May he do Whatever he Would. May he murder that Father of his, may he be Without a Father, may he go from home to a Field, to a Field! Let him sin! May into whatever he Would transform himself, even into a Murderer, a Patricide! And even into a Freak! May he Couple with whomever he would! At such a Thought within me, seized by strong queasiness, I almost threw up, and as if something was Breaking, Bursting in pain, in the most terrible dread . . . but naught, naught, may he, may he, what do I fear, what do I abhor, indeed, may what is to be, Become; may all Break, Burst, Fall apart, Fall apart, and oh, Filistria Becoming, Unknown Filistria! (*T,* 115)

This "queering" of the voice of a garrulous, provincial Polish braggart soldier, a type familiar in the genre of *gawęda,* was certainly among the playwright's greatest literary "seductions" and one of the most difficult to translate across the lines of language and culture. In its surprise finale, all the conflicting parties converge at Gonzalo's estate, but rather than murder and mayhem, the result is a spontaneous orgy of dancing and laughter (overseen by the host in drag in a magnificent black *mantilla*) that drowns all their past differences.

The theme that emerges from *Trans-Atlantyk* is that of the liberation of Ignacy, along with the narrator, from the morbid demands of Poland's mythology of militarism and martyrdom as well as in a larger sense from the traditional definitions of masculinity.[7] Both choose *filistria* over *patria.* Ignacy is never actually seduced by Gonzalo in the novel, but the combined efforts of Gonzalo and Witold have left him free to discover his true inclinations. He may choose to stay with Gonzalo, he may choose to leave, or he may follow the bisexual path of Gombrowicz himself. This sexual liberation is but the open sesame to his further self-definition. For all the dizzying events that take place around him, Ignacy is still an embodiment of unrealized potential at the end of *Trans-Atlantyk,* remaining essentially a passive, uncomplicated, and emblematic character.

The character of Gonzalo is the thematic touchstone of the novel, and its greatest theatrical opportunity (the Polish actor Jan Peszek created a sensation with his performance of the role in the first professional stage adaptation of the text in Łódź in 1981). Gonzalo's cultivated effeminacy and cross-dressing in the novel are central to the liberation of Witold and Ignacy and have ramifications beyond gender and sexuality. Butler writes:

> The transvestite, however, can do more than simply express the distinction between sex and gender, but challenges, at least implicitly, the distinction between appearance and reality that structures a good deal of popular thinking about gender identity. If the "reality" of gender is constituted by the performance itself, then there is no recourse to an essential and unrealized "sex" or "gender" which gender performances ostensibly express. Indeed, the transvestite's gender is as fully real as anyone whose performance complies with social expectations.[8]

Witold and Ignacy's first visit to Gonzalo's estate reveal him to be a kind of demiurge not only of gender but of all that is "natural." Besides having eccentric and eclectic furnishings in his *estanzia,* Gonzalo serves his guests unheard-of combinations of food and delights in showing the unlikely results of his experiments in cross-breeding various species of birds and animals. At Gonzalo's, not only gender but all of nature and culture proliferates in new categories. The full significance of Witold and Ignacy's experiences with Gonzalo is thrown into relief when we recall that the novel is taking place in the first months of World War II, with the violent politics of identity and nationalism enjoying full play in Europe, with particularly disastrous results for Poland. Gombrowicz was obviously conscious that the politics of fascism, nationalism, and militarism were in turn tied to strict and essentialized categories of gender.

The cathartic laughter that ends *Trans-Atlantyk* reveals the deep significance of its anachronistic language and embodies the book's ultimately postmodern sensibility. This laughter, which also disrupts the novel's language, is perhaps best explained by Butler's concept of postmodern pastiche, in which

> the loss of the sense of "the normal" . . . can be its own occasion for laughter, especially when "the normal," "the original," is revealed to be a copy, and an inevitably failed one, an ideal that

> no one *can* embody. In this sense, laughter emerges in the realization that all along the original was derived. (*GT,* 138–39)

The explosion that closes the novel is thus the laughter of a community with nothing more to lose and which therefore is also suddenly freed from its past and a failed national mythology. No sooner has the old Poland died but a new and perhaps more vital one is born on its grave. In Butler's words at the end of "From Parody to Politics":

> If identities were no longer fixed as the premises of a political syllogism, and politics no longer understood as a set of practices derived from the alleged interests that belong to a set of ready-made subjects, a new configuration of politics would surely emerge from the ruins of the old. (*GT,* 149)

Gonzalo's Polish guests for the first time can thus celebrate their status as a community of dispossessed émigrés, pacifists, and queers.

Gombrowicz created his most original self-portrait in *History,* his only play with a protagonist named after himself. Like *Trans-Atlantyk,* the play is openly autobiographical in inspiration, in this case concerning the playwright's life before his emigration in 1939. Gombrowicz began work on the play immediately after writing *Trans-Atlantyk,* and the play's adolescent hero can be seen as the theatrical merging of the characters of Witold and Ignacy in the novel into a more active form. While virginal in nature, Witold is in *History* the agent of change, rather than the passive object of the characters around him. Paradoxically, however, Witold himself never changes, remaining an adolescent throughout the twenty years that pass during the play's action. "Witold" here can be seen as both looking back to Faust (the author/hero regaining his lost youth) and forward to Günter Grass's eternal child Oskar in *The Tin Drum.* In the manuscript of *History,* the protagonist's speeches are initially assigned to "Witold," but later are simply marked "I," curiously dissolving the line between play text and diary, character and playwright. The play's stage directions at times also refer to "me" rather than to "Witold."

"Witold" here is a vital, Dionysian figure: androgynous, barefoot, anarchic, prophetic, and possessing vaguely shamanistic powers at once sought out and feared by those around him. He is alternately a rebel and an intruder figure in the play. He rebels against all the conventional patriarchal structures of his own milieu: his family and class, the educational system, marriage, the military, and eventually the paternalistic dictatorship of Marshal Piłsudski in interwar Poland. In his travels to the doomed courts of Tsar Nicholas II and Kaiser Wilhelm on the eve of World War I, he assumes the role of a Cassandra-like messenger whose prophetic warnings go unheeded. In his climactic scene with Piłsudski, Witold offers the possibility of saving Europe from Hitler, but Witold's "cure" is the rejection of machismo, militarism, and national mythmaking. Piłsudski, already mirroring the Nazi enemy he seeks to destroy, cannot retreat from the role in which he has cast himself. Seeing that Piłsudski cannot be changed, Witold presumably flees Europe for Argentina. Gombrowicz's notes on the unfinished manuscript indicate that the scene with Piłsudski was to be followed by scenes with Hitler and Stalin.

Homosexuality is most openly emphasized in the play's scene at the court of Kaiser Wilhelm, where the barefoot messenger/prophet Witold is initially greeted by the Prussian Prince Eulenburg. Eulenburg was an amateur poet and the closest friend and advisor of Kaiser Wilhelm, as well as the target of charges of homosexuality which compromised his official relationship with the kaiser's court. Witold's unexpected appearance on the very eve of the kaiser's declaration of war along with his ambiguous sexuality arouse fear and suspicion in both the closeted poet and the kaiser's other advisors. The psychological and political precariousness of the kaiser's court on the eve of the war is revealed by its members' hysterical reaction to Witold, who is after all an unarmed and barefoot adolescent and, therefore, seemingly more likely to become the military or sexual servant of the court than its nemesis. The nature of the message Witold wishes to carry to the kaiser is indicated in Gombrowicz's manuscript notes for the scene:

> Keep the soldier close to the Emperor, have the Soldier and
> the Emperor press against each other,
> THE SECRET OF CREATION is between
> the soldier and the Emperor.
> The Younger creates the Older,
> The Lower creates the Higher.

> THE SOLDIER HOLDS THE EMPEROR CLOSE.
> DOES THIS CHANGE THE FORCES OF HISTORY?-?-?[9]

The scene ends with Witold pressing for a private audience with Kaiser Wilhelm, "one on one" in Witold's suggestively repeated words, much to Eulenburg's paranoid, and perhaps jealous, discomfort. Witold's objective is to become the soldier "pressing against" the Emperor, the "Younger" holding the "Older" close, in hope of changing the forces of history. In the emphatic image of the soldier embracing the emperor is a fresh embodiment of the Gombrowiczean dance of homosexuality and pacifism. Witold's attempted private meeting with Kaiser Wilhelm is a variation on the image, with Witold "seducing" the kaiser away from war on behalf of both himself and the anonymous soldiers of his generation in the name of "creation." Witold's theatrical function in this scene is to air precisely the "stuffy and sexually flawed areas" Gombrowicz later wrote about in the *Diary*. This aspect of the play was effectively captured in the commanding image of Jacek Bunsch's 1985 version of the play in Wrocław, designed by Wojciech Jankowiak and Michał Jędrzejewski, in which the set for the production was made up entirely of freestanding wardrobe closets stacked on top of each other, through the doors of which all entrances and exits took place.

Witold's "queerness" in *History* is marked in several ways. His refusal to wear shoes as a proper son of the landowning gentry casts him instead in the role of a barefooted servant with which a member of the ruling class "can do with as one pleases." His eccentric behavior on this score predictably inspires a consternation tinged with scandal wherever he goes. Such a stable lad first emerged as the fetishized object of sublimated male desire in Gombrowicz's novel *Ferdydurke*. Witold's bare feet and apparent indifference drive his fiancée Christine to distraction, causing her to blurt out:

> Why aren't you normal? Why can't you wear shoes like the other boys! Joining the army would do you good! There'd you learn a thing or two![10]

Christine's wish becomes the family's command, and the unwitting Witold is rushed off to a draft board (performed by the same actors who play the family). Witold's brief scene with Christine once again serves to link heteronormativity to militarism.

Witold's rebellion in *History* against both marriage and military service parallels that of Ignacy's diversion from military service by Gonzalo in *Trans-Atlantyk*. Butler suggests the larger significance of such a critique of marriage and kinship systems. For Butler, as well as Foucault and others,

> . . . the association of a natural sex with a discrete gender and with an ostensibly natural "attraction" to the opposing sex/gender is an unnatural conjunction of cultural constructs in the service of reproductive interests.[11]

Where Gombrowicz's writing augments the work of theorists such as Butler is precisely where this rejection of the gender categories required by marriage and kinship systems is combined with pacifism. The figure of a heterosexual woman goading a reluctant fiancé into military service earlier appears in Gombrowicz's short story "The Memoir of Stefan Czarniecki," where the title character's alienation and anxieties are the result of a confusion of ethnic, religious, and ideological identities rather than sexuality per se. Though one of Gombrowicz's few unquestionably heterosexual male protagonists, the half-Jewish Stefan Czarniecki's desire for his hawkish Gentile girlfriend recedes in direct proportion to his growing pacificism. Stefan's fiancée Jadwiga, in contrast, is sexually excited at first by the sight of soldiers marching off to war and, later, most attracted to Stefan when he returns with a hero's medals on his chest. In other words, the economy of marriage is "unnaturally conjoined" in Jadwiga's mind with that of war. Czarniecki's Jewish—and increasingly pacifist and communist—consciousness marks him as "queer."

Both *Trans-Atlantyk* and *History* concern the attempt to historically "mark" the bodies of Ignacy and Witold with military service, even to the point of death. The representatives both of patriarchy (Ignacy's father and Witold's family) and marriage (Christine) give their blessings to the masculine military project. Witold's emblematic bare foot and agelessness symbolize his declaration of independence from history, in terms both of the passage of time and of the forced marking of the militarized heterosexual male body (the wearing of army boots and the risk of being wounded or killed in battle). Gombrowicz's theatrical treatment of history and the body in the play both draws on Nietzsche and anticipates Foucault's 1971 essay "Nietzsche, Geneology, History." In Foucault's reading of Nietzsche:

> The body manifests the stigmata of past experiences and also gives rise to desires, failings, and errors. These elements may join in a body where they achieve a sudden expression, but as often, their encounter is an engagement in which they efface each other, where the body becomes the pretext of their insurmountable conflict . . . Geneology, as an analysis of descent, is thus situated within the articulation of the body and history. Its task is to expose a body totally imprinted by history and the process of history's destruction of the body . . . History becomes "effective" to the degree that it introduces discontinuity into our very being—as it divides our emotions, dramatizes our instincts, multiplies our body and sets it against itself. "Effective" history deprives the self of the reassuring stability of life and nature, and it will not permit itself to be transported by a voiceless obstinacy toward a millenial ending. It will uproot its traditional foundations and relentlessly disrupt its pretended continuity.[12]

Witold in *History* is thus Gombrowicz's theatrical rejoinder to Nietzsche and Foucault's categories. Witold's significance as what Butler dubs a "speaking subject" (*GT,* 130) is born precisely through his refusal to risk corporeal destruction, as his extensive soliloquys demonstrate in the play. After an order to be silent by the Judge and Prosecutor called to decide his case as a draft evader (double cast with the actors playing his father and brother in the play), Witold replies:

> Let me be heard!
> What does this mean?
> Who doesn't allow me?
> What is it about me that is not permitted?
> Who can take my voice away?
> My voice!
> My voice resounds here!
> Ho, ho, ho, hola—my voice!
> My voice!
> My voice!
> I have a voice. A voice you can't take away. I will speak, because I have a voice. No one now or ever will take my voice away. I'm speaking now! Quiet, I'm speaking! Quiet, quiet! I'm speaking, speaking, speaking!

> And what I have to say is very important,
> But let my bare foot accompany my mouth,
> Here at the bottom of my person
> Let it appear
> and barefoot I will speak, barefoot . . .[13]

In reverse symmetry to Ignacy and Witold, who are delivered from both "marriage" and "history," are the silent and suffering female characters of Ivona (in *Ivona, Princess of Burgundia*) and Molly (in *The Marriage*). In the case of Molly, her body is marked both by war (she has clearly been raped and traumatized by various occupying armies) and marriage (Henry's determination to deny her experience, publicly reannoint her as a virgin, and grotesquely "play the script" of their prewar engagement). Ivona and Molly's eloquent silences embody Nietzsche and Foucault's diagnosis of history; Ignacy and Witold embody Gombrowicz's prognosis of the same.

As a playwright, Gombrowicz's performative vision of gender is concretely embodied in a series of related theatrical images, often employing either costume or its significant absence. Witold's bare feet represent his liberation from the social constructions of class and gender. This effect is heightened in Gombrowicz's last play *Operetta,* which ends with the nude "resurrection" of its young heroine, Albertine, an event which embodies the moment of her liberation from the sexual expectations and fashions imposed by the men around her rather than an image of seduction. Albertine's nudity is but the logical extension of Witold's barefootedness and is in symmetry with the image of the nude, sleeping Ignacy in *Trans-Atlantyk*. Gonzalo carries the logic one step further and assumes the costume of the opposite gender. As Albertine removes her skirts and blouses, the shameless Gonzalo is waiting in turn to put them on. In a final bit of gender confusion, Polish critics Jan Błoński and Konstanty Jeleński have argued that Albertine can be understood as one of Gombrowicz's theatrical alter egos.[14] Thus, is "Witold" undressed revealed to be a woman? Or is Albertine "Witold" in drag?

A discussion of Gombrowicz's queer erotics in those works where homosexuality remains coded and embedded in subtext is unfortunately beyond the scope of this discussion. Suffice to say that there is a marked and consistent lack of heterosexual desire in his male characters, which at least in part explains the dearth of scenes of copulation. Gombrowicz's queer erotics are part of a larger philosophical system which forms the true common denominator between the *Diary, Trans-Atlantyk, History,* and his other works, and this system in turn reflects and informs his personal politics. His dualistic philosophical system is related to the existentialism of Sartre, Camus, and Buber, and in its own terms opposes "form" to "anti-form"—with the playwright always valorising "anti-form." "Anti-form" is embodied for Gombrowicz in youth, beauty, nudity, energy, nature, inferiority, chaos, the escape from sclerotic European traditions, and queer sexuality. It is the culture of *filistria:* the realm of displaced persons of uncertain gender and sexuality living in a postcolonial—and now postideological—world. Gombrowicz's politics could be described as leftist with pacifist-anarchist tendencies and, more specifically, characterized as antinationalist, agnostic, anticlerical, anticommunist, and pro-Semitic. In regard to his future role in performance and cultural politics, queer and otherwise, the playwright has provided a key in the *Diary:*

> . . . the sense of someone's life, someone's work is defined between one given human being and another. It is not only I who imposes meaning on myself. Others impose meaning as well. From the clash of these interpretations arises a third meaning, which delineates me. (*D* I, 146)

Here is the key to the playwright's performativity: to move past what *comes* between us to what *becomes* between us. If our relationship to Gombrowicz in performance is therefore becoming a queer one, he has made it clear he is willing to be as queer as we need him to be.

The playwright will play our Gonzalo, and we can perform Gombrowicz.

Notes

1. Czesław Miłosz, "Who Is Gombrowicz?" Introduction, *Ferdydurke,* by Witold Gombrowicz, trans. Eric Mosbacher (New York: Penguin, 1986), xvii.

2. Judith Butler, *Gender Trouble: Feminism and the Subversion of Identity* (London: Routledge, 1990), 147. Subsequent references to this text will be marked parenthetically as *GT.*

3. Reinaldo Arenas, *Before Night Falls,* trans. Delores M. Koch (New York: Viking, 1993), 80–81.

4. Konstanty Jeleński, "Od bosości do nagości: O nieznanej sztuce Witolda Gombrowicza," *Historia (Operetka): Fragmenty, Kultura* (Paris) 10 (1975): 3–28. Available in an English translation by Allen Kuharski and Dariusz Bukowski as an appendix to "The Theatre of Witold Gombrowicz," diss., University of California, Berkeley, 1991, 360–407.

5. A detailed discussion of this aspect of the *Diary* can be found in my article entitled "Gombrowicz and Faust." Allen Kuharski, "Gombrowicz and Faust," *New Theatre Quarterly* 10, no. 40 (1994), 372–76.

6. From a conversation between the author and Rita Gombrowicz in New York City, October 14, 1994. The fictitious nature of the story of the bastard son in the *Diary* is also confirmed by Gombrowicz's widow in her book *Gombrowicz en Europe 1963–1969* (Paris: Denoël, 1988), 327.

7. The novel's significance as a pacifist statement was promptly endorsed in print by Poland's most renowned antiwar writer, Józef Wittlin—whose support helped contain a critical backlash against the novel in the Polish émigré press. See his preface to the 1953 Instytut Literacki (Paris) combined edition of *Trans-Atlantyk* and *Ślub* (*The Marriage*).

8. Judith Butler, "Performative Acts and Gender Constitution," *Performing Feminisms: Feminist Critical Theory and Theatre,* ed. Sue-Ellen Case (Baltimore: Johns Hopkins UP, 1990), 278.

9. Witold Gombrowicz, *History (An Operetta),* trans. Allen Kuharski and Dariusz Bukowski, *Periphery: Journal of Polish Affairs* 1, no. 1 (1994): 65.

10. Gombrowicz, *History (An Operetta),* 62.

11. Butler, "Performative Acts and Gender Constitution," 275.

12. Michel Foucault, "Nietzsche, Geneology, History," *Language, Counter-Memory, Practice: Selected Essays and Interviews by Michel Foucault,* ed. Donald F. Bouchard, trans, Donald F. Bouchard and Sherry Simon (Ithaca: Cornell UP, 1977), 148, 154.

13. Gombrowicz, *History (An Operetta),* 63.

14. Jeleński, "Od bosości do nagości," 14.

Post/Script

Beth Holmgren

11

Witold Gombrowicz in the United States

Very little research has been done on Gombrowicz in the English-speaking world. Unfortunately, a number of American and English critics who have written on Gombrowicz were not familiar with Polish and had to resort to translations which in most cases have been inadequate and often inaccurate.

It is fair to say that the French discovered Gombrowicz and have done the best research on his work. Unfortunately, the majority of these critics used French translations. It is our hope that future research will be done by scholars who are better versed in Polish. It is our opinion that Gombrowicz is worth the pains to study Polish.

Edward Czerwiński and Bronisława Karst,
" 'Berging' Gombrowicz: A Reappraisal of
'Form-Fastening' "

Whenever Witold Gombrowicz is mentioned, we hear of his unjustified obscurity: perhaps no great writer of this century has been so obdurately and celebratedly obscure. Although much of his work was made available in English by Grove Press in the 1960's, Gombrowicz never profited from America's short-lived appetite for arcane Euroculture. He was a bit *too* weird, devoted to gnarled, foggy themes. . . . His American audience remains negligible.

Gary Indiana, "The Classy Creepiness
of Witold Gombrowicz"

These readings of Witold Gombrowicz's reception in the United States—taken at roughly ten- and twenty-year intervals since his death—reflect the sometimes awkward, sometimes irritated, but generally distanced relationship between the Polish writer and his American readers.[1] With every mention of his work, his scattered champions reprise his biography, reassert his worth, and remonstrate against his neglect. Less initiated critics are more liable to blame Gombrowicz himself (a difficult writer too insistent on his "foggy themes") for his obscurity. Rather than frame writer or readers, I submit that we might better explain and expand his American reception by applying Gombrowicz to Gombrowicz, exposing what he would call the peculiarly American Form of publishing and promoting that obscures him and, if we dare, manipulating that Form to a more positive end.

In large part, Gombrowicz, a reliable generator of antinomies, has succumbed to a basic antinomy of the American literary establishment: its uneven division into academic and (for lack of a better term) broadly intellectual spheres. To be sure, Gombrowicz has attracted his few readers both within and outside of the American university system. Yet, as is the case with almost all "serious" writers (and especially writers translated into English), it is the academy that has taken greater control of promoting his image and art—a paradoxical arrangement for a writer who mounted his life work as a campaign against official, academically sanctioned notions of writers and writing.[2] The small, self-appointed group of scholars promoting Gombrowicz compose a curious alliance of adventurous comparatists; Slavists who have dared, despite the exigencies of the academic market, to specialize in a so-called second Slavic literature (second, that is, to the hegemony of Russian); and Polish critics and writers in exile (Czesław Miłosz and Jan Kott serve as the most striking examples here) who land in the position of Slavist by default. For virtually all of these boosters Gombrowicz's importance is an unquestionable fact, yet their focus on his work, in both thematic and formal terms, presumes that the reader thinks otherwise and requires considerable convincing.

The bulk of American scholarship on Gombrowicz therefore concentrates on introducing the reader to his writings, either through a descriptive analysis of his work alone or through representation of his work as an important example in a historical or comparative series. Articles by George Gomori, Robert Boyers, Bettina Knapp, and Maria Baraniecki fall into this first category; Gomori and Boyers offer general discussions of the characteristics of his work, and Knapp and Baraniecki focus more specifically on his drama.[3] The only American book wholly devoted to the writer, Ewa Thompson's extremely useful *Witold Gombrowicz,* can be read as the most extensive elaboration of this approach.[4] Written for the Twayne series of monographs on world authors, this book was literally commissioned by an academic press to package Gombrowicz for the American undergraduate—to describe, in necessarily succinct outline form, his life and work and place in world literature, and to provide a selected bibliography for future term papers.

In most instances, Gombrowicz's critics validate him through juxtaposition.[5] He is accorded, for example, a rather impressive entry in Czesław Miłosz's *The History of Polish Literature,* where he, Witkiewicz, and Schulz are credited with breaking away from nineteenth-century realist prose forms.[6] Elsewhere his work earns survey coverage in Olga Scherer-Virski's rather dated history, *The Modern Polish Short Story* (she includes only stories from the *Memoirs from the Time of Immaturity* [Pamiętnik z okresu dojrzewania] and in various encyclopedias of the drama).[7]

Released from these histories and encyclopedias, Gombrowicz usually appears chaperoned by one or two other writers, artists with whom he shares a notable artistic approach or life experience.[8] A number of these comparisons progress from textual or literary historical description to important insights into Gombrowicz's technique and demonstrations of his originality. Patricia Merivale, for example, draws an intriguing comparison between the uses of Gothic artifice in the work of Gombrowicz and Henry James, arguing that, through this device, their texts "exempli[fy] the Romantic position that the poet is accursed and the artistic process at best morally dubious."[9] Contrasting the theater of Witkiewicz and Gombrowicz, Louis Iribarne ultimately proves Gombrowicz, with his attention to the interhuman dynamic, to be the more genuinely revolutionary writer of the two.[10] My own work traces how Gombrowicz inverts the influential model of the Polish romantic poet, exemplified by Adam Mickiewicz.[11] And two book-length studies afford Gombrowicz a grander, if still co-habited, showcase. Alex Kurczaba's *Gombrowicz and Frisch: Aspects of the Literary Diary* (1980) explores the basic similarities in theme, form, and function between the two writers' literary diaries, proffering splendid insights into the fusion of fictional narrative and philosophical tract in the diary genre, the influence of Montaigne's *Essais* on Gombrowicz's *Diary,* the various narratorial stances of Gombrowicz's diary persona, and the parodic impulses and play principle at work in the text.[12] Tomislav Longinović's intriguing four-way comparison of works by Gombrowicz, the Russian Mikhail Bulgakov, the Serbian Danilo Kiś, and the Czech Milan Kundera posits Gombrowicz as "perhaps the most extreme example of the borderline prosaist," a particular type of Slavic writer whose "fiction examines institutional power from the position of an individuality that has been exploited, scorned, persecuted, and exiled by the instruments of ideological control."[13] As such, the Polish writer is said to deconstruct and disarm the totalitarian visions of his region and, by extension, the ideological delusions of the rest of the world.

As good as these general and comparative studies may be, their basic format and orientation still belie Gombrowicz's marginal status in American letters—even in the rarefied environment of American scholarship. In the best case, Gombrowicz is taught, read, and analyzed in the American university system as an exotic subject ejected from an exotic literature. His works pop up in the occasional course on twentieth-century East European literature and the very occasional Polish literature survey. Beyond the sheltering walls of the academy his situation is precarious indeed. Gombrowicz's "popular" status in America has depended in large part on the respect accorded Polish language and literature in the American publishing market—more concretely, on the effort expended by translators and publishers to preserve both the spirit and letter of original Polish texts in American editions. The history of Gombrowicz's translation into English illustrates the sometimes surprising problems of this dependency.

Czerwiński and Karst's 1978 appraisal implies the missed first step of Gombrowicz's translation into English. His first major works to be Englished—the novels *Ferdydurke, Pornografia,* and *Kosmos*—doubly removed him from his American readers through second-generation translations from French (and in some cases German) versions of the Polish originals.[14] When Grove Press, an American publisher, undertook what it planned as an American edition of Gombrowicz's complete works, it reprinted the translations of translations without revision.[15] These works read like ponderous paraphrases, gutted of the original's strong syntactic rhythm and oral intonation.[16] They remain the only English versions of these novels even today—an irritating reminder of Gombrowicz's initial critical neglect in the United States and a major disincentive for those readers who discover Gombrowicz through these texts.

Predictably, nonspecialist readers at first puzzled over this very dim reflection of Gombrowicz's greatness. Reviews of *Ferdydurke, Pornografia,* and *Kosmos* appearing in *The Saturday Review* are unanimous in their praise of his work—with the caveat that his artistry and originality manage to *survive* the texts' inadequate translations.[17] For most other readers even this survival is in doubt. In *The Hudson Review* a reader of *Ferdydurke* and *Pornografia* complains that "both [novels] are inexplicably titled, both are the work of a careful and immensely serious writer, both are enervating to read and distressing to write about."[18] A review of *Cosmos* in the same periodical (but by a different writer) reinforces this impression, dismissing the novel as "dreary, dragging and dull."[19] D. J. Enright, a British critic writing for *The New York Review of Books,* acknowledges the subtlety and sensitivity of a work like *Pornografia,* but "would like to know what [Gombrowicz] is being sensitive to and subtle about."[20] Enright's longing for clarity and context resurfaces in reviews by John Updike (for *The New Yorker*) and John Ashbery (for *The New York Times Book Review*).[21] Dissatisfied with the stasis, unevenness, and artificiality of *Ferdydurke* and *Pornografia,* both critics anticipate a livelier read in Gombrowicz's more overtly autobiographical writings. Updike looks forward to the "osmotic margins" of *Trans-Atlantyk* and the *Dziennik,* works then slated for future translation. Ashbery admits the same interest:

> Nevertheless, one wants to see more of Gombrowicz; if he is not on the present evidence a very satisfying novelist he is at least not an easy one. On the basis of the digressions in *Ferdydurke* and extracts from Gombrowicz's diaries in the preface to *Pornografia,* one has the impression that speculative rather than narrative prose is his province, and the Diaries, when they appear, ought to be worth reading.[22]

Ashbery and Updike had to wait several decades for gratification, but it was during this period that English-language publication of Gombrowicz became more serious and specialized. Since the late 1960s, scholars and translators "better versed in Polish" have made most of his work available to American readers in more than adequate English approximations of his style. Good translations of *Ivona, Princess of Burgundia* and *The Marriage* appeared in 1969; a fine English version of *Operetta* was issued in 1971; even the posthumous *History* has been ably rendered into English, albeit in 1995.[23] Gombrowicz's narratives (with the nagging exception of his three twice-translated novels) have fared almost as well. His early potboiler *The Possessed* reached the English-speaking reader in 1980; *A Kind of Testament* (the English rendering of Gombrowicz's "interview" by the French critic Dominique de Roux) has provided Americans with a handy "guide to Gombrowicz" since 1973.[24] Thanks to the Herculean labors of translator Lillian Vallee (and the steady backing of Northwestern University Press), we possess excellent English-language versions of all three volumes of Gombrowicz's Diary.[25] No less impressive is the recent translation of Gombrowicz's most difficult text, *Trans-Atlantyk,* the product of a ten-year collaboration between Nina Karsov and Carolyn French and the sponsorship of yet another academic publisher (Yale).[26] This is not to say, of course, that these conscientious efforts remain on the market. Of the three major plays (which were never collected), *Ivona* and *Operetta* have slipped out of print; Gombrowicz's few translated short stories are scattered in various journals.[27] Most astonishingly, *Ferdydurke* has disappeared altogether, leaving *Pornografia* and *Cosmos* to soldier on alone in a joint Grove Press edition. Nevertheless, it is a fact that the American reader can lay hands on Gombrowicz's most engaging and autobiographical works, which, morever, have garnered enthusiastic and consistent critical acclaim. A *New York Times* review of the *Diary*'s second volume assures readers of universal and recognizable themes in "the parade of Polish names" and invites them "to travel through the geographies of this astounding mind . . . and garner the riches of his fascinating work."[28] The *Chicago Tribune* reviewer of the third volume bears out Ashbery's hunch when he applauds the "congeniality" of the diary form for Gombrowicz.[29] Although the stylistic difficulties of *Trans-Atlantyk* might confuse and dismay a new generation of reviewers, most commend the translators "for tackling the challenge with daring and grace" and sense the work's vibrancy through its sometimes rather obscure, but mostly exuberantly inventive English.[30] A most appreciative reviewer for The *Nation* maintains the novel "reads like a deranged Daniel Defoe" and grants it this ringing endorsement: "Critical rule of thumb dictates that a foreign author's weakest tomes are translated last, but this brilliant, bizarre book is an exception."[31]

Yet availability and accolades have not translated into significant sales, even highbrow popularity. Amid the glowing reviews we stumble on the old complaint about Gombrowicz's obscurity, despite the fact that "[n]o consideration of 20th-century literature is conceivable without including his work."[32] In the first version of this article, written just after the *Diary*'s debut, I blithely predicted that its publication "will conclude our introduction to Gombrowicz and commence a period of full-fledged interaction between the writer and his American public as his text 'soaks, drenches, saturates' our ways of perceiving literature, self, and world."[33] This saturation is doubtlessly taking place, but soaking a much smaller area than I had anticipated. Despite the best efforts of translators, scholars, and publishers, Gombrowicz's American readership "remains negligible." It may be that American readers are deterred by the academic imprint of his most recent translations. More probable, however, are the hypotheses volunteered by Gombrowicz's premier American publishers, Northwestern University Press and Yale University Press. Susan Harris, an editor at Northwestern, speculates that American readers perceive Gombrowicz "to be a Polish writer rather than a great writer," ghettoizing him by their own narrow sense of his nationality.[34] It seems that Gombrowicz must be sold by his place of origin, not his place in the canon; in the American mind, an East European may not qualify as a "great," unless perhaps s/he fought hard (on our side) in the cold war. At Yale University Press, editor Jonathan Brent senses a more general dilemma: The American reader no longer buys "great writers" and no longer cares about Gombrowicz's high-culture targets.[35]

Our material disregard for Gombrowicz speaks volumes about our blinkered ways of seeing the world, but it also shows us how we might spring Gombrowicz from our own obscuring Form. If Gombrowicz would sell better and reach further as an *assigned* "great writer," then we should shelve our nuanced reading and resort strategically to the very manipulations Gombrowicz explored and deplored decades ago. For Gombrowicz the cultivation of "the great writer" signified a national pathology and augured personal destruction, but in the vast, diverse, and largely blasé world of American publishing, such cultivation is no more than another marketing ploy. In Poland that status awards adulation and incurs drastic self-sacrifice; in the United States it amounts to better sales and a modest lecture circuit. Northwestern University Press has already moved Gombrowicz in this direction with encouraging results: Its boxed set of the *Diary* has attracted new Gombrowicz customers, presumably by implying his status as a "boxable" classic. Perhaps we can lobby publishers for similarly suggestive packaging, for an English-language collected works or handsome pictorial biographies with portraits of the artist (Gombrowicz was luckily photogenic) and panoramas of his Old World/New World locales.

If Brent's supposition is correct, however, our strategy must be strictly academic. We are obliged to improve Gombrowicz's currency in the university, touting him in all manner of courses and especially those that cross national boundaries and appeal to diverse audiences—courses on world literature, philosophy, nationalism, gay and lesbian studies, to name the most obvious. We can pitch him as a "great" with each required reading, advertising his perspicacity about the dangers of ideological straitjackets, the utter value of the individual, and the aesthetic and moral advantages of being "between" classes, sexes, ethnicities, and worlds. We can mount him on a multicultural, postcolonial pedestal as a prophet for our times, our "classic" anti-classic, our irascible spokesperson for difference. We can hail him as an advance scout for queer theory. Whatever our patter, we must keep in mind that we are the standard-bearers in Gombrowicz's American campaign. Here in the land of the Flipflopping Canon and fifteen-minute fame, it is up to us Pimkos to make Gombrowicz great.

Notes

1. Edward Czerwiński and Bronisława Karst, " 'Berging' Gombrowicz: A Reappraisal of 'Form-Fastening'," *Polish Review* 23 (1978); Gary Indiana, "The Classy Creepiness of Witold Gombrowicz," *The Village Voice Literary Supplement* May 1987. The term *American* in this article refers generally to North America and publishing fora in the United States.

2. For a penetrating discussion of this phenomenon in the United States, see the collection of articles entitled *Criticism in the University,* ed.

Gerald Graff and Reginald Gibbons (Chicago: Northwestern UP, 1985). In contrast to Gombrowicz's situation in France, here there exists no ready *community* of Polish émigrés willing to preserve and extend his legacy. I would hazard to say that for most Americans of Polish descent (I have in mind second-, third-, and fourth-generation Polish Americans, not Polish émigrés of the last two decades), Gombrowicz represents an annoying crank, a challenger of the most popular icons of Polish literature and culture in emigration.

3. See also George Gomori, "The Antinomies of Witold Gombrowicz," *Modern Language Review* 73 (January 1978): 119–29; Robert Boyers, "Gombrowicz and *Ferdydurke:* The Tyranny of Form," *Centennial Review* 14 (1970), 284–312, and "Aspects of the Perverse in Gombrowicz's *Pornografia,*" *Salmagundi* 17 (1971): 19–46; Bettina Knapp, "Witold Gombrowicz: A Faceless Theatre," *Yale French Studies* 46 (1971): 75–87; and Maria Baraniecki, "Gombrowicz's Drama within and without the Absurd," *Canadian Slavonic Papers* 27 (1985): 241–47.

4. Ewa M. Thompson, *Witold Gombrowicz* (Boston: Twayne, 1979).

5. In making this generalization, I am also obliged to point out some important exceptions. Over the last fifteen years, a number of fine articles on specific aspects of or contexts for Gombrowicz's work have appeared in print. See Edward Czerwiński and Bronisława Karst's discussion " 'Berging' Gombrowicz: A Reappraisal of 'Form-Fastening,' " 50–57; David Brodsky's literary historical study, "Witold Gombrowicz and the 'Polish October,'" *Slavic Review* 39 (1980): 459–75; Ewa Thompson's respective analyses of his narrative prose and drama, "The Reductive Method in Witold Gombrowicz's Novels," *The Structural Analysis of Narrative Texts: Conference Papers,* ed. Andrej Kodjak, Michael J. Connolly, and Krystyna Pomorska (Columbus: Slavica, 1980), 196–203, and "Witold Gombrowicz's Plays and the Polish Literary Tradition," *Poetica Slavica* (Ottawa: U of Ottawa P, 1981), 197–204; Jakób Liszka's examination of the model of the facial duel in *Ferdydurke* entitled "The Face: I and Other in Gombrowicz's *Ferdydurke,*" *Philosophy and Literature* 5 (1981): 62–72; and William Veeder's "A Call to Order: *Cosmos,*" *Cross Currents: A Yearbook of Central European Culture* vol. 4, (Ann Arbor: U of Michigan P, 1985), 125–44.

6. Czesław Miłosz, *The History of Polish Literature,* 2nd ed. (Berkeley: U of California P, 1983), 432–37.

7. See Olga Scherer-Virski, *The Modern Polish Short Story* (The Hague: Mouton, 1955), 230; Bolesław Taborski, "Witold Gombrowicz," *Crowell's Handbook of Contemporary Drama,* ed. Michael J. Anderson et al. (New York: Crowell, 1971), 186–88; David Brodsky, "Witold Gombrowicz," *Magill's*

Critical Survey of Drama: Foreign Language Series vol. II (Englewood Cliffs, N.J.: Salem, 1986), 764–76.

8. We can observe the same tendency in the relatively few dissertations written on Gombrowicz over the last fifteen years. Every one of the eight theses (from both the United States and Canada) that I have been able to locate compares Gombrowicz with other Polish or European thinkers and writers. See Maria Anna Crawford, "An Existential Vision of Man in the Fiction of Witold Gombrowicz and Selected Novels by Sartre, Sarraute, Robbe-Grillet, and M. Butor," New York University, 1972; Colleen Taylor, "Polish Experimental Fiction, 1900–1939: A Comparative Study of the Novels of Karol Irzykowski, Stanislaw Ignacy Witkiewicz, Witold Gombrowicz and Bruno Schulz," Columbia University, 1972; Alex Kurczaba, "Gombrowicz and Frisch: Aspects of the Literary Diary," University of Illinois, Urbana-Champaign, 1979; Maya Wesolowska-Frenkler, "Witold Gombrowicz's Theater of Contradictions," State University of New York, Binghamton, 1979; Christine Brown, "The Image of Polish Society in the Novel of the 1930's," University of Toronto, 1984; Bronisława Karst, "The Problem of the Other and of Intersubjectivity in the Works of Jean-Paul Sartre and Witold Gombrowicz" State University of New York, Stony Brook, 1984; Anna Gale, "Antonin Artaud's Theory of Theatre as a Paradigm for the Analysis of Twentieth-Century Drama," University of California, Los Angeles, 1985; and Beth Holmgren, "First-Person Liberties: The Persona in the Work of Witold Gombrowicz and Abram Terc," Harvard University, 1987.

9. Patricia Merivale, "The Esthetics of Perversion: Gothic Artifice in Henry James and Witold Gombrowicz," *PMLA* 93 (1978): 992–1002.

10. Louis Iribarne, "Revolution in the Theatre of Witkacy and Gombrowicz," *Polish Review* 18 (1973): 58–76.

11. Beth Holmgren, "Witold Gombrowicz within the *Wieszcz* Tradition," *Slavic and East European Journal* 33 (1989): 556–70. Other examples of this comparative approach include Kurczaba's "The Impact of Latin-American Exile on Polish and German Literature: The Case of Witold Gombrowicz and Anna Seghers," *Polish Review* 23 (1978): 58–65; Peter Petro's "Four Eccentrics: The Eccentric Character in the Novels of Celine, O'Brien, Gombrowicz and Solzenicyn," *Canadian Review of Comparative Literature / Revue Canadienne de Littérature Comparèe* 8 (1981): 48–60; and Wladimir Krysinski's "Changed Textual Signs in Modern Theatricality: Gombrowicz and Handke," *Modern Drama* 25 (1982): 3–16.

12. Alex Kurczaba, *Gombrowicz and Frisch: Aspects of the Literary Diary* Abhandlungen zur Kunst-Musik-und Literaturwissenschaft, 295 (Bonn: Bouvier Verlag Herbert Grundmann, 1980).

13. Tomislav Z. Longinović, *Borderline Culture: The Politics of Identity in Four Twentieth-Century Slavic Novels* (Fayetteville: U of Arkansas P, 1993).

14. *Ferdydurke* was translated by Eric Mosbacher in 1961; *Pornografia,* by Alastair Hamilton in 1964; and *Kosmos,* by Mosbacher in 1967.

15. These translations have, in fact, gone through several reprintings. *Ferdydurke* was first published by Harcourt, Brace & World in 1961, and then reprinted by Grove Press in 1968. *Pornografia* and *Cosmos* were published separately by Grove in, respectively, 1966 and 1969. Grove then reissued all three novels in a single volume in 1978. They next appeared in a new configuration: *Ferdydurke,* with an introduction by Czesław Miłosz, was reprinted by Penguin Books in 1986 as part of the "Writers from the Other Europe" series, and *Pornografia* and *Cosmos* were reprinted together by Grove Press in 1985. At present, the separate edition of *Ferdydurke* seems to be out of print.

16. See Edward Czerwiński and Bronisława Karst, " 'Berging' Gombrowicz: A Reappraisal of 'Form-Fastening,' " for a sample critical comparison of the Polish and English editions of *Ferdydurke.* They show how the existing English translation actually redefines the syntactic divisions of Gombrowicz's prose (breaking up a long sentence packed with repetitively structured clauses into a series of separate sentences) and alters the intonation of a key statement by inserting different punctuation marks. I would argue that what is primarily lost in these translations is that all-important narrative tone: the emphatic or spellbinding repetitions, the headlong sentence structure, the verbal signals of a narrator seeking to engage, provoke, or coerce his reader. Deprived of this enlivening medium, the philosophical-psychological discussions in his fiction read as rather dull, at times even confusing, harangues.

17. Harold B. Segel, "Tyranny of Form That Deforms," *Saturday Review,* July 15, 1967: 33–34; Vera Mihailovich on *Cosmos* in *Saturday Review,* February 28, 1970: 43.

18. Roger Sale, "Good Servants and Bad Masters," *Hudson Review* 20 (spring 1967): 666–67.

19. Guy Davenport, "C'est Magnifique Mais Ce N'est Pas Daguerre," *Hudson Review* 23 (spring 1970): 156.

20. D. J. Enright, "Dancing the Polka," *New York Review of Books,* June 15, 1967, 26–27.

21. John Updike, "Behold Gombrowicz," *New Yorker,* September 23, 1967, 169–76; John Ashbery, "Ecrivain Maudit," *New York Times Book Review,* July 9, 1967, 4–5.

22. Ashbery, "Ecrivain Maudit," 5.

23. *Ivona, Princess of Burgundia,* trans. Krystyna Griffith-Jones and Catherine Robins (New York: Grove, 1969); *The Marriage,* trans. Louis Iribarne (New York: Grove, 1969); *Operetta,* trans. Louis Iribarne (London: Calder, 1971); *"History (An Operetta):* An Unfinished Play by Witold Gombrowicz," trans. Allen Kuharski and Dariusz Bukowski, *Periphery: A Journal of Polish Affairs* 1 (1995): 58–68. See Kuharski's perceptive essay in the same volume: "Performing *History:* A Translator's Introduction," 54–57.

24. *The Possessed: or, The Secret of Myslotch,* trans. J. A. Underwood, (London: Boyars, 1980); *A Kind of Testament,* published, again, by Boyars in 1982 (with U.S. distribution by Scribner).

25. The first volume of the *Diary* appeared in 1988; the second, in 1989; the third, in 1993. All three were translated by Lillian Vallee and edited by Jan Kott.

26. *Trans-Atlantyk,* trans. Carolyn French and Nina Karsov (New Haven: Yale UP, 1994).

27. The short story "Premeditated Crime" appears in *Ten Contemporary Polish Stories,* ed. Edmund Ordon (Detroit: Wayne State UP, 1958); "On the Backstairs," in *Evergreen Review* 9 (1965); "The Banquet," in *Partisan Review* 54 (1987).

28. Serge Gavronsky, "Don't Ask. Act," *New York Times Book Review,* November 5, 1989, 34.

29. Rockwell Gray, "An 'Uncompleted' Mind. Poland's Witold Gombrowicz: Exile, Diarist, Debunker and Holy Fool," *Chicago Tribune,* August 8, 1993: 6.

30. Jaroslav Anders, *"Trans-Atlantyk" New Republic,* December 12, 1994, 34. Only one reviewer finds unredeemable fault with the translation. An unnamed writer for *Kirkus Reviews* complains: "French and Karsov include a pronunciation guide and a glossary of words they felt would be lost in translation. One can't help wishing they'd thought twice about translating the book at all." *"Trans-Atlantyk," Kirkus Reviews,* March 15, 1994.

31. Bill Marx, *"Trans-Atlantyk," Nation,* July 11, 1994, 63.

32. Betty Falkenberg, *"Trans-Atlantyk," New Leader,* September 12, 1994, 16.

33. Beth Holmgren, "Witold Gombrowicz in the United States," *Polish Review* 33 (1988): 418.

34. Quoted from the author's August 3, 1995, conversation with Susan Harris, editor-in-chief at Northwestern University Press. My thanks to Susan Harris for permission to quote.

35. Quoted from the author's August 22, 1995, interview with Jonathan Brent, editor-in-chief at Yale University Press. My thanks to Jonathan Brent for permission to quote.

Selected Bibliography of Gombrowicz Criticism

Balderston, Daniel. "Estética de la deformación en Gombrowicz y Piñera." *Explicatión de textos literarios* 19 (1990/91): 1–7.

Barańczak, Stanisław. "Nie ten Gombrowicz." *2b: Polish American Quarterly* 2 (1994): 78.

Baraniecki, Maria. "Gombrowicz's Drama within and without the Absurd." *Canadian Slavonic Papers* 27 (1985): 241–47.

Berressem, Hanjo. "Witold Gombrowicz, *Cosmos:* The Case of the Hanged Sparrow." *Polish Perspectives* 36 (1991): 145–59.

———. "The 'Evil Eye' of Painting: Jacques Lacan and Witold *Gombrowicz* of the Gaze." R. Feldstein (ed.), *Reading Seminar XI: Lacan's Four Fundamental Concepts of Psychoanalysis.* Albany: State U of New York P, 1995, pp. 175–82.

———. ". . . die entbrannten Degenspitzen/Von macht'gen Gegnern . . . : Witold Gombrowicz's Lektura Dantis." *Arcadia* 28 (1993): 47–64.

Błoński, Jan. *Forma, śmiech i rzeczy ostateczne.* Kraków: Znak, 1994.

Bolecki, Włodzimierz. "Witkacy-Schulz-Gombrowicz." Trans. Valerie Laken. *Periphery: Journal of Polish Affairs* 2, 75–79.

Boyers, Robert. "Gombrowicz and *Ferdydurke:* The Tyranny of Form." *The Centennial Review* 14 (1970): 284–312.

———. "Aspects of the Perverse in Gombrowicz's *Pornografia." Salmagundi* 17 (1971): 19–46.

Brodsky, David. "Gombrowicz's Spatial Poetics." R. Bauer and D. Fokkema (eds.). *Proceedings of the XIIth Congress of the International Comparative Literature Association.* Vol. II. München: Iudicium, 1990, pp. 277–82.

Brown, Russell E. "Back to School in Poland: A Shared Motif of Witold Gombrowicz and Bruno Schulz." *Polish Review* 32 (1987): 175–79.

Carcasonne, M., et al. (eds.). *Gombrowicz vingt ans après.* Paris: Bourgois, 1989.

Cataluccio, Francesco M., and Jerzy Illg (eds.). *Gombrowicz filozof.* Kraków: Znak, 1991.

Cordua, Carlos. "Alabanza de la inmadurez: Gombrowicz en Argentina." *La Torre* 7 (1993): 355–70.

Czerwiński, Edward and Bronisława Karst. " 'Berging' Gombrowicz: A Reappraisal of 'Form-Fastening.' " *Polish Review* 23 (1978): 50–57.

Dąbrowski, Mieczysław. *Polska awangarda prozatorska.* Warszawa: Semper, 1995, pp. 115–34.

Dedieu, Jean-Claude. *Witold Gombrowicz.* Paris: Marval, 1993.

Delaperriere, Maria. "Exil et conscience de soi dans l'oeuvre de Gombrowicz." Hana Jechova and Helene Wlodarczyk (eds.), *Les Effets de l'emigration et l'exil dans les cultures tcheque et polonaise.* Paris: PU de Paris-Sorbonne, 1987, pp. 253–67.

Falkiewicz, Andrzej. *Polski kosmos: 10 esejów przy Gombrowiczu.* Wrocław: Agencja Wydawniczo-Reklamowa, 1996.

Filipowicz, Halina. "Fission and Fusion: Polish Émigré Literature." *Slavic and East European Journal* 33 (1989): 157–72.

———. "Gombrowicz za dwanaście lat?" *2b: Polish American Academic Quarterly* 2 (1994): 77.

Fisherman, Alberto. *Gombrowicz o la seducción.* 16 mm film. Buenos Aires, 1986.

Fiut, Aleksander. "Forms That Can Sting." Trans. Theodosia Robertson. *Periphery: Journal of Polish Affairs* 2 (1996): 80–85.

Franz, Norbert. "Entblumung statt Trauung: Textstruktur und Interpratationslogik in Witold Gombrowiczs '*Ślub.*' " *Zeitschrift für Slavische Philologie* 51 (1991): 174–95.

García, German Leopoldo. *Gombrowicz: El estilo y la heráldica.* Buenos Aires: Atuel, 1992.

Georgin, Rosine. *Gombrowicz.* L'Âge d'homme, 1977; Cistre-Essais, 1987.

Gębala, Stanisław. "Odczyniane uroków—czyli *Trans-Atlantyk* kontra *Pan Tadeusz.*" *Poezja* 11/12 (1984): 87–95.

Głowacka, Dorota. "Henry-Roi: Strategies of Evasion and the Romantic Tradition in Witold Gombrowicz's *The Marriage.*" *Canadian Slavonic Papers* 36 (1994): 429–38.

Głowacki, Janusz. "Gombrowicz, A Toothpick, and Chairman Mao." *2b: Polish American Academic Quarterly* 2 (1994): 62–64.

Głowiński, Michał. *Ferdydurke Witolda Gombrowicza.* Warszawa: Wydawnictwa Szkolne i Pedagogiczne, 1991.

Gombrowicz, Rita. *Gombrowicz w Europie: Świadectwa i dokumenty* 1963–1969. Kraków: Wydawnictwo Literackie, 1993.

Gomori, George. "The Antinomies of Gombrowicz." *Modern Language Review* 73 (1978): 119–29.

Gonzales Lanuza, Eduardo. "Witold Gombrowicz i jego Dziennik argentyński." *Twórczość* 37, (1981): 95–99.

Grol-Prokopczyk, Regina. "New Gombrowicziana." *Polish Review* 26 (1981): 82–87.

Holmgren, Beth. "Witold Gombrowicz in the United States." *Polish Review* 33 (1988): 409–18.

———. "Witold Gombrowicz within the Wieszcz Tradition." *Slavic and East European Journal* 33 (1989): 556–70.

Hyde, George M. "The Word Unheard: 'Form' in Modern Polish Drama." *Word and Image* 4 (1988): 719–31.

Jarzębski, Jerzy. "Być wieszczem." *Teksty: Teoria Literatury; Krytyka; Interpretacja* 4/5 (1981): 58–59/236–267.

———. "Gombrowicz: ucieczka z rodzinnego domu." *W Polsce czyli wszędzie.* Warszawa: Wydawnictwo PEN, 1992, pp. 19–37.

———. *Gra w Gombrowicza.* Warszawa: Państwowy Instytut Wydawniczy, 1982.

Jeleński, Constantin, and Dominique de Roux (eds.). *Gombrowicz.* Paris: l'Herne, 1971.

Jeleński, Konstanty. "Od bosości do nagości: O nieznanej sztuce Witolda Gombrowicza." *Kultura* (Paris) 10 (1975): 3–28.

———. "Gombrowicz's Heroic Anti-Heroics." *Formations* 1 (1985): 49–57.

Kalicki, Rajmund (ed.). *Tango Gombrowicz.* Kraków: Wydawnictwo Literackie, 1984.

Knapp, Bettina. "Witold Gombrowicz: A Faceless Theatre." *Yale French Studies* 46 (1971): 75–87.

Kok, Nathalie. "Roman et perversion: Une lecture psychoanalytique du roman *Ferdydurke* de Witold Gombrowicz." Henk Hillenaar and Walter Schonau (eds.), *Fathers and Mothers in Literature.* Amsterdam: Rodopi, 1994, pp. 211–22.

Kott, Jan. *The Theater of Essence.* Introduced by Martin Esslin. Evanston: Northwestern U P, 1984.

Krysinski, Vladimir. "Changed Textual Signs in Modern Theatricality: Gombrowicz and Handtke." *Modern Drama* 25 (1982): 3–16.

Kuharski, Allen. "Gombrowicz and Faust." *2b: Polish American Academic Quarterly* 2 (1994): 65–67. Reprinted in *New Theatre Quarterly* 10 (1994): 372–76.

———. "Gombrowicz and Company." *New Theatre Quarterly* 11 (1995): 388–91.

———. "Polish Literature, Postmodernism, and the End of the Millennium." *Periphery: Journal of Polish Affairs* 2 (1996): 72–74.

Kuprel, Diana. "Ludic Form and Formal Ludus: The Play of Masks in Witold Gombrowicz's *Operetta.*" *Canadian Slavonic Papers* 36 (1994): 413–28.

Kurczaba, Alex. *Gombrowicz and Frisch: Aspects of the Literary Diary.* Bonn: Bouvier Verlag Herbert Grundmann, 1980.

———. "Gombrowicz and Conrad: The Question of Autobiography." Keith Carabine et al. (eds.), *Contexts for Conrad.* Boulder: East European Mongraphs, 1993, pp. 73–86.

———. "Witold Gombrowicz's *Princess Ivona* and Joseph Conrad's 'Amy Foster.'" *L'Epoque Conradienne* 19 (1993): 85–105.

Liszka, Jakób. "The Face: I and Other in Gombrowicz's *Ferdydurke." Philosophy and Literature* 5 (1981): 62–72.

Longinović, Tomislav. *Borderline Culture: The Politics of Identity in Four Twentieth-Century Slavic Novels.* Fayetteville: U of Arkansas P, 1993.

Łapiński, Zdzisław (ed.). *Gombrowicz i krytycy: Wybór i opracowanie.* Kraków: Wydawnictwo Literackie, 1984.

———. *Ja* Ferdydurke: *Gombrowicza świat interakcji.* Lublin: Wydawnictwa KUL, 1985.

———. "Une vie et une creation, ou deux creations." Trans. Elisabeth Destree-Van Wilder. *Textual Coherence and Problems of the Autobiography,* (ed.) Hanna Dziechcińska, Wrocław: Polska Akademia Nauk, 1985.

Majchrowski, Zbigniew. *Gombrowicz i cień Wieszcza.* Gdańsk: Wydawnictwo Uniwersytetu Gdańskiego, 1995.

Matamoro, Blas. "La Argentina de Gombrowicz." *Cuadernos Hispanoamericanos* 469/470 (1989): 271–79.

Van der Meer, Jan. *Form vs. Anti-Form: Das semantische Universum von Witold Gombrowicz.* Amsterdam: Rodopi, 1992.

Merivale, Patricia. "The Esthetics of Perversion: Gothic Artifice in Henry James and Witold Gombrowicz." *PMLA* 93 (1978): 992–1002.

Miłosz, Czesław. "Who Is Gombrowicz?" Introduction to Witold Gombrowicz, *Ferdydurke.* Trans. Eric Mosbacher. New York: Penguin, 1986.

———. "Jakby na opak." *Kultura* 6 (489) (1988): 121–31.

———. "Kilka uwag o recepcji Gombrowicza." *2b: Polish American Academic Quarterly* 2 (1994): 75.

Nasiłowska, Anna. *Trzydziestolecie 1914–1944.* Warszawa: Wydawnictwo Naukowe PWN, 1995, pp. 117–22.

Neuger, Leonard. "Polskość jako cel." *Teksty Drugie: Teoria Literatury; Krytyka; Interpretacja* 1/2 (1991): 5–23.

Petro, Peter. "Four Eccentrics: The Eccentric Character in the Novels of Celine, O'Brien, Gombrowicz and Solzenicyn." *Canadian Review of Comparative Literature* 8 (1981): 48–60.

Proguidis, Lakis. *Un écrivain malgré la critique: Essai sur l'oeuvre de Witold Gombrowicz.* Paris: Gallimard, 1989.

Refaeli, Zvi. "Witold Gombrowicz: HaMythos shel I-Bagrut." *Iton=77* 74/75 (1986): 24–25.

Rússovich, Alejandro. "Gombrowicz od wewnątrz." *Twórczość* 37 (1981): 90–94.

Saer, Juan José. "La perspectiva exterior: Gombrowicz en Argentina." *Punto de vista* 35 (1989): 11–15.

Sandauer, Artur. "Gombrowicz and Politics." Trans. Edward Rothert. *Polish Perspectives* 29 (1986): 33–39.

Scholze, Dietrich. "Emporung gegen die Allmacht der Form." *Sinn und Form: Beiträge zur Literatur* 41, (1989): 651–60.

Sem-Sandberg, Sem. "Eksil." Trans. Per Qvale. *Vinduet* 45 (1991): 34–41.

Sławiński, Janusz. "Sprawa Gombrowicza." *Teksty i teksty.* Warszawa: Wydawnictwo PEN, 1990, pp. 159–65.

Smorag, Małgorzata. "L'idiomatique et l'universel chez Gombrowicz." Hana Jechova and Helene Wlodarczyk (eds.), *Les effets de l'emigration et l'exil dans les cultures tcheque et polonaise.* Paris: PU de Paris-Sorbonne, 1987, pp. 269–86.

Sztajnberg, Suzanne. "Witold Gombrowicz's 'I Am Where I Am Not.' " *Cross Currents: A Yearbook of Central European Culture.* 4 (1985): 99–112.

Świderski, Bronisław. "Gombrowicz's Dostoevskij." *Scando-Slavica* 37 (1991): 48–57.

Thompson, Ewa M. *Witold Gombrowicz.* Boston: Twayne, 1979.

———. "Witold Gombrowicz's Plays and the Polish Literary Tradition." *Poetica Slavica: Studies in Honour of Zbigniew Folejewski,* ed. J. Douglas Clayton et al. Ottawa: U of Ottawa P, 1981, pp. 197–204.

Vallee, Lillian. "Rich in Revolution: Witold Gombrowicz's *Diary.*" *World Literature Today* 61 (1987): 186–89.

———. "I Need Gombrowicz." *2b: Polish American Academic Quarterly* 2, (1994): 79–80.

Veeder, William. "A Call to Order: *Cosmos.*" *Cross Currents: A Yearbook of Central European Culture* 4 (1985): 125–44.

Volle, Jacques. *Gombrowicz, bourreau, martyr.* Paris: Bourgois, 1972.

Wilkiewicz, Zbigniew R. *Personendarstellung und Menschenbild im* Kosmos *Witold Gombrowiczs.* Mainz: Liber, 1986.

Ziarek, Ewa Płonowska. *The Rhetoric of Failure: Deconstruction of Skepticism, Reinvention of Modernism.* (Albany: State U of New York P, 1995).

Zielińska, Barbara. "Śmiech Gombrowicza." *Ruch Literacki* 4/5 (1987): 295–308.

Notes on the Contributors

Hanjo Berressem teaches American literature at the University of Bielefeld, Germany. His book *Pynchon's Poetics: Interfacing Theory and Text* (1992) has been published by the University of Illinois Press. *The Lines of Desire: Reading Gombrowicz's Novels with Lacan* is forthcoming from Northwestern University Press in 1997.

Valérie Deshoulières is a novelist and a literary critic teaching at Institut de Litérature Comparée, Université Blaise Pascal, France. She has published widely on modern writers, including Gombrowicz, Cortazar, and Musil.

Dorota Głowacka is Assistant Professor in the Contemporary Studies Programme at the University of King's College, Halifax, Nova Scotia. She teaches critical theory, contemporary fiction, and the literature of the Holocaust. She has published a number of essays on critical theory and contemporary American and continental writers such as Joseph Heller, John Hawkes, John Kennedy Toole, Witold Gombrowicz, Bruno Schulz, Boris Vian, and others. At present, she is working on a contribution to a monograph on Bruno Schulz and on a book project on postmodern sublime.

Marzena Grzegorczyk (Ph.D. in Spanish and Comparative Literature, Stanford University) is Assistant Professor of Spanish at Emory University where she teaches Latin American Literature, critical theory, and film. She has published articles in Spanish, Polish, and

English on Latin American culture. Currently, she is completing a book on space and subjectivity in nineteenth-century Latin America. She is also an independent film maker (*Island at the End of the Word, English Is for Optimists*).

Beth Holmgren is Associate Professor of Slavic Literatures at the University of North Carolina at Chapel Hill. She has published numerous studies of Russian and Polish contemporary writers. Her book *Women's Work in Stalin's Time,* has been published by Indiana University Press in 1993. She is also a co-editor of *Russia, Women, Culture,* Indiana, 1996.

Katarzyna Jerzak is Assistant Professor of Comparative Literature at the University of Georgia. She received her P.d. from Princeton University in 1995. She is currently working on a book on the space of exile in the works of Gombrowicz, Cioran, Tarkovsky, De Chirico, and Tsvetaeva.

Allen Kuharski is Assistant Professor and Resident Director in the Theater Studies Program at Swarthmore College. He is Performance Review Editor for *Theater Journal* and Associate Editor for *Periphery: Journal of Polish Affairs.* He has directed Mrożek's *The Party,* Ionesco's *The Victims of Duty,* and Ròżewicz's *White Marriage.* His articles and reviews have appeared in *Theater Journal, New Theater Quarterly, Theater, Dialog, The San Francisco Review of Books, 2B, Periphery,* and various anthologies. He has also translated Gombrowicz's *History* and is currently working on a book on Gombrowicz's plays.

Tomislav Z. Longinović is a novelist and Associate Professor of Slavic Languages and Literatures at the University of Wisconsin-Madison. He is the author of *Borderline Culture: The Politics of Identity in Four Twentieth-Century Slavic Novels* and the editor of *Words are Something Else,* a collection of essays devoted to David Albahari, forthcoming from Northwestern University Press. He has published widely on critical theory and contemporary Eastern European writers. His novel *Moment of Silence* was published in 1990.

Piotr Parlej (Ph.D., SUNY at Buffalo) teaches at Russell Sage College. He has published a number of essays on critical theory, philosophy of history, and contemporary American and European writers. His book, *The Present Subject: The Theory of the Novel in Romanticism,* is forthcoming from LSU Press.

Agnieszka M. Sołtysik is Assistant in the Faculty of Letters at the University of Geneva. She specializes in twentieth-century literature, literary theory, and film studies. Currently she is working on the epistemology of the Gothic novel.

Ewa Płonowska Ziarek is Associate Professor and Director of Graduate Studies in the English Department at the University of Notre Dame. She has published articles on Derrida, Kristeva, Levinas, Foucault, Kafka, Benjamin, Joyce and Marianna Hauser. She is the author of *The Rhetoric of Failure: Deconstruction of Skepticism, Reinvention of Modernism* (SUNY Press, 1995).

Index